STORIES THAT BIND

STORIES THAT BIND

Political Economy and Culture in New India

MADHAVI MURTY

RUTGERS UNIVERSITY PRESS

New Brunswick, Camden, and Newark, New Jersey, and London

Library of Congress Cataloging-in-Publication Data

Names: Murty, Madhavi M., author.
Title: Stories that bind : political economy and culture in new India /
    Madhavi Murty.
Description: New Brunswick : Rutgers University Press, [2022] |
    Includes bibliographical references and index.
Identifiers: LCCN 2021035346 | ISBN 9781978828766 (cloth) | ISBN 9781978828759
    (paperback) | ISBN 9781978828773 (epub) | ISBN 9781978828780 (pdf)
Subjects: LCSH: India—Politics and government—1947- | Mass media—
    Political aspects—India. | Popular culture—Political aspects—India. |
    Neoliberalism—India. | Hindutva—India. | India—Economic conditions—1947-
Classification: LCC DS480.84 M877 2022 | DDC 954.04—dc23
LC record available at https://lccn.loc.gov/2021035346

A British Cataloging-in-Publication record for this book is available from the British
Library.

References to internet websites (URLs) were accurate at the time of writing. Neither the
author nor Rutgers University Press is responsible for URLs that may have expired or
changed since the manuscript was prepared.

♾ The paper used in this publication meets the requirements of the American National
Standard for Information Sciences—Permanence of Paper for Printed Library Materials,
ANSI Z39.48-1992.

www.rutgersuniversitypress.org

Manufactured in the United States of America

For Juned and Sahar, my comrades, my family . . .

CONTENTS

STORIES THAT BIND

INTRODUCTION
Spectacular Realism and Political-Economic Change

It is no coincidence that India is my first stop on a visit to Asia, or that this has been my longest visit to another country since becoming President…for in Asia and around the world, India is not simply emerging; *India has already emerged*.
　　　　　　　　　　　　　　　　　　　　　　　　—Barack Obama, 2010

We've woken up each day for half a century and wiped the sky clean,
Sieved sunlight from dusty beams.
Sixty years of freedom.
Hindustan is at history's turn,
At the next turn, our feet will be on Mars.
Hindustan is pregnant with hope,
Let's walk together, because if you walk, Hindustan walks too.
　　　　　　　　　　　　　　—From a brand campaign for the Times Group,
　　　　　　　　　　written originally in Urdu and voiced by Gulzar, 2007

I haven't been sent here, nor have I come on my own. I was, in fact, called by the Ganga [the Ganges River].
　　　　　　　　　　　　　　—Indian prime minister Narendra Modi
　　　　　　　　　　　　　　　　in an electoral advertisement, 2014

This book is about stories. Stories about development, a nation's "emergence" and renewal, about time narrated as eventful and about an aggrieved and aggressive masculinity that argues its time has come to assert dominance. It is about stories shaped by geopolitical changes after the end of the Cold War when India ineluctably drifted into the orbit of the sole surviving superpower, the United States. Stories narrated through the idiom of the brand, the medium of the cinema screen, the news report, and the political campaign. This book is also about the worlds that are organized by stories. It is about the narratives that give form, coherence, and a visceral tangibility to the worlds within which we live.

1

When the spectacle of a U.S. president's visit, particularly a president such as Barack Obama, who is narrated as a transformational figure, is conjoined with his announcement of a nation's emergence, the affective weight of the statement transforms it into a tangible truth. Or when both a brand campaign and a political leader narrate time as destiny, a moment that is full of hope in anticipation of the people and their representative to take their preordained place in history, the present is experienced as eventful. This book is about the organizing structures and patterns of political-economic formations as well as those of aesthetic forms. It is about stories of a political-economic conjuncture, in which a set of economic prescriptions bracketed as neoliberalism intersect with the political form of authoritarian nationalism, in India.

This book is about the form neoliberalism takes in India; it is about Hindu nationalism and its form and the popular stories which give form to their conjugation—Hindutva neoliberalism. It makes two arguments: First, it reveals the conjoining of neoliberalism with authoritarian nationalism. I contend that this binding is not a function of coincidence but is the consequence of shared narrative strategies of both Hindu nationalism and neoliberalism. Second, I suggest that the intersection of neoliberalism and Hindu nationalism has an aesthetic form and I label it *spectacular realism*. Let me be clear, I am not arguing that the political right wing in India in the form of Hindu nationalism or neoliberal capital has been more effective or successful at crafting narratives. I am arguing that capital and authoritarian nationalism have given themselves a local, intimate, familiar form through popular aesthetics. Walter Benjamin had argued that fascism organizes the masses or the people without altering their iniquitous material conditions; it does so instead by giving them a form of "expression."[1] Consequently, aesthetics is introduced into political life. The aestheticizing of politics, Benjamin had argued, culminates in war. The aesthetic form of Futurism, with its celebration of gunfire, tanks, gas masks, and smoke spirals from burning villages, was, as Benjamin showed, an instantiation of the aestheticizing of politics. While we could argue that Hindutva neoliberalism is a form of fascism, spectacular realism is not a specific aesthetic movement with a manifesto, like Futurism; it is instead a patterning produced via the entanglement and intersection of a diverse set of popular stories.[2] Its form gives capital and authoritarian nationalism an intimately familiar shape and wins them consent. Unlike the form accorded to both neoliberalism and Hindu nationalism by their critics, which suggests well-formed, articulated projects that intervene in defined areas in planned, strategic maneuvers, I argue that neoliberalism and Hindu nationalism constitute themselves or give themselves form through an immersion in the textual, visual, and sonic sign systems of popular culture.

Instead of conceiving the story as epiphenomenon or the unreal ideological façade that obscures and obfuscates the reality of political-economic formations, I think about the story as the paradigmatic structure through which political-economic formations narrate themselves.[3] Stories have a worldmaking function.[4]

Just as the cultural story is sometimes seen as epiphenomenon glossing over the "reality" of political-economic structures and changes, Hindu nationalism in India, like white nationalism in the United States and Europe, is sometimes conceptualized as the ideological façade of global capital.[5] The lens or framework of epiphenomenon or façade disables us from seeing nationalism's deep and complex imbrication with capitalism; in turn, it discourages us from narrating capital's ability to roll in the soil nourished by nationalism. Defining Hindu nationalism and neoliberalism as intersecting political projects, I examine the cultural forms these projects use to narrate themselves and track their intersection in their conception of the categories *people* and *development*. Stories are therefore the archive and the story is also a heuristic device for the book.[6] So, even as I read the stories that political parties and their campaigns tell, that corporations narrate, that films, advertising, journalism, and commentary circulate, I track, discover, and explore the story that emerges from these many narratives. My assumption is that that story and its form informs us about the making of the temporal and spatial node within which we live.

Some of the questions that the book poses are: What is the relationship between neoliberalism, associated as it is with globalization, and authoritarian nationalism, linked as it is with nativism? How is this relationship forged? The book approaches questions about political economy through material that is often seen as inconsequential to it, namely the popular cultural story. It reveals that the relationship between globalization and nativism is forged in popular culture. Political and cultural theorists have shown us that for a system of thought to become dominant, it must produce and advance itself through a conceptual apparatus that speaks to our desires, instincts, and values.[7] My book argues that the conjuncture that twines neoliberalism with authoritarian nationalism cultivates an affective node by narrating stories about development, emergence, renewal, and mobility, of the nation and its people. Both neoliberalism and authoritarian nationalism or Hindutva in India narrate themselves as political projects that enable the spectacular renewal of the nation and the emphatic mobility of the people.

Economic policy is formulated in elite institutional spaces and is often obscured by jargon that requires expertise to decipher. Neoliberalism is no exception. However, as David Harvey has shown, neoliberalism has used the political ideals of human dignity and individual freedom to legitimize and advance itself. Neoliberalism in India, the book will reveal, narrates itself as a political project about the authentic commoner, marked as such through gender and caste. Moreover, in the story that neoliberalism narrates, that commoner is linked to the spectacle of national economic renewal and anticolonial nationalism. The sutures that produce the linkage are patrilineal in form. While the nation may be narrated as feminine, the spectacular force that conjoins the nation to the commoner is masculinized. Hindu nationalism also narrates itself as a political project about the authentic commoner—the Hindu—and specifically sutures the people so defined to the spectacular Hindu nation and aggressive masculinity or muscular authority.

The intersection of neoliberalism with Hindu nationalism is defined by their co-constitution of the commoner—this category provides both political projects affective legitimacy—and elicits consent for the establishment of authoritarian power.

This book writes a cultural history of contemporary India by tracing the linkages between divergent and multiple temporalities of political and economic processes. In order to do so, I traverse the 1990s, a historical moment about which much has been written,[8] but also the preceding decades of the 1970s and 1980s as well as the two decades after the new millennium. The book is therefore about those times—the 1970s, 1980s, and the 1990s, the time of the ascent of neoliberalism and religious nationalism—and it is about these times—the new millennium, the time arguably of the consolidation of neoliberalism and nationalism. It is about conjunctures—the terrain of struggle for dominance; the dominance specifically of neoliberalism and Hindu nationalism in India. My aim here is to reveal Hindutva neoliberalism as a conjuncture formed through the deliberate and strategic suturing of multiple temporalities. Namely, the time of modernity and modernization, which as anthropologist James Ferguson notes is believed to be the time of industrial economies, scientific technologies, liberal democratic institutions, nuclear families, and secular world views, or, in Walter Benjamin's terms, homogenous empty time. In distinction to the time of modernization, is messianic time, nonlinear, non-secular, unmarked by the clock and the factory and circular where the past, the present, and the imminent future may be experienced in a single moment and may be connected in a spatial node. The form of this conjuncture, we shall see, channels these different temporalities and the affect or emotions associated with them into a single script defined by conceptions of renewal and emergence.

This is a feminist project because the story of the intersection of neoliberalism with Hindu nationalism is a story about masculinity—aggrieved, obstructed, incomplete, aggressive, and on the move—spectacularized into authority. Additionally, as feminist scholar Clare Hemmings has shown us, in the context of feminist theory itself, a focus on storytelling reveals to us the political grammar and the narrative constructs that enable stories to become amenable to dominant discourses of a political-economic conjuncture.[9] Feminist scholarship, in fact, has recently focused on the stories the field has narrated about itself, as a form of loving critique. Attendant to feminism's call to be vigilantly self-reflexive of the epistemological and conceptual categories we use ourselves and how those might enable and disable certain social formations, my specific interest here is to examine culture's imbrication with political economy through the heuristic device of the story. I expressly do not turn to culture to critique the essentialism of political economy, because, as cultural theorists like Robert Young have shown us, the genealogies of culture and race are deeply imbricated and intertwined with the political economy of colonialism and colonial desire.[10] There is no safety, therefore, in culturalism. Moreover, culture often becomes encoded as the feminized appendage to masculinized political economy. It would not be unfair to say that popular culture is, in fact, constituted as the feminine Other of masculinized political economic projects. My intervention here is to trouble this ossified and gendered disciplinary and methodological bind. I therefore read political economy as a story too, as a story about our time. I read it for the sign systems it deploys, the narrative strategies it uses and the affective story it aims to tell. Most importantly, I read both the popular cultural story as well as the story political economy narrates to interpret its form. The attention to stories allows us to intervene in that conjuncture by imagining different ways of telling the stories about our time.

NEW TIMES

In the 1990s, I was a teenager living in the metropolis of Mumbai, on the west coast of India, when the world changed. Or so it seemed to me. A mosque had been demolished by a Hindu mob, Mumbai city burned, computer science and information technology were all the rage, the Miss World beauty pageant came to India a few years after the introduction of Pepsi and Coca-Cola. The television screen pulsed with new images, new sounds, and new voices, as state control of the airwaves loosened. The first Gulf War played itself out in grainy, green imagery on the screen in the living room. We heard that a Black man named Rodney King had been brutally beaten by the police and we saw images of the Los Angeles "riots." We didn't know who O. J. Simpson was but we saw images of the police chasing his white Bronco and later we stayed up very late—or did we wake up really early?—to hear that he was found not guilty of murdering his ex-wife and another man on those newly liberated airwaves. A few years later, we saw the U.S. president Bill Clinton write a zero against the federal budget deficit on those same screens and heard about Tony Blair in the UK and his "new" Labor Party. At home, the Indian national muscle was flexed through nuclear tests, Hindu pride was aggressively articulated, and caste-based affirmative action policies were violently contested. Economic liberalization became a key phrase. Brands were everywhere and the erstwhile angry young man, the man of the city streets, the working-class hero of the Hindi cinematic screen—Amitabh Bachchan—appeared in the advertising campaigns of many of those brands.

It was a bewildering time that I experienced as a knot, a node of tangled threads and provocations of all manner of hues. In the first decade of the new millennium, as I became an adult and now lived outside the nation of my birth, that temporal and spatial node only grew more tangled. Or so I thought. Economic liberalization or neoliberalism, about which there had been strife, ambivalence, and debate in the 1990s, had consolidated itself in India and around the world. India was deemed renewed, it had emerged, the Indian national press informed me. Hindu nationalism that defines India as a Hindu nation was also strengthened. In fact, in 2014, the right-wing Hindu nationalist Bharatiya Janata Party (BJP), the political unit of the larger Hindu nationalist movement, won a majority of seats in the Indian general elections and formed the government. Narendra Modi, who as chief minister of the western Indian state of Gujarat had aggressively narrated Hindu and Gujarati pride, became prime minister. In the story he tells about himself, Modi is an outsider to the elite, upper-caste political establishment that has governed India since independence from British rule in 1947. In 2019, the BJP won a resounding majority again and came back to power. Modi, having consolidated his power both within his own political party and within the broader political discourse, is prime minister once again.

Modi's ascent to power is not a story about Indian exceptionalism; a global conjuncture was taking shape. In 2010 and then again in 2014 and 2018 for instance, Hungary saw the national conservative Fidesz Party win a supermajority in the parliamentary elections against the Socialist Party. Viktor Orban, under whose leadership Fidesz had moved from its traditional center-right position to a hard-right national conservatism, has been the prime minister. In 2016, the real estate developer and reality TV star Donald Trump became the forty-fifth president of the United States. He (in)famously claimed that his predecessor, Barack Obama, the first African American president of the United States, was not a citizen of that nation. Trump had the support of white supremacist organizations including the Ku Klux Klan,[11] had called for and attempted to enact a ban on Muslims entering the United States, and had run for office on a conservative ticket. He has been accused of sexual assault by multiple women and was recorded on tape stating that he simply forces himself on women without waiting for their consent. Narrating himself as a businessman and thus outside the traditional political class, Trump declared that he would "drain the swamp" in the federal capital, Washington DC.[12] Also, in 2019, the far-right politician and former army captain Jair Bolsonaro became the thirty-eighth president of Brazil. Bolsonaro secured a majority of the vote in a runoff against the left candidate, Fernando Haddad of the Workers' Party. Bolsonaro associates himself with a "family values agenda" and is an opponent of affirmative action, same-sex marriage, and abortion. He styles himself as an outsider, an embodiment of the people's disenchantment with the political class, and has linked himself to an "anti-corruption/graft" and an "anti-crime" agenda, calling for the militarization of the police and looser gun laws.

The specificity of the Indian story brings into relief the complex articulations of a conjuncture that is global in shape. India resides within this conjuncture not as an exception but as a significant geopolitical node. The listing of electoral successes around the world—Europe, North America, Latin America, and Asia—over the last decade, in particular, highlights the electoral defeat of the left and the concomitant emergence of a form of right-wing political discourse that enables the consolidation of global capitalism, articulates religious conservatism, is Islamophobic, xenophobic, and anti-immigrant more generally, is anti-Black, anti-LGBTQ, and misogynistic. This globally dominant political discourse is embodied by a form of hypermasculinity that claims outsider (often victim) status for itself and narrates itself as a reflection of the people. This then is the story of our time. It is a story that gives form to a global conjuncture.

NEOLIBERALISM, RACE, AND CASTE

Popular commentary and academic discourse alike has given us a name for the story of our time—authoritarian populism.[13] The argument here is that populism—the rhetoric that conjures up the "people" and vests it with moral and political authority and authenticity—is the mask or the patina that serves to legitimize authoritarianism, described as obedience to strong leaders who project themselves as particularly enabled to protect the people, their traditions, and their customs.[14] Authoritarian populism emerged as an analytical concept (in conjunction with Thatcherism and Reaganism), in fact, to denote the conjuncture of the 1970s and 1980s in Britain and concomitantly in the United States. Cultural and political theorist Stuart Hall used the concept to describe the "swing to the right," that had installed itself from at least the latter half of the 1960s and had sustained its dynamism and momentum.[15] The concept was used by Hall politically as a rallying cry for the Left in Britain to sharpen their analytical and political tools to confront the conjuncture that established the dominance of neoliberalism. He also used it epistemologically to point to the profound contradictions at the heart of Thatcherism wherein "authoritarian closure"—defined as not simply brute coercive force but the insulation of certain political policies and institutions from social and political dissent—was legitimized by a "populist gloss"—wherein the "people" were mobilized against "unions," "class," and other collectives and linked to family.[16] The contradiction here is that an ostensible anti-statism—its exemplary slogans include "a culture of welfare dependency," "a bloated bureaucracy," "small government" and so on—works alongside authoritarianism, marked by narratives about the state's strong role in upholding moral values, strong policing, tougher sentencing, greater family discipline, and so on.[17] In other words, even as the narrative about small government circulated widely, the story about the strong state that protects moral values and traditions traveled with it. This iteration or configuration of the political right in the 1970s and 1980s that the concept authoritarian populism aimed to capture occurred in the context of a recession, triggered in part by a rise in oil prices, the fragmentation of working classes, and the resultant disaffection with the political establishment.

My point of departure here is the category *people* or *populism*. Rather than assume its coherence and legibility, I am asking how people as a category is constituted within a conjuncture that is shaped by a particular form of capitalism. Theorists have argued that the people is an empty signifier, which emerges through the complex operation of naming.[18] As an empty signifier, the people is akin to the concept of zero in mathematics, pointing to a place within the system of signification, which is "constitutively irrepresentable."[19] These theorists ask us to imagine situations where there is disaffection, critique, and perhaps even anger with powerful institutions or those that people these institutions. That disaffection leads to the expression of certain demands, which are placed before these institutions. In the event that these demands remain unmet, the disaffection may grow and find communion with other "isolated, heterogeneous" demands. If these disparate demands are quilted together into a "global demand," leading to the formation of "political frontiers," the institution comes to be constructed as an "antagonistic force." The people emerge as a name in the moment of quilting, when the many heterogeneous demands become a global demand.

Working on the assumption that it is analytically and politically significant to draw a distinction between the people that emerge from the stitching together of equivalent demands and the people that are constituted through the simultaneous repression of that process of quilting and the appropriation of the disaffection that was the precursor to the articulation of demands, I am interested in tracing the complex and hegemonic construction of that empty signifier, the people. The stories we will follow through the course of this manuscript will reveal the contours of the people as constituted by the appropriation of disaffection caused by persistent and obdurate inequity. In chapter 1, we will track the narrative processes through which the people are defined as disaffected as a consequence of obstructed social mobility and as desirous of improved well-being brought about by a form of spectacular masculinity. In chapter 2, we will find the people on the move. That mobility defined as iconic is narrated as transforming the common into the spectacular—the cinematic working-class hero becomes neoliberalism's brand father, the tea seller is transformed into an ordained leader of the people, and the small-town young man and woman leading utterly unremarkable middle-class lives are turned into brilliant con artists reveling in piles of cash. In chapter 3, the people are defined as possessive individuals and entrepreneurs, and in chapter 4, the people in the time of Hindutva neoliberalism are narrated as upwardly mobile men who turn to ideal femininity in order to find a resolution for their sense of alienation. The people so constituted are used in the service of capital and authoritarian nationalism. They become the foundation on which Hindutva neoliberalism constructs its edifice. In doing so, they also serve as the warrant for the repression of the articulation of different demands, which might have produced a people that answered to a different name.

The significance of drawing a distinction between the name *people* as it emerges through the process of articulation and the name *people* as it is constituted by the appropriation of disaffection and the repression of that articulation can be illustrated by considering India in the late 1960s and early 1970s. Political scientist Ranabir Samaddar has argued that the year 1971 saw the repression of agrarian rebellion that sought redress of the "deliberate neglect" on the part of the central and state governments "of the landlessness and indebtedness of millions of peasants."[20] The agrarian rebellion also highlighted a crisis that was defined by debt bondage, an acute food crisis that resulted in famine and food riots in some parts of the nation. This rebellion was transformed into a political movement, particularly in some parts of the east and the south, and was accompanied by urban protests as well. That transformation of an agrarian rebellion into urban agitations and a political movement occurs through the processes of quilting together disparate, equivalent demands into the name *people*—a particularity that necessarily acts as a universality. Samaddar argues that the end of these rebellions through brutal state repression occurred alongside the "entry of the people as 'poor' in institutional politics."[21] *Garibi hatao* (end poverty) became then–prime minister Indira Gandhi's electoral battle cry, suggesting that "reforms would be henceforth initiated from the top."[22] As such, "agrarian struggles for land, justice and peasant power were suppressed, to be replaced now with stabilization developmental programs of the government."[23] The people named in this moment by development programs and institutional politics, as chapter 1 will detail, are linked to aggressive nationalism and the centralization of state power. Already defined as nationalists and in thrall of authority, these people, two decades into the new millennium, are named by Hindutva neoliberalism as possessive individuals, as proud Hindus desirous of authoritarian nationalism and neoliberalism. This book will track the narrative processes through which the people are constituted as such. It will draw out the resonances and the divergence between the people named by public discourse in the 1970s and the people named by Hindutva neoliberalism.

Before we situate the emergence of the people as a category in the context of neoliberalism, a word about the concept itself. David Harvey has succinctly defined neoliberalism as a political economic theory that suggests that human well-being can best be achieved by "liberating" individual entrepreneurial freedom within an institutional framework that guarantees strong private property rights, unfettered markets, and free trade.[24] Neoliberalism has been described as a specific organization of capitalism that has developed to protect capital and weaken labor.[25] While neoliberalism is not a mode of production, its central tenet can be defined as the organized use of state power to "impose (financial) market imperatives in a domestic process that is replicated internationally by 'globalization.'"[26] A range of global events enabled a political-economic theory that had existed in the margins to acquire dominance in what Harvey describes as a pivotal two-year period in the late 1970s.[27] These global events include the slowdown of growth rates in the 1960s, the collapse of the Bretton Woods system—which had systematized monetary relations among nation-states following World War II—in the 1970s, the dismantling of the Soviet bloc in the 1980s, and the balance-of-payment crises in the so-called developing countries in the 1980s and the 1990s.[28] Neoliberalism has also been conceived as a new relationship between government and knowledge through which "governing activities are recast as nonpolitical and nonideological problems that need technocratic solutions."[29] As such, neoliberalism is described as a "technology of government"[30] and the "infiltration of market-driven truths and calculations into the domain of politics."[31]

Hall, using Antonio Gramsci's conceptualization of hegemony, has argued that the "incessant and persistent"[32] struggle to maintain and consolidate neoliberalism's central position necessitated the move to authoritarian populism. The interventionist, strong state, according to Hall, is an "exceptional form of the capitalist state," which constructs popular and active consent around itself and keeps in place formal representative institutions, unlike the more classical fascist or authoritarian state. How was this "popular" consent won? As Harvey has suggested, when narrated through the conceptions of freedom and human dignity, neoliberalism was defined in excess of specific relations between the state and capital. Discussing most specifically the context of the United States, feminist scholar Nancy Fraser uses the term "progressive neoliberalism"[33] to describe the Clintonian state in the 1990s. Even as the Clintonian state consolidated neoliberalism by, for instance, deregulating the banking sector and the telecommunications industry and crafting the North American Free Trade Agreement (NAFTA), it also formed an alliance with the liberal elements of some social movements including feminism, multiculturalism, environmentalism, and LGBTQ rights. This "progressiveness" attempted to insulate the state, capital, and the relations between them from political dissent.

The "progressiveness" of progressive neoliberalism was always supplemented however, by its carceral agenda. The decades of the 1980s and 1990s in the United States, for instance, also saw the exponential rise in the population of the incarcerated despite the plateauing or even decline of crime rates in the 1980s.[34] Queer of color critics and black feminists alike have thus pointed to the paradox wherein racial inclusion within the state has, in fact, expanded as well as made more complex racial and gendered inequalities. Moreover, the institutional spaces and policies that enable racial inclusion simultaneously expanded the tools of "legitimate violence" that serve to reproduce and consolidate inequity.[35] This consolidation of inequity is predictable, the "Black radical tradition" will tell us, because capitalism flowered in a cultural soil that was infused with racialism.[36] The history of capital reveals its racial core. Understood as such, "racial capitalism" did not destroy or revolutionize the old racial order but developed from it. Consequently, racialism—when it Others and marginalizes, thus understood as racism or when it includes particular bodies, understood as multiculturalism—cannot be conceived as the epiphenomenon that allows capitalism to reproduce itself, the "false consciousness" that insulates capitalism from dissent; it is, in fact, the core, the center of capital itself. Historians of South Asia specifically examining the histories of caste, class, and urbanity have similarly argued that urban life and industrial capitalism did not destroy caste; instead, just as capitalism evolved and developed on the soil of racialism in the United States, industrial capitalism in South Asia in the nineteenth and twentieth centuries attached itself to caste and "leeched on it."[37] Capitalism worked with and through caste. Historian Juned Shaikh has thus argued that industrial capitalism and city life more generally made caste more robust even as it came to be "insulated in the garb of modernity."[38] As these histories of capital reveal to us its flowering in a soil rich with racialism and casteism, they also provide an analytical lever with which to pry open and examine the relationship between neoliberalism—this new phase of capitalism—and Hindu nationalism specifically in the context of India and authoritarian nationalism more generally. More specifically, this history reveals to us that Hindutva neoliberalism is as much a story about caste as it is a story about authoritarian nationalism and capital.[39]

Shanker Gopalkrishnan has argued that neoliberalism in India lacked an organized political force, a political foundation, such as Thatcherism made possible in Britain and Reaganism in the United States. The relationship between Hindu nationalism and neoliberalism that was forged in the 1990s was therefore significant and expedient for both projects. "India shining" was the story told by both the Hindu nationalists and India Inc. in the early 2000s—India was shining economically *and* growing in confidence as a Hindu nation, it had "emerged." Gopalkrishnan enumerates some of the resonances between the political projects of neoliberalism and Hindu nationalism in India, arguing that for both projects, "social processes are reduced to individual choice," the state exists in the form of a "supreme principle" rather than as an expression and a guarantor of individual or collective rights, and that the only division that is important within both projects is that between "'society' and its Other," all other divisions being defined as "unnecessary and pathological."[40] Gopalkrishnan's interventions ask us to think about the political resonances between neoliberalism and Hindu nationalism. Examined through the analytic of resonances or intersections, Hindu nationalism cannot be conceptualized as a façade, a patina, or the epiphenomenon that glosses over or obscures neoliberalism. Instead, we are compelled to trace the contours of a conjuncture coming into relief through the linkages formed between two political projects that have intersecting investments and identifications.

HINDUTVA, HINDU NATIONALISM

Historian David Ludden notes that Hindu nationalism gains support from established ideas in Eurasia that seek to define nations, civilizations, and cultures in terms of their religious history.[41] The Hindu nationalist movement therefore seeks to define a "Hindu way of life" and redefine Indian history as Hindu history. It seeks to mobilize and represent a majority, one that is defined by its religion. Scholars note that whereas the terms "majority" and "minority" are considered fluid in a democracy, such that no majority is ever assumed to be "based on a single unchanging identity alone: a majority is constructed from issue to issue and can change from programme to programme," the majority that Hindu nationalism purports to represent is permanent, because this majority is constituted "solely by the fact that 85 percent of the population are, by census statistics, Hindu."[42] Hindu nationalism claims to represent a majority and also attempts to construct a Hindu past for the nation. Achin Vanaik notes that the project of Hindu nationalism involves "recourse to a systematic distortion of history, to the dogmatization and territorialization of Hinduism—centering Hinduism on specific texts, gods and goddesses, places of worship, myths, symbols and so forth, that are made pre-eminent and widely acknowledged as such."[43] Not only does Hindu nationalism define India as a Hindu nation, Ludden notes that it portrays Islam as "foreign and derivative, alien to India."[44]

This definition of a Hindu nation and the role of the Muslim within it is asserted in public space; public culture is the space where it is converted into common sense. Defining public culture as the "public space in which a society and its constituent individuals and communities imagine, represent, and recognize themselves through political discourse, commercial and cultural expressions, and representations of state and civic organizations,"[45] T. B. Hansen has argued that Hindu nationalism has "emerged and taken shape neither in the political system as such nor in the religious field, but in the broader realm of . . . public culture."[46] That public cultural shape of Hindu nationalism was significant to the formulation of a commodity-image. Media and cultural studies scholar Arvind Rajagopal, for instance, has shown that advertising in India, particularly from the 1980s onward, when economic liberalization policies were instituted and the Hindu nationalist movement began to gain ideological and political ascendancy, has turned to Hindu mythology, symbolism, and ritual in order to constitute a popular aesthetic that would reach a broader spectrum of consumers.[47] This is an aesthetic—enabled by the intersection of neoliberalism and Hindu nationalism—that intimates freedom and mobility even as it reproduces cultural and social hierarchies. Manisha Basu has argued that popular millennial authors such as Chetan Bhagat and Amish Tripathi have inserted a kind of "technological and managerial expertise" into cultural forms such that "metropolitan Hindutva" (i.e., Hindutva in the time of economic liberalization), is "cleansed of its communal-genocidal genealogy . . . and made to appear as a force that merely invests, apolitically, in free market economies, digital competencies and smart communication."[48] Arguing that metropolitan Hindutva must be read as an imperializing force, Basu's analysis of its language reveals it to be a "non-regionalized local English" that is digitally savvy and constitutive of a "kind of techno-managerial culture whereby a national elite claims its place on the world economic stage."[49]

The first decade of the 2000s stood witness to the failure of neoliberalism as a project globally, resulting in the fiscal crisis of 2007, rising unemployment and underemployment, profound fiscal inequities, and states in crisis-management mode dictating austerity measures. In India, the BJP faced defeat in the general elections held in 2004, their campaign slogan "India Shining" was repudiated, and that election saw the Left parties making electoral gains. In the United States, Barack Obama became the first African American to be elected to the office of president, championing a message of hope and change. Neoliberalism, however, was neither vanquished nor repudiated. In India, neither was Hindu nationalism. The return of authoritarian populism as a conceptual category (within academic and mainstream commentary) late into the second decade of the new millennium— with the BJP's Narendra Modi in power in India, Boris Johnson in the UK, and

Donald Trump leading the Republican Party in the United States—suggests a conjunctural similarity between our own present and the not-so-distant past of the 1970s.[50] Even as we might argue that the conjuncture that linked neoliberalism with nationalism began to take shape in the decade of the 1970s and the 1980s, an analysis of our immediate present must contend with the spectacular failure of neoliberalism as a political project *and* its continued salience.[51] Authoritarian populism as a concept has therefore also been retooled and worked upon to better describe the story of our own time. One such concept is "authoritarian neoliberalism" (the reworking of authoritarian populism), which describes the reconfiguration of neoliberalism after the 2007 fiscal crisis. One modality of its working is that dominant social groups and global capital itself are less concerned with co-opting resistance through concessions and compromise and instead are more invested in explicit marginalization and exclusion of subordinate groups via the law, political institutions, and the democratic process itself.[52] Once again, the deep contradiction that authoritarian neoliberalism as a concept aims to describe (at least in part) is the manner in which the invocation of the people and their ostensibly innate sense of morality and authenticity serves also to exclude and marginalize their interests and their heterogeneity. "Authoritarian neoliberalism" aims to explicate the continued salience of neoliberalism despite its dramatic failure.

I am interested in tracing the ways in which the constitution of neoliberalism and authoritarian nationalism in the decades of the 1980s and 1990s in India now enable the reconstitution of neoliberalism in the aftermath of its failure. In other words, I believe that the formulation of both neoliberalism as well as Hindu nationalism reveals to us why and how neoliberalism can continue to be salient and it shows us the shared assumptions of these political projects. Here is where we come back to that oft-used category *people* as well as to the significance of the cultural story. It is within the space of the popular cultural story and via its mediation that the category *people* is worked out as an affective sign and as an embodiment. The popular cultural story also provides the form, the shape, and the template through which neoliberalism and Hindu nationalism alike define themselves. In other words, the story reveals a political imaginary in which Hindu nationalism and neoliberalism are co-constituted.[53]

The intersection of neoliberalism and Hindu nationalism via the cultural story brings postcolonial anger about the obstructed promise of independence from colonialism, the violence attending the desire for a Hindu nation, liberalism's emphasis on possessive individualism, the enchantment of conspicuous consumption, global brands and global travel inaugurated by economic liberalization, even anti-caste and feminist political assertions *together* in an unstable structure-in-dominance. Thus, the anger in the 1970s about an obstructed present melded in the 1980s and the 1990s with the political struggles around Hindu nationalism, economic liberalization, and caste-based demands for redistribution. The book tracks the continuities and shifts in cultural stories from this moment to the consolidation of Hindu nationalism and neoliberalism a decade into the new millennium with the election of Narendra Modi as prime minister of India. Even though the book is a cultural history of contemporary India, you will not find the tracing of a linear history here. Instead, what I am most interested in is tracing the disparate cultural and temporal nodes that enable the constitution of Hindutva neoliberalism, such that the vigilantism of the popular angry young man in Hindi-language films of the 1970s becomes the mode through which the political persona of Narendra Modi is constituted and experienced in 2014 even as the actor who embodied the angry young man is transformed into the father of branding, indeed the father of neoliberal India. Or how the idiom of the "commoner" and development from the 1970s finds echoes in Hindu nationalist discourse and corporate advertising in the new millennium. But before we track these linkages, let us reckon with the affective spatiotemporal node that has come to be called "new India."

NEW INDIA

In 1991, the Indian National Congress (INC)—the political party associated most particularly with anticolonial nationalism, Jawaharlal Nehru (independent India's first prime minister), M. K. Gandhi, and, until the 1980s, the single largest political party with a national footprint—was in power. Manmohan Singh of the INC, finance minister of India at the time, laid out the infrastructure for a set of economic policies that were euphemistically labeled "economic liberalization" and tied India's political economy more intimately to global capital. The Indian state at this time had struggled to manage a fiscal crisis that had resulted in an accumulated public debt that stood at 76 percent of the GDP, foreign exchange reserves that fell to the equivalent of two weeks' imports, a deficit that stood at 9 percent of the GDP, and inflation levels that hovered in the two-figure range.[54] Using the urgency of the fiscal crisis as its "call to action," the Indian state unequivocally defined its shift to economic liberalization in its 1991–1992 budget. The reforms included neoliberal prescriptions like devaluing the currency and initiating policies that attracted greater foreign direct investment, resulting in the increased visibility of consumer products in the Indian market. There was opposition, restiveness, and skepticism about these changes from the political left as well as from the right and from some Indian corporations as well.[55] The opposition raised concerns about the effects of liberalization—intimacy with U.S.-dominated global capital—on a struggling Indian political-economy. A joint statement issued by prominent Indian economists argued that even while the "nature and magnitude" of the financial crisis remained "shrouded in secrecy," the state had induced a panic about the state of the economy, "all of which reduc[ed] India's bargaining position with the international financial institutions and international capital markets." They maintained that a reform program must give the highest priority "to raising the productivity of all the Indian workers" even as the "system is debureaucratized and strengthened." This, they argued, was imperative before the economy was subjected to "international competition in a fundamentally iniquitous world system."[56]

The INC labored to tell the story of economic reforms as a story about continuity with change. They insisted that economic liberalization was in line with the vision for the nation envisaged by those who led the anticolonial nationalist mobilization against the British. In a long preamble to a document outlining the industrial policy reforms the finance ministry and the prime minister's office were seeking, the new policy was genealogically linked to Jawaharlal Nehru. A policy that would abolish the requirement for industry to seek clearances under the Monopolies and Restrictive Trade Practices Act (MRTP Act) of 1969 was narrated within the preamble to the cabinet note as "inspired" by the "goals and objectives set out for the nation by Pandit Nehru [sic] on the eve of Independence, namely the rapid agricultural and industrial development of ... [the] country, rapid expansion of opportunities for gainful employment, progressive reduction of social and economic disparities, removal of poverty and attainment of self-reliance."[57] The preamble went so far as to suggest that the Industrial Policy Resolution of 1956 was the fountainhead, the original vision statement on which the new economic and industrial policy was shaped. In this story, economic liberalization was linked patrilineally to anticolonial nationalism and the fervor of the newly independent state. It was articulated to the heady task of nation-building. It also did the work of winning the consent of a cabinet with many trepidations at the time.

P. V. Narasimha Rao, prime minister of India in 1991, traced an even longer genealogy when speaking in the lower house of parliament in July of that year and later in his writing. Quoting from a Sanskrit *subhashita*—a short epigram that contains a message typically in the form of a maxim—Rao asserted that the economic reforms initiated by his government had "salvaged the prestige" of the nation because "the wise [the *pandit* or the brahmin] when faced with untenable circumstances, find a way out by giving up half their possessions"; such a move avoids complete destruction and the wise [the brahmins] can then use the salvaged half of their possessions prudently to win back all that they had lost. Referencing the fiscal crisis and the controversial decision to devalue the currency as well as liberalize certain sections of the economy, Rao eschewed their modern provenance in political-economic theory and linked such policy decisions to brahminism and articulated it to an ancient national culture. The nation here was also feminized and the policy makers (i.e., the embodiment of the state) were masculinized as her sons who had strived to maintain her honor and prestige. The patrilinear linkage to Nehru and the ancient brahmins was a piece of this larger narrative that reproduced the nation and the state in familiar gendered sign systems. To use Pheng Cheah's evocative phrase here, there was a "surfeit of culture" in this narration of economic liberalization.[58]

Let us think some more, though, about this inaugural story of economic liberalization because it establishes a significant link between liberalism and brahminism, that it defines as indigenous and native. That link is crucial to the intersection of Hindu nationalism and neoliberalism. Political theorist Ajay Gudavarthy has argued that liberalism allows for incremental change, accommodating dissent, so that dissent does not flower into a radical challenge to social and institutional hierarchies.[59] More importantly, liberalism's centering of the individual and its conceptualization of freedom as the capacity to separate from social collectives (such as caste- and class-based communities) engenders the spatial and social segregation of the same collectives. Liberalism's philosophical tenets underline freedom in their discourse and in practice effect segregation and separation along the lines of social and economic hierarchies. Gudavarthy has argued that brahminism, similarly, is "essentially a philosophy of separating and segregating social collectives along caste by birth" and that it "co-opts and accommodates moments that emerge in opposition to it and tones them in its own color."[60] Tracing the history of the domestication of the English language (the language of colonialism) in India, gender historian Shefali Chandra has also tracked the history of the amalgamation of liberalism with brahminism. Chandra's work shows us that battles that were waged around the domestication of the English language in the late nineteenth and early twentieth centuries exacerbated caste-based hierarchies and served to "brahminize" Indian culture.[61] Narrating economic liberalization as "continuity with change," as the INC did, was thus in line with the central tenets of liberalism but also brahminism. More importantly, the INC sought to win consent for neoliberalism by narrating it as indigenous, as emerging from the cultural soil of the nation itself. In order to do so, it narrated the nation and its culture through Hinduism, caste (specifically brahminism), and gender. What was established early in the story of economic liberalization was the significance of the patriline and an embodiment that emphasized caste and masculinity, linked to the nation. Even when other elements of the original story about economic liberalization were disavowed in later iterations, the suturing of patriarchal nationalism, caste, and neoliberalism remained in place.

Thus, in the story that has circulated since 1991, the set of economic policies that were instituted in the first decade after independence from British colonial rule, including the MRTP Act of 1969, have been paradoxically defined as "license Raj" or the colonization of capital and the possessive individual by a vast state apparatus that controls (and therefore chokes, according to this story) capital.[62] The INC's narration of continuity with change, which linked the Nehruvian state to economic liberalization, might have only had limited success therefore, but its articulation of liberalization to the affective registers of nationalism and therefore national renewal did find resonance and was consistently reproduced. So, twenty-five years after the 1991 budget speech that heralded economic liberalization, Montek Singh Ahluwalia, one of the key architects of that set of political economic changes, told a story that insisted on the "domestic pedigree of the 1991 reforms." An economist and a former deputy chairman of the Planning Commission of India, Ahluwalia noted in an essay written for a special issue of the *Economic and Political Weekly* that a "constant refrain when the reforms were unveiled"[63] was that the reforms had been imposed on a nation in crisis by the International

Monetary Fund or the World Bank in return for financial assistance. Refuting that assertion, Ahluwalia tells a different story, one in which "there was a home-grown process of rethinking on economic policy that had been underway" from at least the 1980s. Ahluwalia traces a genealogy for the budget speech of 1991 within this story: Marking the decade of the 1980s as a significant turning point, he notes that the "strategy of industrialization, fashioned in the 1950s and early 1960s, in which the state played a very active role with the public sector as a major investor," was dominant until this point. According to Ahluwalia, the shift occurred in the 1980s when bureaucrats and technocrats working within and on the margins of the state apparatus wrote white papers or think pieces that argued for rethinking India's political economy. Ahluwalia delinks economic reforms or Indian neoliberalism from the Nehruvian state but insists on its national, native pedigree. Circumscribing the ideas that produced economic policy initiatives within the boundaries of the nation-state was still deemed significant, twenty-five years after the budget speech of 1991–1992.

The 1980s are seen as a crucial turning point for the Hindu nationalist movement as well, as this is the decade when the mobilization to construct a temple in the place of a mosque in northern India gained momentum. In 1992, a year after the budget speech that had heralded economic liberalization, the Hindu nationalist movement destroyed a sixteenth-century mosque in the north Indian city of Ayodhya, the birthplace of the mythic king Rama, worshipped as a Hindu god. The demolition triggered anti-Muslim pogroms in different parts of the nation. Twenty-two years after these events, in 2014, the Hindu nationalist BJP, which had been at the center of the mosque demolition movement in 1992, won a thumping majority in India's general elections. While the BJP had formed the government earlier, briefly in 1998 and for the full five-year term in 1999, the political party won the 2014 election with a simple majority, a scale of electoral supremacy that had not been witnessed by any party since 1984. Narendra Modi, a politician from the western Indian state of Gujarat who until that point had been denied a visa to travel to the United States or England because of his leadership during anti-Muslim pogroms in his state, became prime minister. A regional politician who had worked as the liaison between the Rashtriya Swayamsevak Sangh (RSS)—the ideological unit of the Hindu nationalist movement—and the BJP in the state of Gujarat, Modi was propelled onto the national stage during and in the aftermath of the 2002 Gujarat pogrom. In 2009, five years prior to his election as prime minister, Modi had received a resounding endorsement from large corporations and champions of economic liberalization in India. The *Economic Times* had reported this endorsement under the headline "Narendra Modi Becomes India Inc. Poster Boy."

Popular commentary and scholarly analysis have also listed the social, cultural, economic, and political changes that have transformed India since the 1980s and described the last decade of the twentieth century in that region as a rupture. Rupal

Oza thus notes that "the political economic changes in the early 1990s began to materially and discursively construct a *new* India," such that the nation had to forge an image of a "vibrant new economy that welcomes foreign investment."[64] Nivedita Menon and Aditya Nigam define the years between 1989 and 1992 as constituting a "truly ruptural moment in contemporary Indian history." Some of the events that they list as constituting this rupture include the decline of the INC and the rise of coalitional politics, the implementation of affirmative action policies for a set of castes categorized as Other Backward Castes through the realization of the Mandal Commission report in 1990, and the emergence of the regional, lower-caste political parties as significant players in national politics. Menon and Nigam also point to the "beginnings of the media explosion that was to gather momentum through the 1990s and 2000s," marking the "beginning of the end of state-run media and the advent of a whole series of new media technologies that radically transformed the nature and form of politics and the terrain of social and cultural life in this period,"[65] as yet another transformation defining this time.

The moniker of "new" for the nation has been used in academic discussion to define and name the transformations that have taken place since the 1990s but it has also been used within branding and advertising campaigns to describe shifts wrought by economic liberalization. And most recently, "new" has been adopted by the BJP to describe the national polity that has enabled it to secure a commanding majority in the 2019 general elections. "Newness," in fact, signifies a much more complicated story about temporality and transformation. "Newness" in the stories told by both neoliberalism and Hindu nationalism, as we shall see in greater detail in chapter 1, temporally links the present to the past—sometimes that past is the inauguration of the nation or the birth of the nation-state in 1947 (or Year One), sometimes it is an ancient past (the nation-state may have been born in 1947, but the nation is timeless, the story goes)—as well as to the affective future in a single node. The multivalent temporality that the term "newness" gestures to always centers the nation as the affective ground that legitimizes political-economic shifts.

CULTURE AND STORY

Let me now discuss a couple of key concepts, specifically culture and story, in order to lay out the methodological stakes of the book before delineating spectacular realism as a form. We know through the work of feminist postcolonial and critical race scholars as well as cultural theorists that the separation of culture as a space distinct from the spheres of the political and economic is symptomatic of liberal conceptions of modernity and is observable in liberal legal and political philosophy. We also know from the work of postcolonial theorists that colonialism and its conception of modernity defined modern societies (read: the white West) as "having" culture while nonmodern societies were deemed to "be" foundationally cultural. Consequently, cultural critique working to decolonize the very conception of culture has argued that "rather than adopting the understanding of culture as one sphere in a set of differentiated spheres . . . 'culture' [should be discussed] as a terrain in which politics, culture, and the economic form an inseparable dynamic."[66] This work has also argued that rather than view culture as purely aesthetic or in terms that we might deem "anthropological" (the culture of a tribe, a community, a region, a nation) that culture must be posited as the space within which socioeconomic relations are reproduced and in which simultaneously antagonisms to that reproduction are articulated.

Literary theorists have argued that cultural productions such as the literary text perform the labor of resolving contradictions produced by sociopolitical and economic transformations. Literature or the cultural artifact, in this formulation, "has a problem-solving vocation" in that it labors to assuage the tensions created by a "symbolic overload" that follows such transformations. These symbolic overloads, which are a consequence of ideological contradictions, "risk rendering social cohesion precarious, and individual existence wearisome" and it is culture that makes existence more comprehensible, and more acceptable. "And . . . make[s] power relations more acceptable too—even their violence."[67] Turning from literature to productions that are seen as the effluence of a society, cultural and political theorist Lauren Berlant has argued for reading "the waste materials of everyday communication in the national public sphere as pivotal documents in the construction, experience, and rhetoric of quotidian citizenship in the United States."[68] Berlant thus suggests that varied cultural artifacts including propaganda materials produced by fringe political groups, mass entertainment media, viral images and videos, magazine covers, news stories, zines, and so forth are significant texts shaping the foundations of what constitutes citizenship. Media and cultural studies scholar Sarah Banet-Weiser has thought about consumer citizenship and the ways in which the 'brand,' which she defines as the intersection between marketing, a product, and the consumer, has become the "cultural context for everyday living, individual identity, and affective relationships."[69] As such, branding, she has argued, is more a cultural phenomenon than an economic one. Distinguishing between commodification, which she discusses as a marketing strategy that monetizes different spheres of life, and branding, Banet-Weiser has argued that as a broader cultural phenomenon, branding shapes the very ways in which we organize ourselves and importantly, the stories we tell "ourselves about ourselves."[70]

When examining the relationship between capitalism and culture or more specifically the commodity and the image, scholars have argued that capitalism compels the conjoining of image with commodity in a manner that alters both entities. Arvind Rajagopal, for instance, suggests that the translation of a commodity's use value to exchange value is mediated by the image and that in the relationship that is thus forged between the two, both are altered. The commodity does not remain a purely economic entity nor does the image function as only aesthetic.[71] Theorists of popular culture[72] and feminist media studies scholars have argued that the variegated modes of consuming the popular image as commodity have the ability, on occasion, to "open aperture-like into a social network yet to come."[73] In other words, while the cultural story or the cultural sign might be fashioned to win consent for a hegemonic project, the consumption of that self-same sign as a commodity that has a materiality and circulates has the potential to rework the sign into a historical actor around which a proto-social network or nascent social formation can be intuited.

Indebted to these interventions, as well as the work of Fredric Jameson and Michael Warner, I posit that the popular cultural story is crucially significant to both global capitalism and nationalism generally and neoliberalism and Hindu nationalism specifically. I suggest that the popular cultural story, which attempts to actualize ideals, including the people as a unit, is the model or the template for political-economic systems such as neoliberalism and Hindu nationalism to constitute themselves. We will therefore track the ways in which neoliberalism in India will constitute itself, mold itself through the affective registers of national renewal. This is a contradiction, a paradox that could have unraveled the conjuncture that was coming into relief. An old project that traces its genealogy to at least the 1920s, Hindu nationalism was being reformulated at the same time. It was also constituting itself as national renewal; more significantly, it was immersing itself in the popular stories that had voiced anger, anguish, and despair at the lost promise of anticolonialism. Hindu nationalism was fashioning itself as the solution to historic inequity and disenfranchisement. This was a contradiction too, for Hindu nationalism centers the brahmin and the upper castes, reinforces caste and Hindu patriarchy, and violently Others the non-Hindu, particularly the Muslim. This contradiction could also have created instability in the social formation. The *intersection* of cultural stories within which neoliberalism and Hindu nationalism were formulating and constituting themselves enabled first, the circulation of national renewal and authoritarian masculinity as sign systems and second, sutured neoliberalism to aspiration and Hindutva to righteous anger, and established an articulated relationship between the two systems of political and ideological thought. As such the contradictions of both systems of thought, for the moment at least, remain repressed.

Culture's co-belonging with politics means eschewing the epistemological binary that conceptualizes culture as ideology or resistance.[74] This epistemological binary assumes the culture of the state and the political institution as ideology and the culture of the people as radical, resistant. I think instead about culture as the story, the paradigm that gives form, that makes sensible or tangible, politics, economics, development, nation, *and* the people. I envisage stories as the medium that gives form to economic and political instances and as the sutures that link these diverse instances together into a complex unity or structure. "Stories" therefore are not reflective of the economic or the political in the last instance; instead they are assumed to be *constitutive*. As such, "stories" do not represent a false consciousness, instead they are the only modality through which we attain, maintain, and reinforce consciousness itself. Seyla Benhabib has argued, in fact, that culture presents "itself through narratively contested accounts,"[75] and that "to be and to become a self is to insert oneself into webs of interlocution; it is to know how to answer when one is addressed and to know how to address others."[76] Stories are a significant terrain of political struggle—they are the ground on which hegemony is attained, struggled over, and reinforced. Stories work to express political projects in ways that will win consent. Stories are complex, unstable scripts themselves encoding several different stories into a contingent unity.

Let us recap the argument thus far: Neoliberalism in India intersects with Hindu nationalism. This intersection is not merely a function of timing—the *coincidence* of Hindu nationalism resurrecting itself at the same time as economic liberalization was being formulated—but one that occurs because both these political projects are similarly constituted via the template of the popular cultural story. The *form* of the popular cultural story as well as the stories neoliberalism and Hindu nationalism narrate is our methodological point of entry.

SPECTACULAR REALISM

Let me now tell you three stories—a story drawn from popular culture, a story about Hindu nationalism, and a story about neoliberalism and global capital—as a way to narrate the form that brings Hindu nationalism and economic liberalization together. These stories are the archive and the story is the heuristic device for the book. I have thus culled stories from popular media and those composed by various narrators of Hindu nationalism and economic liberalization and, through a critical reading practice that is attentive to form, I track the emergent *story* from these many stories. *The story* defined through monikers of authenticity and realism is a story about common folk, the people. But there is more: *the story* is a story that links and articulates the people to a spectacle—the nation, spectacular power, a superpower. Each chapter outlines distinctive iterations of this articulation. Here, through a reading of these three disparate stories, I will define the contours of the narrative form that I am calling spectacular realism. While I will reveal the shapes, lines, and curves of spectacular realism in each of these three stories, I want to emphasize that it is only through the methodological maneuver of reading them together and consistently holding the three stories within a single analytical frame that the form comes into relief. In what follows, I aim to both define that narrative patterning and demonstrate my reading and interpretive practice. Let us begin.

In the hugely popular 1987 Hindi film *Mr. India* (Shekhar Kapur), the nation comes to be embodied by a commoner, specifically a common *man*. This *aam Hindustani* (common Indian) ekes out a living by teaching the violin. Orphaned himself, he is the caretaker of and *bhaiyya* (brother) to a group of orphans who live with him and his friend Calendar in an old, decrepit home he rents from a ruthless landlord. He struggles to make the rent and pay the bills to run the house each month. The ordinariness of Arun Verma, our common Indian, is emphasized through the ill-fitting sport coat, trousers, and unpressed, stained shirt and a misshapen hat that he wears through the length of the film. It is also represented through both his guileless voice as well as his quiet dignity in the face of tribulations. What transforms this common man into Mr. India is a device that was invented by his scientist father, which when activated renders its user invisible to the eye. Arun bhaiyya is thus an *everyman* because as an orphan who appears to know very little about his parents, he is ostensibly unmarked by the patriarchal family's investments in class and caste lines; but he is also *the man*, Mr. India, via an invention that belongs to him through the patriline. The film literalizes the invisibility of the commoner—he is unremarkable, unnoticeable, one in a mass— and transforms it into a superpower. When literally invisible, the commoner Arun Verma is transformed into the superhero Mr. India. The film pits Mr. India, the invisible common man against a spectacular supervillain. Mogambo, the antagonist, is an over-determined embodiment of evil: he alludes to fascism, specifically Hitler, is invested in territorial conquest, he foments and encourages violence along religious and caste lines. And he is invested in "corrupt capital" and drug and arms smuggling. He is a misanthrope who enjoys watching his subservient lackeys leap into a vat of acid. His Mephistophelian costume in red, black, and gold, his garish makeup and hair, his menacingly booming laugh and catchphrase, where he speaks about himself in the third person, "Mogambo khush hua," [(That makes) Mogambo happy] all work to transform him into both comic-book evilness and a spectacular super-villain.

Mr. *India*, the film, makes two significant narrative and representational moves that are central to the story that this book tells: 1) The film defines commonness or the commoner through heteronormative masculinity that is nevertheless subdued, un-heroic, unremarkable, and mundane and articulates or links this narration of commonness to realism. To narrate in the modern form of realism, *Mr. India* suggests, is to tell the story of the un-heroic, invisible common *man*, dressed in unremarkable clothes, unshaven and sans makeup, much like the real middle-class or lower-middle-class, middle- to upper-caste aam Hindustani. Realism as a form (as opposed to the melodrama or the romance, for instance) here connotes demystification and an intimacy with sociological, cultural and historical detail. In other words, the character of Arun Verma can be read as realistic not because he is "lifelike" necessarily but as a consequence of conventions that define realism as the narration of sociological details and an embodiment of unremarkable un-heroicness.[77] Sociological details render Arun Verma a commoner; as a common man he is the antithesis of the larger-than-life hero, and his embodiment does not encode a metaphysical or transcendental meaning; as such, he is real and through him the narrative alludes to realism. 2) But *Mr. India* does more. Cinematically, the film links this particular investment in realism to the narration of that which is spectacular. In other words, the film links realism to sensationalist drama and indeed, the distinctly unreal. Arun Verma may be unremarkably real, but Mr. India is sensationally unreal, spectacular, and literally invisible.[78] Mr. India and Mogambo are larger than life; they come to embody mythic conceptions of good and evil and as such they are spectacularly in excess of the conventions of characterization deemed necessary by sociology, history, and ethnography. We can thus define the narrative form of *Mr. India* as spectacular realism.

To be clear, realism here is defined as the simple enumeration of sociological, cultural, and historical detail through textual, visual, and sonic signifiers. These would include costume; makeup or the lack thereof; spatiality entailing shooting on location rather than on a set; referencing or alluding to known and established historical events; using local dialects, slang, and colloquialisms in dialogue; and, starting from the new millennium, increasingly shooting with in-sync sound rather than dubbing the dialogue over the visuals. While *Mr. India* is set in the metropolis of Mumbai, realism as a form has come to center the small-town, upper- to middle-caste male, particularly in cinema in the new millennium. This form of realism is associated with modernity itself and the coming-into-maturity of both the nation and its predominant storytelling processes.[79]

Historically, realism as a form has been significant both to the projects of colonialism as well as to the endeavors of artists and critics working out an anti-capitalist, anti-fascist aesthetic. Influential film theorist and critic Andre Bazin, writing in the aftermath of Nazism and the destruction of World War II, advocated a cinema of "transparency," wherein the ambiguity and complexity of "reality" could be grasped despite the condensation and reordering that was inherent to the art of filmmaking. A film culture that is attentive to and advocates for this cinema of transparency and which eschews "ideological abstraction and self-aggrandizing technique" would, he suggested, also be aware of the distinction between the reality of its *own* desires and the desires that "an entire production consortium, a State, even a civilization or a culture" wants the audience to *mistake* as their own. In other words, the assumption here was that a minimally controlled camera would capture the complexity of the real in a manner that would allow the audience to more clearly see the ideological apparatus within which they resided and distinguish ideology from desire.

For literary and political theorist George Lukacs, realism needed to exhibit an "immediate, unworried grasp of material fact."[80] He believed that realism as a form meditated on the coming-into-being of a particular social formation, revealing both the conditions which formed this world and its consequences.[81] Realism revealed the world as the "living result of the (class) human relations" between people as well as the living relations between people and the political economy. Lukacs argued that as capitalism got more oppressive and the artist felt a greater sense of alienation from his/her society, realism as a form degenerated to a type of naturalism that simply enumerates detail and experience: "the breath of life is gone" and the artistic creation "declines to photographic reportage."[82] In the context of capitalism and the concentration camp, these film and literary critics underlined the importance of a form of artistic creation that did not reproduce the world, power, and oppression as abstractions or reproduce the individual as an alienated being progressively withdrawing inward into their psyche. This type of literature was, in fact, sometimes called "modernist anti-realism" to distinguish it from realism's critical potential.[83] If "modernist anti-realism" reproduces the alienation and abstractions that are engendered by and central to capitalism, then as film scholar Priya Jaikumar has shown in the context of films produced in the 1930s within the political economic structures and institutions of British colonialism, the narrative form of imperial realism "reproduces spatial divisions between colonizer and colonized as obvious." Additionally, it renders the colonized as consumable through documentary-style naturalism. Thus, film and literary critics have revealed the ways in which realism as a form is deeply intertwined with the processes of capitalism (and therefore modernism) as well as with colonialism. But, as these critics reveal, realism as a form also carries the potential of critique. As we shall see, the stories of new India signal this potential even as they use realism often as a simple and simplistic deployment of sociological detailing that aims to articulate the commoner or aam admi with the spectacular power of capital or the nation.

The spectacle or the spectacular harkens to the tradition of melodrama, which film scholar Ravi Vasudevan has narrated as a form of storytelling that formulates subjectivities that are at once personal, intimate, *and* public. Melodrama, Vasudevan has argued, pointedly addresses its audience as a public rather than as individuals and is a loose assemblage or what the Hindi film industry refers to as *masala*, a food flavoring agent formed by the intermingling of various spices. The spectacular, as we are defining it here then, draws on intimate, personal, and specific cultural, social, and political experiences and narrates it in big, bold strokes using the loudest of colors and sounds. The spectacular *feels* real but does not look or sound real. The emphasis is, in fact, on the sensational and on the creation of memorable spectacle. More specifically, the spectacular is a strategic (and often cynical) appropriation of the melodrama and its ability to twine the intimate and the public. Let us also be clear that the spectacle, as we are defining it here, makes specific allusions to the nation and capital as affective concepts. The spectacle defines a concept, idea, or belief as transcendental; in other words, as outside the bounds and limits of the mundane tasks of meaning making and analysis. As such, it connotes an irrefutability to the concept or belief. Mogambo's villainous deeds— land grabbing, violence engulfing neighborhoods, the exploitation of the poor, and the violent extortion of surplus value—feel real (these can be analyzed and a critique can be formulated through that analysis) but Mogambo himself does not look or sound real (he signifies 'evil' and that evilness is irrefutable because it transcends the limits of analysis). His unreal, sensational persona makes him memorable as a character. His antithesis is the spectacular Mr. India. To be read as the embodiments of good and evil, Mogambo and Mr. India must be larger than life, which means they must transcend the conventions of meaning-making that require the reader/the listener/the viewer to complete the chain of signification.[84] At the same time, in order for Mogambo and Mr. India to be affective signs, they must not be rendered as abstractions. Instead, Mogambo and Mr. India are authoritatively defined as good and evil through the spectacle. As a narrative form, spectacular realism combines and deliberately entangles realism—with its emphasis on ethnographic and sociological detail—with the sensationalist melodrama (the masala) of the spectacular. Realism provides the warrant for the authority of the spectacle. To put it differently, the spectacle rests on the foundation provided for it by realism.

Narrative form has typically been studied in the context of film and literature but we will track the form of spectacular realism within political and economic discourse as well, which will reveal to us the ways in which nation and capital are narrated as transcendentally given authoritarian conceptions backed by the analytical weight of the real commoner. Let us then consider another instantiation or expression of the form of spectacular realism, this time from the arena of party politics. In 1992, five years after the release of *Mr. India*, the Hindu nationalist movement destroyed a sixteenth-century mosque in the north Indian city of Ayodhya. The demolition, as mentioned earlier, triggered anti-Muslim pogroms throughout the nation. As scholars such as Arvind Rajagopal have shown, various mobilization strategies were used by different Hindu nationalist groups in the 1980s to galvanize a public that culminated in the demolition of the mosque. One key mobilization strategy was the *rath yatra* [journey by chariot] undertaken by L. K. Advani, a senior and seasoned political leader of the BJP. The chariot is a significant symbol within Hindu mythology, particularly within the stories that are a part of the epic *Mahabharata*. Here, Krishna, described as an avatar of Vishnu (designated as the "creator" in the Hindu trinity of gods) and worshipped as a god himself, takes on the role of a charioteer during the climactic battle scenes of the epic and renders a set of arguments about morality, ethics, and creation itself. Those arguments have circulated as the *Bhagawad Gita*, which has been defined as one of the central texts of Hinduism by British colonialists, native elites during colonialism, and by Hindu nationalists. Within this narrative, Krishna is both common (as the mere charioteer) and spectacular (he reveals himself as the supreme, transcendental power, God himself). During the rath yatra, the chariot and its representation within the *Mahabharata* was yoked to the symbolism associated with the second significant epic in the Hindu pantheon, namely the *Ramayana*, which narrates the story of Ram as a morality tale. The rath yatra as a performative event and a tool for political mobilization used this accreted symbolism of the chariot and was designed as a spectacle. A Toyota minibus was dressed to look like a chariot.

The discourse of Hindu nationalism has consistently described the cities of Somnath, Ayodhya, Kashi, and Mathura as holy temple cities for the followers of Hinduism that were deliberately desecrated by "Muslim kings" or Mughal emperors like Aurangzeb and Babur. The BJP's chariot traveled from Somnath, in the western Indian state of Gujarat to the northern city of Ayodhya, thus tracing the geography of wounded Hindu pride as narrated by the discourse of Hindu nationalism. Advani writes that the movement to build a temple in Ayodhya "was not . . . merely about reclaiming a holy Hindu site from the onslaught of a bigoted foreign

invader in the past . . . it was [instead] about reasserting our [Hindu] cultural heritage as the defining source of India's national identity."[85] Moreover, he notes that
Ram "is a unique symbol of India's national identity, unity and integration . . . he is
an ideal for Indians' aspiration to live a life of higher values. Thus, it is hardly surprising that the place of Ram's birth in Ayodhya, which was the capital of his king-
dom, has been the focal point of deepest devotion for the Hindus through the
millennia."[86] Writing his memoir over a decade after the rath yatra and the demolition of the mosque, Advani links the spectacle of the Hindu nation, complete
with the narration of a king who embodied morality itself and an epic battle between
"invaders" and the nation defined as bounded space and culture, with the mass of
"real" Indians, namely, the Hindus. The rath yatra was a performative instantiation
of this linkage.

   The chariot as a symbol of the Hindu nation played a central role in the narration of the journey as a spectacle. Thus, Advani notes, "the principal messenger of
the Rath Yatra [sic] was the Rath itself. And it was worthy of worship as it was
headed for Ayodhya for the sacred mission of construction of the Ram Temple at
his birthplace."[87] Through the symbolism of the chariot, Advani and the BJP
demanded that the rath yatra be read as more than a political rally, and instead as a
spectacle in which the Hindu nationalist movement sought to define the Hindu
nation as irrefutable. What is also significant for our purposes here is the manner
in which this spectacle twined the intimate with the public. In Advani's narration
of the experience, people came out to see, greet, and pay obeisance to the chariot;
they were less interested in the political agenda of the BJP and its particular stake
in the temple mobilization. This reverential and curious interest in the chariot is
narrated by Advani as the reality of popular, common Hinduism. The chariot,
argues Advani, "acquir(ed) divinity" as a consequence of a popular form of Hindu
worship through which "common people see (the) manifestation of the Divine
[sic] in any idol or object—a tree, a mountain, a river, or a lake etc. that they
believe is sanctified."[88] Using this "deep-rooted religiosity" that is intimate (not
private, necessarily, as defined by liberalism's distinction between the public and
private) in the sense that it is a relationship between an individual-in-community
and an object, the rath yatra, twined it with the public (i.e., a particular discourse
of nationalism). Advani notes that "although the people's response to the Rath
Yatra was mainly religious, the focus of my speeches was on nationalism."[89] Defining the rath yatra public's reverence as the reality of the common Hindu, it was
also then twined with the spectacle and the mythic symbolism of the chariot and
thus to the Hindu nation by the story told by Hindu nationalism. This story of the
rath yatra as told by Hindu nationalism relies on the character of the common
Hindu (read: "real") to narrate the spectacle of the Hindu nation. To be clear, the
common Hindu is a character within the story told by Hindu nationalism and as
such as "realistic" as Arun Verma from Mr. India.

   Let me tell you a third story now; this is a story that I will develop in greater
detail in chapter 1, so for now, here are the highlights. In the summer of 2008, the

Indian parliament debated and voted on an India-U.S. civil nuclear cooperation initiative. This nuclear deal, as it has come to be called, is a significant element of the form neoliberalism has taken in India. It is also central, as I will discuss in the next chapter, to the story of development. The India-U.S. agreement resulted in India separating its civil and military nuclear facilities, subsequently placing its civil nuclear facilities under safeguards instituted by the International Atomic Energy Agency, and, more significantly, it hoped to increase India's nuclear power generation—in which the U.S. expected to have a share—through the purchase of reactors from nuclear vendors in the U.S. and elsewhere and the transfer of equipment and technology. The debate that took place in the Indian parliament became a media spectacle. The speeches—some witty, some acerbic, some passionate, some dull—made in parliament were telecast live on English- and Hindi-language television. This was followed by lively commentary, interviews, a rebroadcast of some of the best speeches, and discussion.

Political parties on the left—such as the Communist Party of India and the Communist Party of India (Marxist)—were vehemently opposed to the agreement and coded their opposition through the citation of the excesses of globalization, the enormous disparities instituted by neoliberalism in India, and by discussing American imperialism. This argument aimed to sketch out the reality of "new India" and raised the figure of the commoner—the poor worker in urban landscapes, the landless in rural villages—in the hope of arguing that economic opportunity, the alleviation of poverty, and food security were real imperatives that the spectacular story about nuclear technology would not and could not address. Proponents of the agreement in parliament, most significantly members of the Indian National Congress, also raised the figure of the commoner. In the case of Rahul Gandhi, son of the late prime minister Rajiv Gandhi and grandson of another late prime minister, Indira Gandhi, the figure of the common woman was the sign through which to argue *for* nuclear technology. Rahul Gandhi, in his speech in parliament, described two women (both dalit, poor)—Shashikala, a landless laborer who had three sons and Kalawati, who had nine children and whose husband had committed suicide—to argue that the energy security that nuclear technology would provide would work to alleviate the poverty of people like them. Subtly alluding to then Senator Barack Obama's speech at the Democratic National Convention in 2004, Gandhi said he had decided to speak not as a member of a political party but as an Indian and concluded his speech by suggesting that Indians should no longer be worried about how the world would impact them, but instead should focus on how *they* could and would impact the world. This argument, unlike that of the Left parties, twined the commoner with nuclear technology and the spectacular with the real. It was an argument that won the day in parliament; perhaps even more significantly it was the story that resonated most powerfully within Indian popular culture.

The three stories we have tracked here are located in distinct analytical, disciplinary, and narrative spaces—*Mr. India* within popular cinema, the rath yatra in realpolitik, political science, and history and the nuclear deal debate within political economy—but all three share a narrative form, that of *spectacular realism*. Literary critics have argued that narrative form is an ideological act in its own right with the "function of inventing imaginary or formal 'solutions' to unresolvable social contradictions."[90] In other words, ideology does not precede and then "invest" and "inform" symbolic production, rather the "aesthetic act is itself ideological." The story of our time is a story about spectacular realism. To reiterate, in the story of Hindutva neoliberalism, the spectacle of capital and the nation is sutured to the realism of the commoner, in order to win consent for the conjuncture. In the story of Hindutva neoliberalism, the spectacular requires realism. Stories are unstable scripts however, so, even as I track *the story* of the intersection of neoliberalism with Hindu nationalism, I also trace the contours of an unruly story. This unruly story is a narrative that does not quite follow the semiotic and affective logic of *the story*. It speaks in a different cadence sometimes, it can function as a deconstructive lever unravelling the story of spectacular realism sometimes, and at other times it employs its worldmaking function to point to the shape of a world undefined by neoliberalism and Hindu nationalism.

LAYOUT OF THE BOOK

Each of the following chapters tells a story, about the conceptualization of development, iconicity, the entrepreneur, and love in order to reveal the narrative processes through which neoliberalism is conjoined with Hindu nationalism. Each chapter also highlights the narrative patterning that articulates the realism of the commoner with the spectacle of the nation and capital. The chapters will detail how the commoner is constituted as such and how the nation and capital are translated into spectacles and sutured together. In order to do so, I read across disciplines, narrative genres, and media to constitute an archive that includes stories from news reports, commentary, and editorials that have discussed the economy, poverty, caste, electoral campaigns and outcomes, advertising campaigns that center the nation as a brand, and electoral campaigns, popular Hindi films that narrate love, new times, the entrepreneur, and works of popular nonfiction. In the first chapter, "The Development Story: Caste, Religion, and Poverty in 'New' India," we begin to track the story of Hindutva neoliberalism with an examination of the concept of development. Development sutures together the nation as spectacle with the authentic or real figure of the commoner and as such enables Hindutva neoliberalism to build its edifice on this foundation. Both Hindu nationalism and neoliberalism in India narrate themselves as centering development and therefore the commoner. The stories about development crystallize the figure of the commoner as desirous of mobility, consumption, and change but obstructed and shackled. To understand how development becomes foundational to Hindutva neoliberalism, I read the stories that discuss caste, socioeconomic mobility, economic growth, electoral politics, and equity across a range of media including film, electoral campaigns, political speeches, journalism, nonfiction, and commentary. Through this reading, I trace the variegated narrative threads that constitute development. Additionally, I trace the contours of the form spectacular realism within these stories.

An unruly moment within this story of development occurs in 2006 when the relevance of the concept of equity to development is discussed in the English-language mainstream press. The discussion was initiated by the publication of that year's World Development Report titled "Equity and Development." Tracing the contours of this moment where equity as a concept is disarticulated from development will reveal to us the distinct shape development as a concept-image takes in the time of Hindutva neoliberalism.

If development is the keyword through which neoliberalism is linked to authoritarian nationalism, the second chapter, "Iconicity: Moving Between the Real and the Spectacular," reveals the embodiment of Hindutva neoliberalism in iconic personages. In other words, this chapter discusses how Hindutva neoliberalism is given corporeal form. It analyzes three icons, namely, Hindi film actor and superstar Amitabh Bachchan, Hindu nationalist politician and current prime minister of India Narendra Modi, and Mayawati, the nation's first dalit female chief minister. Bachchan as the "angry young man" character he played in films in his youth, Modi as the son of a tea seller, and Mayawati as *dalit ki beti* (daughter of a dalit) represent and embody the commoner. As such, they represent the body of the people. However, as icons, they are also cast as spectacular. The commoner is defined as obstructed (fettered/shackled) and angry. The chapter reveals that Hindutva neoliberalism is narrated as unshackling the commoner, allowing movement and transforming that common person into an icon. Bachchan becomes brand father or the father of neoliberal India, Modi becomes the prime minister, and Mayawati an acute political strategist. This is the embodiment of spectacular realism and therefore also of Hindutva neoliberalism. The chapter also points to the manner in which Mayawati's story is an unruly one. In the brief moment when her story appears to seamlessly fit the narrative requirements of the iconic form, she is cast to narrate national renewal. The assertion of caste as a political identity, however, marks the limit of the narration and defies appropriation. Mayawati's iconicity both uses and disrupts the form of spectacular realism. Moreover, her iconicity uses the signifiers of Hindutva neoliberalism but sutures them to a different set of signifieds, creating new and disruptive sign systems. Both the first and second chapters examine the problem posed by caste for Hindutva neoliberalism. These chapters reveal that the story of caste can only be narrated through the form of spectacular realism, such that the lower-caste body defined as the commoner is articulated with the spectacle of the nation and capital. An assertion of caste identity that critiques Hinduism, the concept of the nation and capitalism, and a demand for recognition or redistribution of resources on the basis of caste is repudiated by *the story*.

Development links authoritarian nationalism to neoliberalism and iconicity gives corporeal form to Hindutva neoliberalism. Both the key word of development and iconicity as I discuss it in chapter 2 constitute and give form to the category *people*. In the third chapter, "The Entrepreneur: New Subjectivities for 'New' Times," I reveal the narrative processes through which the entrepreneur becomes *the* subject position or identification for the people. The people deemed unshackled by the advent of Hindutva neoliberalism are narrated on a trajectory (a teleology) that starts with rejection and moves to euphoric embrace, as they occupy the identity of entrepreneur. The possessive individualism of the entrepreneur is narrated by Hindutva neoliberalism as the apogee of subalternity itself. Despite its claims of universality, the chapter will show that the entrepreneur is a very particular form of embodiment. It is not available for identification to all who may aspire for it. The Muslim woman distinctly marks the boundary of the category. It is in this context that the chapter also investigates the tragic case of Zaheera Shaikh, a victim of the anti-Muslim pogrom in Gujarat in 2002. Shaikh attempted to trade her story—arguably the only possession she owned that was marketable—like a commodity in the market. She could not be represented through the category of entrepreneurialism however, and was convicted of perjury. Her story and its inability to be narrated through hegemonic categories reveals the contradiction at the heart of liberalism's possessive individualism and unravels Hindutva neoliberalism's possessive investment in the category entrepreneur as the apogee of subalternity. The story of the entrepreneur is told through the narrative form of spectacular realism, where the little boy serving tea at a roadside stall and the girl selling flowers at a traffic light are articulated to home-grown millionaires and billionaires and through them to the spectacle of neoliberal capital.

In the fourth chapter, "Love in New Times," I reveal that contemporary Hindi-language cinema uses the love story to define the neoliberal male as adrift and incomplete. These films then narrate love and the feminine ideal as redemptive for such a male. The Hindu right's concept of "love jihad" flips the coin on love and narrates it as the danger that threatens the purity of Hindu society; the Hindu feminine body is the vulnerable breach in such a conceptualization. The cinematic love story since the 1970s has variously used love to reinforce the nation and Hindu patriarchy but also to point to a radical space unbounded by both global capital and Hindu patriarchy. In the chapter, I strive to stay with these dissonant stories about love. By pointing to the ways in which love is narrated as the radical possibility of the formation of a new world that is built on the ground of difference as well as the ways in which the heterosexual, consuming couple are constructed as the ideal citizens of neoliberalism and as the instrument of Hindu patriarchy, the love story reveals the persistent iterative work necessary to maintain the contours of the conjuncture and the gendered and sexed ground on which this work is carried out. This chapter also points to the radical potential of the cinematic love song as a disruptive audiovisual that aims to construct a world outside the bounds of both Hindu patriarchy and global capital. Most importantly, this discussion of love points to the stories that challenge the dominance of Hindutva neoliberalism. I argue that the popular conception of love in India is rooted in difference and invested in world-making and as such is a threat. It is therefore either de-fanged by celebrating it on screen, appropriating it so the adjustment to Hindu patriarchy and capital is made easier, or it is labeled as jihad and violently repressed.

In the conclusion, I work with the 2015 film *Tamasha* (Spectacle, Imtiaz Ali) to underline the stakes of the book's arguments. As such, the conclusion emphasizes that the intersection of neoliberalism with Hindu nationalism is *the story* of our time and it is the archive of popular media stories that enable that intersection to narrate and speak.

1 · THE DEVELOPMENT STORY
Caste, Religion, and Poverty in "New" India

What enables the narration of neoliberalism, Hindu nationalism, a nuclear deal between the United States and India, affirmative action, the consumption of multinational brands, and the burgeoning economic might of the diaspora as development? What, then, is development? Development has been discussed as an unstable concept, sometimes narrated as a discourse, other times as a policy or a project blueprint.[1] Scholars have argued that a "vision of development as improved well-being" has gained ground and that this is especially true in former colonies.[2] The movement from "underdeveloped" and "developing" to "developed" political economies signifies improved well-being, opportunities, and greater equity in postcolonial nation-states like India. This movement from underdeveloped to developed or emerged also, of course, signifies a teleology— movement across time. The seductive allure of development can be attributed to its allusion to movement, in both material and temporal terms. That movement is, in turn, defined as progression and improvement. As anthropologist James Ferguson has argued, development and modernization theory in the mid-twentieth century transformed a "spatialized global hierarchy" into a "temporalized historical sequence," such that poor people and poor nations were no longer seen as at the bottom but at the beginning. To follow Ferguson's argument, the concept of development in the twentieth century broke the dominance of the idea that the "various creatures of the world formed a great and continuous chain, ranked from highest to lowest."[3] The concept of development enabled hierarchies to be instead conceived in terms of historical or evolutionary progression. Or at least this was the promise development offered newly formed nation-states, including India, in the mid-twentieth century. Contrary to the narrative of hopeful movement and progression, however, the postcolonial story, as David Scott reminds us, is often defined by the experience of time as painfully mundane, stalled, and obstructed.[4] In other words, even as the end of World War II and the formal end of colonial rule in parts of Asia, Africa, and the Caribbean from the late 1940s onwards ushered in a sense of moving progressively through time via the conception of development, the experience of living in postcolonial contexts was apprehended in reality as movement that had been obstructed. Time, in the postcolonial context, Scott has argued, is the "endlessly extending" present "stricken with immobility and pain and ruin."[5] Yet, the conception of development has endured. Despite its instability and capaciousness as a conception, development has remained significant in postcolonial contexts since the Truman doctrine of 1949.[6]

An important stake of this book is an investment in tracing the intersection of neoliberalism and Hindu nationalism in India, an intersection for which the popular discourse around conceptions of the commoner, newness, and emergence is pivotal. Development in the time of neoliberalism and Hindu nationalism in India becomes the concept-image through which to tell the story about the coming of new time. I describe development as a concept-image in order to highlight the range of narratives, images, and affects that have come to be associated with this concept.[7] I use it also to emphasize that development as a concept bears the imprint of this diverse, sometimes contradictory set of narratives, images, and affects. In the story that I will track in this chapter, development serves as a justification (the warrant) for specific political-economic projects *and* it helps define the nation as renewed and new. As a concept-image, development simultaneously signifies the commonness of the commoner and their lived struggles for an improved life and the spectacle of nuclear technology, global conglomerates, the stock markets, and a muscular vision of Hindu nationalism. As such, the concept-image of development conjoins the spectacle with realism.

If development in the mid-twentieth century convinced its public to think about hierarchy temporally—indeed, to think about inequity as the beginning of the story and not its foregone conclusion—then development now is a strategic echo (or the reiteration) of that idea. As an echo, development in new India draws its affective sonic textures from that earlier iteration but also registers a different, altered sound. I will argue in this chapter that in the time of Hindutva neoliberalism, narrative processes commodify the experience of obstruction, of time painfully stalled, and then produce and reproduce the concept-image of development as movement, renewal, and emergence in order to win consent for specific political-economic projects. In other words, the conception of time as teleological progress as well as stalled and obstructed is crucial to the concept-image of development in the time of Hindutva neoliberalism. Obstructed time and time as progress form the beginning and end points of the story, with development signifying movement across these nodes. Moreover, the narration of obstructed time necessitates sociological and ethnographic detailing and is therefore constituted as realism. The renewal of the nation and unchecked capital are signified spectacularly as time unfettered and fluid.

Much of this chapter will focus on detailing the stories that constitute obstructed time and unfettered time in order to reveal the narrative processes through which development as a concept-image provides the justification for Hindutva neoliberalism. Development works to resolve ambivalences about economic reform and violent conservative political agendas (as we shall see with the case of Hindu nationalism in the western Indian state of Gujarat), it sutures the seduction of the nation and nation-building work to questions of political economy in new India, and it manages anxieties the middle class and the elite (who have disproportionately benefited from economic reform) have about the poor (who have not). Development performs the *political work* of winning consent for exclusionary political economic projects, and yet, development is crucially defined as an *apolitical* concept. This, as we shall see, is resolutely what development must mean in new India; the concept-image's ostensible "apoliticalness" is also a part of its allure. In the next section, I will discuss the story of nuclear technology and the India-U.S. nuclear deal first to provide a snapshot of this argument before turning to the narrative patterning of spectacular realism in the context of development.

NUCLEAR POWER AND NEW TIME

In 2015, then–U.S. president Barack Obama traveled to India to attend the nation's sixty-fifth Republic Day parade on January 26. The date celebrates the promulgation of the Constitution of India in 1950, formally marking the end of British colonial rule. The visit also served to complete administrative arrangements for an India-U.S. civil nuclear cooperation initiative. The Republic Day celebrations are always marked by a performance that links a conception of the nation with that of the state.[8] In 2015, that performance of sovereignty was conjoined with the signing of a deal that the Indian Left had critiqued as an instantiation of American imperialism. This conjoining was not seen as a contradiction within public discourse. On the contrary, it was narrated as a spectacle that defined the *assertion* and *renewal* of the Indian nation itself. The concept-image of development played a crucial role within these narratives, which translated nuclear power into a spectacle of national might and sutured it to the realism of the commoner.

On the occasion of Obama's visit, Hindu nationalist leader and current Indian prime minister Narendra Modi announced that six years after a bilateral agreement had been signed, India and the United States were finally moving toward commercial cooperation. Indeed, in the summer of 2008, the Indian parliament had debated and voted on the India-U.S. civil nuclear cooperation initiative. But the deal had a much longer genealogy than the debate in 2008 and had, in fact, been in the works since the collapse of the Soviet Union and the liberalization of the Indian economy in 1991. As such, it firmly turned the page on frosty geopolitical relations between the United States and India, which was a legacy not just of the Cold War but also of India's anticolonial investment in the Non-Aligned Movement, and it formally made India a strategic U.S. partner in Asia.

India first conducted nuclear tests in 1974, under the helm of then–prime minister Indira Gandhi and her Indian National Congress party. Sanctions were imposed on India under the Nuclear Non-Proliferation Act of 1978. These sanctions served U.S. foreign policy interests then. The United States was critical of India's relationship with the Soviet Union and the regulatory mechanisms in place within India's economy at the time, which did not allow foreign capital to establish itself.[9] The disintegration of the Soviet Union and India's moves to liberalize its economy in 1991 changed the terrain. The sanctions imposed after the first set of nuclear tests in 1974 now began to be seen as a hindrance to a more complete form of liberalization, and the Bill Clinton administration in the United States made attempts to alter the situation. India's refusal to sign the Comprehensive Test Ban Treaty in 1996, on the grounds that it created a nuclear divide by refusing to stipulate a time-bound process of nuclear disarmament for the nuclear states (the United States being the largest of such states), followed very quickly by a second round of nuclear tests in 1998, this time carried out by the Bharatiya Janata Party–led coalition government, put a spanner (albeit a minor one in these altered geopolitical circumstances) in these negotiations. A new set of sanctions were imposed but were soon lifted as talks between the two states continued. Negotiations between the George W. Bush government and Manmohan Singh's Indian National Congress–led coalition government (which had come into power in 2004) then cemented the terms of the nuclear deal. The agreement came to be called the "126 for 123" deal: India would purchase 126 fighter aircraft in exchange for an amendment of section 123 in the U.S. Atomic Energy Act by the U.S. Congress in order for nuclear trade to take place between the United States and India.

When the terms of this deal were debated in the Indian parliament in 2008, the Communist Party of India and the Communist Party of India (Marxist) opposed the agreement through an argument that focused on the enormous disparities instituted by neoliberalism in India and by discussing American imperialism. This argument by the Left raised the figure of the poor and landless laborer. Moreover, the Indian Left argued that "the bilateral nuclear agreement must be seen as a crucial step to lock in India into U.S. global strategic designs . . . [and] for closer military collaboration."[10] Proponents of the agreement in parliament, most significantly members of the Indian National Congress, also raised the figure of the commoner. In the case of Rahul Gandhi, a leader of the party, the figure of the distinctly gendered commoner was the sign through which to argue *for* nuclear technology. In his speech in parliament, Gandhi described two women (both dalit, both poor)—Shashikala, a landless laborer who had three sons and Kalawati, who had nine children and whose husband had committed suicide—to argue that the energy security that nuclear technology would provide would work to alleviate the poverty of people like them. Gandhi concluded his speech by suggesting that Indians should no longer be worried about how the world would impact them, but instead should focus on how they could and would impact the world.

The nuclear-deal debate was a dense semiotic node: globalization, recolonization, development, nation, nation-ness, and neoliberalism were all discussed. While the Indian Left attempted to narrate the debate as a story about imperialism— the nation pitted against the advance of global capital—the nuclear-deal debate instead became a story about national renewal in which an emergent nation would direct global capital that was in its thrall. The narrative pivot was the concept-image of development. Signifying improved well-being, mobility, and renewal (all signifiers attached to development through a process of layering and accretion), development helped define the nuclear deal as the empowerment of commoners like Kalawati and Shashikala.

As such, this story in 2008 was an echo of the story that was crafted in the early decades of the 1970s. Indira Gandhi (Rahul Gandhi's grandmother) and her wing of a splintered Indian National Congress won the 1971 general elections on the slogan "Garibi Hatao, Desh Bachao" (Remove/Eradicate Poverty, Save the Country/Nation). Gandhi had argued that whereas her opponents were consumed with "Indira Hatao" (Remove Indira), she was more interested in development, poverty, and the Indian common person. It was the same Indira Gandhi who authorized the 1974 nuclear tests in the wake of the war between India and Pakistan, which resulted in the formation of Bangladesh in 1971. The war was seen as a successful flexing of India's military might and the nuclear test in 1974 put more nationalist aggression into that flexing. Here then was a narrative that had linked development (poverty eradication), nationalism, and nuclear power. In 1998, when the second set of nuclear tests were conducted, this articulation of nationalism (this time Hindu nationalism), development, and nuclear power was reiterated by the BJP-led government that had sanctioned the tests months after taking power. The BJP's campaign in the subsequent general elections argued that India was "shining" on the basis of a surging stock market, its declaration about being a nuclear state, and economic reforms. These linkages were reproduced again during the nuclear-deal debate in 2008. Understood as a concept-image, therefore, development can be seen as signifying social mobility, poverty eradication, muscular nationalism, and even nuclear power. It can be understood as linking the realism of the people with the spectacle of nation and capital.

There was one crucial difference between the narrative of the 1970s and the one from 2008: Development linked to nationalism in the 1970s was defined through state-controlled capitalism or a weak form of socialism, a planned economy, modernization theory, and even Malthusian economics. It was wrought in the crucible of the Cold War, the Non-Aligned Movement, and postcolonial conflict in South Asia. It entailed therefore the nationalization of banks and the abolition of the privy purse but also a vehement and often violent focus on population control, family planning, and even sterilization. In 1998 and again in 2008, contrarily, development was defined through *deepening* the articulation of the Indian economy with global capital. Acute power shortages and inequity were sought to be ameliorated through neoliberal economic policy and by forging an alliance with the world's preeminent superpower. *This* was narrated as emergence and renewal, specifically national renewal, linked as it was to nuclear power. Even as the difference between the discourse of the 1970s and more contemporary rhetoric is crucial, there is an analytical and political danger in overstating it. The narrative of development that was stitched together in the 1970s allowed for the story of development to be fashioned as such in 1998 and 2008, and as this chapter will argue, also crucially enabled development to become the concept-image that binds Hindu nationalism with neoliberalism and the spectacular with the real.

The story about nuclear technology in the decade of the 1990s and then again in the first decade of the new millennium was an echo of the narrative of the 1970s. It narrated the commoner's painful experience of immobility and obstruction (realism), then defined development as improved well-being by translating nuclear technology into a spectacle whose adoption would bring renewal, both for the commoner and the nation. In 2008, this story about nuclear technology and development was narrated even as the deep fiscal crisis in the United States and Europe was revealing the failure of neoliberalism. Development as a concept-image that references progression, improvement, and mobility was now used strategically to win consent for neoliberalism in the new millennium and for Hindu nationalism.

To return to Obama for just a moment: The visit in 2015 was not Obama's first official trip to India. In the fall of 2010, when the Indian National Congress–led coalition government was in power, Barack Obama had made his first official visit to India. In a speech made to the joint session of the Indian parliament, Obama revealed why India had figured significantly on his itinerary and why it loomed large in a rapidly globalizing world: "It is no coincidence that India is my first stop on a visit to Asia, or that this has been my longest visit to another country since becoming President . . . for in Asia and around the world, India is not simply emerging; *India has already emerged*."[11] In one simple and pithy statement, Obama had powerfully echoed a cultural story that had been taking shape within Indian popular culture over the past decade and a half: that the nation had arisen and come forth renewed and rejuvenated from a moment of rupture. The headline of an article that appeared in the *Economic Times*, analyzing Obama's speech a day later, therefore stated the matter equally pithly: "It's True, India has Emerged."[12]

Emergence suggests a powerful, radical, and exhilarating sense of newness. The "newness" of emergence in this context, much like the newness of New York, Nouvelle Orleans, or Nieuw Amsterdam, "has the meaning of 'successor' to, or 'inheritor' of, something vanished";[13] it suggests an alignment between the "old" and the "new" such that, in Benedict Anderson's words, "the former appears always to invoke an ambiguous blessing from the dead."[14] The "dead," the "old," or the "treasured past," as Obama would put it in the Indian case, is the event of independence from British colonialism. The popular Indian narrative will suggest that even though the nation itself is ancient, the event of independence ushered in new time; it was a moment when the turning of time could be witnessed. That was Year One. Linked to the exhilaration of Year One, the present is signified as "new," renewed; it is a present that hasn't simply followed the past, it has emerged.

Jawaharlal Nehru, independent India's first prime minister, in an act of enunciation that has since been called the "Tryst with Destiny" speech, had said in 1947, "Long years ago we made a tryst with destiny, and now the time comes when we shall redeem our pledge, not wholly or in full measure, but very substantially . . . at the stroke of the midnight hour, when the world sleeps, India will *awake to life* and freedom ... a moment comes, which comes but rarely in history, when we step out from the old to the new, when an age ends, and when the soul of a nation, long suppressed, finds utterance."[15] At the precise moment in historical time, when a new nation-state was formed, Nehru narrated it as an awakening, an *emergence* from slumber, from suppression to, most significantly, "utterance," from silence to narration.

Nehru's narration of the nation marked the end of colonialism and the awakening to a form of freedom that needed to be qualified ("not wholly or in full measure, but very substantially"), coming as it did in the wake of genocidal violence, euphemistically called partition. Obama's narration of the nation, one that was simultaneously an echo and a validation of narratives in Indian popular culture, marked another shift in political economy. This shift, the popular cultural story will argue, was initiated quite specifically in historical time—in the early 1990s through the liberalization of the economy. While the shift in Indian political economy has accurately been named neoliberal, the cultural story narrates it through the eccentric temporality of the nation: this is a story of emerging, awakening, and about the new being the inheritor of a distinctly defined old. Both neoliberalism and Hindu nationalism, in fact, are narrated as eruptions that radically alter the immediate past, which is defined as obstructed. They are narrated as enabling the nation that had awakened from a deep slumber in 1947 to emerge renewed from time that had been obstructed and stagnant since.

In 2004, Manmohan Singh, then prime minister of India, defined the moment of reform as "epochal." "A decade is not a long time in the history of an ancient land like ours," Singh argued in a speech that year, "yet, for a people who for centuries have seen very little change, the past few decades have been *epochal*."[16] By defining the shift in political economy as "epochal," Singh had read and enunciated the emergence of new time, which he claimed was driven by economic change. This turn is radical, he had argued, precisely because it was unpredictable and because it was preceded by dead time where very little or nothing had changed, much like Nehru had narrated the awakening of the nation at the stroke of midnight as new time. In a similar narrative register, the BJP during the 2014 general elections centered its campaign on its prime ministerial candidate Narendra Modi and named it "Achche din aane wale hain" (Good/better days are coming). It referenced the melancholy and anger of the past and the present and suggested that "history was turning a page,"[17] time itself was now "pregnant with possibility,"[18] and the future was imminent. What we are tracking here then is the manner in which this conception of new time connotes development. As a concept-image, development bears the imprint and resonances of these various narrations of new time. The diverse set of popular cultural stories focused both on economic reform and Hindu nationalism that we will sift through here are stitched together by the concept-image of development. Signified as "improved well-being," development allows public discourse to speak simultaneously in two registers: the personal (the improvement of individual well-being) and the public (the improvement of national well-being, formulated as national renewal). Thus, it is possible to narrate the India-U.S. nuclear deal as a radical shift that would light the bulbs in the homes of poor, dalit women like Shashikala and Kalawati *and* resignify India as an *emerged nation*. In other words, development allows the spectacular (the nation, capital) to be articulated with the real.

This then is a story of the processes through which development emerges as the concept-image of the contemporary conjuncture. Even as it relies on the semiotic and narrative structures constructed in the early decades of the conjuncture we are tracking through this manuscript (the 1970s and the 1980s), this contemporary story about development defines those decades as stalled and obstructed and the later decades (from 2010 onwards, in particular) as new and emerged. In the narrative that I chart in this chapter on development, we will examine the modes through which the obstructed present is narrated as such; we will focus on the stories that allude to social, economic, and cultural hierarchies created by caste in the discussion of development while simultaneously disavowing it as a political discourse; and we will track the processes through which development is used as a concept-image to win consent for Hindutva neoliberalism. Finally, we will discuss an unruly moment in this story of development. This moment, which is quickly managed, is a consequence of the World Development Report of 2006 linking the concept of equity to development. That linkage threatened to transform development into a political concept and suggested that the promise of progressive movement and improvement that defined development could be achieved through the redistribution of resources and even wealth. Discussion in Indian's English-language media quickly managed that threat and repositioned development as an apolitical concept that acknowledged the pain of socioeconomic immobility and addressed it through not only neoliberalism but also Hindu nationalism.

THE OBSTRUCTED PRESENT: ANGER

Let us begin then by examining the story about obstructed time; we will do so through a focus on popular cinema and advertising, political advertising specifically. In the development story, these narratives about obstructed time are constituted through the processes of realism. The cultural story about a present that is obstructed and stagnant is narrated in one of two ways: 1) through anger, which is then linked to vigilantism and authoritarianism, and 2) through a tale about two Indias: one that is straining at the leash, ready to take the great developmental leap forward and a second that is mired in traditional, premodern ideas and attitudes and as such obstructed. The first of these narratives is strongly resonant in the 1970s but is also echoed in Hindu nationalist discourse in the new millennium, and even though the second story about two Indias has loudly been in circulation since the first decade of the new millennium, it makes allusions to older discourses about economic and social inequities in India as well as to the modernizing, post-colonial state's attempts in the 1970s and 1980s to construct a public that valued reason and rational thought over superstition and dogma. Development as a concept-image therefore feels both familiar and new. Even as this chapter trains its analytical attention on the story about development that is told in the time of Hindutva neoliberalism, we will also track the story's allusions and citations of an older discourse. And, we will trace the ways in which the story about development in the time of Hindutva neoliberalism does specific political work: Development is defined as a set of technocratic, apolitical strategies and policies. Development is, in fact, untethered from those sociopolitical movements that demand redistribution of resources and the redress of systemic and institutional discrimination on the basis of caste and religion. But let's not get ahead of ourselves.

Let us focus our attention on the narration of time as obstructed, painfully mundane and stalled. The narrative about an obstructed present has a genealogy that can be traced to the "angry young man" films of the 1970s. Almost a quarter century after independence from British colonial rule in 1947, the angry young man films were a popular instantiation of narrating the postcolonial condition of a stalled present through the affective register of anger and vengeance—vigilante, extralegal even. We will discuss these films in greater detail in the next chapter, but here it is important to note that these films, which were created by the script-writing duo of Salim Khan and Javed Akhtar and turned the actor Amitabh Bachchan into a super-star, conceptualized the time within which they were produced and circulated (the 1970s) as stalled or violently obstructed. The films, including *Zanjeer* (The Chain, Prakash Mehra, 1973), *Deewar* (The Wall, Yash Chopra, 1975), *Kaala Pathar* (The Black Stone, Yash Chopra, 1979), and *Coolie* (Porter, Manmohan Desai, 1983) drew a connection between the experience of obstructed time and the corruption of the idea of the nation itself as well as the apparatus of the state. The hero—the angry young man—was a vigilante who was strong, aggressive, a man outside the system but who espoused a deep and powerful understanding of it.

The link between obstruction, anger, and strong, muscular leadership that brooked no opposition was forged not just on the screen but on the political stage as well during the decade of the 1970s, except that in the latter scenario, a woman came to embody the articulation. At a time of political turbulence, political-economic crisis (including Cold War tensions), and flux, facing protest and opposition from within her own political party and from her political opponents, then–prime minister Indira Gandhi suspended civil liberties, instituted clamp-downs and transfers of personnel seen as oppositional in the judiciary and bureaucracy, censored the press, and arrested political protestors between 1975 and 1977, a twenty-one-month period that is remembered as the Emergency. The Emergency was narrated by the authoritarian state that it created as strong, muscular leadership necessitated by the obstructions that were in turn constituted by political opposition and political-economic crises. As we have already noted, obstructions during this time were addressed by nationalizing banks, abolishing the privy purse, and by flexing military and nationalist muscle through the war with Pakistan and nuclear tests.

An iteration of this muscular anger about a present that is defined as obstructed, combined with a discourse of development, can be found in Hindu nationalist discourse several decades later. Bear with me, therefore, as I fast-forward our story to the 2014 BJP campaign for the general elections. This campaign began by narrating its version of the story about the stalled present and postcolonial melancholy and anger. Titled "Janta maaf nahin karegi" (the people will not forgive), a series of television commercials circulated on the airwaves, each of which featured an individual cast to embody the category *janta* (the people) as well as an issue deemed significant to the discursive climate of the 2014 general election cycle. Framed in close shots and shot in stark black-and-white tones, each advertisement narrated a story about people living and striving in the face of economic and social hardship. Each of the six advertisements focused on one issue—power, unemployment (two ads), inflation (two ads), and women's safety. Each commercial focused on one individual and yet the story narrated by the individual was constituted as a universal. This story has two distinct consequences, both of which involve the process of abstraction: 1) The story constitutes the common person as a composite image formed through the assembling (collage-like) of several embodiments and particularities and transforms the common into an abstract category, and 2) moreover, the story translates the socioeconomic specificity of inequity into the abstract category of the stalled present and links the affect of anger to it. The focus on the unremarkable, unheroic, toiling people helps categorize this story as realism.

The commercial on power featured an elderly man, a villager, noting that electricity was available in the village for just a couple of hours a day, and that without power he faced the torment of the heat, that he needed to buy diesel to irrigate his land, but that he had never complained; he simply lived and toiled. The affective register of the commercial shifts from powerful stoicism to anger when the man starts to talk about the durability of inequity (i.e., when he narrates an instantiation of the stalled present), as exemplified in this instance by the story of the man's children (but also therefore "the people's children") continuing to read under the flickering light of the oil lamp—an iconic sign of the "unmodern"—while the homes of the elite dazzled with lights. "Ab bahut ho gaya" (now, we've had enough/ now, we've crossed the threshold), says this man, this embodiment of the people, adding emphatically that the people will not forgive anymore. The advertisement does not specify who or what will not be forgiven. Certainly as a campaign commercial, the ire is meant to be targeted at the Indian National Congress—the two-term incumbent government that had persisted in its failure to bring basic necessities to the people—but the deliberate lack of specificity makes it possible to narrate a more abstract form of anger about the postcolonial condition.

The conception of the stalled present unmoored from the material, empirical world thus becomes myth. The obstructed present could therefore allude to many diverse and sometimes contradictory conditions; it could reference analyses of social conjunctures that are at ideological and political odds. For instance, in the 1970s, it could reference the state's failure to provide its citizens with basic necessities amid unemployment, food shortages, corruption, and an absence of a social security net; in the discourse of the politically powerful Indian National Congress and its leader Indira Gandhi, obstruction could also be defined as political opposition directed against its policies. In 2014, it could reference enduring economic inequity and the strangulation of radical redistribution measures including land reform, but *also* and *contradictorily* the correction and plateauing of stock market indexes and growth rates after the global financial crisis of 2008. It could reference the ostensible stalling of the liberalization of the economy and, in fact, this was a key issue for corporate leaders who supported Narendra Modi's campaign in 2014. It could allude to the durability of caste, religion, gender, and class as axes of difference that structure the social, such that the upper-caste, upper-class Hindu male is rendered as the legible and legitimate citizen subject. However, and again contradictorily, it could *also* be used to narrate reservations or affirmative action programs as *casteist*. This was and continues to be an issue for the BJP's upper- and middle-caste electoral base that has defined the support for affirmative action as casteist. In other words, as an abstract category, the stalled present could and did make allusions to diverse and contradictory sets of politics and experiences.

Moreover, this narration of the stalled present often encodes the affective register of angry vengefulness, an unforgiving sense of being wronged that is sutured to a masculinist ethos of vigilantism or authoritarianism. By the time we get to the 2014 general elections, in fact, the conception of obstruction is a dense affective node—an anger about being stalled is tethered to a *political* investment in Hindutva neoliberalism that is nevertheless deemed *apolitical*. In the 2017 Gujarat state elections, the BJP was facing a restive and demoralized electorate. Agrarian distress and a significantly depressed economy as a consequence of a couple of major economic policy decisions of the BJP were two important election issues. In its audiovisual election campaign advertising titled "I am development," the BJP allowed for the expression of some of these complaints, but that expression was immediately supplanted by an angry didacticism by a male authority figure who claims for himself as well as for Modi and the BJP an injury—an injury, he claims, that was inflicted by a self-indulgent elitist discourse that could not tolerate power in the hands of an "outsider" and by a gullible citizenry in the thrall of this elitism. The stalled present as a myth then is flexible and adaptive to diverse situations. This lack of specificity within the narrative about the obstructed present is significant because as we will see, it allows development—seen as the solution that will unclog this obstruction—to *also* acquire a nonspecific character. Crucially, obstruction can be narrated in this nonspecific manner only because it alludes to sociological and political detailing within narratives from previous decades that were constructed as realistic.

THE OBSTRUCTED PRESENT: TWO INDIAS

The obstructed present post–economic liberalization was often also narrated through constructing the imagery of two Indias. The concept-image of development with its accreted allusions to movement towards improved well-being is foundational to many of these stories. The 2005 caper film *Bunty aur Babli* (Bunty and Babli, Shaad Ali) begins by painting the dichotomy between two Indias through multiple signifiers. The film follows the travails of a young man (Rakesh) and woman (Vimmi) who shed their small-town beginnings and personas to become "Bunty" and "Babli," respectively, so they can live the metropolitan life. As Rakesh and Vimmi, the characters embody realism. Rakesh and Vimmi are given life by drawing on journalistic, sociological, and autoethnographic accounts of small-town India post–economic liberalization, which describe brand-conscious men and women reading magazines like *Cosmopolitan* and dreaming of becoming the next Bill Gates.[19] Bunty and Babli are spectacular characters, untethered from the restrictions imposed by realism and as such unobstructed. The next chapter will discuss the film at length; here I want to sample it for a few key narrative themes. The introductory sequence of the film situates the narrative in its political frame: Though the film is a catch-me-if-you-can caper about two crooks, it is *also* a particular kind of a story about the contemporary conjuncture in India. The film's narrative in its introductory sequence itself distinguishes between two Indias, a distinction that is both visual and political. The "shining, glittering" India that urges you to dream big is metropolitan India; glimpsed in fading, pale light through a handheld camera that refuses to stay still, this metropolis surrounded by a whispering sea, with the silhouettes of buildings glimmering and rising to meet the night sky stands in contradistinction to that other India. This other India, symbolized by a torn kite that hangs forlorn from a TV antenna and visual vignettes that are bursting with color but static, frozen in time, suffocates even as that first India beckons. The political distinction that defines the two Indias in the story that the film narrates pivots on the desire for the excessive and dynamic life lived in the throes of transnational capital within the spaces of the metropolis. In this narrative, obstruction was defined through the *absence* of desire—desire for wealth, fame, glamour and excess. Unlike the angry young man films in the 1970s where obstruction was defined through the narration of the oppressions of poverty, hunger, hard labor whose attempts to organize were violently suppressed, unemployment, a failed system of formal education whose degrees were as valuable as pieces of paper, and gendered violence and assault, films like *Bunty aur Babli* made post–economic liberalization told the story of obstruction through desire and an entrepreneurial attitude.

In commentary published in the English-language newspapers in the first decade of the new millennium, the two-Indias imagery was used to draw the distinction that neoliberalism as an ideology has attempted to make since its early instantiations—that is, the distinction between the spaces of the economic and the social.[20] The space of the economic or the market is deemed apolitical and is narrated as new India. It is defined by the apparatus of the economy, but particularly India's growing "world-class business community," through growth rates, reports of the gross domestic product, and the fortunes of stock indices. In these stories, the market is constituted as an irrefutable success without an alternative and therefore spectacular. The space of the social is narrated through statistics about poverty, farmers' suicides, descriptions of villages sans infrastructure, and discussions of the rural and urban poor voter and the fear that "his" (this individual is consistently gendered male) voting decisions may veer to the "extreme left." The social is also narrated through discussions of the "rot" of Maoist or Naxalite violence, and in discussions of education (or the lack thereof), healthcare, squalor, reservations, or affirmative action–like programs and labor reform.[21] Seen in the persistent iteration of corruption and the presence of persons with a criminal record in the legislature and in descriptions that stress the breakdown of law and order—listing the number of murders, dacoit-related activity, rapes, and riots— old India is seen at worst as a threat to the stability of the economic and at best as a condition that disallows a sustained celebration of the economic. The social is narrated in the familiar codes of realism. This sharp delineation between the social and the economic sets the stage for development to be defined as the solution for old India and, importantly, enables the concept-image to be narrated as apolitical, technocratic strategy. Development signifies movement from old India to new and conjoins realism to the spectacular.

The content of this story about two Indias, the obstructed present, and development has a relationship to the structural changes that the English-language news media went through in the time of economic liberalization. Much like other forms of media, it had undergone transformations in the late 1990s and the first few years of the new millennium. The Times Group, for instance, one of the most prominent media conglomerates in India, is integral to the story of economic reforms or economic liberalization in India.[22] The publishing group was established in 1838 in colonial India and became Indian-owned in 1946. Its flagship newspaper, *The Times of India*, reportedly has a circulation of over 2.14 million and the *TOI Mumbai* accounts for approximately 60–70 percent of the Group's revenues.[23] In the early 1990s, as the Indian state was being liberalized, the Times Group was being restructured with the aim of turning around an old family business that was in decline.[24] The story of the Times Group's transformations during that decade runs parallel to the story of changes wrought by economic liberalization policies of the Indian state. Thus, the Times Group, under the leadership of Samir Jain (who had taken over the operations of the Group in 1986), redefined the newspaper as a consumer product, hired people with a background in marketing and selling fast-moving consumer goods (FMCGs) such as soap and shampoo, and "played with every element in the product mix."[25] The Times Group's strategies included introducing glossy color supplements, shutting down a number of publications that included magazines that were respected for their editorial content but were not seen as "money-spinners" such as *The Illustrated Weekly*,[26] price-cutting, pricing the newspaper differently on different days of the week, "cross-brand advertising packages," and allowing advertising content to encroach on editorial content space.[27] The *Times of India* was not alone in witnessing these changes; many newspapers in the country saw such transformations as "young newspapermen . . . took over their fathers' businesses in the early 90s," though none were as aggressive or as big as those initiated by the Times Group. The content featured in the media produced by the conglomerate narrated these structural changes in the language of renewal, newness, and emergence from obstruction. It wasn't just the print news industry that was seeing change though: government monopoly over airwaves in India ended in 1995, an event preceded by the entry of satellite television in 1990.[28] Thus, "state agencies no longer dominate broadcasting, and privately-produced and domestically-owned content dominates the scores of channels."[29]

One of the consequences of these industry changes for English-language newspaper content was a consistent emphasis on the brand of the media conglomerate and the linkage between that brand and the brand of the nation. Thus, using a model that had worked to produce economic data analysis that could then generate ideas for news content in the financial newspaper, the Times Insight Group was set up to produce campaigns that would build the brand equity of the *Times of India* and strengthen its news content (the *Times* had been criticized for its journalism following the changes that were instituted in the 1990s).[30] One of the results of this analysis was the India Poised campaign, which included television advertisements and a set of stories that appeared in the *Times of India*, that took the form of report cards on various sectors (such as Information Technology, Health, and Oil and Gas) deemed important to the nation by the editorial team of the newspaper. The television advertising of the India Poised campaign specifically and unequivocally used the two-Indias imagery to suggest that the only leash holding a "pulsating, dynamic new India" was the skepticism, fear of failure, and traditional conservatism of old India. The conclusion drawn by the report card–like news stories that formed a significant portion of the *Times of India*'s India Poised campaign was that the key constraint (the leash) to new India was the political leadership of the nation; the Times Group therefore titled its next campaign "Lead India" and organized it as a competition—screened on television—to find "new leaders for new India." Stories in the English-language press, such as the *Times of India*, consistently followed the two-Indias imagery by hailing the state to devise strategies to present reform as revolutionary. More importantly, these stories called for the state to be embodied by a muscular visionary.

Transformed into an individual, the state was urged by commentary in the English-language press to animate the hearts and minds of the "common man" with the spirit of reforms by addressing the gap between the social and the economic, a distinction that narratives fueled by neoliberalism have constructed in the first place. Columnist Sagarika Ghose, for instance, writing in the *Hindustan Times*, noted that, "The government, by restricting reforms to financial measures and the corporate sector, is depriving India of the passion and romance of reforms. By confining the spirit of reforms to the economic sector, the *aam aadmi* [common man] is being deprived of the energizing force of reforms."[31]

Ghose went on to argue that "reforms should be a magnificent new design, a new way of thinking, a civil and democratic leap forward."[32] At the precise moment when the Indian state opens up to transnational capital, it is hailed as a paternal, even evangelical figure that must powerfully persuade the nation of the "spirit of reforms." It is here in the twists of this narrative about the obstructed present that we can trace the intersection of neoliberalism and Hindu nationalism. Both political projects, even when they sometimes distance themselves from each other, narrate their present as similarly obstructed and both call on muscular visionaries to unclog the trajectories of the commoner and the nation.

It is not surprising, therefore, that in 2018 Indian public culture saw the release of a film that neatly ties these many threads together. The Hindi-language film *Parmanu [Atom]: The Story of Pokhran* (Abhishek Sharma) was released a year prior to the Indian general elections in 2019, which gave the Narendra Modi–led BJP government an overwhelming majority of seats in the lower house of parliament and a second term. The film told the story of the 1998 nuclear tests conducted by the then-BJP government led by Atal Bihari Vajpayee and was therefore seen by some critics as propaganda.[33] I want to call attention to the narrative processes through which the film discusses the time frame within which its plot is situated as obstructed. *Parmanu* defines obstruction through geopolitics. The film begins in 1995, three years prior to the formation of the Vajpayee-led BJP government. Its opening frame describes this period as tense and turbulent: The Soviet Union has collapsed and India has lost a strong ally, even as its neighbor Pakistan has grown in strength through alliances with the United States and China. Moreover, the film states, "western powers" have been placing increasing pressure on India to sign "one-sided" deals to "weaken it economically and militarily." And China had conducted yet another nuclear test that year, part of a series of tests that the nation had undertaken from the mid-1960s until the late 1990s. *Parmanu* argues that these geopolitical factors and events had left India isolated and vulnerable and had obstructed its own growth as a superpower in the region. Setting the stage thus, *Parmanu* narrates nuclear technology as empowerment and the muscular, obsessive male patriot as a visionary. The combination of this male visionary, nuclear technology, and the resurrection of the Hindu nation via the BJP clears the obstruction, or so the film suggests. Time, it suggests, lurches forward again, for both the common Indian and the nation itself.

UNCLOGGING THE OBSTRUCTION: "APOLITICAL" DEVELOPMENT

Conjoined to the story about the obstructed past and the anger of the common person who will not forgive is the story about renewal and a new dawn. In other words, sutured to the conception of the stalled present is the desire for the affective register of good times, that better days are imminent. Here now, is the release of the libidinal charge, where the coiled anger of the stalled and obstructed present is discharged and soaked up by authoritarian masculinity. This story about emergence was central both to the processes that stabilized neoliberalism in India as well as to the narrative of Hindu nationalism. Consider, for instance, the following lines from a verse penned by poet and lyricist Gulzar for the "India Poised" campaign in 2007:

> We've woken up each day for half a century and wiped the sky clean,
> Sieved sunlight from dusty beams.
> Sixty years of freedom.
> Hindustan is at history's turn,
> At the next turn, our feet will be on Mars.
> Hindustan is pregnant with hope,
> Let's walk together, because if you walk, Hindustan walks too.[34]

This verse in particular and the India Poised campaign in general narrates the melancholic and seemingly unendingly arduous work of making do and finding hope while living in postcolonial times as culminating in *this* moment, a decade after liberalization, when time (historical time) turns a corner. The poet uses the Hindustani phrase "umeed se hai," often used to announce a woman's pregnancy (she/her body itself is filled with hope, *umeed*), to narrate the nation's temporality. In another verse, written for the film *Guru* (Mani Ratnam, 2007), Gulzar had narrated the nation's and the film's protagonist's present as a restful, recuperative pause (the pause of nightly sleep) after an arduous, working, wakeful day (read: the past) when new dreams could be sown. New dreams thus planted would germinate into a new dawn. This new dawn is signified as development, brought about by economic liberalization. Here, that metaphor of reproduction is taken to its conclusion, where the nation is itself pregnant with the hopeful future. The use of the metaphor of reproduction to affectively narrate a temporal node as new sets in place a storyline wherein agency is masculinized and time is feminized. Moreover, development itself is circumscribed within a heteropatriarchal universe even as femininity is appropriated to create an affective charge around this conception of temporality.

The popular story that narrates time as obstructed also suggests that the unclogging of temporality can be achieved through a muscular visionary and an apolitical conception of development. In other words, the story about obstructed time is inevitably followed by a story about new India, a shining future that is imminent, and about good days that are just around the corner. Eschewing the space of the social, popular stories suggested that development was most effectively pursued and cultivated by global capital and its professionals, namely corporate business houses, the urban elite, and visionaries. The space of the social narrated through the form of realism is used to define obstruction, and the spectacular tells the story of capital, the nation, and the market. As such, the story went, development would melt hierarchies that mired the rural and urban poor. It is this script that allowed and enabled the constitution of Hindutva neoliberalism and its particular embodiment in the political figure of Narendra Modi. Constituted and defined hegemonically as apolitical technocracy, fueled and supported by global capital that enables improvement, development as a concept-image has allowed Hindutva to link itself to neoliberalism and translate itself (on the back of the commoner) as an ethical, moral nation-building political movement. Development, constituted as such, thus enables a limited and circumscribed political ideology that emphasizes Hindu supremacy to market itself as a righteous social movement. Relatedly, transformed into a ventriloquist's dummy, to use Gayatri Spivak's provocative formulation, the *aam admi* (commoner) becomes the voice and the body through which this ideology resurrects itself. For global capital, the articulation first with the concept-image of development and then with Hindu nationalism works to manage and repress the threat posed to it by subaltern demands for equity and redistribution. The Indian corporate elite's support for Narendra Modi is a specific instantiation of these articulations. I will come back to the story of the visionary, but for now, let us work out the conception of development as apolitical strategy that will enable time, the nation, and the commoner to progress.

In order to trace the contours of development as a concept-image that is deliberately defined as apolitical, we must discuss caste and specifically the relationship that is forged in stories about new India between caste and development. In order to do so though, we must travel back in time to the first decade of the new millennium when the BJP had lost electoral power. In the middle of the year 2006, when the Indian summer was at its harshest, students—particularly those living and attending universities and professional institutions in metropolitan cities like Mumbai and Delhi—led a series of protests against the proposed extension of "reservations" or affirmative action–like policies to elite engineering and medical institutions in the country. Human Resource Development Minister Arjun Singh's announcement that the state planned to reserve 27 percent of seats in the Indian Institutes of Technology (IITs), the Indian Institutes of Management (IIMs), the central-government run medical colleges—including the All India Institute of Medical Sciences (AIIMS)—and some other elite institutions for Other Backward Castes (OBCs) was the immediate provocation for these students. The Supreme Court decision that finally paved the way for such reservations was delivered two years later in 2008. This case was widely referred to as "Mandal II" after the Mandal Commission Report, tabled in 1980 and enacted in 1990, which first called for reservations for lower castes listed within the category of "Other Backward Castes." "Mandal I" had sought 27 percent reservations for OBCs in Central Services. Prominent public commentators termed the policy "destructive" and a "great rip-off in the name of development." They argued that reservations would lead to a "dilution" of the "high standards" of these institutions and that students in the "reserved category" would find it "difficult to cope and end up sidelined and mentally fatigued."[35]

Massed under the organizational banner "Youth for Equality," students participating in the agitation against the reservations represented themselves as a "non-violent," *"non-political"* group and decried the "loss of meritocracy" as a consequence of caste-based reservations. Repeatedly defining Indian politicians as "vote beggars," the students saw Arjun Singh's announcement as yet another attempt by the "dirty" political establishment to cater to their "vote banks." Additionally, Youth for Equality accused those who favored affirmative action policies or advocated for them of "casteism" and divisiveness. A press release, for instance, issued by the Mumbai branch of Youth for Equality (http://yfepress.blogspot.com/), on May 2, 2006, which was marked by this organization as a day of "nationwide protest" against reservations, stated the following:

> It is time that the Government of India stop using petty "vote bank politics" and realizes its responsibility to empower these marginalized communities with good primary education, better infrastructure and opportunities so they may compete with the so called "upper castes" and not against them. As members of the student community we urge the nation to raise its voice so it may be heard above the din of political hogwash and *their attempt to divide us on the grounds of casteism.*

The press release worked specifically to define development—good primary education, better infrastructure, and the ambiguous term "opportunities"—as *apolitical* and positioned it in opposition to that which is political, namely caste-based reservations. It argued that caste-based affirmative action policies were divisive and that the form of politics that institutes such policies reeks of "casteism." A similar argument was made by a range of public commentators, including prominent journalists, bureaucrats, and social scientists writing in the English-language news media. In this argument, development was constituted as the *apolitical* redress to marginalization.

To substantiate this argument, a number of these texts constructed a narrative for "deprivation" and constituted caste and class as distinct categories, such that class (and *not* caste) was deemed the "authentic," "genuine" indicator of deprivation. For instance, after noting that "the government's quota policy is not only divisive but also encourages mediocrity in education ... [and that] by compromising on quality for its youth, India will never be able to ride the wave of globalization," a commentator, identified as a senior Fulbright scholar, writing in the

Hindustan Times, noted that "reservations" display an "unconcern with excellence," do away with merit, and usher in a "regime of mediocrity and mendacity" interested in "retaining power without genuine concern for the uplift of the impoverished and economically backward."[36] Another social scientist, writing a column in the *Times of India,* argued that "public policy . . . should be based on evidence and logic, not glib sociological babble . . . whether caste is a good indicator of socio-economic deprivation remains an unsettled issue" and that "by using caste as a criterion in public policy, India's government is effectively treating the rich and the poor equally . . . this [reservations] helps co-opt the elite among the lower castes to the ruling coalition, and keeps the poor divided along caste lines . . . but it is hypocritical to argue that this [reservations] does anything to eliminate poverty."[37]

Caste was deemed an inconsistent and often false marker of marginalization by such discourse because caste-based oppression could not be quantified. Development in post–economic liberalization India insisted on the quantification of oppression through a "deprivation index." An editorial published in the *Times of India* in 2007 stated that "the government must rethink the entire reservation policy and move towards affirmative action," and that options must be considered that "replace quotas based only on caste."[38] One such option the *Times* advocated in this editorial was the use of "points awarded for disadvantages based on caste, community, gender, type of schooling and family background" in order to create a "deprivation index." Similarly, Kirit Parekh, then a member of the Planning Commission writing a column in the *Times of India,* argued that admissions to elite institutions identified in Mandal II should be "based on a merit list adjusted in a transparent manner for differences in nurture to reflect true potential" and that therefore "marks" could be given for "different types of handicaps" or "different attributes of disadvantage, which may include religious background."[39] Parekh insisted that any mark or point system should be "empirically defensible and dynamic" so that this index can be adjusted over time. Television journalist and anchor Barkha Dutt, writing a column for the *Hindustan Times,* similarly insisted that a "comprehensive assessment of whether there is an empirical relationship between quotas and social/economic upliftment"[40] was necessary. These narratives represent class, caste, religion, and gender as a "disadvantage" or "handicap" that they then suggest can be measured and quantified through "marks" or "points" that would make up a "deprivation index." Such an index would in turn help, these stories argue, in the formulation of a "transparent" development agenda. The emphasis on the quantification of marginalization and the creation of a "deprivation index" in these texts must be read as the manifestation of what John Gledhill has termed as a characteristic of neoliberalism, namely "audit culture." Gledhill argues that "audit culture"—the "continuous assessment and demands for evidence that goals are being realized"—highlights a "paradoxical feature of neoliberalism"[41]: where the strengthening of the bureaucracy is achieved through an emphasis on empiricism and social scientific inquiry even as the state signals a loosening of its grip by divesting the task of auditing onto other bodies. The case of "reservations" in India presents us with a very particular manifestation of audit culture. Here, the state—as a direct consequence of the political struggle and the concomitant power and legitimacy garnered by political parties and groups representing lower castes in India since the late 1970s and 1980s—reveals its presence by instituting "reservations" in elite educational institutions in the nation. The middle class and the bureaucracy (note that a member of the Planning Commission was one of the commentators calling for a "merit list" of disadvantage) through the medium of the elite press attempt to circumscribe the state and its presence by emphasizing a "value-neutral," "scientifically sanctioned" audit culture in the specific form of a deprivation index.[42] The commentators are not always clear about the specific bodies or organizations that would work to constitute a deprivation index—while some suggest the educational institution in question should be centrally involved others point specifically to the state. As such, the state remains a key presence within the social formation, and audit culture is used not so much to call for the state's withdrawal; instead it is used to define development as apolitical, while simultaneously castigating caste-based assertions as political.

Neoliberalism draws a distinction between the social and the economic and concurrently repudiates the social as the appropriate space for justice. As Wendy Brown has argued, this renders invisible "the social norms and inequalities generated by legacies of slavery, colonialism and patriarchy,"[43] and in the Indian context, caste as well. As we have been noting, the story about the social is told through the form of realism. The merit list and the deprivation index, on the other hand, are defined as certitude.[44] As numbers, the list and the index are ostensibly irrefutable, transcendent, and as such spectacular. While this characteristic of neoliberalism is more familiar to those who have followed the ideology's rise to hegemonic status, my contention is that this is a feature that neoliberalism shares with authoritarian nationalism, specifically, in our case, Hindu nationalism. Moreover, a focus on narrative form and storytelling reveals that Hindutva neoliberalism articulates the social (narrated through realism) to the economic (narrated as spectacular) to win legitimacy for the market and the nation, even as conceptions of justice are simultaneously disarticulated from the space of the social. This is precisely why the rendering of development as apolitical via the bracketing of the space of the social is necessary to the stories that have circulated in public culture in the time of Hindutva neoliberalism—it enables the centering of upper-caste, middle-class urbanity as the ideal identification in new India. By turning to popular cinema in the concluding portion of this section, I will trace the ways in which caste and corruption get interlinked and development defined as apolitical gets associated with upper-caste, middle-class urbanity.

Back to Mandal II then. The middle-class, upper-caste youth that protested Mandal II specifically defined politicians and politics itself as dirty and corrupt. The institution of reservations, they argued, was evidence of the corruption of the very conception of development by the political class. Popular Hindi cinema produced during this time reinforced but also reconstituted this argument, and some of these films were specifically referenced by Youth for Equality in their literature. *Yuva* (Youth, Mani Ratnam, 2004) and *Rang de Basanti* (Color Me the Colors of Spring/Color Me Saffron, Rakyesh Omprakash Mehra, 2006) were both popular mainstream Hindi films released in the first decade of the new millennium that specifically foregrounded the question of youth and politics. While there were other films, most notably director Farhan Akhtar's *Lakshya* (Goal, 2004) and *Dil Chahtha Hai* (What the Heart Desires, 2001), that also focused on youth and were coming-of-age stories that included middle- and upper-middle-class Indian males as their protagonists, *Yuva* and *Rang de* explicitly linked questions of political awakening with youth in India. Moreover, films like *Rang de* were foregrounded by youth groups who even adopted some of the strategies of protest represented in the film. *Yuva*, the older of the two films, traces the lives of three young men in the city of Kolkata, in eastern India. Two of the three protagonists, Michael Mukherjee and Arjun, are characterized as belonging to the urban Bengali middle class; Lallan Singh, the third protagonist, is placed in a different socioeconomic category. Lallan has run away from a village and makes a living by roughing up the opponents of Bengali politician Prosenjit Bhattacharya; in other words, he survives through *goonda gardi*. In classical Marxist terms, he is part of the lumpen proletariat. Michael and Arjun, on the other hand, are students. The former—the son of Bengali *bhadralok* parents—is deeply involved in student politics and is a student leader, while the latter is the son of a bureaucrat and on his way to the United States to complete a graduate degree and is mainly interested in having a good time before he catches his flight.

The narrative of the film defines the politics of Prosenjit Bhattacharya as corrupt, dirty, and savage. While his political ideology is not clearly defined within the film, he is identified as being part of the ruling political party in the state of Bengal. In real life, Bengal was governed by communist parties for thirty-four years before they lost power in 2011. The start of the new millennium, which coincided with the resignation (due to ill health) of a stalwart of the Left Front and the chief minister of the state of West Bengal, Jyoti Basu, initiated a weakening in the communist electoral hold over the state. The character Bhattacharya, thus, can be read in two ways: 1) He signifies the corruption of left politics in Bengal specifically but also across the nation more generally, and 2) He symbolizes the viciously violent politics of regional satraps. The regional political party, it must be stressed, is often associated with representing particular caste groups. Bhattacharya, as a character without redemption, can work to condemn the Left Front in the time of the Hindutva neoliberalism as well as strategies of political recognition that foreground caste.

Lallan is closely linked to Bhattacharya not simply because he works as his lackey, but also because Bhattacharya himself traces a genealogy when he states with some paternalistic pride that Lallan reminds him of his younger self. There is another genealogy at work here as well: we could think of Lallan as a descendent of the angry young man character from the 1970s. Or we could think of him as a mimic, a copy of the cinematic angry young man. As such, Bhattacharya is also linked to the angry young man character. He is the older avatar of the 1970s cinematic hero, wizened and now part of the system, but he nevertheless retains the dirt, the filth, and the violence that had defined the angry young man.

Lallan is played by Abhishek Bachchan, son of the actor who embodied the angry young man character, Amitabh Bachchan. Following a string of box office failures in which he played largely middle-class characters, Abhishek Bachchan won critical acclaim for his role in *Yuva* where he mimicked his father's embodiment of the angry young man: moving his long, lean body with a muscular, uninhibited swagger and using his voice with powerful restraint. While Lallan does have an understanding of the structures that keep him powerless, he is a mercenary who indulges in violence for a payment and harbors a desire for the kind of unadulterated power that he believes the politician Prosenjit Bhattacharya enjoys. The cinematic angry young man of the 1970s was also interested in upward mobility; he was in some iterations interested in working-class politics, fighting for the right to lead a life of dignity. His violence was always distinctly directed towards those who ruthlessly kept him and his community of laborers powerless. He may have sought wealth, but he was not narrated as power-hungry—that, the angry young man films suggested, was the preserve of the wealthy and powerful elite. This is precisely why, as we have seen earlier in this chapter, the angry young man's muscular anger continues to be useful for popular stories. Sociologically, Bhattacharya and Lallan are identical to the angry young man of the cinematic 1970s but their violence in *Yuva* is deemed selfish at best, mercenary at worst. Lallan's masculinity is scruffy, loud, boisterous—he is rough and physical with his wife when expressing both love and anger. In *Yuva*, Lallan meets the same fate as the angry young man did in the cinematic 1970s. He cannot be legitimated even though he is often endearing and it is his raw, unvarnished masculinity that gives a seductive charge to the narrative.

What we get instead is the absorption of that seductive charge enabled by violent masculinity within the body of a middle-class, urbane male, namely Michael Mukherjee. Michael is introduced to *Yuva*'s audience through a fight sequence in a shopping mall and is distinctly positioned as the leader of a group of young urban men. He has a steely, unwavering eye and his moves have the precision of a martial arts expert. His clothes remain immaculate even after this fight where he takes on and vanquishes another group who are quickly defined for the audience as political thugs. The audience, in fact, views the sequence in slow motion and the shots emphasize Michael's deliberateness; this is a purposeful masculinity. It is aggressive, violent, but legitimate because it is deemed to be in service of the nation (as opposed to self-interest and the interests of a caste or regional group as is the case with Lallan and Bhattacharya) and the violence deliberate and defined.[45] Angry, even violent masculinity had long been a preserve of the subaltern classes in the

cinematic narratives of Hindi films, as evidenced by the angry young man character of the 1970s. Sociologically dissimilar to the cinematic angry young man, what
Michael nevertheless has in common with him is the narration of righteous anger,
violence, and brooding masculinity. In *Yuva*, not only does a distinctly middle-
class, urbane character embody this angry, violent masculinity, he is represented
as heroic precisely because of it. Thus, even as the descendant of the angry young
man stands delegitimized in the story that *Yuva* narrates, his defining characteristics transform the upper-caste, middle-class urban male into a heroic figure. In a
context where realism is narrated through the unremarkable, the mundane and
the common and the spectacular as singular and sensational, we could read Michael
in *Yuva* as spectacular.

The narrative describes the political awakening of the third protagonist in the
film—Arjun—through his contact with Michael and his friends. Michael and
Arjun along with a third friend successfully contest an election, and in the last
scene of the film enter the state legislative assembly. The three strapping young
men, clad in denims, stand in contradistinction to the majority that peoples the
assembly—these men who are in the majority are significantly older than our protagonists, they are clad in traditional Indian political garb (*dhoti, kurta,* and what
has come to be known as the Gandhi *topi* or headdress, because of its links with
the independence struggle and Gandhi's *swadeshi* movement). Yet, the staging of
this scene suggests that the state legislative assembly is the rightful home of our
middle-class, upper-caste urban young male protagonists and that the dhoti-clad
politician is, in fact, the outsider—the benefactor of subaltern men like Lallan and
the limit of subaltern success. *Yuva* thus makes a specific argument; it suggests that
middle-class youth must find their calling in the cause of the nation. More importantly, it calls on the middle classes to reclaim the space of electoral politics that
has been sullied by the "dirty, vote bank politics" practiced by political representatives representing or claiming to represent the interests of rural subaltern classes
and castes. *Yuva* also suggests that the middle-class urban youth are the *legitimate*
representatives of the marginalized. Even as global capital advances into the small
town and the space of the rural, *Yuva* seems to suggest that the Indian middle
classes must assert their *political* selves not just in the spaces of the city and its
markets but also outside the city so they can reclaim their hegemonic authority
over the villages of India, which are perceived as threatening spaces following the
political assertion of the subaltern classes and castes. The middle class that *Yuva*
urges on is the Indian bourgeoisie—upper and middle castes, with well-educated
(often English-educated) parents who are professionals (university professors,
bureaucrats, business executives) and whose grandparents were cultivated by the
colonial state to form a native elite. Socioeconomically, this is not the "new middle
class" that burgeoned post–economic liberalization.[46] Importantly, *Yuva* makes its
narrative argument by enabling its male lead to appropriate and absorb the angry,
brooding masculinity that had come to cinematically embody the obstructed lives
of subaltern classes in postcolonial India. Realism twined with the spectacular is

the narrative form through which this story is told. Moreover, development is the sign through which the link between the middle class and the subaltern rural groups is forged, here within the space of electoral politics.

In a similar vein, *Rang de Basanti* suggests that youth in India, in particular middle-class urban youth, should "awaken" to their history and find themselves in the nationalist cause. The primary objective of its narrative, which is set in Delhi, is to depict the realm of politics—more specifically electoral politics—as dirty and corrupt. The motley group of friends who are the centerpiece of the film are university students who are drifting along for various reasons. They represent various religious groups, including Sikhs, Hindus, and Muslims, and a budding Hindu nationalist is thrown into the mix for good measure. The young men also represent the different socioeconomic strata that compose the middle classes in India; thus, while one young man's father is a rich arms broker, another young man's mother runs a *dhabba*—a restaurant that offers cheap meals to truckers and others on transit. In this, *Rang de* is different from *Yuva*. In the cinematic world constituted by *Rang de*, the middle class encompasses both the old and new formations that have come to define this socioeconomic category in India. This group, in the film, considers patriotism and nationalism passé, is always cynical of what the nation had given them in tangible terms, and is "awakened" when they perform the roles of young, radical revolutionaries who fought British colonial rule (for instance, Bhagat Singh and Chandrashekhar Azad) for a film being made by a British documentary filmmaker. Nandini Chander has accurately noted in this context that the iconic figure of Bhagat Singh has become a commodity within Indian national popular culture much like the figure of Che Guevara is within transnational popular culture allowing (oftentimes) an inchoate notion of revolution to be marketed and consumed.[47] Bhagat Singh, much like Che, has come to represent youthful masculinity, political passion, and, ironically, a joie de vivre (Bhagat Singh was executed in his early twenties by the British colonial state) within Indian national culture. *Rang de* expertly reveals this form of consumption through the easy transformation that the protagonists go through from being young, middle-class, and adrift to focused and intent on a violent task by simply taking on the personas of Bhagat Singh and his comrades that they were performing for camera. Like *Yuva*, here too we encounter an instantiation of the absorption of youthful, radical masculinity by characters distinctly marked as the middle class, in order to constitute a legitimate form of political masculinity. The difference here is that the youthful masculinity that is being appropriated in *Rang de* resided with a political revolutionary and not a cinematic hero. Both *Yuva* and *Rang de* thus constitute legitimate political masculinity through the consumption of angry, youthful masculinity by the middle-class male. It is not a coincidence that this middle-class male as the native elite and the beneficiary of institutional and structural privilege is, in fact, the target of the angry young subaltern man. The middle class in these cinematic narratives consumes/eats/appropriates its nemesis and his angry purpose and as such is deemed legitimate.

The narratives of *Rang de* and *Yuva* enable the audience sutured to their stories and their protagonists to construct a model for post-liberalization middle-class protest. *Rang de*, in fact, became the inspiration for Youth for Equality's protests against reservations and later for the urban middle-class's outcry against the murder of a model, Jessica Lal, in Delhi and its subsequent cover-up. *Rang de* was also an inspiration for the form of the protests that took place in Delhi in 2012 demanding action for the brutal and vicious rape and murder of a young woman on a bus. Much like the protagonists in the film who are "awakened" by noting parallels between their lives and the lives of the young revolutionaries they were performing for camera, Youth for Equality saw parallels between the "corrupt" defense minister in the film and the "vote bank"–obsessed Human Resource Development minister who had called for reservations for Other Backward Castes. Some students saw parallels between the events unfolding during the student-led protests against the extension of reservations and those depicted in the film—educated, rational youth against a corrupt, dirty political system. The film was screened during student meetings and become a rallying cry for youthful frustrations. The viewing of the film provided the moment of "awakening" *and* the model for protest. Youth for Equality used new media technologies—online forums, blogs, discussion boards, and social networking sites like Orkut—much like *Rang de's* protagonists had used the radio to articulate their stance to a sympathetic audience. The narrative of the film constructed and reinforced the distinction between the spaces of civil society that belonged to the youth and the middle classes and a "political" society that was corrupt and abusive of power.[48]

Our discussion of popular cultural stories surrounding the debate around the extension of reservations for OBCs, as well as cinematic narratives produced at the same time that tell the story of "dirty, corrupt" politics, suggests that the middle class is being narrated as the rightful and legitimate wielders of political power and that development works within these narratives as the sign that aims to suture subaltern groups or commoners with a middle-class-led new India. Our cultural analysis also suggests that the distinction between a civil and a political society does not always already exist within India; it is, in fact, constantly constructed, re-inscribed, and reinforced discursively, precisely because this distinction serves to delegitimize the political practices of the subaltern classes and castes and positions the middle classes as the masters of the state and its apparatus. This discursive construction and reinforcement may be seen to have assumed significance starting from the 1980s, when what Christophe Jaffrelot has termed the "second democratic upsurge" brought increased political legitimacy to subaltern classes and castes in India.[49] The beneficiaries of an epistemology that draws a distinction between civil and political societies remain the middle classes and the upper castes, as the commoner can only be imagined as residing at the peripheries of an otherwise modern world.

I will conclude this section about the strategic use of caste while obfuscating its violence and eschewing its annihilation with a story that I hope brings into even sharper relief the form and shape that development as a concept-image takes as a consequence of this setup. In 2017, two years prior to the general elections in 2019, a Hindi-language film called *Toilet: Ek Prem Katha* (Toilet: A Love Story, Shree Narayan Singh), starring the superstar Akhsay Kumar as the lead was released. The film's plotline focuses on the absence of a toilet within the home of a newlywed couple—an absence that is common to the village within which the groom resides. The young bride who has grown up in a home with indoor plumbing refuses to rise early and trek to the open fields on the outskirts of the village along with other women to complete her ablutions. Having defined the conflict as such, the rest of the film centers on the groom's efforts to save his marriage by convincing his conservative brahmin father and the village elders to allow him to build a toilet in his home. In the process, he seeks the intervention of the state as well. This state is not an abstract entity; it is quite specifically identified in the film as the institution governed by the BJP. The filmmakers thank this state—Narendra Modi's government—and its Swachh Bharat Mission (Clean India Mission). This project began in 2014 to build toilets in rural India and aimed to make rural India "open defecation free." The film, in fact, served to popularize the Modi government's narrative about its development agenda via the Clean India Mission. In 2019, two years after the release and success of the film, and a few months after the BJP's electoral victory in the general elections, Modi was awarded the Bill and Melinda Gates Foundation's "Global Goalkeeper Award" for the Swachh Bharat Mission, despite a mobilization that petitioned against it.[50] The happy conclusion of the film, wherein a toilet built in the home of the protagonist is inaugurated by his wife, intermixed with scenes of product and brand placements for such corporations as eBay and Kajaria Tiles (representing new and old economies), was complemented by the recognition that Modi received from the world's preeminent philanthropist and his foundation, which in turn is at the forefront of setting the agenda for development globally. The award therefore was another semiotic node, tying together global capital, the global nonprofit, and Hindu nationalism, such that development gets defined yet again as a technocratic solution that does not disrupt either neoliberalism or authoritarian nationalism.

There are two contentions I want to make through a reading of the film *Toilet*: First, that obstructed time here, as in so many other popular narratives produced in India post–economic liberalization, is defined through a narrative about old India. Moreover, even as the narrative makes an allusion to caste via old India, it deliberately obfuscates the hierarchies constituted by the caste system. Even as it alludes to the caste system's emphasis on rituals of purity and pollution, it renders invisible untouchables, lower castes, and non-Hindus, who have been and continue to be violently affected by those diktats. Second, the film defangs any radical potential that might be associated with development as a concept-image by recentering the caste system and by emphasizing the salience of the *Manusmriti* in new India. The *Manusmriti* is a Sanskrit text of medieval provenance that was used in the precolonial and colonial eras to codify conduct, duties, and so forth and is one of the foundations of the caste system (the British colonial state used the *Manusmriti* to codify Hindu law). The film suggests that an incomplete reading of the *Manusmriti* is at the core of the village elders' insistence against the building of a toilet and that a more detailed reading would reveal that the text argues against defecating near streams, rivers, and other water bodies. Development in this formulation does not critique the *Manusmriti* as anti-caste movements do; it does not seek to annihilate caste or even the patriarchal conservatism of old India, it simply gives it a proximal toilet. Significantly, this re-centering of the caste system and its foundational text, the *Manusmriti*, occurs through the centering of women, their bodies and bodily functions, and the ostensible preservation of their honor. In the film, it's the open defecation of women that is defined as a problem in new India.

The popular narrative, including such mass-mediated messages as the BJP's electoral campaign, transform the experience of caste-based oppression, of a gendered self, of the experience of marginality as a consequence of religious and class-based identities, into the abstract category of *aam* or the common. Defined as the common or the ordinary, the abstract retains the earthy seduction and the enchantment of the real but does not demand redistribution or even justice. The anger associated with the experience of obstructed time is thus managed through a happy resolution and is strategically used to legitimize or win consent for authoritarian, muscular leadership. Read together, the stories in this section reveal spectacular realism as a narrative patterning that defines the space of the social through the anger of the commoner, which is then strategically and spectacularly used to legitimate the ostensibly apolitical space of the economy, technology, and the upper-caste middle classes as the space for justice.

UNCLOGGING THE OBSTRUCTION: THE VISIONARY

Rebecca Klenk has noted that India's developmentalist paradigm embeds a deep contradiction as a consequence of the diverse visions and philosophical predilections of two of its most significant leaders: Jawaharlal Nehru, independent India's first prime minister, and M. K. Gandhi, the man who gave the Indian National Congress its political and strategic vision during the anticolonial movement. Klenck notes that while Nehru's vision of the developmentalist state revolved around rapid industrialization, a vision of revived village-level economies formed the cornerstone of Gandhi's national development agenda.[51] The narrative processes through which development emerges as the dominant concept-image in the contemporary conjuncture resolves this contradiction. By linking economic liberalization—read as a modernizing drive and as modernity itself—with the figure of the commoner through the concept-image of development and transposing this articulation onto a personage defined as a visionary, the popular narrative resolves the historic contradiction that has defined not just public policy but also the narrative form in India. Using (and constituting) this narrative, Narendra

Modi's BJP, for instance, asserted that it would be a better, more effective, less corrupt reformer of the economy than Manmohan Singh, the architect of liberalization and his Congress party, precisely because Modi was a visionary (and Singh was not) *and* was not alienated from the *aam aadmi*. Approached from the angle of narrative form, it is spectacular realism as the preeminent form of the conjuncture that attempts to bridge the disparities in socioeconomic and cultural capital between the rural and the urban, and between the large majority that is poor and the wealthy, that have been exaggerated by neoliberalism in India.

The nonprofit, corporate responsibility, and the visionary are key institutions, ideas, and embodiments for this conception of development. Nandan Nilekani, cofounder of one of the most prominent IT firms in India, a bureaucrat in the Manmohan Singh–led government where he directed a unique identity card program for the Indian state, a failed politician but a popular public intellectual, narrates the nongovernmental organization (NGO) as a sign of the growing might of the middle class in new India and therefore also as a "sign of the changing nature of India's democracy."[52] Nilekani offers us another iteration of the distinction between civil and political societies, situating the middle classes and the nonprofit within civil society and caste, religion, and regional identities of the poor and the working classes within political society. The nonprofit in neoliberal India, in this narration, would reshape caste, religious, and regional divisions such that they are in fact seen to be melting away, thus rendering the subaltern more modern. Thus, Nilekani notes in his hugely successful book, *Imagining India: Ideas for the New Century*, that:

> This bottom-up civil consciousness, non-political and non-partisan as it is, is a sign of a new kind of democracy in India. These organizations [NGOs] are emphasizing an approach towards political democracy that is rooted in the idea of "civil society" rather than in the divisions that now dominate India's politics. And while it is still early days here, this trend carries a great deal of promise, especially when we consider that the growth of such NGOs has been enabled by a middle class with an active interest in political reforms. This ever-widening group of middle-class Indians is using NGOs to come face to face with India's poorer and working classes, and to *plant* the ideas of secular rights and liberties across these communities.[53]

Nilekani's narrative ascribes potency to non-governmental institutions precisely because they are deemed "non-political" and "non-partisan." Other commentary had made similar ascriptions about large business houses and the urban elite, urging them to act as a supplement to the Indian state by making the alleviation of poverty a core corporate strategy. The nonprofit, the business house, and the urban elite are lauded because such institutions are seen to be formed by the melting of caste-, religion-, and regionally based identities and therefore deemed "non-political" and "non-partisan." More importantly, it is global capital, these narratives argue, that allows for the melting of old categories: "The need for social capital and mutual trust in India's market economy—to form working networks, supply chains and non-family business relationships—is reshaping India's divisions across religious, caste and regional lines," Nilekani notes.[54]

Public discourse in the first decade of the new millennium argued that pro-business policies had produced high growth rates and that the state must therefore not be deterred from the path of sustaining such policies. The deterrent—the rage and the consequent vote of the subaltern, for whom inequity continued to define the present as obstructed—must therefore be managed, not just by the state but also by urban elites and business houses dependent on the state's pro-business policies. This should be of particular significance to urban elites and business houses because, as this discourse argued, the rage of the common voter toiling in poverty could allow the "decrepit extreme left a second wind."[55] The electoral gains that Left parties had made in the 2004 general elections loomed large here. Thus, commentators demanded that urban elites and business houses make poverty alleviation an integral part of their corporate strategy, since the presence of poverty was a threat to the state's pro-business policies. This is not a prototypical neoliberal call for a rollback of the state, but an argument for business to act as its *supplement*. The argument pivots on defining the common as agentive and also as a threat to the tenuous political-economic conjuncture that is new India. Both the agency of the commoner and the threat she poses is sought to be managed under the sign of development, but specifically through a visionary, inside and outside the apparatus of the state. Let us first consider the narration of a visionary working within the apparatus of the state and then pick up a story about one working outside the bounds of the state.

In October 2008, Tata Motors relocated its Nano manufacturing operation from Singur in the eastern state of West Bengal to Sanand in the western state of Gujarat. The Nano was branded as the "people's car" and marketed as the most inexpensive car in the world. Tata Motors had faced sustained resistance from farmers in Bengal and the Mamata Banerjee–led political party, the Trinamool Congress, at Singur over the farmland that was allotted to the corporation for its use. On moving to Gujarat, a state that has seen the BJP dominate politically since the mid-1990s, Ratan Tata, chairman of the Tata Group, proclaimed that "there is a good M and a bad M."[56] Tata was referring to the then chief minister of Gujarat, Narendra Modi, who had succeeded in bringing the company to the state and who had "impressed" him with what he had been able to do in terms of "administering and managing the state,"[57] and Mamata Bannerjee, leader of the Trinamool Congress and the politician who became the face and voice of the Singur protests against Tata Motors and the West Bengal government (which had Left Front parties in power during this time). For Tata, Modi was the "good M" and Mamata Bannerjee the "bad M," because Gujarat had aided and promoted the interests of the corporation. In early 2009, a few months after Tata Motors' move to Gujarat, Modi was lauded as prime ministerial material by industrialists in the telecommunications sector such as Anil Ambani and Sunil Mittal. The *Economic Times*, reporting this endorsement under the headline "Narendra Modi Becomes India Inc. Poster Boy," noted that "Modi is a brilliant orator who has a reputation for battling corruption to bring development to Gujarat, but [is] also accused of turning a blind eye to the murder of hundreds of Muslims during riots in 2002 and is fiercely critical of Pakistan."[58] The English-language news media in India was captivated by what they perceived was a transformation, from what one *Times of India* article termed "Moditva"—referring to Modi's central role in the project of Hindutva or Hindu nationalism—to "Modi-nomics."[59] In an interview for the magazine *Business India*[60] in 2009, on the eve of the Vibrant Gujarat Global Investors' Summit—a biennial event that had attracted much press and corporate and industry attention and was the occasion for the announcement of new memoranda of understanding (MoUs) between the state and industry—Narendra Modi noted his "vision" for the state:

> We need to sustain growth. For this, we need to develop our own model in which overall development comprises one-third industries, one-third agriculture and one-third service sector. If all these three sectors achieve balanced development, the strongest of recession [sic] cannot slow down the economy. The common man will never be in difficulty . . . we believe in inclusive growth. We want mass production and also production by masses. This will take the money to the poor. Wealth creation is not the function of the state. The function of the state is wealth distribution.[61]

Development, inchoately defined through a model of thirds, a mention of the common man, and wealth distribution, is the concept-image that enables Modi to articulate Hindutva with global capital. Through development, Modi narrated the story of "good governance" and noted that the state of Gujarat was "progressing because we are providing [a] political vision," and that "things are good because of . . . [his] *proactive political interference*."[62] As columnist Praful Bidwai noted in an essay in the magazine *Frontline*, "since 2003, Modi has been 'normalized' in the eyes of Indian business," and "after more than a decade of economic neoliberalism, which was supposed to reduce their dependence on politicians,"[63] industrialists and corporations have, in fact, assiduously linked themselves to the kind of "proactive political inference" from the state that allows them a "peaceful industrial climate, good infrastructural backup and policy continuity." In a passionate lament, Bidwai therefore asked in the context of Gujarat: "How can anyone talk about 'progress' and 'development' in 'Gujarat Unlimited' without a reference to the worst carnage since 1947? Why did not business barons present at the event feel emboldened to ask questions about the rule of law in Gujarat?"[64]

Development can be and is talked about without raising the dissonantly violent images and sounds of the "worst carnage since 1947" because that concept-image itself now signifies the articulated relationship between capital and a muscular state that interferes, violently if necessary, to pave its way. It carries with it the libidinal charge of a muscular visionary whose individual will alone can light bulbs in villages and whose fifty-six-inch chest can bring self-pride and self-respect back to the emasculated masses of the nation. Journalist Nandini Oza, writing in the magazine *The Week*, cited political analyst Achyut Yagnik to note that "Modi uses development to absolve himself of his alleged involvement in the 2002 riots and to switch over to national politics"[65] and reports that despite all his shortcomings Modi's voters favor him because "for them he is a *vikas purush* [man of progress/ development] who ushers in progress."[66] Rajdeep Sardesai, a prominent broadcast journalist and writer, teased out the story about Modi's twin personas that Oza alluded to in her article:

> The darker side of . . . [Modi's] personality cult had been seen in 2002, when Modi converted a terrible human tragedy into a personal *gaurav yatra* [journey of pride]. He was then the "tough-on-minority-terror" [minority here refers to the Muslim population, a religious minority] Hindu Hriday Samrat [The King of Hindu Hearts]. In 2007, the propaganda was designed to build Modi's appeal as a more inclusive *"vikas purush"* [man of progress/development], a hard-working CM responsible for pushing Gujarat on the fast-track to development, someone at ease in both corporate gatherings and political rallies.[67]

For Sardesai, as for a majority of the English-language press, the story about Narendra Modi pivots on the description of his twin personas created through political propaganda: Modi as "King of Hindu Hearts" and Modi as "Man of Progress." Moreover, the press argues—as exemplified by Sardesai here—that Modi has been so successful in "merging muscular Hindutva with Gujarati *asmita* (self-respect) with a commitment to good governance,"[68] that the violence from 2002 has been all but forgotten and Modi stands "retooled" as "a typical, middle-class politician."[69] The assumption underlining these narratives is that development and good governance are apolitical categories while Hindutva or Hindu nationalism is a political appeal and that Modi and his propaganda machine have successfully used the apolitical category development (*vikas*) to produce amnesia about the political category (Hindutva). These stories suggest that the Jekyll-like figure of Modi as vikas purush espousing "Modi-nomics" has all but subsumed the Hyde-like figure of Modi as *Hindu Hriday Samrat* (King of Hindu Hearts), the proponent of "Moditva." In fact, "Moditva" is integral to and complementary to "Modi-nomics"; they are conjoined, not twin, figures. In its Hindu nationalist iteration, development is narrated through an aggressively masculine discourse of pride (*asmita*), machismo (Modi was described as a leader with *chhappan nee chhatti*—a fifty-six-inch chest—in his political campaign), and unapologetic authoritarianism and as such is identical to the discourse of Hindu nationalism itself.

In the general elections held in 2014, the BJP, from the position of a two-term opposition party, centered its campaign on its prime ministerial candidate Narendra Modi and named it "Achche din aane wale hain" (Good/better days are coming).

Using the traditional development idiom, this campaign signified an imminent future and linked it to a visionary (i.e., Narendra Modi). The tagline for the advertisement underlined this sense of futurity that was available in the present: "Hum Modiji ko laanewale hain, achche din aane wale hain" [We are going to bring Modi to power; better days are coming] it said. A song titled "Achche Din Aane Wale Hain" [Better Days Are Coming] was recorded in ten languages and recomposed in five regional genres. A "music video" was also created and a series of TV commercials featured eight advertisements focused on the themes of "inflation, education, infrastructure, electricity, rural empowerment, corruption and farmer empowerment."

This series was distinct from the *Janta Maaf Nahin Karegi* series we have discussed earlier. Shot in color, all eight commercials in this series feature a conversation between two individuals. Unlike the *Janta Maaf Nahin Karegi* series, here the audience is listening in on a dialogue that is seemingly taking place independent of the audience's own position. In the *Achche Din* series, the audience as a diegetic spectator is spoken to and narrated; the audience is *told* that good/better days are coming. Here, even when the individuals in the commercials articulate the condition of a stalled present—an incomplete road construction project, a degree or training but no employment opportunities, not being able to earn enough in the city to send money home to the family in the village—they do so with a gentle shrug, a knowing smile or laugh, precisely because good days are now imminent. The angry masculinist sensorium of the *Janta Maaf Nahin Karegi* series is transformed here into hopeful joy. That narration of optimism and joy is linked to the arrival of a visionary. Each commercial in this series ends with a refrain that is similar to the chorus line in the song and music video that proved central to the BJP's 2014 campaign: "Hum Modiji ko laanewale hain, achche din aane wale hain" [We are going to bring Modi to power; better days are coming].

In chapter 2, we will discuss the narrative processes through which an icon is constituted by first constructing a commoner as a commoner and then telling the story of movement or progression through which this commoner becomes a spectacular icon. Using Modi's electoral branding campaigns, what I am calling to attention here is the ways in which development in new India is defined through a visionary who is also a commoner. More specifically, development is narrated as renewal and emergence through the arrival of a visionary who is also a commoner. That arrival in and of itself is deemed significant enough to be narrated as renewal, newness, progression, and therefore development. In the 2014 general election campaign, Modi was defined as a visionary and an ordinary tea-seller (*chaiwallah*); in the 2019 campaign he continued to be narrated as a leader with an unselfish vision but also a *chowkidar* (a watchman/guard). It was in 2013, in fact, that Modi had first used the term *chowkidar*, suggesting that he wanted to be the nation's chowkidar or protector and not its prime minister.[70] In the campaign for the 2019 general elections, the opposition party—the Indian National Congress—had attempted to use the term to critique the incumbent Modi government's handling of a multibillion dollar deal with France's Dassault Aviation for fighter air-craft. The Congress alleged corruption and used the phrase *chowkidar chor hai* (the watchman/guard is the thief) in its campaign, specifically targeting Modi. In other words, the Congress alleged that the prime minister who had defined himself as the nation's watchdog was, in fact, a thief. The BJP's response was to link the visionary (Modi) to the commoner by translating the term, *chowkidar*, into a sociological category, defined by socioeconomic class and caste. It created the hashtag *main bhi chowkidar* (I too am a watchman/guard), which was taken up by most BJP politi-cians and thousands of the BJP's supporters on social media. In Modi's original usage, the term *chowkidar* could be read as setting up an analogy, drawing a com-parison and a similarity between the watchman's and the prime minister's work/labor. In the second iteration, as a hashtag, *chowkidar* was translated into signifying not just a form of labor but an identity category—the commoner defined through class and caste. Of course, this second iteration was made possible by the first. The assertion *main bhi chowkidar* in a context where *chowkidar* is now an identity cate-gory suggested that if the visionary was being called a thief then all who identified with that category were being defined as thieves. The visionary linked as such to the commoner manages the anger that the selfsame common person might feel about her experience of an obstructed present. The narrative form of spectacular realism makes this resolution of obstruction possible.

Let us consider an instantiation of the narration of a second type of visionary, one who works outside the bureaucracy and apparatus of the state. To encounter this second type of visionary, we will venture into the world of the Hindi cine-matic imagination, specifically the 2004 film *Swades* (Homeland): *We the People* (Ashutosh Gowariker). Lauded by film critics in India as an exception to the urban-themed films produced by the Hindi film industry post–economic liberal-ization, *Swades* articulates a specific narrative about development and centers the visionary—not the politician or even the political activist, but the Non Resident Indian (NRI) engineer.

Swades traces the story of an NRI who returns home (read: village, rural India) to do development work. The protagonist, Mohan Bhargava, works for the U.S. National Aeronautical and Space Agency (NASA) and has earned a significant amount of capital in the United States—education, wealth, and social and cultural capital. He returns to visit India, represented in this narrative by a village defined by relations of caste and poverty, sans electricity, and struggling to maintain a school. Bhargava's character—sketched by filmmakers who were inspired by a true story of NRI engineers who returned to set up electricity generators for vil-lage schools—decides to leave the life that he had created for himself in the United States and return to India permanently. He would return to *swades* to, in the words of his American boss, "light a bulb." In other words, he would return to do devel-opment work. Let me briefly describe one sequence from the film to highlight how this narrative constitutes development. The protagonist Mohan Bhargava first returns to India in order to find his nanny—the woman he had lost touch with as he built his life in the United States—and finds Kaveri amma in the village of Charanpur. Soon after Bhargava's arrival to the village, Kaveri amma takes him to a *panchayat* (village council) meeting that is led by five (*panch*) elected representatives and where most of the villagers have gathered. An elderly man, who the audience later learns was an anticolonial activist and had participated in the Indian National Congress's anti-British Quit India protests in 1942, argues with the Block Development Officer (BDO), who represents the state in the meeting about the lack of electricity in the village. The elderly man, who the viewer learns commands a certain amount of respect but is also treated in a patronizing fashion by the wielders of real power, namely the *panch* and the BDO, expresses his frustration at what he perceives to be the absence of urgency on the part of the state to bring facilities like electricity imperative for the development of the village. The BDO patiently attempts to explain that the state realizes the significance of ensuring that power is available to the village and that the matter was being discussed by concerned authorities. The elderly man is not assuaged by this response and is in fact agitated even further. With voice raised and face flushed with frustration, he asks the BDO how long the state needed to consider a matter as imperative as electricity, noting with an edge in his voice that perhaps it would finally resolve the matter in time to light a bulb at his funeral. The BDO then states that *he* (read: the state) had a complaint against the village as well, which was that some villagers were stealing power from the power lines that did run across parts of the village. As the elderly man hangs his head, having been shamed by the complaint, the villagers break out into loud accusations labeling each other guilty of power theft.

This seemingly mundane encounter between a state representative and a representative of the generation that engaged in the movement for independence from British rule on the issue of development is quite central to the film's core themes. It establishes the film's representation of development as improved well-being and as a matter of collective responsibility. This is why even though this sequence depicts the state as largely inept at bringing power and other resources significant for the development of rural India, its citizens are also represented as having failed *it* by indulging in activities such as power theft. The elderly anticolonial activist at this point in the narrative is represented as being in an untenable position: he (carrying the weight of being part of and having defined a utopian moment in Indian history) must represent a village, members of which indulge in activities deemed criminal to a state that he sees as largely derelict in its developmental tasks.

The resolution of this small drama is achieved in the film's narrative through a single character, namely our NRI engineer, Mohan Bhargava. For it is Bhargava, using the technical, monetary, and cultural capital that he has acquired in the United States, who brings power to the village. Here, it is the NRI who occupies the role of visionary. Lying on a bed under the bulb that Bhargava's efforts had helped light, the elderly anticolonial activist holds Mohan's hand and says that he could now die in peace. The film's narrative thus forges a link between the generation that brought independence to the nation and the middle-class

male professional who has amassed capital abroad through a patrilineal relationship. Note that while the subaltern patrilineal linkage between Lallan and
Prosenjit Bhattacharya in *Yuva* was the ground on which both characters were
repudiated, this relationship forged between upper-caste, middle-class men, one
linked to the anticolonial nationalist movement and the other to the diaspora, is
validated. The resolution that Bhargava embodies to the question of development allows new India to move away from defining the welfare state as being
pivotal to the improved well-being of the nation without necessarily calling for
its demise. Moreover, *Swades* shows us evocatively how development as concept-
image links two disparate conceptions of time. As an embodiment of modernity—
technological, cultural, and social—Mohan Bhargava, the NRI, signifies the linear
progress of calendrical, homogenous, empty time, but as the man the anticolonial activist had been waiting for his entire life, he also signifies messianic time.
The fervor of anticolonial nationalism is linked to the excitement of the diasporic
male's success not just through a linear progression, but also through an affective node. This is the significance and the enchantment of development, *Swades*
argues.

   Swades thus links the rural with the urban, indeed with the diaspora; it articulates the anticolonial activist with the Non Resident Indian, old and new technologies, the Nehruvian drive towards modernization with the Gandhian emphasis
on village economies, and the concerns of art-house Hindi cinema—rural India,
caste, and inequity—with the routines of commercial cinema—the love story, the
spectacular climax, and the song and dance. Moreover, it suggests that development combines the spectacular with the common and it is the visionary's *apolitical* zeal that will improve both the individual's and the nation's trajectories. *Swades*
is thus apiece with the public discourse that argued that the apolitical and professional zeal of the corporate house and the urban elite would work to alleviate poverty, assuage the poor, and bring development to these groups mired in old
hierarchies.

AN UNRULY STORY: EQUITY AND DEVELOPMENT

Development, as we have been tracking, is constituted in the time of Hindutva
neoliberalism as a concept-image that alludes to the radical reconceptualization of
hierarchies as being on the move (moving towards equity), but is a simple echo of
that idea. Development in the time of Hindutva neoliberalism appropriates and
uses the story of time obstructed (realism) in order to narrate progression, the
unclogging of time itself, as apolitical technocratic strategy and the emergence of
a visionary who can give muscular voice to that scheme (the spectacular). Development in the time of Hindutva neoliberalism appropriates the story of oppression wrought by caste-based hierarchies, gender, religion, and the experience of
historic and burgeoning inequity but eschews the call for the redistribution of
wealth, land, resources, and opportunities that accompany that story of subjuga-

tion. There was an unruly moment, though, within this conjuncture when development did get linked to the concept of equity, which in turn alluded (and *only* alluded) to the idea of redistribution. It was an unruly moment—and as we shall see was defined as such—because it referenced redistribution and suggested its linkage with the concept-image of development. As such, it disrupted the story about development that was curdling into place. Its disruptive potential was therefore quickly managed by the more powerful narrative.

The 2006 World Development Report (WDR) published by the World Bank began by asking its readers to consider the life stories of two children born on the same day in post-apartheid South Africa, one black and female and the other white and male: "Nthabiseng is black, born to a poor family in a rural area in the Eastern Cape province, about 700 kilometers from Cape Town. Her mother had no formal schooling. Pieter is white, born to a wealthy family in Cape Town. His mother completed a college education at the nearby prestigious Stellenbosch University."[71] Tracing the probable life trajectories of Nthabiseng and Pieter, the report noted the striking differences in life chances between the children, concluding that "such disparities in opportunity translate into different abilities to contribute to South Africa's development."[72] The report thus linked difference— racial, gendered, social class, nationality—to "national development" and aimed to analyze "the relationship between equity and development." The phrase "equity and development," in fact, was the title of the WDR 2006. The WDRs have been produced annually by the World Bank since 1978, and they are often credited as functioning as the public face of the bank. Each year, the WDR focuses on a theme seen to be central to the thinking around development. In 2006, the theme was "equity." The research, production, and publication budget of the WDRs is often higher than those for other significant publications put out by "comparable institutions such as the United Nations Development Program, and the United Nations Conference on Trade and Development."[73] Scholars have argued that the WDRs create a global shared sense around development that reinforces neoliberalism and eschews alternative or radical positions on the conception of development. They claim that the WDRs use a "soft talk, hard policy" approach, such that even when there is an ostensible discussion of alternative trajectories for development—for instance, the criticism of large-scale irrigation projects and an advocacy of small-scale solutions—in the final instance, that alternative is jettisoned for a technocratic strategy that reiterates neoliberalism, such as the World Bank funding for large dams around the world.[74] The 2006 WDR's narration of "equity" was in line with this larger discursive strategy, such that the allusion to redistribution and even to the failure of markets to correct historic and institutionally sedimented inequity remained just that, an allusion. In the final instance, the WDR 2006 reiterated neoliberalism as the framework within which development policy must be undertaken. Its narrative form could also be seen as an iteration of spectacular realism whereby sociological and ethnographic detailing becomes the warrant or the justification for reinforcement of the market and the

nation (the spectacular). Yet the report created a moment of disruption and con-
sternation among the advocates of neoliberalism in India, who felt compelled to
intervene and correct the narrative.

The report defined "equity" as "equal opportunities to pursue a life ... [of an
individual's] choosing and be spared from extreme deprivation in outcomes."
"The main message," the report noted, was that "equity is complementary, in some
fundamental respects, to the pursuit of long-term prosperity."[75] The report noted
that while markets provided the best route to the distribution of wealth and
power, in the event of missing or imperfect markets (and where correcting market
failures was not feasible) "some forms of *redistribution*—of access to services,
assets, or political influence" could increase economic efficiency.[76] This was the
unruly turn in the narrative: Not only did the report link difference to development, it also seemingly linked development to redistribution ("of access to services, assets, or political influence"). In this one narrative moment, the social was
not delinked from the space of the economic and realism did not function as
merely the staging ground for the spectacle of capital.

Discourse in the elite English-language press in India seized on this narrative
unruliness. This discourse discussed and debated the WDR 2006 with a particular
focus on the concept of "redistribution." In a scathing column in the *Economic Times*,
Arvind Panagariya, an economist, public commentator, and head of the Planning
Commission (renamed the NITI Aayog) in the Modi administration between 2015
and 2017, stated that the 2006 WDR was a "great leap backward in development
thinking." [77] This was so, he argued, because "virtually all agree that the central goal
of development policy should be to tackle poverty, not inequity."[78] Inequity and
poverty were thus represented as mutually exclusive concept-categories. Such a
representational strategy was made possible by the enabling assumption that development is *not* redistribution. Panagariya made this point explicitly by noting that
"greater equity does not guarantee less poverty ... take one billion dollars away
from Narayana Murthy [one of the founders of Infosys, credited with spearheading
India's IT revolution] and distribute it equally among 1,000 existing millionaires ...
you will get greater equity but not less poverty ... indeed, given the prospect that
as a billionaire Murthy is likely to engage in greater philanthropy than the 1,000
millionaires, the redistribution may reduce the potential for future poverty reduction."[79] His argument hinged on defining equity as "anti-growth" and as such, "anti-
poor." He noted therefore that "virtually all anti-growth and anti-poor policies
India has been dismantling for the last two decades have their origins in the pursuit
of equity." Citing policy examples from India's pre-reform political economy,
including the nationalization of banks, import licenses, and regulatory mechanisms
for private industries, Panagariya noted that the driving force behind such "anti-
growth" policies was the push for equity. He also critiqued the report for not
"confront[ing] the question [of] whether *politics* would allow the government to
selectively choose those equity-oriented policies that promote growth and reduce
poverty or force its hand in the opposite direction." Panagariya's evocation of "poli-

tics" as the specter that would haunt and force the state's hand on choosing anti-growth policies is a reiteration of neoliberalism's old adage that the realm of the sociopolitical must be separated from the economic, which we have discussed earlier in our analysis of the narration of caste and its relationship to development. This distinction defines the dichotomy between the two Indias we had discussed earlier as well. Panagariya's narrative suggested that even the allusion to redistribution via the concept of equity in the WDR was unruly. That narrative unruliness needed to be corrected or discredited.

Francisco Ferreira and Michael Walton, co-directors of the World Development Report 2006 on equity and development, used the "guest column" space of the *Economic Times*, more than two months after Panagariya's comment appeared in the newspaper, to respond to him. Here now, we get the management or the curtailment of the disruption caused by the narrative unruliness. Ferreira and Walton noted in response to Panagariya's critique that the "World Development Report defines equity in terms of equality of opportunities, rather than of incomes" and that the "difference is not purely semantic."[80] In other words, they insisted that the WDR was not, in fact, advocating redistribution. They clarified that the "report argues for policies that expand the educational, productive and political opportunities of the poor and excluded, whilst *avoiding capture of public policies* by influential interest groups at all levels."[81] Here again, we are confronted with the specter of politics. "Influential interest groups" or those communities that narrate historic discrimination and seek redress through redistribution are delegitimized. Instead even as development is linked with difference and therefore equity, this conception of equity must continue to foreground market-based growth *and* be defined in terms of equality of opportunities. Thus, Ferreira and Walton note that their "main emphasis was not on income redistribution . . . [instead] the emphasis was on the losses to India from not giving millions of the poor in rural and urban areas the same starting chances as the wealthy had."[82] The market and market-based growth are pitted against "politics," "influential interest groups" and politicians within these narratives and development itself is therefore conceptualized as apolitical. The narrative unruliness and disruption created by their WDR 2006 is managed by Ferreira and Walton finally by the suggestion that poverty exists precisely because the market has not expanded enough.

The argument I have attempted to make throughout this chapter has been that such a conception of development, which draws a distinction between the spaces of the sociopolitical and the economic, repudiating the former as dirty, corrupt, and as a form of capture and valorizing the latter as clean, technocratic vision enables the intersection of Hindu nationalism with neoliberalism in India. In other words, such a conception of development does not simply reiterate neoliberalism, it enables Hindutva to narrate itself as a mobilization of the common person through the assertive vision of a muscular but ostensibly apolitical form of development. Hindutva's claims of political hygiene rest on the constant narration of caste and other identity-based demands for redistribution as dirty and corrupt.

This complex pattern of representation that constructs the concept of development as an apolitical instrument that will nevertheless result in equity works by naming the *political* demand for equity through redistribution as its "other." Moreover, it is caste and caste-based demands for redistribution that are defined within the discourse as "political" or politically motivated. Conceptions of equity, redistribution, and indeed, politics are thus disarticulated from the concept-image of development even as it articulates diverse narrative threads and political commitments into a complex unity.

Development is *thus* the concept-image of the contemporary conjuncture in India. It binds the spectacle of emergence and national renewal with the figure of the commoner. It can act therefore as the justification for the rollback of the welfare state and the incorporation of both foreign capital and the visionary diasporic male engineer, as in *Swades*; it can also act as the warrant for strategic geopolitical and economic deals such as the nuclear initiative and can act as a sanction for Hindu nationalist authoritarianism. This is because development is a concept-image constituted by the affective register of time—new time and the time of event in particular—and by the enchantment of capturing the real. It is for this reason that development speak will also always raise the dead—that midnight hour when a tryst with destiny was made and that freedom fighter who fought for that first emergence of the nation—and sutured to these forefathers, the story that development narrates argues that *this* conjuncture is new, renewed; it is true, it says, we have emerged.

2 · ICONICITY

Moving between the Real and the Spectacular

An icon, simply put, is an image, and the examination or analysis of images is iconology. Images, though, are rarely simple. W. J. T. Mitchell has argued that "images are not just a particular kind of sign, but something like an actor on the historical stage, a presence or character endowed with legendary status."[1] An image, any image, thus carries the potential to be powerful, incendiary, subversive, and legendary, and engender idolatry. An icon, commonly understood as an image that is revered or idolized, is that potential of the image realized. Icons link or articulate various ideologies, affects, and systems of thought into a potent symbol or a mythology. Icons constitute norms, but also disrupt them. Icons could articulate new technologies, aesthetics, and representations of the self with purportedly older modes of being in the world, such as a transcendent belief in a god, a faith, and so forth. This chapter reveals the seductively affective ways in which the form of spectacular realism is realized within the iconic. It showcases the embodiment of Hindutva neoliberalism in iconic personages. I have been arguing that spectacular realism is the narrative form of Hindutva neoliberalism. If Hindutva neoliberalism is the conjoining of Hindu nationalism and Indian neoliberalism, then the narrative form that gives it shape, texture, and an affective visuality is formed at the intersection of the spectacular, the fantastical *and* the real, the plausible. By staging icons and their iconicity, we will dwell on this intersection, revealing the ways in which the icon embodies the abstract category, the people, *and* the authoritatively singular, magically spectacular individual. Moreover, by following the iconic narratives of three key characters, namely Amitabh Bachchan, Narendra Modi, and Mayawati, the chapter will reveal how the iconic is defined through movement.

In tracking the story of these three iconic personages, I am also tracing the production of a sensory apparatus that I call the idolatrous eye. The idolatrous eye—vision itself constituted as idol worship—in a conjuncture defined by the articulation of Hindutva and neoliberalism is the crucial sensory and affective link that holds this otherwise unstable structure in dominance in place. Icons—particularly iconic public figures—are the material instantiation of the idolatrous eye in this conjuncture. Combining neoliberalism's emphasis on the individual, but particularly on the possessive individual (the individual as the owner of themselves) and the caste system's construction of the brahmin as the mediator between the common and the divine—between, in fact, the common eye and the divine text—icons in this conjuncture perform the critical task of becoming the cultural link that holds the conjuncture in place.

Literature focused on the image in the Indian context often opposes aesthetics—the separation between image and beholder that produces a disinterested evaluation of images demanded by, in the Indian context, white European colonial schools of philosophy—to "corpothetics,"[2] the native's or the colonized's (or the subaltern's) desire to fuse image and beholder such that the efficacy of the image for the beholder is the central criterion of its value.[3] Efficacy is defined in terms of the image's ability to bring good fortune or luck or a blessing for its beholder. As such, the East more generally and India more specifically is narrated as producing and sustaining a particularistic visual culture that defines the image as powerful, subversive, and efficacious—in short, a divine and magical material. This is despite the colonial state in conjunction with the native elite and then the postcolonial state's attempt to produce modern subjects with a modernist eye. Within this literature, this visual culture, in fact, serves to signify the popular. More importantly, this visual culture, defined in opposition to post-Enlightenment visual cultures of the white Western world, is also characterized as authentically about the people and as inherently a negotiation with dominance. This argument is made in large part by drawing on the religious idiom—specifically Hinduism—and its shaping of the eye and of vision itself. For instance, the practice of "darsan," which assumes that the divine deity is present in the image, is defined as an act of "visual apprehension" that is "charged with religious meaning."[4] Darsan is seen to shape the interaction between the eye and the image in a distinct manner.[5] Christopher Pinney thus makes an argument for conceiving of South Asian visual cultures through the concept of the "optical unconscious," defined as "a visceral domain in which objects become sensorially emboldened in a magical technology of embodied knowing."[6] Drawing on Pinney's argument, Sumati Ramaswamy in her visual history of the nation form in South Asia reads the convergence of the divinized gendered form of the goddess—Mother India—with the cartographed map of India as a disruption of the state's cartographic productions by the "anthropomorphic, the devotional, or the maternal."[7] The argument about icons and iconicity, given this context, is that much like other mass and popular commodities, icons are "re-territorialized, re-signified in consumption to embody 'local' aspiration," and that the "images and lives of bio-icons" (i.e., public figures as icons) are continually "migrating media content that is constantly repurposed to serve local ends."[8] Thus, Bishnupriya Ghosh argues that icons are best understood as "technologies" that can on occasion open aperture-like into a social network yet to come, and that it is the "icon's capacity as media (practical arts, techne) that they can summon to action."[9]

My contention here is that rather than setting corpothetics, the practice of darsan, or the idolatrous eye at an epistemological remove from concepts such as aesthetics and the public,[10] rooted as they are in liberalism, that we analyze the worlds that are constituted by the conjoining of these conceptions. I am suggesting that the conjoining of the idolatrous eye of "darsan" with the possessive individualism of neoliberalism and liberalism's public icon as the representative of the people produces the very particular public icon of Hindutva neoliberalism.[11]

THE COMMONER

Popular Indian texts have often concatenated on the figure of the commoner—the ordinary (*aam*) man and woman defined *as* ordinary through the appellations of femininity, lower caste or class status, and/or religious identity. In some of the most popular Hindi films of the 1970s, this commoner was accorded a mythic status; the ordinariness of this deliberately and specifically male figure defined him as the outsider, the vigilante and the marginal.[12] But in this very ordinariness resided the mythic and magically potent power to destroy that world that rendered this ordinary man as subaltern (i.e., a person of inferior rank). As such, this angry, young and ordinary man in the popular cinematic texts of the 1970s was already iconic. To go further back in historical time, the 1957 Hindi cinema classic *Mother India*, directed by Mehboob Khan, featured an ordinary rural peasant woman as the iconic "Mother India." Her femininity, particularly her motherhood, rendered her both common and representative of the nation itself, but simultaneously signified her as iconic. Just like the cinematic angry young man of the 1970s, the smoldering moral power of the peasant woman of *Mother India* had always been iconic.

A decade after the inauguration of economic liberalization policies, however, when popular media industries in India were claiming a renewal themselves and when Hindu nationalism had worked to mobilize a Hindu people, the valence accorded to the ordinariness of the aam man and woman in popular Hindi film and a diverse range of English-language texts had changed. No longer mythic or magically potent, ordinariness in new India served to legitimate and authenticate the *text* within which it appeared as real/reality. The narration of ordinariness came to be defined as realism, as we have noted, and the text deemed as realist in this manner was recognized as authentic. The renewal that media industries (particularly Hindi cinema) claimed for themselves now was linked to the assertion that the narration of social worlds signified modernization and growth.[13] In other words, the presence of the commoner placed within his or her common world now functioned to define the text and the medium itself as having come of age. The narration of that common world, for many media industries, including advertising, meant a turn to Hindu symbolism. We have already noted in the introductory chapter that Indian advertising turned to Hindu mythology, symbolism, and ritual in order to constitute a popular aesthetic that would reach a broader spectrum of consumers following economic liberalization and the mobilization of Hindu nationalism.[14] As such, the semiotic and affective power now resided in the discourse or the text—the texts of economic liberalization and Hindu nationalism that justified and legitimated themselves through the figuration of the commoner—rather than *in* the figure of the aam man and woman, who now remained resolutely ordinary. By itself, such a characterization of the commoner—resolutely rather than mythically common and resident in a common, ordinary world—was not necessarily a rupture. As Satish Poduval has shown, a cinematic template for such a characterization already existed and was, in fact, also a production of 1970s Hindi cinema—namely, the character that Poduval has termed "the affable young man," the distinctly middle-class, urban male whose conflicts as well as their resolution are entirely individual and centered on the self.[15] Chapter 4 discusses the "affable young man" of the 1970s in greater detail in the context of the love story. I raise his figure here to show that while the presence of the common or ordinary person in an ordinary world (particularly a Hindu, upper-caste, middle-class world) was not a definitive break, the post–economic liberalization text's focus on the ordinary in order to reinforce the power of the *text* itself was novel. I also raise his figure to showcase Hindutva neoliberalism as a conjuncture of multiple temporalities, where the 1950s and the 1970s are sutured to the 1990s and the decades of the new millennium through the invocation and allusion to affective images and characters.

The realist text peopled by ordinary people channels its power to narrate and showcase the ordinary man on a journey—a journey that would transform him from the ordinary into the extraordinary. This transformation is deeply personal and utterly individual. This journey and the transformation that it produces is not simply about socioeconomic mobility; rather, this radical change is affectively powerful because it claims to be reality itself, a reality whose time has come. The transformation of the ordinary person is now narrated as both the product of and constitutive of the nation itself. Indian neoliberalism's focus on deregulation and possessive individualism can be narrated as an unfettering and renewal by defining the commoner on a transformative journey. Concurrently, Hindu nationalism's story about the unshackling of the Hindu nation and its renewal can also be narrated by the commoner on a journey of transformation.

Over the past couple of decades, popular media like Hindi cinema has loudly claimed to represent the *real* and has been particularly adept at defining an audiovisual idiom and a set of signs that center on the commoner (the aam). This claim takes one of two forms: 1) The film claims to represent the *real* Indian film audience's desire and demand for larger-than-life heroism, the song-and-dance routine and glamour.[16] This claim is often based on a dichotomy that is constructed between that which is defined as artistic and films deemed as escapist catharsis. This is also a dichotomy that is set up between rational intellect and libidinal desire.[17] As film studies scholar Tejaswini Ganti has shown, this is both a conception of the film's audience and an estimation of their own aspirations in the self-expression of Hindi filmmakers rather than a sociological analysis. The filmmaker dreams about the creative but must work with the ordinary person's desire for catharsis, which is, in fact, the *real*. 2) Or the film claims to represent the *reality* of life for the common Indian. In other words, it eschews all the elements that defined the real in the previous instance.[18]

Consider one of 2005's most successful Hindi films, *Bunty aur Babli* (Bunty and Babli, Shaad Ali), which we have mentioned in the previous chapter for its narration of the "two Indias" imagery. The film follows the travails of a young man (Rakesh) and woman (Vimmi), who shed their small-town beginnings and personas to become "Bunty" and "Babli" respectively, so they can live the metropolitan life. *Bunty aur Babli*'s assertions about the real occur in both the forms identified above. Thus, the caper film includes all the essential ingredients of a *masala* movie—humor, heroes functioning at the margins of the law and morality, song-and-dance sequences, and glamour—believed to be the kind of cine-going experience the *real* Indian cine-lover desires. And its narrative centers on characters plucked from *real* India. The significance of *Bunty aur Babli*, in fact, hinges on the narrative's choice of protagonists. *Bunty aur Babli* constructs the young man and woman living in small Indian towns with access to the mesmerizing stories of wealth, innovation, individualism, entrepreneurialism, fame, glamour, and success circulating within popular media as desiring subjects. Prakash and Vimmi desire the excess of the metropolis, but by donning the personas of Bunty and Babli, they begin to actively realize that desire. As a direct consequence of arriving as desiring subjects, such common men and women ("the people") are legitimated and applauded within stories such as those told by the film *Bunty aur Babli*. As this desiring, agentive individual, the common man or woman has the potential to become iconic.[19] Put more baldly, as ordinary people, Prakash and Vimmi are indistinguishable from the mass; they are common. But, transformed into Bunty and Babli, they can be powerfully iconic. The iconicity that *Bunty aur Babli* initiates enfolds a linear trajectory, where the protagonist moves from claustrophobic oppression to becoming an agent or a modern subject. This iconicity has a political consequence; it suggests that the space of new India allows the commoner to achieve his or her potential and that it is the technologies of new India that can truly grasp and represent the *real* commoner. As we have discussed in the introduction, and in the previous chapter, the narratives of both neoliberalism and Hindu nationalism in India conjoin in the enunciation of newness and renewal. Hindutva neoliberalism claims to have constituted new India.

The film *Bunty aur Babli* was produced by Yashraj Films, one of the largest film production studios in India. Since 2005, Yashraj's filmography has included an increasing number of small- and big-budget films that have focused on characters drawn from small-town India or middle-class urban settings—in short, the aam man and woman or the commoner. It bears noting that the founder of the studio,

Yash Chopra, was the director of one of the classic angry young man films from the 1970s, namely *Deewar* (The Wall, 1975). However, neither Prakash nor Bunty from *Bunty aur Babli* are similar to Vijay from *Deewar*. We will have more to say on both Vijay and *Deewar* later, but for now, I want to acknowledge a certain continuity and a break: Vijay from *Deewar* and Prakash/Bunty from *Bunty aur Babli* are characterized as common men, with origins in the lower middle classes of small-town India who come to the understanding that money matters over all else. Vijay and Prakash/Bunty as characters are also the product of the same film production house and they signify the salience of patriliny within public discourse: Vijay was played by Amitabh Bachchan, and his son Abhishek Bachchan plays the part of Prakash/Bunty (Bachchan Sr. played the part of the cop who chases down the notorious duo of Bunty and Babli in the film); the father Yash Chopra directed *Deewar*, and the son Aditya Chopra was at the helm of Yashraj when *Bunty aur Babli* was produced (and remains so). These then are the continuities. The break that distinguishes Vijay and Prakash/Bunty is the relationship that the two films construct between the common man and the world within which he resides. In *Deewar*, Vijay is persistently obstructed by his world; his ambition to take on this world is fueled by rage and the cynical understanding that money is the name of the game. Prakash believes the world is a stage waiting for him to perform, and the shackle holding him back is traditional conservatism and not the social hierarchies of the world. While Prakash's desire for money is playfully celebrated by *Bunty aur Babli*, Vijay's accumulation of illicit wealth is repudiated by *Deewar*. Most importantly, Prakash is on a journey, a trajectory of self-transformation, whereas Vijay walks the more weathered road of tragedy. This is the break. The journey from Vijay in *Deewar* to Prakash/Bunty in *Bunty and Babli* is, in fact, iconic and signifies itself as national renewal produced by Hindutva neoliberalism. What I am aiming to emphasize, in other words, is that *Deewar*'s Vijay from the 1970s is crucial to the story of Hindutva neoliberalism in the new millennium. In the previous chapter, we discussed how the story of an obstructed present which is then unshackled by the development promised by both neoliberalism and Hindu nationalism relies on the narrative universe created by the angry young man films in the 1970s. Here, I am suggesting that the distance between the angry young man of the 1970s and the cheery commoner of the new millennium is defined as iconic and emblematic of the transformations wrought by Hindutva neoliberalism.

In the linear narrative trajectory that is traced for commoners, the climactic moment often arrives when the commoner is transformed into an entrepreneur (chapter 3 deals specifically with this identity category). This, in fact, is the moment when the common becomes iconic. This is the moment when Prakash becomes Bunty. In his international best-seller *India Unbound: The Social and Economic Revolution from Independence to the Global Information Age*, "management guru" and self-styled public intellectual Gurcharan Das argues that India has entered the twenty-first century "on the brink of the biggest transformation in its history"[20] because the 1991 economic reforms have "released entrepreneurial energies the like of which we have never seen before."[21] In his conclusion, Das reiterates his arguments about a "brave new India" by drawing on a motley set of characters— all common, all representative of *real* India—including "Vikas, the proud Dalit[22] in feudal Uttar Pradesh, who would prefer to make steel trunks rather than bribe someone to become a bus conductor"; "Sushila, who makes shoes for Florsheim and Hogarth and a dowry for herself"; and "Kum Kum, the 'flower girl' at the traffic light in Delhi, who stores her flowers in a refrigerator because it gives her competitive advantage."[23] In Das's story these commoners and their gendered and caste work—selling flowers, working with leather (a task that has historically been associated with ritual pollution and therefore performed by lower castes)—play as significant a role as "Naryana Murthy, who not only created India's most successful software company but has become the role model of ethical corporate behavior" and "Pravinder Singh, who built India's biggest pharmaceutical company, Ranbaxy," precisely because they are all defined as entrepreneurs.[24]

These narratives are doing two types of "work": Firstly, the particular experience of marginality of Prakash and Vimmi in *Bunty aur Babli* as residents of small-town India and the subalternity of Vikas, Sushila, and Kum Kum defined through their caste, class, and gendered identities is transformed into the abstract category of the common or the commoner, such that Prakash, Vimmi, Vikas, Sushila, and Kum Kum can all and interchangeably be termed the common (aam) people of India. As common people, they are also defined as *real*. Note also that although some of these characters are lower-caste or dalit, none of them is defined specifically as non-Hindu. As such, even as neoliberalism transforms the subaltern into the commoner, that commoner is defined as Hindu by Hindu nationalism. Aam or the common—a product both of the cinematic imagination as well as the narrative strategies of journalistic reportage—is a composite, formed through the assembling (collage-like) of several embodiments and particularities. Realism here is used less to reveal structural and institutional inequity, more to claim authenticity and authority over the space of the social. This composite, however, obscures the ideological processes that produced it. It also obscures the violence and oppression of socioeconomic hierarchies by drawing an equivalence between the heterogeneous bodies and histories that are brought together in the category. The management of Infosys as well as the sons and heirs of the founder of Ranbaxy have recently been accused of financial impropriety and the misappropriation of funds, among other charges.[25] Drawing an equivalence between characters like Vikas and Sushila and corporations through the category *entrepreneur* does the ideological work of legitimizing neoliberal capital on the backs of the subaltern. Importantly, that ideological work is also obscured. Secondly, in narrating these ordinary and real people on a journey that culminates in them becoming desiring consumers and entrepreneurs (as well as denizens of a Hindu nation), these narratives constitute an iconic image. My suggestion is that the valence and affective charge of this iconicity comes from the narration of movement—the trajectory along which the commoner moves to become a desiring consumer and entrepreneur. Though the start (subalternity) and end points (entrepreneur) of this journey are significant, the *movement* itself is formulated as iconic. I am approaching icons and iconicities then as a provocative opportunity to ask two questions: 1) Why do certain types of iconic figures become popular at certain historical moments? and 2) Through what processes are these iconic figures constructed as such?

Here, through a reading of three iconic figures and their iconicities, we will track the ideological construction of the common (the aam) and the real as well as its link to the formulation of the conjuncture, namely Hindutva neoliberalism. Second, icons and their iconicities enable us to investigate the ways in which the eye, vision, and the popular are constituted as such and whose interests such constructions serve. In other words, we will track the ways in which a specific image and a particular embodiment is constituted as iconic and the processes—visual and sensory—through which such a constitution is made possible. In the previous chapter, we had tracked the processes through which development is narrated as apolitical, which in turn effects the repudiation of caste-based arguments for redistribution of resources. This chapter will argue that Hindutva neoliberalism's reproduction of the idolatrous eye reveals the narrative processes through which caste and caste-based hierarchies are reproduced as common sense.

In this chapter, I will narrate three stories—the narration of some stories will require the telling of other stories as well—or I might say that this chapter will feature three protagonists, namely Hindi film star Amitabh Bachchan, Hindu nationalist politician and current Indian prime minister Narendra Modi, and dalit politician Mayawati. Each of these protagonists embodies the commoner through appellations of caste, gender, religion, and socioeconomic class. However, each of these protagonists is also cast as the chosen one. As commoners, Bachchan, Modi, and Mayawati signify realism; as icons, they embody the spectacular. They acquire iconic form through movement: Bachchan traverses the distance between angry young man and brand father, Modi from son of tea seller to prime minister, and Mayawati from dalit queen to political strategist. The specific form of their embodiment differs; whereas Bachchan performs the character of the common man on cinema screens, Modi and Mayawati are political actors, and as leaders of their political parties they espouse and define a political vision. These stories thus bring together the fictional and the lived, the cinematic screen and the street and the electoral campaign, in order to trace the concatenated image of the commoner. Through the narration of these stories, the chapter will trace the processes through which the eye, vision, and the popular were constituted in the period between 1973 and 2014. We will trace the narrative modes through which the commoner is first defined as shackled and therefore angry. We will discuss how the chains that shackle the commoner qua the angry young man, the son of the tea seller, and the daughter of the dalit are defined as those that were put into place by postcolonial liberal secularism. Unshackling—narrated through a deeply masculinist idiom— and the assertion of presence (defined as Hindu presence) is deemed to be spectacular. The unshackling is made possible by a conjuncture that sutures neoliberalism to Hindu nationalism, or so the story goes.

The protagonists of these stories will also help us tell the story about iconicity itself: the processes that helped constitute the iconic, the negotiations of actors with the form of the iconic as well as what constitutes the failure to become iconic. They will reveal the ways in which the iconic is a powerful form through which Hindutva neoliberalism acquires its own shape. Mayawati's story is an unruly one in this context. In the moment when her story appears to seamlessly fit the narrative requirements of the iconic form, she is cast to narrate national renewal. However, Mayawati's own narration of the common and the commoner through a political, social, and historically specific category (*bahujan samaj*, or the society of the oppressed majority) that demands political recognition and redistribution of essential resources disrupts the form of spectacular realism. Mayawati's narration of the spectacular is also unruly because it insists on the assertion of caste as a political identity and uses both the built environment as well as the narration of genealogy to assert the political presence of the untouchable castes. As such, Mayawati's iconicity both uses and disrupts the form of spectacular realism and marks the limit of this form of narration.

Even as these stories are centrally about the three protagonists, material objects such as bridges, masks, and statues play a significant role as well. In other words, these stories feature iconicities constituted as much by public personages as they do by specifically powerful objects, namely the bridge, the mask, and the statue. Through these material objects, spectacular realism can be touched, felt, and sensed through brick, mortar, concrete, steel, sandstone, paper, and string. These objects give spectacular realism a material form and translate Hindutva neoliberalism into a story of cultural emergence that is etched onto the cityscape (through the bridge and the statue) and on the body (through the mask). Each material object is integral to the specific iconicity of each of the three protagonists and helps give shape to their iconicity. A word about the narrative form of the chapter: I stage the stories of the three protagonists through significant scenes; framed as such, the stories distinctly foreground the movement that transforms the protagonists from the commoner into the spectacular icon.

AMITABH BACHCHAN: THE BRIDGE

Amitabh Bachchan was voted "Indian of the Year" in 2004 and 2005 by a poll conducted by the *Times of India*.[26] As film scholars and the audiences of Hindi cinema will note, while there "have been many stars of the Hindi cinema ... the undisputed star is Amitabh Bachchan."[27] Through Bachchan—an actor and public personality—we will track the story of the movement from one powerful symbol, namely the angry young man, which is a cinematic embodiment and symbol, to yet another sign, which I will name brand father or patriarch of neoliberal India, a public persona that was constituted via advertising, the public relations industry, and television. While I have drawn a distinction between the narration of ordinariness in the angry young man films in which Bachchan starred, and the embodiment of the commoner in popular cultural contexts in the new millennium, my contention is that the cinematic character of the angry young man is fundamental to the narration of movement that spectacular realism as a form demands. Moreover, as we have noted in the previous chapter, the anger expressed by the angry young man is strategically alluded to by the stories told by Hindutva neoliberalism to narrate obstruction and its resolution. Indeed, the angry young man character as an instantiation of vigilante and powerful masculinity is foundational to the conjuncture we are naming Hindutva neoliberalism.

Scene one: In Hindi cinema of the seventies and the eighties, Bachchan played the character of the angry young man or the urban industrial hero. Even though he began his cinematic career playing the middle-class hero, it was his embodiment of subaltern characters—a dockworker who leads a rebellion of his fellow workers, a porter who directs a labor strike, a brooding policeman who turns into a vigilante to destroy a smuggling racket, a son rebelling against his principled but rigid father—that transformed Bachchan into a superstar. Created by the scriptwriting duo of Salim Khan and Javed Akhtar, the angry young man was an intertextual character produced at the intersection of such diverse sources as Hollywood films, such as *On the Waterfront* (Elia Kazan, 1954), that focused on mob violence, union politics, and corruption; popular American fiction; Hindi films such as *Mother India* (1957, Mehboob Khan), mentioned earlier, an allegorical tale of a newly independent, postcolonial nation struggling with the ancient and the modern alike; as well as Urdu literature.[28] The angry young man films were also constituted in the sociopolitical ferment of India in the seventies and the eighties; scriptwriter Javed Akhtar has noted that the angry young man character was a "reflection of his time."[29] Literary and film studies scholars Priya Joshi and Rajinder Dudrah have noted that while the decade of the 1970s witnessed "political turmoil, economic stagnation and civic despair"—a state precipitated by the global oil crises, "wars with China and Pakistan in the 1960s and the Bangladesh War in 1971," labor unrest, massive food shortages, and finally the state of emergency declared by then–prime minister Indira Gandhi in 1975—Indian media culture saw "an expanded repertoire of technical and narrative impulses."[30] The angry young man films were one instance of a "politically engaged popular cinema" being consolidated in this particular experience of the stalled present or time experienced as obstructed and stuck. Film scholars have argued that Bachchan as the angry young man brought a "new physicality" into Hindi cinema: while he was not muscular, "he was particularly tall and long limbed, slim and hard bodied,"[31] and, most significantly, Bachchan's voice was integral to the character. In fact, Bachchan as the angry young man used "his voice as a weapon, to control, to show his temper and to mark his intelligence."[32] He may have been inexpressive about romance and love, but he was eloquent when he was speaking about the "system" and the exploitation of the laborer. Bachchan's voice, consistently described as a baritone, materialized or gave form to the angry young man.

Scholars such as Priya Joshi have argued that Bachchan's 1975 film *Deewar* (The Wall, Yash Chopra) is emblematic of angry young man cinema. It exposes the collapse of the newly independent nation's "myth of opportunity and justice" and narrates India in the 1970s as the stalled present. For instance, in a scene from the film, filmed at the docks in a bustling new metropolis, a character—an old dockworker, who has worked at the same spine-bending job for twenty-five years—notes wryly that he has seen nothing change in all his time on the docks: the laborers still haul massive weights under inhumane conditions and their meager incomes are still extracted as rent by extortionists under threat of violence. "People say the world has changed," he says; if it has, "I haven't seen it." This is *Deewar*'s pithy and evocative summary of the conception and experience of the stalled present for the subaltern toiling in postcolonial India.

At the center of the film breathes a family: first, a father, a coal miner and a labor activist, who is forced to betray his comrades to the owner of the mine in order to save his wife and two sons; second, a wife who is forced into the position of a single mother when her husband cannot live down the shame of his betrayal and abandons them. This is a mother who is compelled into another kind of a grotesque betrayal when she enables her older son to forego his childhood and school education and enter the working classes so her younger son could have a chance at middle-class status. In the coal miner, labor activist father who abandons his family and now rides the trains, the film gives us yet another iteration of the stalled present: When he is asked by a fellow passenger where he is going, the father's one-word response sums up his own obstructed, stalled life and that of a world—particularly a world that espoused his moral and political principles: "Nowhere," he says.

Joshi argues that *Deewar* is focused on the conception of "provision," which serves to capture "above all the shortages of the decade."[33] Vinay Lal, in his short manuscript on the film, notes that as its protagonist—Vijay, the older son of the family, first a child who polishes boots on the street, then a dockworker, and finally a smuggler—is transformed into the angry young man when he witnesses the utterly mundane and inhumane death of a fellow dockworker, the audience of the film "also senses the explosion of urban India . . . the 'angry young man', a new urban hero, represents the anger of a generation whose dreams lie in tatters."[34]

In addition to the angry young man, *Deewar* put a set of significant visual and audiovisual sequences into circulation. When the mother moves to the city with her sons, she is compelled to live in abject conditions under a bridge. She works in construction, doing the hard labor of breaking stones and mixing concrete to build the kind of high-rise buildings that would come to visually signify the metropolitan city of Bombay. The bridge under which Vijay, his younger brother Ravi, and their mother live is the contrasting visual that also signifies the city. Here people live, transforming their patch of the bridge's wall into a personalized, if not private, space with God posters and narrow shelves precariously holding their small set of belongings. As adult men, when Vijay the smuggler and Ravi, the cop intent on breaking his brother's smuggling ring, confront each other, Vijay contrasts the lived, shared space of the bridge with the literal and moral wall (*deewar*) that separates them. The bridge signifies the shared experience of childhood, but also (or so Vijay hopes) the communal knowledge of oppression, humiliation, and abjection. This bridge is the *only* place, Vijay tells his brother, that could now contain their differences. Dissociated from its function of connecting two places (we never see where the bridge leads) or from signifying a path that leads elsewhere, the bridge in *Deewar* is an unchanging reminder and a sign of the stalled present, of the postcolonial condition itself. Affectively, the bridge and the angry young man collude to paint a tragically evocative portrait of postcoloniality as bristling with energy but stalled and obstructed. While Vijay leaves the abject living conditions of the bridge, his road does not lead him elsewhere; that trajectory belongs to Ravi.

The radical potential of the angry young man, particularly his ability to articulate his subalternity as a powerful critique both of the nation and the state, was repressed within the film itself. In *Deewar*—arguably the most powerful and explosive of the angry young man films—Vijay is killed and his murder is scripted by his mother (read: the nation) and his brother who is a police officer (read: the state). His end is deemed necessary to the moral and political universe of the film and therefore also to its audience's political imagination. What the angry young man films did particularly effectively was foreground individual vigilante deeds and violence over collective political action. Even though the protagonist of *Deewar* is transformed into an angry young man while wearing the uniform of a dockworker, the narrative of the film does not place him within the proletariat; rather, it centers the individual—Vijay—and his transformation from a dweller of the pavement and the bridge to the owner of skyscrapers. When Vijay as a dockworker refuses to pay his extortion money to the gang that controls the docks where he works, he does not mobilize his comrades into collective action (unlike his father); instead he (singlehandedly) physically subdues the extortionists. His victory is celebrated by the other dockworkers, but the consequence of his rebellion is Vijay's elevation (or devolution?) to a smuggler. His rebellion brings him to the attention of a rival smuggler and businessman who gives him the ticket out of the docks and the working-class life associated with its spaces. While the legacy of the angry young man films is rich and varied, my contention is that one of its consequences was to put into circulation a particular narrative about the postcolonial condition in India—it conceptualized its own temporality (the time of its production and circulation) as stalled, and more specifically, as violently obstructed; it linked the experience of this stalled, obstructed time with the corruption of the idea of the nation itself and the apparatus of the state (even though the idea of India and the state itself is always affirmed in the last instance) and the affective register of anger was sutured to this conception of the stalled present. Bachchan as the angry young man also constituted desire and an affective allegiance for the vigilante; a masculinist construction, this vigilante was strong, aggressive, a man outside the system but who espoused a deep and powerful understanding of it. This is precisely the set of signifiers that Hindu nationalism would later turn to in order to constitute its critique of liberal secularism. Narendra Modi would constitute himself in the likeness of the angry young man. But we must not get ahead of ourselves. Back to Bachchan.

Scene two: Five years after Manmohan Singh's 1991 budget speech that unequivocally set the wheels of economic liberalization in motion, Amitabh Bachchan launched his own corporation—the Amitabh Bachchan Corporation Ltd. (ABCL)—with the aim of becoming a mega entertainment and film production company by the beginning of the new millennium.[35] ABCL, in fact, became emblematic of the turbulent flux within the political economy and public culture in the nineties. Its most spectacular investment and failure was the staging of the Miss World contest in the southern Indian city of Bangalore, billed as India's Silicon Valley, in 1996. As Rupal Oza has argued, the staging of a beauty contest, which was a global franchise, became the grounds for a vehement discussion about modernity and national culture—in short, about the home and the world. On the one hand, anxieties about liberalization and globalization from both the political left and right were mapped onto the feminine body showcased in a beauty contest. On the other hand, flexing the cultural and media technology muscle on the gendered ground (and body) of the beauty pageant was a narrative modality through which economic liberalization could be represented as national renewal. Amitabh Bachchan, no longer the vigilante or the angry young man, thus narrated India's hosting of the pageant and ABCL's organization of the show as an opportunity "to get into people's living rooms all over the world and show them what India was capable of . . . to promote India to a captive audience that we would not have otherwise reached."[36] In the turbulence and instability of the 1990s however, neither this narrative nor ABCL found the soil fertile enough to take root. As Inderpal Grewal has argued in the context of the initial failure of the Barbie doll to find consumers in India, "the cultural work required to create consumer desire for a product is not as simple as producing a marketing plan; rather, the plan contributes to and participates in wider cultural changes within which the product can become meaningful (or not) in ways that often cannot be predicted."[37] The transition from angry young man to brand father of neoliberal India had not yet occurred for Amitabh Bachchan in the nineties and ABCL declared bankruptcy in 1999, with losses of Rs. 70.82 crore (almost 94 million USD at the current exchange rate) and debt of another Rs. 70 crore. As a reporter for *India Today* wryly noted: "If only it was reel life. The angry young man of the '70s would have straddled the 70 mm screen, delivered well scripted dialogues in deep baritone—peppered with a few left-handed punches—and saved the day . . . unfortunately, this one is for real. The not so young Amitabh Bachchan today has to resort to rather unheroic ways to wriggle out of the financial mess his dream venture Amitabh Bachchan

Corporation Ltd (ABCL) has landed him in."[38] The angry young man had exited the stage and the brand father had not made his entry yet.

Following the collapse of ABCL, Bachchan turned to a new television industry that was seeing dramatic changes following the entry of satellite television and foreign investment in the late nineties to rebuild his fortune. As the host of *Kaun Banega Crorepati*—the Indian version of the British game show *Who Wants to Be a Millionaire* (the format of the show is owned and licensed by the Japanese production company Sony Pictures Television International)—Bachchan resurrected his "star value." He now endorsed such diverse products as chocolates (Cadbury's), beverages (PepsiCo.), menswear (Reid and Taylor), even cars and hair oil. An India Abroad News Service story had suggested that Bachchan's stint as anchor of *Kaun Banega Crorepati* in 2000–2001 gave him a new persona and new credibility that manufacturers have exploited to market a range of different products to a broadly defined audience—both the urban and the small town, the Hindi speaker and the English speaker. In this context, the story cites filmmaker Ravi Chopra, stating that "people look at him [Bachchan] as a fatherly figure and believed that he will not give wrong suggestions . . . When I see an ad that has Amitji, I feel 'he is saying it, then it must be true.'"[39] We are getting now to the scene where Bachchan's transformation is complete.

Scene three: In the year 2007, one of India's largest media conglomerates, the Times Group, launched a branding campaign titled "India Poised." Inaugurating the campaign, the editor of the *Times of India* (TOI), Jaideep Bose—who was the editor of the Times Group's business publication *The Economic Times* until he was made editor of the group's flagship publication the *Times of India* in 2004—wrote that the year 2007 could well be the "Year of India," because combined with "new-found economic and political clout," an "increasingly influential diaspora," the status of a "global soft power or superwower [*sic*] (from Bollywood and Indian art to yoga and spirituality)," "Brand India" was on a "roll like never before."[40] Thus linking economic policy, politics, the perception of a louder diaspora, and the commodification of such diverse elements as the practice of yoga and "Indian art," Bose went on to note that at this unique moment, the *Times of India* would use its space to "highlight areas of hope and despair," with the anticipation that along with readers' responses the publication would be able to "put together a few transformational ideas and solutions for an India whose real obstacle to progress is itself."[41] And the Times Group turned to Amitabh Bachchan—the fatherly figure in a suit who can sell anything because his audience believes he is speaking the truth—to sell its own brand. The Amitabh Bachchan who appears in the India Poised ad in 2007 is an older man, no longer angry, no longer dressed in the dirt and sweat-stained uniform of the "coolie" or the dockworker; instead, with his salt-and-pepper facial hair and fashionable suit, Bachchan stands transformed into the patriarch of "new" neoliberal India.

The India Poised campaign was, as previously discussed, as much about Brand *Times of India* as it was about Brand India. The campaign included a television advertisement, featuring Amitabh Bachchan in the English version, and a set of stories that appeared in the *Times of India* that took the form of report cards on various sectors (such as Information Technology, Health, Oil and Gas, etc.) deemed important by the editorial team of the newspaper.

In a short article with the headline "Big B Gives Baritone to Big Idea," published on the day the campaign was introduced in the newspaper, the TOI editorial team let their readers know that they had asked Bachchan to voice the India Poised campaign. The link between the angry young man and the patriarch of neoliberal India is his baritone. That baritone, which had materialized a particular kind of physicality—a masculinity that was angry, brooding, controlled, intelligent, and eloquent about power and the condition of subalternity—to the character of the male hero in the seventies and eighties now becomes the voice of the burgeoning middle classes of "new" India, urging "old" India to come over to "this side." In the India Poised campaign, the baritone materializes a wizened masculinity, more paternal than youthfully rebellious, yet still controlled, intelligent, and eloquent, this time about the historic moment facing the nation. More importantly, the baritone now performs the significant labor of marking time, calling the event of national renewal into being. The angry young man's baritone marked him as the outsider, on the margins of the nation's hegemonic moral and political imaginary, which is why it was seductive at the time, but the baritone that belonged to the patriarch of neoliberal India now voiced hegemony; its husky tonality stated that it was the nation and its time was now. The vigilante was home. The baritone links the two personas—"angry young man" and "patriarch of neoliberal India"— together. The persona of the "angry young man"—a creation of the cinematic imagination—is integral to Bachchan's new persona of "brand father"—a creation of both Bachchan's public relations machinery and the advertising and television industries—because it is the *movement* from one persona to the second that now becomes iconic. In other words, the affective valence of Bachchan's persona as patriarch of neoliberal India is engendered by the movement from angry young man to brand father. The narrative form through which the story of that movement is realized is spectacular realism.

The baritone is an auditory and therefore a deeply sensory bridge that links the angry young man with the brand father, but the Times Group's campaign also featured another bridge. Bachchan was filmed for the India Poised ad at the Bandra–Worli Sealink in Mumbai, a bridge which at the time was still under construction. The Times Group and Bachchan himself sought permission from the state government of Maharashtra to shoot at this high-security location. The controversial bridge links the city's northern suburbs with central and south Mumbai. The *Times* noted that the bridge was an ideal location for the ad because they had wanted a backdrop that was "as symbolic as it was stunning."[42] Comparing the Sealink to San Francisco's Golden Gate Bridge, the newspaper also stated that "to all of Mumbai, it [the bridge] is the giant totem of the urban dream . . . to everyone, it stands for India unleashed, bridge and country leaping powerfully into the future, leaving behind the carping and dithering which had held back both for so many years."[43] Dismissing the protests of the fishing communities and other residents of Worli who had petitioned against the construction of the bridge on the grounds of environmental degradation as "carping" and "dithering," the *Times of India* transformed the Bandra-Worli Sealink into a visual spectacle—a signifier with multiple signifieds. As a visual, the Sealink recalled the spectacle of the Golden Gate Bridge, and as such the urban topography of bustling Mumbai could now be compared with the urban spaces of cities like San Francisco and signified the Indian nation's arrival on the world stage. As a bridge, the Sealink physically connected the suburbs with such symbols of capital and industry as the stock exchange and the port (both located in southern Mumbai) and could symbolically connect present time—a moment created by the neoliberal turn in economic policy—with future time, a moment that was imminent, or so the India Poised campaign would argue. Moreover, in the advertisement, the bridge—itself a signifier of new India—marked new India's movement away from old India. As such, the bridge in the India Poised campaign is a powerfully different sign from the bridge in *Deewar*. That older bridge was a sign of the stalled present, a symbol of the abjection and humiliation that produced the angry young man. This newer, incomplete bridge is a road to elsewhere; it signifies time unstuck, it connotes movement from the stalled and tragic time of the angry young man to the dazzlingly renewed time of the brand father.

The visualization of the India Poised ad is starkly austere: the colors are a muted gray, black, and white and the frame holds just two powerful symbols, namely Amitabh Bachchan and the Bandra-Worli Sealink. Both of the symbols tell a tale of movement from the "old" to the "new," from the angry and constrained to the desiring and expansive; moreover, both symbols *link* the "old" with the "new" and as such define the space of the "new" as a rupture. In other words, the India Poised ad, working evocatively through the persona of Amitabh Bachchan and the Bandra-Worli Sealink, narrates new India *as* a rupture that is spectacularly real.

The text of the ad—as narrated by the Bachchan baritone—works to name the rupture *as* rupture by defining a nation that is split within. One India—the India that is tied to a past of "license raj" and "inspector raj"—is defined through skepticism and fear. This was the India within which the angry young man resided and seethed. The other India (new India) is "pulsating, dynamic and new," it leads instead of following, it desires rather than hopes and is straining at the leash that is old India so it can fly. Bachchan goes on to note that "history is a bad motorist" because "it rarely ever signals its intentions when it is taking a turn." Taking over that task of signaling from the time of history, this popular cultural artifact marks its intervention by *naming* precisely the moment of turn. Thus, Bachchan states, punching the empty space around him for emphasis: "*This* is that rarely ever moment, history is turning a page." The advertisement concludes by asserting that "our time is now." Undefined, empty space—the space created by the changes within economic policy—is thus filled and named as event through an act of intervention.

Scene four: The concluding scene of this story completes the picture; it reveals the contours of new India (the elsewhere) that the India Poised ad had proclaimed was imminent. Amitabh Bachchan lent his iconic image and baritone for the state of Gujarat's tourism advertising campaign on the specific request of its then–chief minister Narendra Modi in 2010. The next section will focus on Modi's story, but for now, it is important to note that when Bachchan agreed to become a part of the Gujarat tourism campaign, Modi had already earned the dubious distinction of being chief minister of the state when it was torn asunder by programmatic violence against Muslims leading to several hundred deaths, assaults, and displacement.[44] Modi's chest-thumping machismo, his consistent and strategic narration of his origins—that he was the son of a tea seller—to mark his outsider status (i.e., on the outside of the upper-class, upper-caste dynastic hold of political power), and his uninhibitedly aggressive rhetoric link him to the legacy of the cinematic angry young man.[45] The coming together of Amitabh Bachchan and Narendra Modi for an advertising and branding campaign at a time when the vigilante outsider was home was not a coincidence; it indicated the conjoining of neoliberalism with Hindu nationalism through the form of spectacular realism. The angry young man, however, had also signified powerful subaltern anger about consistent disenfranchisement and so, Amitabh Bachchan, the man who embodied and voiced the angry young man, was questioned about his motives for joining hands with a Hindu nationalist. When pressed by the journalist Barkha Dutt on the news program *The Buck Stops Here*, for instance, on why an "icon of secularism" such as Bachchan would endorse Modi, the Hindu nationalist, Bachchan noted that he was endorsing the state and not its chief minister. He noted that he was impressed by all the "progress" the state had made. The ad campaign with the tagline "khushboo Gujarat ki" (the scent of Gujarat) featured Bachchan in different locales of the state—the desert of Kutch, the Somnath Temple, and the Gir Forest. Bachchan narrates the locales in the campaign, transforming the desert, the temple, and the forest with its population of Asiatic lions into embodiments of Gujarati endurance and artistry, untrammeled devotion and pride, and ends each advertisement by urging his audience to spend a few days in Gujarat. As such, the narrative of pride, strength, endurance, aggressive devotion, and Hindu nationalist symbolism were sutured to the image of new India by the erstwhile angry young man, now patriarch of neoliberal India. The character of the angry young man—a symbol of obstructed time—had gone traveling and come home (now the Hindu nation) as the brand father, the patriarch of neoliberal, new India—a symbol of renewal. The iconicity of Amitabh Bachchan becomes the bridge that links neoliberalism with Hindu nationalism.

NARENDRA MODI: THE MASK

If the angry young man became the brand father, then the journey that the political actor and Hindu nationalist Narendra Modi takes moves *this* commoner from being the tea seller's son to the prime minister of the nation. His entanglement with the symbolism of the angry young man on this journey is crucial to the form of its apogee. Let's trace that journey. In 2015, then U.S. president Barack Obama traveled to India to attend the nation's sixty-fifth Republic Day parade on January 26. This was Obama's second visit to India. In the previous chapter that focused on development as a keyword, I have discussed Obama's first visit to India, in the fall of 2010, when the Indian National Congress–led coalition government was in power and Manmohan Singh, economist and chief architect of economic liberalization, was the prime minister. In that first visit, Obama had sealed the story of emergence and renewal. The second visit in 2015 served to transfer the powerful sign of transformation to an Indian political leader who had, until then, been disallowed from entering the United States on the grounds of human rights violations. The encounter between Modi and Obama pivoted on the concept of difference. Emptied of its political valence and its cultural struggle, difference became the narrative trope through which Modi was legitimized by the global superpower. Moreover, difference enabled the constitution of an equivalence between Barack Obama and Narendra Modi. Difference was the abstraction that erased the particularity of race, gender, and class in the United States as well as the particular history of caste, gender, and class in India. As an abstraction, enabled by the politics of liberal multiculturalism in the United States and liberal brahminism (as discussed in the introduction) in India, the concept of difference could constitute an equivalence between Blackness, even anti-racist and Black power movements, and Hindu majoritarianism via the personages of Obama and Modi. During his visit to India in 2015, Obama repeatedly cited Modi's trajectory from humble, common beginnings as the son of a tea seller and domestic worker to prime minister. It is this simple tale, which pivots on the signifier of difference, that articulates Obama, the first Black president of the United States, with Modi, who is consistently represented as a transformational figure as well. Obama, in fact, authored a short piece on Modi for *Time* magazine's mid-April 2015 issue, which listed the Indian prime minister as one of the world's 100 most influential people. "As a boy, Narendra Modi helped his father sell tea to support their family. Today, he's the leader of the world's largest democracy, and his life story—from poverty to Prime Minister—reflects the dynamism and potential of India's rise," begins the piece on Modi. "When he came to Washington, Narendra and I visited the memorial to Dr. Martin Luther King Jr. We reflected on the teachings of King and Gandhi and how the diversity of backgrounds and faiths in our countries is a strength we have to protect. Prime Minister Modi recognizes that more than 1 billion Indians living and succeeding together can be an inspiring model for the world," Obama concluded.[46] Invoking the powerful and radical iconicities of King and Gandhi and his own voice, which signified transformation and the "audacity of hope," Obama had authored a legitimizing narrative for the *Hindu Hriday Samrat* (the king of Hindu hearts) that underlined Modi's journey, starting humbly as a tea seller and ending at the prime minister's office. This is a narrative that effectively reinforced the movement as iconic.

Scene one: *Hindu Hriday Samrat* was a moniker Modi took on in the wake of the Gujarat pogrom in 2002. In the state assembly elections held that same year, the Modi-led BJP (in the state of Gujarat) won 126 of the 181 seats it had contested with a 49.8 percent vote share.[47] An editorial in *Frontline* magazine called the result "a turnaround in the fortunes of the Hindu Right" because this sweeping victory had come after a period where the "BJP suffered a demoralizing series of electoral defeats in States across India . . . its political stock was in uninterrupted decline and its prospects of returning to power in the next general election . . . were widely believed to be non-existent."[48] Several commentators read this election result as a grim and sordid warning for the polity. Historian Mushirul Hassan, writing in the *Indian Express*, warned that "the Modi victory has established a sinister precedent for the future of democracy . . . one cannot help feeling that Modism, rather than the tired Hindutva ideology, will be the new mantra of a Hinduised polity that is being constructed with the aid of militant Hindu jehadis."[49] Hasan was accurate. Even though the BJP lost the subsequent two general elections, this victory in the state of Gujarat in 2002, preceded by the "genocidal anti-Muslim pogrom"[50] that same year, brought the erstwhile RSS worker, who had not been seen as a mass leader early in his career and was, in fact, remarked upon as creating dissidence within the party, into the national spotlight. Scholar of politics and international relations Harsh Pant lamented in vehement terms: "Accepting this verdict as merely an acknowledgment of democracy in India is reneging on one's responsibility as a citizen of India. . . . Why is it difficult to tell the people of Gujarat that they have made a wrong decision and that its consequences will be borne not only by Gujarat but by the entire nation?"[51] That poignant lament reverberates in 2019, when the Modi government in its second term has passed legislation that aims to create a national registry of citizens that links citizenship with religion and creates a graded hierarchy of citizenship. In the context of Gujarat 2002, the warning was deemed necessary because, as one English-language magazine put it, "Trampling on poll surveys and using a communally polarized populace to full advantage— with a lot of assistance from a motivated organizational structure that raised the Hindutva pitch to a new high," Modi, the "former RSS pracharak turned the Gujarat elections on its head, winning in a style that none predicted."[52] In 2002, Modi had led an election campaign that systematically beat the drum of Gujarati pride (*gaurav*) and a chest-thumping sense of self-consciousness (*asmita*). It was a campaign that had linked terrorism with Pakistan ("miyah Musharraf") and thence to Muslims.[53] Modi's campaign insistently referenced the deaths of more than fifty people in a fire on a train—the Sabarmati Express—that was carrying Hindu nationalists (party activists and volunteers) back to Gujarat from Ayodhya on February 27, 2002. Ayodhya, as discussed in the introduction, is the northern Indian city where Hindu nationalists have attempted to build a temple on the site of a mosque that was destroyed by their mobilization in 1992. The fire erupted in a compartment that was largely occupied by Hindu nationalists. The anti-Muslim Gujarat pogrom of 2002 is narrated by Modi and the Gujarat state as the spontaneous eruption of violence in response to this tragedy on the train. The election campaign, conducted barely a few months after the train tragedy and the pogrom, repeatedly referenced the gruesome details of the fire, deemed it murder, and identified the culprits as Muslims (despite a botched and broadly repudiated investigation into the fire), without any recognition of the state's complicity in the anti-Muslim programmatic violence that followed. Consider a portion of Modi's speech in Modera, north Gujarat, on the last day of electoral campaigning as reported by the *Telegraph*: "I have been to Godhra. I have seen the bodies, the shrunken, charred, shriveled bodies of women and children and boys on the railway platform. I cannot forget Godhra. For me, Godhra is not an election issue. It is an issue that concerns humanity. I swear to you that the criminals of Godhra will not go unpunished. How the women, children, and men must have shrieked when they were being burnt! Can man be so evil? And I am asked to forget Godhra. How can I!"[54] This speech ended by noting starkly that a vote for the Congress party would be celebrated in "Miyah Musharraf's Pakistan."[55] The speech thus explicitly defined the loss of life at Godhra as the wanton and inhumane murder of Hindus by the evil "other"—the Muslim—whose real home was Pakistan; because Modi would never forget Godhra, he was and would always be the "King of Hindu Hearts." Even in his televised message to the state ostensibly seeking calm and restraint after the Godhra tragedy, Modi stressed that this act of "cannibals" would never be forgiven and would not be tolerated—this before any form of an investigation had been completed to ascertain the cause and nature of the fire on the Sabarmati Express. The Hindu Hriday Samrat was thus fashioned through the deliberate, insistent, and violent representation of the Muslim Other, through unabashed chest-thumping machismo that called on the public to a self-conscious acknowledgment of their Hindu identities.

Modi's identification as the "King of Hindu Hearts" was in line with the ideology of the RSS and the Hindu Mahasabha that have argued, following such ideologues as V. D. Savarkar, that the true Indian was a Hindu—one who considered the land mass of the subcontinent as both his religious and national home (both his "holy land" and his "fatherland").[56] Muslims, in particular, are singled out as the minority group in the subcontinent who are inimical to such a definition and therefore can be second-class citizens of India at best. More importantly for our purposes here, Hindu nationalist ideologues like Savarkar had always exhorted a loud assertion and acknowledgment of Hinduness. "Down with the apologetic attitude that makes some of us feel shy to proclaim themselves as Hindus, as if it was something unnational [sic], something like a disgrace to be born of the line of Shree Ram and Shree Krishna—Shivajee and Pratap and Govind Singh. . . . You must henceforth vote for those who are not ashamed themselves of being Hindus, openly stand for the Hindus, and pledge themselves not to keep burning incense, always at the cost of the Hindus before the fetish of a dishonorable unity-cult," Savarkar had argued in a speech made to the Hindu Mahasabha in Gujarat in 1937.[57] As Hindu Hriday Samrat, Modi had—in line with the Savarkarite diktat—consistently asserted his Hinduness. He has campaigned on the concepts of Hindu pride and self-consciousness and will not publicly acknowledge or apologize for the horrific violence that scarred Gujarat in 2002.

The Modi mask has been a feature of the politician's electoral and public relations since his days as a political leader and chief minister of the state of Gujarat. Just as the bridge was a central symbol for Bachchan's iconicity and crucial to the conjoining of the realism of the commoner with the spectacle of new India, the mask is central to the fashioning of Modi's iconicity as Hindu Hriday Samrat and important in twining neoliberalism with Hindu nationalism. The mask, as we shall see, enables the assertion (through multiplication) of Hindu presence as well enacting neoliberalism as the realization of a common dream. The mask (or the metaphor of the mask) has been central to the critique leveled against the BJP by those opposed to the strategic muddling of the Hindutva agenda by BJP politicians aiming for a broader reach in an electoral cycle. The first BJP politician to acquire the mantle of prime ministership—Atal Bihari Vajpayee—was famously critiqued for being the mask (*mukhauta*) of the RSS. In other words, Vajpayee's ostensibly more moderate political agenda was seen as a mask that shielded the harder Hindutva ideology at the core of the RSS and the BJP. Critique of the Vajpayee-led BJP was therefore often posited as an unmasking, which would reveal the real face of the party's ideology. The Modi mask is not a metaphor. It is, on the contrary, a material tool central to his electoral campaign and is distributed at rallies and public events and can be purchased from variety stores that stock political party merchandise during election season. The Modi mask radically alters the chain of signification that is typically central to the mask as an object that hides or derides: the mask, in this instance, does not hide or cover a secret; on the contrary, it marks presence. It proclaims allegiance loudly and powerfully and such a proclamation is central to the discourse of Hindu pride within Modi's BJP and to Savarkarite Hindutva. The chest-thumping, saffron-marked-forehead assertion of Hindu identity is defined as self-respect, self-consciousness (asmita), and pride (gaurav) and an eschewal of perceived historic emasculation. Parul Dave Mukherji has remarked, "The very act of appearing in a public space with the Modi mask becomes a newly invented ritual which assures that Modi's presence is literally multiplied and his megalomania acquires a public dimension and sanction."[58] More significant than megalomania for our purposes here is the ritualistic manner in which the Modi mask results in the multiplication of the *Hindu Hriday* (the Hindu heart), asserting the presence of a Hindu majority by claiming its self-confessed *samrat* (king).

In this context, consider another election campaign in which Modi was once again the protagonist: the BJP's 2014 general election campaign centered Modi as the prime ministerial candidate and included a music video titled "Hum Modiji ko laanewale hain, achche din aane wale hain" (We are going to bring Modi to power; better days are coming). We have discussed this video for its narration of development in the previous chapter. Even though Modi is the protagonist here, he does not feature in the visuals that accompany the music video; his photograph appears at the very end. Instead, a common man or woman representing the diverse regions of the nation takes center stage. In the *Achche Din* music video moreover, the commoner wears the Modi mask. The mask here is a semiotic node: it signifies that difference can be subsumed behind the mask, but in this case also that Modi is common like the *aam aadmi* (common man) and that in the aam aadmi resides the visionary Modi. The congruence between the commoner and Modi as visionary (or samrat) is underlined in the campaign. The image of the commoner wearing the Modi mask is an instantiation of spectacular realism, conjoining the reality of the ordinary citizen with the spectacle of Modi's public persona. The mask—particularly as it appears here in a circulating commodity image—also functions as a screen, in the sense that the audience watching, listening, and sensing the music video knows that a particular face lies behind the mask and yet this audience's senses are utterly captured by the mask itself. The audience evinces no interest in unmasking the face, and there is no interest in learning about the particularities of that face. The mask as screen is all that matters; it is thus entirely captivating. As such, the mask—much like the screen—constitutes the mass as a mass.

The Modi mask is reminiscent of, and in fact alludes to, another mask that appeared in another advertising campaign, namely the television commercial for Pepsi India produced in 1998. The ad featured the best-known sports personality in India, the cricketer Sachin Tendulkar, and the tagline "yeh dil maange more" [the heart desires more]. Yeh dil maange more was the translation of one of PepsiCo International's slogans, "ask for more," that the Indian advertising industry's process of glocalization produced. It became a popular anthem, appearing as an epitaph for an Indian soldier killed in a military operation (Capt. Vikram Batra, who died in 1999 during the India-Pakistan Kargil conflict), as the title for a Hindi film in 2004, and perhaps most significantly as the popular signifier for India post–economic liberalization. The Pepsi commercial—titled "The Mask"—uses the same rustic aural, melodic, and visual idiom that would appear sixteen years later in the *Achche Din* music video and advertising campaign. It features a group of young boys—visually coded as residents of rural India—wearing Sachin Tendulkar masks and "desiring more." Tendulkar himself appears in the advertisement, wearing the mask, which he then lifts to reveal his real self, but also his celebrity iconicity to the enthrallment of the boys. The commercial suggests that in every boy resides a Sachin Tendulkar and that the icon and the commoner are linked through both the desire for more, which as an aspiration necessitates a sense of futurity, as well as the commodity itself. This Pepsi commercial acts therefore as an intimation of the *Achche Din* campaign advertisement and that intimation and allusion is yet another instantiation of the twinning of Hindu nationalism and neoliberalism in India.

A creation of Genesis, an ad production house helmed by filmmaker Prahlad Kakkar, this particular film was an anomaly in the advertising that was created for PepsiCo during the 1990s. Other films produced for PepsiCo by Genesis emphasized celebrity endorsement of the fizzy cola—Sachin Tendulkar and other members of the Indian cricket team and film stars like Shahrukh Khan were shown sipping the drink—and often included entertaining gags. Moreover, the Pepsi "Mask" commercial employs an audiovisual and melodic idiom that encodes a demographic that PepsiCo, in fact, was not interested in speaking to at the time. The boys featured in the commercial did not belong to the English-speaking, urban middle- and upper-middle classes with ambitions for global citizenship that PepsiCo was interested in marketing its products to. Genesis insisted though that the Pepsi campaign slogan, yeh dil maange more, signified dreams and desire and the signifier that most potently completed that chain of signification was the unfettered effervescence of the common child and not the child who lived in a high-rise and actually consumed a bottle of Pepsi or might potentially run into Sachin Tendulkar at a restaurant or at the airport.[59] The distance between the material realities of the boys featured in the commercial and their ostensible dream of becoming a cricketing superstar like Sachin Tendulkar (or even having the opportunity to meet him) was significant, impossible even. Genesis convinced PepsiCo that it was the impossibility of that distance that, in fact, constituted the most powerful affective register for yeh dil maange more. The Pepsi "Mask" commercial and the tagline "yeh dil maange more" have had an afterlife in the Indian popular imaginary beyond the immediacy of localizing PepsiCo in India in the 1990s. The "Mask" commercial enabled an idiomatic constitution of the "common/the commoner/the people" and this commoner's aspirations. The circulation of this image within the popular imaginary allowed the BJP campaign to allude to it, and translate this instantiation of the common created for a multinational corporate brand into a political imaginary. Moreover, the concatenation of the Modi mask with the Pepsi "Mask" commercial is an instantiation of the conjoining of Hindutva and economic liberalization within the spectacularly real form of the popular narrative. The mask links realism with the spectacle, it links Hindutva to neoliberalism, and the assertion of Hindu presence to the narration of neoliberalism as the dream of the commoner. I moved forward to the BJP's 2014 electoral campaign to draw out my argument about the Modi mask; the key, though, to this first scene in the Modi story is 2002 and the first few years of the new millennium, when Modi is fashioned as the "King of Hindu Hearts." We will move more specifically now to the 2014 electoral campaign that brought Modi to the prime ministerial chair, to track the movement in the symbols and chains of signification that constitute his persona.

Scene two: "Na mujhe kisine bheja hai, na mein yahan aaya hoon, mujhe to Ganga ne bulaya hai." "I haven't been sent here, nor have I come on my own. I was, in fact, hailed by the Ganga [the Ganges River]." These words spoken in a muted, reverential tone by the then–prime ministerial candidate Narendra Modi inaugurate a campaign advertisement used by the BJP in the 2014 Indian general elections. By early 2009, Modi was lauded as prime ministerial material by Indian industrialists such as Anil Ambani and Sunil Mittal. The *Economic Times*, reporting this endorsement under the headline "Narendra Modi Becomes India Inc. Poster Boy" noted that "Modi is a brilliant orator who has a reputation for battling corruption to bring development to Gujarat."[60] This endorsement of Modi as a champion of development was followed by the caveat that he had turned a "blind eye" to the "murder of hundreds of Muslims" in 2002. In September 2013, four years after the public endorsement by Indian industry, the BJP declared Narendra Modi its prime ministerial nominee. English-language political journalists such as Rajdeep Sardesai have noted that Modi "presented himself as India's [first] post-liberalization politician . . . someone who has sought to combine a certain cultural rootedness with the vaulting desire of millions of Indians to get onto the superhighway to prosperity."[61] Popular commentary such as this has deemed development as a secular apolitical project as opposed to the project of Hindu nationalism and presented Modi's persona as renewed by the fact of its transformation from Hindu Hriday Samrat to *Vikas Purush* (man of development). While we have discussed the constitution and circulation of the concept of development in the time of Hindu neoliberalism in the previous chapter, what I will track through this scene is the manner in which the story of a transformation from religious bigotry to secular developmentalism obfuscates the twinning of Hindutva with economic liberalization and constitutes Modi into an icon of the conjuncture. This is not a scene of transformation but of movement, such that the Hindu Hriday Samrat becomes the embodiment of a nationalist figure responding to "new time," a time that the superstar icon Amitabh Bachchan had signaled was imminent. A central feature of the Modi mask is that it does not hide a secret and instead marks presence; the key to Modi's iconicity is that the persona of the Vikas Purush does not hide or mask the Hindu Hriday Samrat. The King of Hindu Hearts is the centerpiece, the fulcrum, the nucleus from which movement itself becomes possible. In this sense, every move is a reassertion and reiteration of that pivotal figure of Hindu Hriday Samrat.

Let us return to our scene. The advertisement that began this scene features visuals drawn from Modi's campaign rally in Varanasi, including shots of a surging crowd of people, some dancing, others waving their arms and the party flag. It features Modi on an open campaign truck bedecked in marigolds, waving to this crowd and greeting them with folded hands. As the male voiceover talks about a "people's storm" (*jan sailaab*) that is speaking in one voice, low chants of "Modi, Modi, Modi" gently fill the soundscape. The sensory world constituted by the advertisement through sound, visuals, voice, and pacing is deliberately placed at a remove from the hypermasculine braggadocio that claimed a *chappan nee chatti* (56-inch chest) and the title of Hindu Hriday Samrat for Modi, even though it relies on that precise foundational narrative to construct its affective scaffolding. It is no coincidence, for instance, that Modi chose to contest a seat from Varanasi, the temple town and Hindu pilgrimage center in the northern state of Uttar Pradesh in this election. The BJP had seen a waning of its electoral fortunes in the state of Uttar Pradesh prior to the 2014 election, but knew that it had to do well in the state in order to regain power at the center. Modi's campaigning from the pilgrimage town of Varanasi was a part of the campaign strategy to center Uttar Pradesh.

The pilgrimage, as Benedict Anderson evocatively informed us, is a "meaning-creating experience." Not only do pilgrimage towns become centers of sacred geographies, the journey itself—the "constant flow of pilgrims moving towards them from remote and otherwise unrelated localities"—constitutes fellow travelers and potential travelers as a distinct community separate from travelers journeying to other sacred centers.[62] Modi's decision to contest from Varanasi, despite the lack of any prior commitment to the city or the larger state, was therefore an invocation of Hindu identity and community, just as much as his masculinist assertion of being the King of Hindu Hearts was at another time. There is more, though, to the use of the pilgrimage town: In Anderson's narration of the pilgrimage, the journey constitutes the sacred geography of the religion and the secular geography of the nation. Moreover, the pilgrimage enables the discovery of community itself—we Hindus, who travel to Varanasi. In the Modi campaign, the pilgrimage town, even as it invokes the community of Hindus, functions emphatically to signal messianic time and a new political figure.

The advertisement, in fact, acts as narrative scaffolding for this signaling: the intermixing of the visuals, the melody, the low chant, the narrative of the voiceover all aim to engender a reverence, a deep sense of awe not simply for the man, prime ministerial candidate Narendra Modi, but more significantly for this moment in time, when a "rising tide," a "people's storm" even, has compelled the Ganges to call on her "son." In an interview to the press agency ANI at the time of this rally in 2014, Modi made sure to begin and end the interview with the line about the river having hailed him and how his visit to Varanasi made him feel like a child returning to his mother's lap. There are at least two metonymic constructions embedded within this textual and visual assertion: The goddess figure of the river Ganges stands in for the Hindu pilgrimage town of Varanasi, which in turn stands in for the sacred center of the nation (read Hindu nation). Unlike the pilgrimage, where a diverse collection of peoples is transformed into a mass of Hindus or Muslims, Buddhists or Jews or Christians, Modi journeys alone, precisely because he (in his claim) is responding to a divine call. As such the narrative conjoins him to the mass—Modi is a Hindu like all the other Hindus who journey to Varanasi—but also sets him apart from the mass—he was the chosen one, he was called. The narrative underlines his presence as spectacularly real. The advertisement, moreover, makes a specific assertion about time itself. It argues that this is a time-turning or revolutionary moment: both the gods and the masses recognize it as such and are hailing the one man who can help realize the potential of the moment. The narrative of the advertisement thus suggests that this moment itself is calling the iconic personage of Modi to meet it at the crest, thereby constituting a new Indian polity.

My suggestion is that the constitution and circulation of this conception of time has two consequences: 1) It sutures messianic time—as in, time as full and filled—together with homogenous empty time—as in, time as empty continuum and linearly progressive. The time of the commodity (and of the clock and the calendar), with its consistent emphasis on repetition, is thus linked to moments in the past and in the future nonlinearly. The constitution and circulation of this desire thus articulates instantiations of the secular with those of the sacred and the religious. "Na mujhe kisine bheja hai, na mein yahan aaya hoon, mujhe to Ganga ne bulaya hai." ("I haven't been sent here, nor have I come on my own. I was, in fact, called by the Ganga [the Ganges River]."), prime ministerial candidate Modi says in the campaign advertisement. As such the advertisement sutures the regularized clock-time of an election (every five years in the schema of Indian parliamentary democracy) and its homogeneity (every election's processes are regularized and repetitive) with a messianic moment when the gods call on a man to embody this moment. 2) In a global conjuncture that has witnessed a consolidation of the authoritarian political right, such a constitution and circulation delinks or disarticulates the conception of revolution or the turning of time from any association with radical left political thought and action, allows neoliberalism to be represented as national renewal, and intertwines it with Hindutva. Modi's political persona moves from the King of Hindu Hearts to the Man of Development and finally to the Chosen One, even as he moves from the position of a party worker to the chief ministership of a state and finally to prime ministership. That movement of his public persona and his political ambitions gives corporeal form to spectacular realism and to Hindutva neoliberalism. That movement, moreover, is deemed iconic. The Modi mask signifying Hindu assertion and presence and a form of economic liberalization that defines development and the economic itself through such an assertion[63] is the centerpiece of this iconicity.

MAYAWATI: THE STATUE

Finally, I want to turn to the story of the making of a dalit iconicity. Mayawati, the first dalit female chief minister of India and the leader of the Bahujan Samaj Party (BSP) [understood and translated as the party of the marginalized who constitute a numerical majority in India], is the protagonist of this story. Within the narrative of Hindutva neoliberalism, dalitness, transformed into the category common or aam, signifies national renewal. This narrative often pivots on the category of the dalit entrepreneur. Chapter 3 deals specifically with the constitution of the category entrepreneur in the time of Hindutva neoliberalism; here, I reiterate the argument that dalit entrepreneur as a category and an identification narrates the story of movement—from oppression to liberation—without necessitating the annihilation of caste itself. The Dalit Indian Chamber of Commerce and Industry, founded in 2005 to promote entrepreneurship among dalits as a "solution to their socio-economic problems," notes in its pithily stated aim that the dalit entrepreneur as a category signifies "fight[ing] caste with capital."[64] Such a narrative defines capital as a secular force and the market as a nondiscriminatory public space. Narrated in this fashion, the rise of the dalit entrepreneur is appropriated to tell the story of national renewal post–economic liberalization, as we have seen with management guru and public commentator Gurcharan Das's concatenation of the stories of the growth of the IT and pharmaceutical industries with that of the young girl selling flowers at the traffic light and the dalit small business owner through the category entrepreneur. More importantly for our purposes, this story about the dalit entrepreneur can be twined with the Hindutva story of caste as well.

In Hindutva ideologue V. D. Savarkar's argument, caste was invented by Hindu society as a method to "restore political, religious and social stability in the society and the nation,"[65] prior to and after "the Muslim invasions of India" and thus "facilitated the stupendous consolidation and remarkable stability of the Hindu society under certain peculiar circumstances and in particular contexts."[66] Savarkar has argued that the caste system was created and consolidated with the "sole object of protecting" Hindu "racial seed and blood, preserving their caste-life and tradition and keeping them absolutely pure from contamination."[67] In other words, the argument is that caste as a system was foundational to Hindu society and not only marked it as distinct from the Muslim other (also the Christian other) but "protected" it from the contamination of the non-Hindu, specifically the Muslim. As such, Savarkar argues, caste as a system must be lauded. However, his argument continues, caste also produces the "seven fetters"—including a system of segregation that prohibits castes deemed untouchable from using the same drinking water and food as upper castes and disallows inter-caste marriages and travel across the seas. It defines the touch of whole groups of people as polluting and prohibits the "purification of religious converts" (shuddi). These "fetters," Savarkar argues, impair daily life and, most importantly for the ideology of Hindutva, have prevented Hindu society from brutally and ruthlessly vanquishing the "Muslim invader" because caste, in the final instance, segregated rather than consolidated Hindu society. For Savarkar, the caste system's prohibition of shuddi, a ritualistic cleansing that would enable those who had converted to Islam or Christianity or had lost caste as a consequence of travel across the seas or through inter-caste/inter-religious marriage to "return" via purification to Hinduism, was a significant problem; he believed this allowed a depletion in Hindu ranks. Savarkar thus calls for a loosening of the "fetters" imposed by caste without seeking the dismantling of caste, precisely because caste is seen as definitive of Hinduism itself. The celebration of dalit success— particularly if it can be cast within the category of entrepreneurship—is precisely the kind of loosening of caste fetters that Hindutva seeks. This celebratory narrative serves the purposes of neoliberalism or economic liberalization in India as well. As I have discussed in the introduction, economic liberalization was constructed in its inaugural moment through a story that reproduced caste as foundational to Indianness. Such a celebration enfolds the dalit into the story of national renewal and strategically uses her dalitness to mark the conjuncture as new without repudiating the persistent inequities of caste.

Through the story of Mayawati's iconicity, we shall track the ways in which caste is employed to stage newness and renewal but we shall also trace her own improvisations in a field of constraint, such that she enables the constitution of an iconicity—a dalit iconicity—that both exploits the Hindutva narrative on caste and explicitly critiques it. Her story, therefore, unlike Bachchan's and Modi's, is an unruly one. In some moments, her story allows for the strategic use of dalitness to define renewal but in others her political assertion of caste necessitates repudiation and disarticulation in the time of Hindutva neoliberalism. In order to stage the unruliness of Mayawati's story, I will first discuss the moment when her political success could be narrated through the form of spectacular realism, followed quickly by the scenes of her repudiation. With Bachchan and Modi, the scenes followed each other to chart movement, twining realism with the spectacle and Hindu nationalism with neoliberalism. With Mayawati, the sequence of scenes narrates a strategic appropriation by Hindutva neoliberalism followed almost immediately by a disarticulation. Caste, particularly gendered caste, produces fissures in the neat story that Hindutva neoliberalism wants to tell through spectacular realism.

Scene one: When Mayawati won the Uttar Pradesh state elections in 2007 through a simple majority and formed a single-party government in the nation's most populous state, she and her party accomplished a feat that had not been achieved by any political party in Uttar Pradesh since 1991.[68] More significantly, this was a victory that had not been won by a political party of dalits such as the Bahujan Samaj Party since Indian independence.[69] In the narration of this victory, Mayawati's dalitness was centered as the significant characteristic of the story. The BSP victory in 2007 was marked as a historic dalit victory and narrated as an instantiation of new time and a renewed nation where hierarchical categories of differentiation were deemed to have melted away. In other words, much like the story of the rise of the dalit entrepreneur was used to signify the unshackling of capital and through it the unfettering of caste hierarchies, the story about the 2007 Uttar Pradesh elections suggested that this time was new and signified renewal because the fetters imposed by the caste system were dissolving. A dalit female politician's resounding electoral victory in a state where caste affiliations have always had a historic significance was proof, the story suggested. As such, the BSP's 2007 electoral result was defined as a dalit victory only insofar as it could be appropriated to signify the loosening of caste fetters.

The plotline of the narrative therefore consistently emphasized the BSP's 2007 strategic electoral alliance with dalits, brahmins, and other upper castes, even as it narrated the story of a dalit female politician's electoral victory.[70] In fact, this alliance was appropriated to narrate a story about movement—from the old identitarian forms of politics to new forms of political strategizing that did not rely on caste. Using the term *sarva samaj* (the entire society) in juxtaposition with *bahujan samaj* (the marginalized who make up a numerical majority in society), the BSP had formulated a complex alliance between dalits, brahmins, and Muslims in order to broaden its electoral base. This alliance was translated into a story about the melting down of caste, where brahmins and dalits comingle. For instance, Barkha Dutt, a senior journalist and then managing editor of the news channel NDTV 24 × 7, wrote a column in the *Hindustan Times* titled "Art of Reinvention." Dutt wrote that "caste matters just as much as it always did, but it is both malleable and dynamic . . . the BSP may have been born and rooted in anti-Brahminical rebellion . . . but social churning made it possible for Mayawati's elephant [the BSP's electoral symbol] to shed its traditional symbolism."[71] Dutt argued that "politics is the art of reinvention" and that Mayawati had proved this "in her dramatic evolution from Dalit queen to Brahmin messiah."[72] Or consider Rajdeep Sardesai, a senior journalist and then editor in chief of the news channel CNN-IBN and IBN7, writing a column for the *Hindustan Times* and noting that "to see Dalits and Jats standing side-by-side at a BSP rally in the Jat bastion of Baghpat, to hear Brahmins actively considering voting for the BSP, to listen to Thakurs who are ready to vote for the elephant, is nothing short of a social miracle, a grand melting down of caste in a state frozen in age-old divisions."[73]

If Dutt characterized movement as Mayawati's evolution from a "dalit queen" to a "brahmin messiah," then in Sardesai's account, jats and dalits come to stand side-by-side because Mayawati had evolved: "From being a rabble-rouser who reveled in the abuse of the upper castes to a political strategist consciously wooing them, the evolution of Mayawati has easily been the most fascinating aspect of the battle for UP, an illumination of how, in order to win more votes, one simply has to shed an *extremist stand*."[74] What is interesting about this "melting down of caste" within such representations is that it is seen as Mayawati's successful experiment with "social engineering." Thus like Dutt, Sardesai also defines Mayawati's political strategy to form alliances with upper castes as "evolutionary."

As we have seen in the preceding discussion, the narration of movement from that which is deemed static and old to that which is putatively dynamic and new is important for signification processes discussing Hindutva liberalization and the consequent changes produced in India. Defining the commoner on this journey transforms the movement into an iconic sign. In the story that the 2005 Hindi film *Bunty aur Babli* narrates, small-town "Vimmi" who was being compelled into defining herself through "old" India's gendered norms (an arranged marriage, the identity of a housewife) transformed herself into "new" India's cosmopolitan "Babli" who was still a normatively gendered subject, but the norms now belonged to a "new" India (beauty pageants, love marriages, and conspicuous consumption). In the story that prominent journalists like Dutt and Sardesai narrate, Mayawati, a dalit woman and a commoner, undergoes a transformation as well, from occupying the distinctly "old" Indian political and gendered subjectivity of "dalit queen" or "rabble-rouser"—the "queen" of a community that can only be defined through caste status and more significantly through an assertion of that caste status for political recognition—to the "new" Indian subjectivity of "brahmin messiah" and "political strategist." When Mayawati asserts the political demands of the bahujan samaj she is a dalit queen; she "evolves" and stands transformed when she represents sarva samaj. In a political culture where politicians are often worshipped as "messiahs," the moment when a dalit woman comes to be seen as the representative of dalits and brahmins is euphorically new, or so the story goes.

In this scene then, Mayawati is constituted as a miraculous icon. The political and visual spectacle of upper castes mingling with dalits and attending rallies of dalit political figures such as Mayawati in a state where caste distinctions appear "frozen" in time is deemed magically new. Even as the historic and continued oppression of dalits is acknowledged by marking the BSP's alliance with upper castes as remarkable, in a double move, an expression of anger against caste oppression is simultaneously marked as extremist. For the story of the time, the possibility that a figure like Mayawati evoked could be represented through the modality of her dalitness—her embodiment of this category and her putative play with it in the moment when her party emerges with the largest number of seats in the Uttar Pradesh state assembly. In these representations, Mayawati's dalitness is itself seen as agentive. Her dalitness is imbued with historic potential and can be representative of progress—a movement from oppression to power. Her supposed play with the politics of caste but particularly with the politics of dalitness is therefore also represented as powerful.

Mayawati's *femaleness* poses yet another interesting possibility. In the BSP's image-making processes, Mayawati is consistently defined as both a woman and a dalit. In his monograph *Women Heroes and Dalit Assertion in North India: Culture, Identity and Politics*, Badri Narayan argues that "Mayawati's acceptance as a leader of the masses was made possible . . . by the BSP's projection of brave women heroes as symbols of Dalit identity and by building her image as an incarnation of these heroes."[75] Mayawati, in the BSP's representations of her, is seen as a *woman* like Udadevi, Jhalkaribai, Avantibai, Pannadhai, and Mahaviri Bhangin—iconic figures in the oral traditions of dalit cultures—and a dalit. Thus, in Badri Narayan's reading of BSP's image-making processes, Mayawati had to be both a woman and a dalit. Mayawati, in fact, refers to herself as "dalit ki beti" (daughter of a dalit), marking both the inheritance of caste as a marker of difference as well as her gendered subjectivity; as the daughter of a dalit she marks her intersectional subjectivity (she is a subaltern woman) and the "double disadvantage" that such a subjectivity carries in its name. Rajdeep Sardesai notes that as a woman and a dalit "in feudal north India," Mayawati is "doubly disadvantaged" and compares her to other Indian female political figures. He argues that unlike a "majority of South Asian women political leaders, who were beneficiaries of the principle of female accession to male martyrdom," Mayawati had succeeded in her own right after benefiting initially from mentorship offered by BSP founder Kanshi Ram. Moreover, he argues that unlike other female political leaders like Mamata Banerjee and Uma Bharti who have been "pushed to the margins by their self-destructive penchant for the theatrical," Mayawati is "focused and single-minded, a politician more than capable of dealing with her male rivals."[76] In this scene, where Mayawati is being marked as a figure of possibility largely through a focus on her dalitness, her femininity works to amplify the discussion. In this moment, Mayawati is thus narrated as an icon most suited to affectively narrate the story of new India. The constitution of Mayawati's iconic image in this scene by the English-language press and editorial commentary is an instantiation of Indian liberalism coinciding with Hindutva on the issue of caste wherein the system of caste is defined as a set of fetters that are loosened when dalits and brahmins stand together, even as a politics of recognition and redistribution is deemed casteist.

Scene two: The project of constituting Mayawati as an icon of new India was always fraught. Writing just a year after the 2007 Uttar Pradesh elections, Sagarika Ghose, then senior editor of the TV news channel CNN-IBN, argued in a column for the *Hindustan Times* that "Identity politics in the 21st century, in times defined by economic change, mobility and the free flow of ideas and information, is a supreme condescension to the voter. Vote for me simply because I am a Dalit or a Hindu or a Muslim may work in the first election, to secure an initial mandate. But the mandate fritters away if the demagogue fails to grow up and become a bridge-builder between communities."[77]

In an India that is "new," where economic change and the mobility of both socioeconomic status and ideas is deemed possible, Mayawati's dalit identity a year after the election was remarked upon and represented as "identity politics" because—or so Ghose notes—she is "angry again, raging again, on the warpath again." Even as Ghose acknowledges that "every upper-caste, however progressive and liberal, must *never* be allowed to forget his civilisational guilt," she nevertheless critiques Mayawati for having slipped from her role as a "social reconciler" to "being the upper-caste hater."[78] Within the hegemonic story about the commoner and new India, a dalit leader like Mayawati can only be legitimated and narrated within its plotlines if she enables a tale about movement from rabble-rousing anger to social reconcilement. An assertion of dalitness qua dalitness stands repudiated as anger and mocked as self-aggrandizement; here Mayawati slips back into the category dalit queen. The difference between Modi's "King of Hindu Hearts" persona and Mayawati's "dalit queen" must be underlined here. For Modi, the iconic movement to "man of development" and "visionary leader" still retained the sign of Hindu Hriday Samrat; it was the foundation, in fact, that produced the acceleration to iconic status. This was true, as we have seen, for Bachchan as well. Without the angry young man, the brand father could not exist. The angry young man gives the brand father his affective force, just as the Hindu Hriday Samrat is the fulcrum of the visionary leader. Yet the political and discursive demand on dalit ki beti Mayawati is that she renounce her political assertion of dalitness in order to retain her iconic status.

The assertion of a dalit identity is discursively marked and then repudiated by a sustained interest in the construction of statues and memorials in Uttar Pradesh under Mayawati's leadership. *India Today* magazine noted a few months after the BSP's electoral victory in 2007 that Mayawati was "using the state machinery aggressively to imprint Dalit imagery on to the public consciousness."[79] The construction of the "Kanshi Ram Memorial," the "Kanshi Ram Research Center," the "Kanshi Ram Auditorium," and the "Rama Bai Ambedkar Memorial" is recognized within the story as "dalitising the landscape,"[80] and is defined as being at odds with the social reconcilement project that the BSP had initiated in the election campaign. The *India Today* article thus goes on to argue that "sarvajan hitaya, sarvajan sukhai (welfare and prosperity of all sections of society)" might be Mayawati's rhetoric, "but her actions are a far cry from such lofty ideals."[81] Mayawati's interest in constructing her own statues is particularly censured as a "policy of self-glorification" and conceit.[82] Her humble beginnings are discussed in order to point to her new wealth. In an article titled "Poor Little Rich Girl," *India Today* notes that "this daughter of a post office employee now owns, among other things, a house in Delhi's diplomatic area, Chanakyapuri, worth Rs 18 crore [about $2 million at the current rate of exchange], commercial properties in the Capital's business district Connaught Place, diamonds and jewellery worth Rs. 1.5 crore [about $140,000 at the current rate of exchange]."[83] Here then is also a second iteration of Mayawati's gendered subjectivity, the impossibility of her iconicity is marked by a discussion of her acquisition and display of feminized objects such as diamonds and silks. Mayawati was also censured by the liberal press for organizing an elaborate display of power to celebrate the BSP's twenty-fifth anniversary. At the event, Mayawati conspicuously received a garland made of 1,000 rupee notes. Her display of wealth and cash (even though she has never been found guilty of tax fraud and the large sum of money she pays as tax is on record) is consistently repudiated within a public culture that has nevertheless turned to the celebration of cash as a marker of "new" India.

Mayawati's wealth (read: corruption) and her caste politics are sometimes depicted as in line with and similar to the strategies adopted by most politicians in India, but particularly in UP. Thus Rajdeep Sardesai argues that "in the journey from dirt to the high citadels of power, one sometimes does not have the luxury of being a *mahatma*."[84] In a similar vein, Sagarika Ghose notes that political behavior in the state of Uttar Pradesh is about "business opportunity" and argues that "no ideology or belief systems or loyalty to a leader ties them [politicians in UP] to a party . . . what motivates them is purely the calculation of future opportunity."[85] In this particular narrative about subaltern politics in Uttar Pradesh there is both the acknowledgement of the oppression that is seen to have produced particular political strategies and behavior (and thus Mayawati can be cast as a political entrepreneur) and a simultaneous repudiation of it, specifically when there is a political assertion of caste and a demand for recognition. Rajdeep Sardesai writes: "In a sense, the rise of Mayawati only exposes the utter bankruptcy of the political system, a system increasingly devoid of morality or ideology."[86] In this double move, Mayawati as the first dalit female chief minister in independent India is the pride of Indian democracy and an icon of "new" India, but as the conceited and corrupt "dalit queen" is also its lament.

Scene three: In the winter of 2009, I set out in search of Mayawati's autobiographical text. The autobiography appears as a trace within the popular cultural stories that purport to report on, make sense of, and explain Mayawati for their largely middle-class, English-speaking audiences. I call the appearance of the autobiography within such representations a trace because the text appears as both a presence and an absence within these representations—it is mentioned, defined as an autobiography, and then not referenced at all, to the point where its title remains absent, unknowable. As such, the autobiography functions as the "foreclosed figure of the native informant"[87] within such representations; in its absence-presence it helps authenticate knowledge about the dalit, seen as the historical other. The simple and simplistic gesture of citing the autobiography, even in the absence of any engagement with the text itself, nevertheless identifies and marks the author of the representation as an expert on the dalit other. Having read many stories about Mayawati's self-aggrandizement, I assumed that I would be able to easily locate her autobiography in the city of Lucknow, the capital of Uttar Pradesh, the state she governed at the time. Surely, a politician who purportedly commissions spectacular statues of herself would also make available her autobiographical narrative. Mayawati's Hindi-language autobiography—*Mere Sanghursh-may Jeevan evam Bahujan Movement ka Safarnama* [The Journey of My Life in Struggle and that of the Bahujan Movement], published in two volumes in 2006 by her political party, the Bahujan Samaj Party, is—contrary to expectation—not an easily available text. It cannot be found in bookstores even within the state she governed. Moreover, it cannot be purchased from the Bahujan Samaj Party's own bookstore and publishing unit in Lucknow. My quest to locate the book took me to the BSP headquarters in Lucknow, where I obtained an appointment with Mayawati's personal assistant. The office was sparse; it did not contain a framed picture of Mayawati, nor could I locate any material announcing or celebrating the chief minister's tenure. I was seated with petitioners who had come with more immediate requests about employment, education, and healthcare. After some polite conversation comparing the Hindi-language press with the English-language press, Mayawati's assistant gave me the names of a couple of people who he said would help me locate the autobiography. I was however unable to procure the book even after contacting the two sources that Mayawati's assistant had directed me to. The manager of the BSP bookstore informed me that the book could not be purchased directly from a bookstore because Mayawati and the party publish and circulate limited copies of the book only on particular occasions to raise funds for election campaigns. The two-volume autobiography, as he rightly informed me, can only be procured from a BSP minister. I was finally able to procure the *Safarnama* through a journalist and friend who had purchased the two volumes from a BSP minister on my behalf (for a sum of Rs. 2000 or $27).

What do we learn about the iconicity of a political actor like Mayawati when we read popular media's descriptions of her self-aggrandizement in conjunction with the deliberate invisibility of her authorial, writerly voice? Following Michael Warner, we could argue that the stories of self-aggrandizement that regularly appear about Mayawati in popular representations enable the "public" constituted by these representations themselves to "appropriate" her iconic status by "reminding us that . . . [she] do[es] not possess the phallic power of [her] images—we do."[88] In other words, if the construction and the visual spectacle of memorials, parks, cash, diamonds, and elaborate birthday celebrations intend to signify the burgeoning "public" might of Mayawati, then the reiteration of the trope of self-aggrandizement by the English-language press enables the "public" it constitutes through its narratives to appropriate the power of that iconicity by "reminding us" that "we" are its final arbiter. By deliberately making 'private'—in the sense of its inaccessibility—a purportedly "public" autobiographical volume (such that the desire to procure the *Safarnama* necessities embarking on a journey ourselves), Mayawati can be read as attempting to trouble this form of "publicness" engendered by her iconicity that necessitates the performance of universality, openness and access.[89] Or to put it differently, the inaccessibility of the autobiography can be read as enabling Mayawati to appropriate the power of her own iconicity, reminding us that *she*, in fact, remains its final arbiter.

More importantly here, I want to reiterate that the *Safarnama* be read as a material cultural artifact that serves the function of "poetic world making,"[90] constituting a public through the modalities of kinship and genealogy. The *Safarnama* is a 2,000-page text (each volume encompassing close to a thousand pages) made with rich, glossy paper, with gold-brushed edges. It is a weighty book and is intended to be seen as significant; in its materiality it demands the distance and respect accorded to an encyclopedia or religious scripture. This is not a book that calls on its public to consume its narrative and digest it. As its first few pages clearly indicate, the *Safarnama* is presented as a "blue book" on the bahujan samaj and the BSP. It is thus presented as the seminal text—*the* textbook, in fact—on Mayawati, the bahujan samaj, and the BSP.

The *Safarnama* constructs a lineage, calling on the past, the present, and descendants in the future. The autobiography positions its author as a powerful political actor fated to lead the "public" that she is a part of, and thus the text points to the uncanny (the fact that Mayawati was born the year Ambedkar died) as well as to deliberate agency (the book was released in 2006, the year which marked Mayawati's 50th birthday, Ambedkar's 50th death anniversary, the Indian constitution's 55th year in promulgation, and the 2,550th year of Buddha's nirvana) to represent and constitute the dalit public it then addresses and to define Mayawati as the leader of this public. She is represented as being the descendent of the political agents who first hailed and constituted the dalit public.[91]

Scene four: In the fall of 2011, Mayawati inaugurated a large memorial park called the Dalit Prerana Sthal or the Dalit Inspiration Space in Noida, now a suburb of the Indian capital city, Delhi. The mainstream English-language news media in India broadcasted the event live, reiterating now-familiar tropes and representational patterns associated with the then chief minister of Uttar Pradesh, including feminizing her iconicity through a discussion of her clothes, her purportedly "favorite" color pink, the conspicuous consumption of expensive technology, and other products as well as dwelling incessantly on the scale at which the cityscape had been altered, to define and underline her actions as selfish, greedy self-aggrandizement. The derisive focus of most of the broadcast was the massive statue of Mayawati herself (unprecedented, according to the broadcast, for a politician to commemorate herself with her own statue) situated within the memorial park. This was the final piece of evidence, the broadcast suggested, of the chief minister's megalomania. The cost of the park—estimated at $113 million—was reiterated along with the argument that the large sum of money could have been better spent elsewhere, but particularly for the education of dalit girls. The ceremonial presence of Buddhist monks during the inauguration, the positioning of the Mayawati statue in the park with statues of B. R. Ambedkar, the most significant political and intellectual leader for dalits and the framer of the Indian constitution, as well as Kanshi Ram, the founder of the Bahujan Samaj Party, and other dalit leaders was conspicuously not remarked upon.

In the summer of 2015, when the BSP was no longer in power in Uttar Pradesh and had not been since 2012, I visited the much-vilified Dalit Prerana Sthal in Noida. Its vastness was my first affective perception of the space. There is an attempt here to enthrall and construct awe in the mind of the visitor.[92] Sitting on the banks of the Yamuna, straddling UP and the capital city of Delhi, such that you witness the park before you head into Delhi from Uttar Pradesh and experience it as you leave Delhi for Uttar Pradesh, the park beckons and demands attention. The Prerana Sthal seeks to create a specific spatial experience through vastness and the enormity of the memorial structure itself. The park is both horizontally and vertically vast: it occupies 82 acres of garden and park space and the visitor must consistently direct her gaze upward in addition to looking from a distance in order to take in the structure in its entirety. The massive statues of dalit leaders B.R. Ambedkar, Kanshi Ram, and Mayawati inside the main structure of the Prerana Sthal command attention. From a distance, the beautiful sandstone memorial structure appears like a secular monument, but the experience of walking up to the building, climbing its stairs, and walking along its vast foyer that leads into a darkened enclosure where the three statues are housed feels similar to entering the sanctum sanctorum of an extremely well-endowed temple. In this, the Prerana Sthal establishes a "way of seeing": This space commands a respect, a distance, and the "object" (the statue) is imbued with an aura, an enchantment, and a mythos that has power precisely because it cannot be consumed but must be gazed upon. The statues of Ambedkar, Kanshi Ram, and Mayawati look out onto a horizon that cannot be perceived by the visitor. These are not gods then that grant *darshan*. They are behemoths that command—take up—space, that forcefully mark their presence. In doing so, they demand that you account for your presence as well. The Prerana Sthal enables a visuality (a mode of seeing) and a spatiality (a mode of moving the body within a space) that appears familiar but is also distinctive. In its expansiveness, which appears to pause time itself, it is reminiscent of the Mughal-era monuments that have fashioned the landscape and topography of the region, but in its centering of the statues within a chamber that must be accessed via a flight of stairs and around which you are compelled to circumambulate, the Prerana Sthal is also reminiscent of the modern Hindu temple. The statues of dalit heroes deliberately eschew darshan; the visitor must direct her gaze upward but can never hope to catch the eye of the statue. The circumambulation does not reward you with idols of other heroes but is designed to narrate the mythology of the bahujan movement. The Prerana Sthal appears to write a history, but also eschews historical time. The Prerana Sthal is replete with statues of elephants—the BSP's electoral symbol—and is a distinctly political space. If this is a temple, it is unlike any Hindu temple you may have visited.

The Prerana Sthal is insistent that it marks, commemorates, inserts, celebrates a movement—the bahujan movement. The murals behind the statues aim to tell a story of this movement. B. R. Ambedkar, Jyotirao Phule, Shahu Maharaj, Kanshi Ram, and Mayawati are etched as the vanguard of this movement. The bronze murals also register significant moments in the movement: the 1927 Mahad satyagraha, the campaign by Ambedkar to allow untouchables to drink water from a public tank in Mahad, Maharashtra; the conversion of Ambedkar and almost 60,000 other dalits to Buddhism in 1956; the formal presentation of the constitution in 1950; the formation of the All India Backward and Minority Communities Employees Federation (BAMCEF) in 1971 by Kanshi Ram; and the induction of Mayawati into the BSP and the subsequent recognition of her as a legatee of Kanshi Ram. The murals also mark Mayawati's stints as chief minister of Uttar Pradesh.

The Prerana Sthal captures space, asserts presence, and demands recognition for the bahujan movement but also and significantly establishes a kinship and a community for the bahujan. While the commanding statues assert presence and demand that the role of dalit scholars, activists, and politicians be recognized, the murals could almost function like a family album. Cast in metal that freezes for posterity significant moments in the kin's history, it thus simultaneously defines the shape and form of the kin itself. One of the murals depicts dalit leaders meeting with Muslim leaders; this particular mural does not commemorate a specific meeting, and there is no date or location attached to the mural that would allow the visitor to recognize it as a specific historical event. The Muslim leaders participating in the meeting are not named and the purpose of the meeting is not defined either. In these absences, the mural must be read as marking the inclusion of Muslims within the bahujan kin.

Mayawati's statues are a dense semiotic node. If the Modi mask is an assertion of presence, specifically the aggressively masculine presence of a Hindu majority, Mayawati's statues spectacularly stage the presence of a bahujan samaj. The form

that this assertion of presence takes—enabled by the statues, the presence of Bud-
dhist monks at the inauguration, and the spatiality of the Prerana Sthal—disallows
any appropriation into a Hindu public or new India. The Prerana Sthal constitutes
kin and kinship ties, formulating a genealogy for the bahujan and does so in public; in doing so, it tempts appropriation only to subvert the attempt.[93]

If the violence of caste specifically and the constitution of outcastes (racial and
religious others) more generally dwells at least in part in the sundering of genealogies and the debasing of kinship ties,[94] then the *Safarnama* and the Dalit Prerana
Sthal are most productively read as artifacts performing the labor of publicly constructing a genealogy. It is this labor that produces the play between notions of
the public and private and engenders a discourse about aggrandizement and
megalomania in the public sphere even as the narrative about the life and times
of Mayawati and the political party remain elusive. More importantly, this labor
articulates the spectacular with the real through strategies that are different from
those we have been tracking thus far. The suture between the spectacular (the
memorial park, the *Safarnama*, and Mayawati's iconicity itself) and the real (the
bahujan samaj) in this case is *political*. The *real* man and woman—dalit, lower-
caste rural poor—in the space of the memorial park or within the text of the *Safarnama* are not transformed into the abstract category common, but are instead
grouped within the political category bahujan samaj (the majority society). The
Safarnama, much like the memorial park, constitutes a spectacular discursive and
material space for the bahujan samaj to recognize and assert itself as a public—a
political public. The movement that Mayawati's iconicity tracks, moreover, is genealogical. For the constituency that the *Safarnama* sees as its own—the bahujan
samaj—it constitutes a historiography. Thus, even as there is an insistent assertion
of Mayawati as a political actor within the text, she is also continually placed
within a long line of dalit political actors. This is true about the memorial park as
well. She is represented as the legatee (albeit *the* chosen one) of a rich history of
dalit political thought and action rather than a founding figure. This assertion is
as much about self-respect as it is about a public constitution of genealogy and
kin.[95] The constitution of kin and genealogy for the historically dispossessed
requires both the public spectacle—read by those outside the samaj or the public
as aggrandizement—*and* the private and more strategically constructed narrative.

The twining of the spectacular with the real, such that Hindutva neoliberalism
is mythologized into the spectacular event of national renewal and then articulated to the abstract but affective category of the common or the ordinary has, as I
have been arguing, been a significantly popular narrative strategy to win consent
for both economic liberalization and Hindu nationalism. The constitution and
circulation of iconicity is an important modality through which the common as
an abstract and emotive category is formulated. Movement—from subalternity to
desiring consumer and entrepreneur—rather than embodiment or assemblage is
what gives the iconic image of this conjuncture its affective charge. This movement is, in fact, emotive and iconic of its time, popular discourse will suggest,

precisely because it is apolitical. Mayawati's iconicity is an unruly one in this context. It twines the spectacular and the real in modes that are distinctly political, the spectacles that constitute her iconicity labor to trace a movement for both Mayawati the individual and the bahujan samaj that is genealogical. Rather than trace the possessive individualism of the entrepreneur as the apogee of subalternity, Mayawati's iconicity performs the loving work of constituting kin and family.

Despite rising unemployment, agrarian distress, and a slump in industrial production, Narendra Modi's BJP won a second term in the 2019 general elections. Standing under a shower of rose petals, Modi claimed that the people of the nation had emerged victorious.[96] Large corporations across a range of industries had supported Modi, and the chairman of Vedanta Resources, Anil Agarwal, exulted that as Modi took "another step" towards the "next progressive innings . . . his vision will help India take a leap in its journey of growth."[97] In tangible terms, these corporate leaders expected foreign fund inflows to continue, a cut in corporate taxes and a "healthy ecosystem for businesses and entrepreneurs."[98] Hindu nationalism had twined with neoliberalism through the narrative form of spectacular realism. It was only appropriate that at the end of the year that brought Modi back to political power for a second term, Yashraj Studios announced that it began filming a sequel to its 2005 hit *Bunty aur Babli*. Spectacular realism and Hindutva neoliberalism had dug their heels into the cultural soil.

3 · THE ENTREPRENEUR
New Identities for New Times

> The story of India's rise has clearly been … [the] story of the Indian entrepreneur, who after a long, painful period in shackles has been allowed to come out into the sun …
>
> —Nandan Nilekani, *Imagining India: Ideas for a New Century*, 2008

The entrepreneur plays a significant role within the narrative patterns that seek to connote, signify, and represent new India. The renewed and emergent nation, as we have been tracking, is narrated through the advent of new time. This conception of new time is narrated by linking together multiple temporalities. As such, Hindutva neoliberalism as a conjuncture is narrated through the deliberate articulation of diverse temporalities, yet it is nevertheless described as new. The entrepreneur as an embodiment, identity, and identification is crucial to new India precisely because he is narrated as both familiar and new.[1] Just as the architects of economic liberalization, including Montek Singh Ahluwalia, insist on the home-grown quality of liberalization and thereby eschew the argument that neoliberalism was an import forced on the common people of the nation, the entrepreneur is described as a familiar identity, a recognizable aspiration that was once obstructed but is now free. The story about obstructed time that we examined in chapter 1 is therefore crucial to the story of the entrepreneur. The freeing of the entrepreneur, the story goes, enables time to move unimpeded and allows for the construction of new India. In 2004, when Manmohan Singh, then prime minister of India, had defined economic liberalization as "epochal,"[2] he had also argued that this event had released the innovative and "entrepreneurial spirits" latent in the nation, allowing the economy to grow at a fast pace.[3] In a similar register, the *New York Times* had written about the lower-caste and untouchable entrepreneur, for whom the story suggested economic liberalization had enabled the shedding of caste-based oppression and allowed for his transformation into that which was "unthinkable a generation ago": a wealthy businessman.[4] In chapter 2, we tracked the narrative processes through which this movement is constituted as iconic. Here, we trace the stories that narrate the entrepreneur as the culmination of that movement; entrepreneurialism is narrated as the spectacular mountaintop for the journeying commoner. The entrepreneur thus comes to embody the renewal of the nation.[5]

The hegemony of the entrepreneurial subjectivity is, in fact, a global phenomenon linked inextricably to the new forms that global capital has acquired, which includes the information technology boom, the rollback and critique of the welfare state, and rapid urban growth. In 2009, the *Economist* published a special report on entrepreneurship in which it argued that entrepreneurialism encouraged creativity and economic dynamism, passionately suggesting that the "revolution for the current generation is the entrepreneurial one."[6] Moreover, the magazine listed the encouragement of entrepreneurial capitalism as a possible solution for the economic woes of various European nations and the sluggish economic growth rates in the United States. Essayist and critic William Deresiewicz, writing in the *New York Times*, had argued that "the small business is the idealized social form of our time ... our ... hero is not the artist or reformer, not the saint or scientist, but the entrepreneur (think of Steve Jobs, our new deity)," and linked this preponderance of money and business to "the heroic age of dot-com entrepreneurship" plus a "distrust of large organizations, including government, as well as the sense ... that its every man for himself."[7] Extending this argument, Deresiewicz noted that the "self today is an entrepreneurial self, a self that's packaged to be sold."[8]

Wendy Brown has argued that the "entrepreneurialization" of the self in the late twentieth century, wherein the self becomes a "portfolio of self-investments" ("including childcare, education, health, appearance and old age provisions"), where urban households "transform their possessions, time, connections, and selves into sources of capitalization" (think leasing out rooms of your home on Airbnb, driving for Lyft or Uber, and other part-time sources of income), and where "the family is retasked with providing for every kind of dependent—the young, the old, the infirm, the unemployed, the indebted student, or the depressed or addicted adult," has resulted in not only bringing capitalism back from the brink following its crises in the 1970s and in the new millennium but has also recuperated "both the individual and the family at the very moment of their seeming extinction."[9] In other words, the entrepreneurialization of the self is a retooling of capitalism following the crises caused by its failures but it is also a response to the critique leveled against it. In chapter 1, we examined the narrative processes through which development as a concept-image is used similarly to respond to the failure of capitalism and to manage the threat posed by the critique of capital. Development as a concept-image appropriated the lived experience of obstruction, of inequity and disparity, and narrated the muscular, individual visionary as well as technocratic strategies seen as apolitical as the resolution of that experience of stalled movement or immobility. The entrepreneurialization of the self responds specifically to the massification of society and the ostensible destruction of what we might call pastoral patriarchy by capitalism through urbanization, the disintegration of the joint family, and so forth. If capitalism was critiqued for producing a deindividualized mass that nevertheless threatened a socialist revolution, then entrepreneurialization was and continues to be a counter by "reindividuat-ing" as well as "regrounding" the self "in practices of self-provisioning."[10] This is achieved *not* through the dismantling of capitalism but through shoring it up. Entrepreneurialization is thus an appropriation of the critique leveled against cap-ital that paradoxically works to reinforce and entrench capitalism.

While entrepreneurialization has a distinct history,[11] we have also noted that the entrepreneur as an identification or identity category in India is narrated as both familiar and new. The familiarity of the entrepreneur can be understood by considering the longer genealogy of the narration of the self as a package that can be sold. In other words, the narration of the entrepreneur as an identity category may have a specific and shorter history but the narration of the self as a proprietor of capabilities that can be traded or marketed has a longer genealogy. Political theorists such as C. B. Macpherson have argued that possessive individualism was in fact a key element of liberal democratic theory, the roots of which can be traced to seventeenth-century Western thought. In his groundbreaking work published in 1962, Macpherson argued that divergent thinkers of liberal philosophy never-theless shared an assumption about the conceptualization of the individual. The individual, he argued, was conceived by thinkers such as Hobbes, Locke, and others "as essentially the proprietor of his own person or capacities," or as the "owner of himself."[12] Such a conceptualization suggests that "human essence is freedom from dependence on the wills of others, and freedom is a function of possession."[13] Macpherson suggested that this was a form of individualism that was "possessive." It was a form of individualism where the relation of ownership had acquired such primacy that it was deterministic of the self's freedom, the real-ization of their full potential, and most importantly, ownership was read back onto the very nature of the individual or the self. This form of individualism assumes that society is composed of a series of market relations and that the indi-vidual as the "proprietor of his person and capacities" did not owe society any-thing.[14] Possessive individualism is the unquestioned, covert but foundational assumption, MacPherson argued, of much liberal-democratic thought.

So, the possessive individual is a familiar character. He has appeared in stories about freedom, democracy, and the self for a while now. In India too, this posses-sive individual or the businessman, the proprietor, or the trader was a familiar fig-ure, except that he appeared in a body that was specifically identified by caste and was often denigrated as a harasser of the common person and as dishonorable. Within the Hindu four-order (*chatur-varna*) caste hierarchy, the trading and bank-ing occupations are assigned to Vaishya castes. As Harish Damodaran details in his study of entrepreneurs and caste in India, "The Vaishya held a higher position than the Shudra (peasant and manual laborer), but was vastly inferior to the Brah-min (priest) and the Kshatriya (warrior)."[15] Business, including the work of the moneylender, shopkeeper, wholesaler, or factory owner has often been associated with distinct caste communities and has relied on the community networks that

are defined by caste. As such, Damodaran has argued that business in India is associated with "distinct communities and capitalism developed correspondingly
through a number of business communities rather than an integrated business
class."[16] As we have been tracking throughout this book, capitalism but also liberalism roll in the particularity of the soil in India to acquire a form that recasts the
hierarchical power of the locality (caste) even as capitalism and liberalism position themselves as familiarly local. To put it simply, the possessive individual as a
character fundamental to liberalism is *not* new or alien to the political-economic
or cultural landscape of India. Recast within a type of soil that is saturated by the
caste system, the possessive individual in India is often instead associated with a
caste and as Damodaran's work reveals, embeds his "economic behavior" within
"concrete social relations."[17]

Grouped with the landlord and the moneylender, the businessman who was
often also narrated as a smuggler in popular discourse in India was linked to either
one of the Vaishya castes in the Hindu four-order hierarchy or to Christianity
(particularly true of the smuggler characters) and Islam as well as to conceptions of moral corruption, unscrupulous ruthlessness, and criminality. As Pankaj
Mishra noted in the *New York Times*, one of the consequences of the anticolonial
nationalist movement led by political leaders like M. K. Gandhi was a "low opinion" in public discourse "of profit-seekers" and "private wealth creators" and a concomitant focus in popular cinema and state television on the "rural poor."[18] In
entrepreneur, public intellectual, bureaucrat, and politician Nandan Nilekani's
story about the unshackling of the entrepreneur in his best-selling book *Imagining
India*, business more generally and the entrepreneur more specifically stood inval-
idated in the early years following independence because of the political ideology
and concomitant policy that maintained hegemony in postcolonial India. Nilekani argues in his popular history of India's political economy since independence
from British colonialism that the "anti-business policy" of those early years was
shaped by two factors—"the determination to take the country as far away as possible from the institutions that dominated colonial India and an enthusiasm to
embrace the promise of a new, rising world order, socialism."[19] This political hegemony of socialism, motivated by the desire to define the newly formed nation as
distinct from its colonial master, ensured that business remained largely in the
hands of specific caste groups, according to this narrative. Films such as *Mother
India* (Mehboob Khan, 1957), *Namak Haraam* (Betrayor/Traitor, Hrishikesh
Mukherjee, 1973), *Amar Akbar Anthony* (Manmohan Desai, 1977), *Jaane Bhi
Do Yaaro* (Let It Go Friends, Kundan Shah, 1983), and the angry young man films
like *Deewar* (The Wall, Yash Chopra, 1975), among many others produced until
the 1990s, cast the possessive individual as morally decrepit. Even in *Mr. India*, the
1987 Shekhar Kapur film we discussed in the introductory chapter to define
the contours of the form of spectacular realism, Mogambo or the spectacular villain's plans are given material or real form by the shopkeeper, the landlord, and the
businessman.

How then does the entrepreneur become the ideal identification in the time of Hindutva neoliberalism? To answer that question, we must pay closer analytical attention to the stories that crafted the shopkeeper and the businessman as the villain. Such an analysis will, in fact, reveal to us that the visionary individual and resolute, masculine individualism continued to be reinforced even in narratives that espoused a "low opinion" of "profit seekers." In the award-winning 1976 film *Manthan* (The Churning, Shyam Benegal) for instance, the village businessman, whose ruthless self-interest, which includes setting arbitrary prices and extends to willfully destructive manipulation as well as criminal behavior such as arson, is cast as a foil against a state employee and a veterinarian who enters the village to help set up a dairy cooperative. *Manthan* narrates the cooperative or community ownership of the means of production as the route to equity. While the dairy owner suggests that development efforts for the village should be focused on health and "family planning" or birth control, the employee of the state insists that equity must be any development effort's goal. That equity, he argues, can only be achieved if the villagers exercise control over the production and sale of milk. Recall that in chapter 1 it is the appearance of the term *equity* in a World Development Report that sets off a little storm in the commentary and opinion sections of India's English-language press. That little storm assumed that equity signified the redistribution of wealth or the radical reshaping of the means of production. The use of the term *equity* was therefore seen as a threat that needed immediate re-narration. The dairy owner in *Manthan* attempts the same re-narration of the "ideals" of equity espoused by the state representative. He insists that his paternalistic relationships with the villagers who are also his customers ensures that they are well taken care of. He suggests that his work had helped build the economy of the region, that he had personal connections and relationships with all the villagers built over a period of thirty years, and argues that those relationships would be sundered by the inevitably short life of the cooperative. In other words, he narrates his transactional relationships with the villagers through the idiom of paternal and paternalistic care. This ostensible relation of care, which is founded on and draws sustenance from caste and patriarchal hierarchies, is in fact the re-narration of equity. The film uses the character of the dairy owner to narrate the particularity of the possessive individual in India. In the context of Hindu patriarchy shot through with caste hierarchies and feudal relations of extraction, the businessman/dairy owner narrates possessive individualism in the idiom of familial and paternalistic relations. Here, the possessive individual is still the proprietor of his own person and capacities, but individualism is defined through patriarchal and caste-based hierarchies. The authority of caste and patriarchy imbues the possessive individual in India with authoritative force. *Manthan* sets such a possessive individual against the conception of a cooperative. The film itself was a cooperative effort, being produced by the Gujarat Co-operative Milk Marketing Federation, and the posters marketing the film announced that *Manthan* was a story presented by 500,000 farmers of Gujarat. Each of the 500,000 farmers contributed

Rs. 2 to the production of the film.[20] The film's narrative was inspired by the movement to constitute milk cooperatives in the western Indian state of Gujarat starting in the late 1940s that culminated in the formation of a nationwide milk grid that connected farmers with consumers.

The contradiction at the core of *Manthan*'s narrative, however, is that it feels compelled to tell the story of a cooperative through the chronicle of an individual. Dr. Rao, the veterinarian and state employee, comes to embody the conception of the cooperative. This embodiment centers a masculine ethos: Rao is characterized as a hard worker, incorruptible, principled, steadfast, and unflinchingly committed to the idea of a dairy cooperative. In previous work, I have traced the genealogy of such popular masculinities that embody an unflinching and singular moral commitment that is defined as duty to nationalist discourse, both anticolonial nationalism as well as Hindu nationalism.[21] Here, my contention is that even as *Manthan* aims to tell the story about the struggles to form a milk cooperative in rural Gujarat, the hero of the tale is a duty-bound, morally upright man. The narrative works to construct a libidinal charge for this character, done in part by linking the commitment to an ideal to a narration of masculine morality and more overtly through the characterization of sexual tension between Rao and a woman from the village (Bindu). The woman is characterized as feisty, self-assured, and self-efficient, a perfect feminine foil for Rao, the embodiment of unflinching masculine morality. Rao's wife, on the other hand, is narrated as a sickly, complaining woman. She remains largely unaware of her husband's moral force. To put it plainly, the character of the sexualized woman of the village (the feminized subaltern) is used by the film's narrative to constitute a libidinal charge around the central male character. In turn, the very conception of the cooperative acquires a masculine ethos.

There is a second contradiction in the narrative: The film plots out for its audience the cynical use of the rural woman by the businessman and the upper-caste chief of the village to destabilize the cooperative. Bindu's husband is first emasculated and then manipulated by the dairy owner and the village head to falsely implicate Rao in rape. Bindu's thumbprint, acquired under false pretenses, is used to file the police complaint. In revealing the machinations of the businessman and the village chief, *Manthan* critiques the cynical use of the subaltern woman's body by the upper castes and the businessman. Even as it reveals this manipulation though, *Manthan*'s narrative *also* appropriates Bindu to serve its own textual ends, which are to constitute Rao as the moral, masculine core of the narrative and to imbue his moral force with a libidinal charge.

We have previously discussed how the masculine visionary is central to the concept-image of development in India. In the post–economic liberalization 2004 Ashutosh Gowariker–directed film *Swades: We the People* (Our Land) that we discussed in chapter 1, this visionary is a diasporic male. He is an engineer and uses his own capital to bring electricity to a village. The story that emerges when we read *Manthan* alongside *Swades* is that this masculine ethos is central to nationalist

discourses, for development as well as for the narration of economic liberalization. Moreover, we can see how Mohan Bhargava, *Swades*'s central character, is a
descendent of Dr. Rao from *Manthan*. Secondly, both films present caste and
caste-based hierarchies as an obstacle: in the case of *Manthan*, for the realization
of the cooperative and therefore for the structural constitution of equity, and in
Swades, for development conceived as improved well-being. *Manthan* narrates
an especially harsh indictment of caste and reveals the violence used to maintain
caste-based hierarchies. When a dalit becomes the chair of the cooperative board,
defeating the upper-caste village head in an election, the film reaches its climax as
violent vengeance is meted out on the lower-caste residents of the village. *Manthan*'s
critique of the possessive individual, moreover, emphasizes the businessman's
reinforcement of caste-based hierarchies and his cynical use of those hierarchies
in their gendered form to maintain his own dominance and control over the means
of production. This critique deploys morally upright masculinity as the embodiment of the cooperative and as the foil for the possessive individual. Even though
the film ends with the villagers (particularly those belonging to the lower castes)
running the cooperative following Rao's departure, the narrative does not dis-
abuse its audience of the moral authority of the individual. Almost thirty years
later, in the character of Mohan Bhargava in *Swades*, the individual is a visionary,
unsaddled from the state and the conception of a cooperative; he takes on the
entrenched hierarchies of the caste system individually and quite literally brings
light to the village.

Dwelling on *Manthan*'s narrative enables us to see that even the critique of the
possessive individual in popular Indian discourse centers the individual and his
masculine ethos. As a consequence, possessive individualism itself was never rigor-
ously repudiated and continued to hold ground in public culture. *Manthan* aimed
to reveal the articulations between caste-based hierarchies, feudal forms of patron-
age and power, and capitalism; in order to do so, however, it continually reinforced
the might of the upper-caste male committed to his duty and sexualized the rural
lower-caste woman. In other pieces of contemporary popular discourse, such as the
angry young man films, the critique of the possessive individual focused on his
investment in caste-based hierarchies in ways that often caricatured the middle
castes and their occupations in trade, commerce, and finance.

This popular discourse from the 1970s is the foundation for the insistent narration of the entrepreneur as a new yet familiar identification in new India. Continuing to center the individual (even when a collective was being described), this
discourse had suggested that the problem with the possessive individual was his
investment in caste-based hierarchies. The shift that occurs in the characterization
of the possessive individual in new India is therefore the narration of a rupture in
the link between caste and entrepreneurialism. It is this rupture that is deemed as
the unshackling of the possessive individual and as having engendered the newness of the nation. Thus, Nilekani, in a foreword to Damodaran's *India's New Capitalists*, notes that "the market has ... been opened up to anyone with the talent

and energy to take advantage of it . . . and existing business houses based within traditional communities have had to adapt in order to make the necessary transition from a 'community bazaar' to a modern global and structured marketplace."[22] As such, the entrepreneur is central to the narration of both neoliberalism in India but also Hindu nationalism. For neoliberalism, the entrepreneur helps suture the spectacle of the commodity and the brand to the reality of the commoner. Economic liberalization, this story insists, unshackled the commoner so he could become the ambitious entrepreneur, a possessive individual who is no longer beholden to the whims and fancies of social relations. For the leaders of Hindu nationalism, as we have discussed in the previous chapter on iconicity, the caste system did not necessitate an eradication; caste simply needed to be hidden in plain sight, in other words within a universalized Hindu identity.[23] The dissociation of the possessive individual's link with caste and its recasting or re-narration as the unshackling of the commoner's true nature within popular discourse found resonance with Hindu nationalism's own narrative about new India freeing the Hindu to embrace his own true identity with pride. It bears reiterating that the BJP's traditional constituency has been the middle castes, including the trading and business communities. We will explore the linkage between Hindu nationalism and neoliberalism in the context of the middle-caste trader and businessman a little later in the chapter.

The possessive individual in India, who until the 1990s had been attached to a caste identity, thus becomes an entrepreneur who is defined as a cosmopolitan figure. The cosmopolitanism of the entrepreneur is linked with global capitalism, indeed with neoliberalism, and it is precisely this link that allows it to be valorized. A word here about cosmopolitanism: Discourse that valorized globalization, such as the arguments a reader encountered in the writing of a columnist such as Thomas Friedman in the *New York Times* or Nandan Nilekani, linked cosmopolitanism to modernity. It might be hard to imagine now in the midst of the resurrection of ethno-nationalisms the world over but globalization and indeed neoliberalism were enthusiastically heralded as the death knell for nationalism in the new millennium. Friedman had famously argued that the world would become flat post-globalization. This intellectual climate of the late 1990s and the early years of the new millennium celebrated globalization and ostensibly rejected nationalism as a "particularistic mode of collective consciousness or a private ethnic identity that disguises itself as a universalism," and cosmopolitanism was seen as a political alternative.[24] It was considered the liberal, political substitute to a putatively discredited nationalism in the time of globalization. This was the argument made by Nilekani, Friedman, and indeed much of the commentary in India that celebrated the entrepreneur, even though political and cultural theorists even at this time had argued that holding a wake for nationalism was premature. And they were right: nationalism did not die with globalization or neoliberalism, and in fact, as we have been tracking through the course of this book, it neatly intersected with it. What we are discussing here with the entrepreneur is in fact the ways in which his ostensible cosmopolitanism serves to constitute and reinforce the potency of the nation and of national belonging within popular narratives in India. Cosmopolitanism did not portend death for nationalism; it reinforced it by enabling it to hide in plain sight. Through the cynical use of cosmopolitanism (i.e., by translating possessive individualism as cosmopolitanism and then defining it as belonging to the people), nationalist discourse claimed newness and suggested a disarticulation from ideas deemed retrograde by modernists, such as caste and patriarchy. The cosmopolitan entrepreneur did not annihilate caste or patriarchy; what he did instead was construct a new universal that relied on and reinforced an old particularity—specifically the possessive individual and the Hindu male. We will see through this chapter that cosmopolitanism linked distinctly to the entrepreneur, who is in turn linked to globalizing capital, serves to signify caste and gender *and* reinforce the nation as an affective concept. We will thus see that cosmopolitanism signified as freedom within popular stories in India anchors people to the nation and defines its renewal.

This chapter tracks the narrative processes through which possessive individualism is reconstituted and valorized through the subjectivity of the entrepreneur in the time of Hindutva neoliberalism. We are also tracking the recasting of the relationship between caste specifically but subalternity or inferior status more generally and possessive individualism. This is done by constituting the entrepreneur as the embodiment of possessive individualism and second, the hegemonic position of the subjectivity is justified by narrating a tale that sees the subaltern as having arrived at "freedom" through his or her transformation into an entrepreneur. As such, popular cultural stories construct and reinforce a possessive investment in the subjectivity of the entrepreneur, which is seen as the apogee of subalternity. George Lipsitz has argued in the context of the United States that the dissemination of cultural stories and systemic political economic efforts from colonial to contemporary times has worked to create "a possessive investment in whiteness for European Americans,"[25] such that "people who left Europe as Calabrians or Bohemians became something called 'whites' when they got to America and . . . that designation made all the difference in the world."[26] In other words, Lipsitz argues that political economy and culture alike institutionalized a possessive investment in whiteness in the United States. What this chapter will show is that by working out a hegemonic position for possessive individualism through the subjectivity of the entrepreneur, cultural stories circulating in popular media in neoliberal India constitute a possessive investment in entrepreneurialism. This possessive investment in entrepreneurialism is achieved through narrative processes that delink castes traditionally associated with business and entrepreneurialism from their caste moniker (this is the unshackling), even as lower-caste groups qua lower-caste groups are seen to attain radical mobility by becoming entrepreneurs. Hence, the headlines celebrating dalit entrepreneurs, or small-town lower-caste entrepreneurs. These cultural stories thus also suggest that the ethnic subaltern's possessive investment in cosmopolitan entrepreneurialism "makes all the difference in the world" (both to the subaltern and the renewed nation). Chapter 1 had revealed to us that the subaltern's demand for recognition and redistribution of resources through an assertion of caste could be defined as *casteist* through a simultaneous narration of development as *apolitical*. Here, we track the narrative processes through which the subaltern is mobilized to occupy the position of the entrepreneur; indeed, to invest in it. That possessive investment is defined as the resolution of historical, institutional, and structural marginalization.

This chapter's epigraph is a quote from Nandan Nilekani's immensely popular book *Imagining India* and succinctly captures the core of the popular narrative that has served to twine the entrepreneur to the nation and thereby articulate the spectacular with the real as well: "The story of India's rise has clearly been ... [the] story of the Indian entrepreneur, who after a long, painful period in shackles has been allowed to come out into the sun."[27] *Imagining India* was shortlisted for the *Financial Times* and Goldman Sachs Business Book of the Year in 2009 and sold over 50,000 copies in its hardcover edition within a few months of its release.[28] Nandan Nilekani, an entrepreneur himself, is one of the cofounders of Infosys Technologies, a corporation that is credited with leading the "information technology (IT) revolution" in India. As a bureaucrat in the Indian National Congress–led government in 2009, he was responsible for executing the "Unique Identity" program for the Indian state. The program aimed to provide an identification number for all Indian residents and create a database of the entire population of the nation, including biometric information. Nilekani is thus seen as a corporate leader, a political leader, and a public intellectual both nationally in India and internationally—he is cited often by *New York Times* columnist Thomas Friedman, who even credits Nilekani for the central thematic at the core of his own popular book, *The World is Flat*. Nilekani, much like Freidman, has fashioned himself into a public intellectual who can help his public understand the complexities and possibilities of this purportedly new moment constituted by economic liberalization. In *Imagining India*, Nilekani charts a story about the emergent nation where the entrepreneur as a subjectivity is narrated as always already existing, albeit in shackles. In Nilekani's narrative, economic liberalization seen as the event of national renewal does not produce the entrepreneur; rather it *frees* the subjectivity, allowing it to claim its "rightful" place in the sun. The unshackling of the entrepreneur, moreover, is seen within narratives such as Nilekani's, as defining and shaping new India and its rise. The story of renewal is scripted by narrating the entrepreneur as a subject position that has been newly unshackled; the nation has been made new because, this story argues, economic liberalization policies first instituted in the 1990s and maintained in various forms since, have allowed the entrepreneur to become a legitimate and dominant subjectivity.

Nilekani's narrative is not a unique story. Popular films in India narrate an extremely affective version of this story wherein new India is defined as a space that cultivates and fosters a particular attitude—a space that will satiate all forms of hunger, a dreamscape itself, it will nevertheless encourage you to dream and allow those dreams to be realized. It is a space, these films suggest, where entrepreneurship is rewarded unconditionally. Nilekani notes in the conclusion of his chapter on the entrepreneur, aptly titled "From Rejection to Open Arms: The Entrepreneur in India," that "there was an old wag of a saying that 'India has potential, and it will always have [only] "potential"' . . . it is as Indian attitudes towards entrepreneurs have transformed—from criticism and suspicion to a new appreciation of the 'animal spirit'—that this potential was realized."[29] In the cultural story that Nilekani and other popular texts chart, the move from "rejection" to appreciation and embrace of the entrepreneur's "animal spirits" unshackles both the subjectivity embodied by the entrepreneur and the nation itself—the nation becomes new at the precise moment when the entrepreneur acquires hegemony within popular discourse. Possessive individualism, unshackled from caste, comes to symbolize renewal itself. These stories take the narrative form of spectacular realism. Capital and the nation are narrated within these stories as the undisputed, spectacular truths and the realism of the commoner—defined by caste, gender, and socioeconomic indicators—buttresses that spectacle.

In this chapter, we will specifically track the construction of this entrepreneurial subjectivity through an examination of two significant popular histories, Nandan Nilekani's *Reimagining India* and Gurcharan Das's *Nation Unbound*. Das, who took early retirement from Procter & Gamble to establish a writing career, is seen as a management guru and a public intellectual, much like Nilekani. He writes columns in English-language news dailies and appears frequently on broadcast media talk shows as an expert on globalization, identity, capitalism, and corporate culture. Das and Nilekani are thus elites whose commentary and analysis have a potent influence both on public culture as well as the state apparatus, whose ear they have always had access to. Nilekani's and Das's writing have appeared in previous chapters in this book along with other important cultural stories that produce a narrative about "new" India. These narratives, moreover, will be put into conversation with popular Hindi film texts that have addressed the entrepreneur as a significant subjectivity, including Mani Ratnam's successful film *Guru* (2007), Shimit Amin's modestly budgeted film *Rocket Singh: Salesman of the Year* (2009), and Sharat Katariya's *Sui Dhaaga: Made in India* (Needle and Thread, 2018). We will put these popular texts in conversation with the Modi government's "Make in India" initiative, which was launched in September 2014 to "transform India into a global design and manufacturing hub."[30]

The story about the entrepreneur within popular stories consistently traces a telos: linked in pre–economic reform India to distinctly defined caste groups, he is delegitimized. Unshackled in post-reform India from his moorings in caste *and* the post-independence hegemonic hold of socialism, he finally finds himself. We will trace the narrative processes through which the entrepreneurial subjectivity is inextricably linked with the conception of freedom to show that this link is central to how the entrepreneur is conceived. Rather than assume what freedom as a concept means, we will trace the meanings that are linked to this signifier. Freedom as it is embodied by the entrepreneur in new India is signified through three interconnected narrative strategies, constituting the entrepreneurial subjectivity itself as an affective political construct. Firstly, the entrepreneur's ability to dream and articulate those dreams in language that validates global capital are a significant motif through which freedom is constituted. Secondly, the entrepreneur in "new" India is represented and constituted as a cosmopolitan subjectivity. Thirdly, freedom is constituted as possessive individualism within stories circulating in Indian popular media.

Having traced the narrative and representational strategies through which possessive individualism is constituted as the pinnacle of subaltern agency, we will examine the limits inherent to such a conception of subalternity by turning to the tragic story of a young Muslim woman, Zaheera Shaikh. Through her story, we will see that even as subalternity works as a foundational justification for possessive individualism, it simultaneously works to mark its limits. A poor, teenaged Muslim woman whose family home and business were burned down in anti-Muslim genocidal violence, Shaikh trades the one thing that she possesses—her story—like a commodity on the market. Her agency derived from an assumption that she owned her own story, that she was its proprietor. That proprietorship, however, did not work in any way to validate global capital and as such could not be accommodated within popular representational categories. Shaikh's gendered subalternity and her case thus unravel the liberal conception of possessive individualism and its embodiment in the entrepreneur. Shaikh's story is an unruly one because it could not be told within the confines and strictures of spectacular realism.

COSMOPOLITAN ENTREPRENEUR: COMMERCE OVER POLITICS

Let us begin with instantiations of stories that translate the businessman, the trader, and the shopkeeper into a cosmopolitan entrepreneur. These stories, as we shall track, use caste and gender, appropriate critiques of misogyny, and translate particular identities into the ostensibly universal category of the possessive individual. These narratives also constitute economic liberalization as an event that produces a rupture and enables the unshackling of the Indian entrepreneur. That unshackling is narrated as the shift in public culture from an emphasis on politics to commerce, such that the entrepreneuralization of the self comes to be defined as the resolution for inequity and injustice. To put it differently, the resolution of historic inequity, including caste- and gender-based inequality, is narrated within these stories through the argument that the event of economic reforms produced a prioritization of the space of commerce over politics, which in turn enabled the unshackling of the subaltern. These stories use caste and gender in at least a couple of different ways. First, they translate the traditional middle-caste trader and businessman into the cosmopolitan entrepreneur; second, they insist on narrating success and justice for the lower-caste man or woman through the entrepreneuralization of the subaltern self.

The character of the entrepreneur finds an important place in these texts, which I will call popular histories of India's political economy. I have already referenced one such text, Nandan Nilekani's *Imagining India*; we will also discuss Gurcharan Das's *India Unbound: The Social and Economic Revolution from Independence to the Global Information Age*, a text we have encountered previously.[31] Written by entrepreneurs, business leaders, and journalists, popular histories such as *Imagining India* and *India Unbound* have helped transform their authors into commentators and public intellectuals. These popular histories perform the cultural labor of writing new India into being and constitute economic liberalization specifically into an event, in the wake of which the authors suggest, new time comes into being and the nation itself is renewed. Moreover, these texts spectacularize capital, narrating economic liberalization as irrefutably productive for the formation of new India by articulating the commoner, whose story is told through sociological and ethnographic detail, to the aspiration for capital. Das's *India Unbound* was published at the turn of the twenty-first century and has been translated into several languages; it was the subject of a British Broadcasting Corporation production. Popular histories such as *India Unbound* thus circulate inter- and intranationally, constituting new India through an act of narration. Das, moreover, publishes regular columns in national broadsheets such as the *Times of India* and regional broadsheets such as *Eenadu* (In Today's Day), as well as guest columns in international news media publications such as *Newsweek* and *Foreign Affairs*. His career, both as a top executive in the multinational Procter & Gamble and as a writer, has enabled him to occupy the position of a native informant internationally and a public intellectual domestically. In the story that Das narrates about new India, which he defines as a "revolution" in ideas and attitudes brought about by economic reforms, the entrepreneur plays a distinct role.

Das argues that while India has always had entrepreneurs, those of the 1990s "are creatures of a competitive economy" and "no longer embarrassed about wanting to be rich."[32] Recall that the 2005 film *Bunty aur Babli* (Bunty and Babli, Shaad Ali) discussed in chapter 2 made a similar visual argument, portraying the protagonists of the film playing, dancing, and reveling amid piles of cash. This uninhibitedness set Bunty and Babli apart from their parents. As such, the film *Bunty aur Babli* contended, a shift had occurred within public culture. In Das's account, this shift or unshackling is a consequence of a swing in emphasis from politics to economics within Indian public culture. Das suggests that since 1991, he has encountered a "new mind-set" in India, which he argues will "increasingly determine India's identity and future."[33] Das defines this new mindset as that which is engendered by commerce and is innate to the subjectivity of the entrepreneur.

Spatializing "commerce" and "politics," or to put it differently, translating elements of a political economy into distinctive spaces/urban landscapes, Das tells a story about the significance of commerce over politics. Narrating his return migration to India after voluntarily retiring from a successful career with Procter & Gamble, Das describes his decision to live in the Indian capital city of Delhi rather than the commercial capital Mumbai. He reveals to his readers that this was a decision that did not please his wife. Using his wife's discomfort with life in Delhi as a narrative peg, Das proceeds to define Mumbai's cosmopolitanism, distinctly linking it to commerce. More significantly, Das narrates the cosmopolitanism of Mumbai in gendered and caste terms:

> They say that the measure of a civilization is how it treats its women. Since coming to Delhi I have met many women who long for Bombay [*sic*]. My wife explains that Bombay gives women dignity. If Bombay respects women, Delhi looks on them as sex objects. In Bombay, she can take a taxi at midnight; in Delhi, a girl cannot walk freely on the street in the evening. It seems that it takes more than education to bring civilization. Bombay has this civilizing quality, I think, because of its origins as a city of commerce ... [as Samuel Richard notes] through commerce, "man learns to deliberate, to be honest, to acquire manners, to be prudent and reserved in talk and action." (p. 231)

Das uses an oft-repeated storyline about women's safety in public spaces in Mumbai in opposition to urban centers such as Delhi, which belies the complex experience of vulnerability that gendered and sexual minorities in Mumbai have consistently narrated.[34] He uses this storyline to constitute cosmopolitanism through liberal-humanist notions of reason, deliberation, and prudence. He argues that the city of Mumbai, the commercial capital of the nation, "gives women dignity" and respect, even as Delhi, the nation's capital and as such its political center, "looks on them as sex objects." Using his wife's discomfort with inhabiting and moving in public spaces within the urban landscape of Delhi, Das first transforms the capital city into a voyeur, imbues its urban landscape with the aggressive, masculine power of the scopophilic gaze, and links that "dirty" power to politics itself. In opposition, commerce and Mumbai's urban landscape is embodied by a sanitized, civilized, controlled, and prudent masculinity. As such, *India Unbound* states that the business*man* or the *man* of commerce embodies the civilized ideal. The man of commerce or the possessive individual is narrated as the idealized citizen-subject. In this moment in the text, the particularities that define him are his location—Mumbai—and his gender—he is a man—but both of these specificities are translated into the universal identification of the possessive individual. In fact, both commerce and masculinity are particularities that are foundational to the possessive individual.

Das goes further. He writes that his experience of "businessmen—*Marwaris, Jains, and Gujarati banias*—is that *they* possess these qualities [thrift, hard work, self-reliance, and self-discipline] in abundance, particularly the virtue of restraint."[35] In this second textual moment, Das defines the businessman or the possessive individual through his caste markers—he belongs to one of the middle castes traditionally associated with business and trade. Having defined the businessman through his caste, *India Unbound* in this textual moment labors to transform him into the putatively unmarked possessive individual. Having established commerce as liberalism itself and the man of commerce as the ideal citizen, this introduction of caste markers works to translate a particular ethnic subjectivity into the normative cosmopolitan entrepreneur. In a double move, *India Unbound* defines the businessman through his regional, religious, and caste-based identity and *simultaneously* describes him in the universalist terms of the cosmopolitan entrepreneur. In these textual moments of this story, the particular is defined and transformed into the universal.

On the other hand, when the story turns toward defining the event of economic reforms and its consequences for the entrepreneur, the particular ethnic/caste and gendered identity of its characters are consistently kept in play in order to define the unshackling and inclusivity of the category *entrepreneur* and to constitute economic reforms as a radically new event. Thus, when Das describes the changes wrought by economic reforms, his story shifts to characters like fourteen-year-old Raju, who works at a coffee stall in a village near Chennai in southern India and wants to become like Bill Gates; or to the twenty-year-old woman named Sushila who works for 40 dollars a month at a leather factory that produces shoes for multinational corporations like Florsheim, Hogarth, and Marks and Spencer and carries a small bottle of Oil of Olay in her bag. In the story that Das narrates, the characters of Raju, Sushila, and the dalits living in a northern Indian village who have moved from leatherwork to farmwork are significant because they help define the shift in emphasis from politics to economics. In this moment, the story says, when as a consequence of economic reforms public culture shifts to prioritize economics and commerce over politics, subalterns (defined as such through their caste and gendered identities) become cosmopolitan by acquiring the *language* and *aspirations* of the entrepreneur. Thus Das says, "Raju and Sushila ... were already a part of the global economy—Raju in his dreams of Bill Gates and Sushila in the way she thought about her customers ... Liberalization in trade, besides information technology, tax reform, and free access to the airwaves, was beginning to change Sushila's and Raju's minds."[36] Here, the particularities of Sushila and Raju's subjectivities—their rural subalternity, their caste and gendered identities—are consistently narrated to define and constitute the inclusivity and "civilizing" impulse of commerce and economics. While the traditional entrepreneur is unshackled by economic reform, liberalization, the story says, *changes* the minds of subalterns like Sushila and Raju. In other words, the story talks about subalterns, consistently defined by their caste, gender, and regional identities, as possessively investing in the entrepreneuralization of the self, in new India. In doing so, it claims, they transform themselves into cosmopolitan entrepreneurs who seek social mobility through commerce. As such, to follow through with the narrative logic here, they transform themselves into ideal citizens.

It is clear in Das's story that traditional caste businessmen were always already cosmopolitan and entrepreneurial; for them, economic reforms are seen to have produced an unshackling that allows them to fully express, articulate, and act on the impulses that they have innately possessed. On the other hand, liberalization is narrated as unshackling for the rural poor and lower-caste groups because it transforms their minds and their subjectivities from those anchored in the realm of the political to the space of commerce. Raju and Sushila can be defined as cosmopolitan and entrepreneurial within Das's story, not because they have established businesses or enterprises or even because they have acquired greater material success, but because they *consume* and *speak* aspirationally in terms legitimated by globalizing capital. Freedom here is thus narrated in two distinct ways: one form of freedom is material, the other is more abstract, and it signals a shift in the imagination from politics to consumption. Economic liberalization frees the traditional-caste businessman to acquire greater material wealth and dominance, whereas what excites Das about subalterns like Raju and Sushila is their imagination of themselves as consumers and aspirants of global capital. What is common to both textual moments is the spectacularization of capital, such that commerce and its embodiment in the form of the possessive individual is narrated irrefutably as a moral good. Sociological and ethnographic detail, through the narration of caste and gender identifications, becomes the foundation on which this spectacle is built.

As Raju and Sushila's ethnicity is used to narrate the inclusivity of the entrepreneurial subjectivity and simultaneously used to mark them as modernity's "other" now brought into its fold through the civilizing impulse of commerce, their gendered subjectivity is signified through old masculine-feminine binaries. Sushila becomes a cosmopolitan, in Das's story, through her consumption of feminine beauty products and Raju through his aspiration to become an entrepreneur like Bill Gates. The new subjectivity that Das thus constructs for Raju and Sushila reinforces and circulates old gendered norms—the female is constituted through the consumption of commercial products that, in fact, define her as feminine and the male is constituted through his aspiration for economic and social mobility. In Das's narrative then, both the unshackling of the traditional-caste businessman and the change in the desires of subalterns (from political to economic dreams) are represented as freedom.

Nandan Nilekani also narrates a tale about the entrepreneur and the role of commerce in India. In *Imagining India*, he charts a story about the emergent nation where the entrepreneur as a subjectivity is narrated as always already existing, albeit in shackles. Here again, economic liberalization does not produce the entrepreneur; rather it frees the subjectivity. The entrepreneur moves from a position of "rejection" in pre-reform India to one of euphoric acceptance and embrace post-reform. Both Nilekani and Das suggest that a crucial difference between pre-reform and new India is the significance accorded to commerce in public culture. While Das uses the circulation figures of trade and business newspapers to bolster his claim that public culture had shifted its emphasis from politics to economics, resulting in the "freeing" of the entrepreneur, Nilekani marshals popular Hindi films to provide evidence for his argument about the increased relevance of the entrepreneur in public culture. The films produced post–economic reform, Nilekani argues, "reflected the Indian transformation." "The films of today are highly aspirational," he states, elaborating that they present "very different profiles of ordinary people passionate about success":

> And as India's human capital—its entrepreneurs, consumers and its millions of workers—has become the country's Atlas, holding the economy high up on its shoulders, films like *Rang de Basanti* [Color Me the Colors of Spring] and *Swades* [My Land] channel a growing belief that ordinary Indians can bring about enormous change.[37]

We discussed both *Rang de Basanti* and *Swades* in chapter 1 as we tracked the constitution of development as a concept-image in the time of Hindutva neoliberalism. Both films, we must recall, performed the semiotic labor of defining the space of politics as well as the state itself as corrupt at best, dirty at worst. *Rang de* made the argument that the dirty space of politics needed to be cleaned up by middle-class urban masculinity. *Swades* resolved the inequity experienced by rural lower-caste villagers through the capital of the middle-class, upper-caste male who is a part of the Indian diaspora. Thus, the "ordinary Indians" that Nilekani invokes via these two films are not so ordinary after all; the narratives within which they reside use the category *ordinary* to signify realism even as they interpellate a very particular form of masculinity that they contend has come to signify new India. In *Imagining India* too, the films are used to signal the ostensible shift from politics to commerce. That shift, Nilekani's text suggests, makes all the difference for the lives of "ordinary Indians." In the teleology that Nilekani traces through his narrative, "ordinary Indians" only truly find representation as *agents* within popular culture in the post-reform period. This is precisely because agency, within this story, is defined through consumerism and commercial enterprise. *Imagining India*, much like *India Unbound*, pivots on the assumption that commerce, not politics, makes the subaltern an agent. It is when, and only when, the subaltern speaks in the language of global capital and becomes a desiring subject (i.e., desirous of consumer goods) that he or she is recognized as a legitimate agent—a cosmopolitan entrepreneur.

The most recent iteration of this story is the 2018 film *Sui Dhaaga: Made In India* (Needle and Thread, Sharat Katariya). The central protagonist of the film, Mauji Sharma, is one of the "ordinary Indians" that Nilekani and Das wrote about more than a decade prior. Mauji lives in a small town and works for a small-business owner who consistently demeans him, whereas his father retires from a clerical position in a government office. The early part of the narrative dwells on the father and son's emasculation as a direct consequence of their form of employment, which is narrated as humiliating servitude. Mauji Sharma is unshack-led, via his wife's gentle goading, when he becomes an entrepreneur and enters the garment industry, first when he sets up a sidewalk tailoring shop, second when he designs and stitches comfortable but also attractive hospital gowns for women, and lastly when he designs and stitches a line of clothing that wins a coveted fash-ion industry prize. Importantly, Mauji's entrepreneurship harkens back to his grandfather's skill and artistry as a tailor, according to the story that the film nar-rates. The collapse of traditional and also caste-based labor such as tailoring and weaving in the town had compelled Mauji's father to seek employment with the state. It had also, according to the narrative of the film, engendered in the father a rigid and fearful avoidance of business or entrepreneurship of any kind. Mauji's unshackling is therefore a return to traditional caste-based work, except that that work is now deemed cosmopolitan and he can now be translated into an entrepre-neur. Mauji's grandfather's labor could only be narrated as caste-based work; Mau-ji's work, on the other hand, can be narrated in the form of spectacular realism and through the category of the entrepreneur.

A decade prior to the release of *Sui Dhaaga*, Nandan Nilekani had concluded his chapter on the story of the entrepreneur in India by stating that "Nehru had once expressed contempt for what he called the 'bania civilization' [*bania* is a caste-based derogatory term for the small shopkeeper/businessman], and Indira Gandhi had spoken of businessmen as 'the dark and evil forces' that threatened to destroy the country; but in the new era, Manmohan Singh lauds businessmen as 'the source of India's confidence, and our optimism.'"[38] Nilekani thus trium-phantly narrates the arrival of the entrepreneur into a position of deserved legiti-macy and hegemony within Indian public culture. He traces a genealogy that links the "contemptible *bania*" from the 1950s to the "evil businessman" of the 1970s to the entrepreneur of the late 1990s, who is the source of the nation's confident emergence. Characters like Mauji, who return to caste-based labor wearing the label of entrepreneur rather than their caste identity papers, are the filmic or cel-luloidal manifestations of that genealogy. The arrival of the entrepreneur, more-over, is signified by narrating another entrance—that of the nontraditional (defined as such through caste, habitus, and gendered terms) businessperson. Thus, Nilekani notes that "some of the most prominent entrepreneurs who emerged post-1980, such as Sunil Mittal and Dhirubhai Ambani, had built their firms from scratch, and were a breed far apart from the closed circle, family entre-preneurs of the 1960s and 1970s."[39] As in *India Unbound*, both the return to tradi-tional caste-based work in the guise of entrepreneurship as well as the subaltern's possessive investment in possessive individualism in *Imagining India* serves to renew the nation, define its emergence, and underline commerce over politics as a space for justice.

Social scientists such as Achin Vanaik have pointed to the "ideological-philosophical shift" that underlie the strategies of economic liberalization and have named the "post-1991 reforms" a "neoliberal turn."[40] Scholars like Vanaik have defined both the shift in political economy as well as its constituent elements as a *political* shift. Commentators and popular public intellectuals like Nilekani and Das, on the other hand, narrate the shift and the subjectivities that constitute and give form to it as *apolitical* and therefore legitimate. Such a narration, as we have been tracking through the course of the book and as we will continue to do in this chapter, acquires a hegemonic position in new India. Public cultural discourse thus transitions from the dairy owner in *Manthan*, who is described as ruthless because he reinforces caste and patriarchal hierarchies, to characters celebrated as entrepreneurs like Mauji, Raju, Sushila, and Dhirubhai Ambani, without a *political* resolution to the oppression of caste and patriarchy. The motley cast of characters who are defined as entrepreneurs in new India are, instead, narrated as disinvested and disarticulated from caste (unlike our dairy owner from *Manthan*) and therefore unshackled and legitimate. My contention is that narratives like *Manthan*, which critique the greedy, ruthless businessman, simultaneously reinforce the force of the resolute individual and thereby leave a discursive space open for the continued salience of the possessive individual.

ENTREPRENEURSHIP AS DEMOCRATIC AND INCLUSIVE

Commentary, popular histories, and other stories suggest that there were at least a couple of problems with the way in which the businessman was narrated in old India (post-independence, pre-reform India). One, the businessman reinforced caste-based hierarchies and inequity and two, that he was ruthlessly greedy. In the previous section, we discussed the narrative resolution of the first of these problems: Popular histories such as those authored by Nilekani and Das narrated the entrepreneur of new India through a story about caste and inequity that enabled it to hide in plain sight. As such, the category *entrepreneur* is defined as cosmopolitan, inclusive, and foundationally freeing. Popular Hindi cinema, in particular critically and commercially successful films like *Guru* (2007) and the less commercially successful but critically appreciated *Rocket Singh: Salesman of the Year* (2009) provide an aural and visual narrative to the story that popular histories such as those written by Nilekani and Das tell. Moreover, *Guru* and *Rocket Singh* constitute the entrepreneur not just as cosmopolitan but as innately democratic, and they work to transform rather mundane, middle-class masculinities into a heroic form. Here, the form of spectacular realism enables the narratives to render their protagonists as utterly ordinary and then, as these protagonists transform themselves into entrepreneurs, the narratives convert them into heroes. These popular films thus contend with the second problem associated with the businessman, namely greed. The entrepreneur in these films is transformed into a morally resolute, upright, and ethical individual. Recall our hero in *Manthan*? Even as the reviled businessman from films like *Manthan* is now translated as a cosmopolitan entrepreneur and is made legitimate, the morally upright hero invested in building and working with collectives is transformed into an entrepreneur.

Raja Sen, film critic for the news and features website rediff.com, noted when reviewing *Rocket Singh* that "the best films about sales are [often] compelling narratives about savage closers, like David Mamet's *Glengarry Glen Ross* or Oliver Stone's *Wall Street*, [with] audiences lapping up the con-games used by piranhas in action, but [the] *Rocket Singh* story is the exact antithesis of the 'greed is good' dictum: this is about a straightforward, sincere lad who believes in sharing."[41] Nilekani had argued when constructing a telos for the subjectivity of the entrepreneur in India that it had been a despised category in post-independence, pre-reform India because it was associated with greed and particular castes at a time when hegemonic socialist thought espoused equality and the eradication of poverty. As Sen notes, films like *Rocket Singh* constitute the entrepreneur as a legitimate, hegemonic ideal not by validating that which had thus far stood as illegitimate in Indian public culture, namely greed, but by transposing that which is seen as moral and good onto it. In other words, the entrepreneur in films such as *Rocket Singh* is constituted as inherently democratic by producing a mongrel subjectivity that draws on Gandhian ethics, socialism's emphasis on parity, and neoliberalism's valorization of the market as the ultimate equalizer. Thus, even as films such as *Rocket Singh* provide the narratives constructed by *India Unbound* and *Imagining India* an embodiment in celluloid, these filmic entrepreneurs also diverge in significant ways from their textual counterparts. The possessive individualism of the entrepreneur in a narrative like *Rocket Singh* draws from a range of ideological formations, including a sense of morality grounded in religious discourse, socialism, liberalism, and Gandhian thought, some of which ostensibly contradict each other.

The protagonist of *Rocket Singh*, Harpreet Singh Bedi, is an unassuming young man leading a simple middle-class life. He is specifically situated in the opening sequence of the film in an identifiably middle-class home—gaudy wallpaper, kitschy artifacts, plastic plants and flowers, appliances without an identifiable brand, and bland furniture upholstered with flowery prints. He is a young man who lives with his retired grandfather, and has just (barely) graduated from college with a degree in commerce. The film's narrative also deliberately distinguishes him from his closest friends who belong to the elite classes. Harpreet believes that a career in sales and marketing will allow him social mobility and success. Having secured a job as a salesman in a company that sells assembled computers called AYS (short for At Your Service), Harpreet learns soon enough that success in the organization is acquired through practices that he defines as unethical. When a potential customer offers him a "cut" to secure his order at a particular price, Harpreet files a complaint against him; he is shocked when this action earns him the intense ire of his own boss. Harpreet is humiliated and is told to simply complete his training period and leave the company. As he sits shocked and afraid at his desk, which is located near the restrooms, his colleagues add indignity to his disillusionment by throwing paper rockets at him. Having had enough, HP, as he is known to his friends, transforms himself into an entrepreneur and establishes his own computer marketing company within AYS, running it on his own terms. It is not incidental, as Sen reminds us, that Singh is called HP. The narrative makes a neat allusion to the computer giant Hewlett-Packard, formed as Silicon Valley mythology would have it, in a garage in Palo Alto, California. In fact, HP's "About Us" page defines the garage where college friends Bill Hewlett and Dave Packard came together to establish their own enterprise, "as the enduring symbol of innovation and the entrepreneurial spirit." For this other HP, located in another time and in a place far removed from the neighborhoods near Stanford University, the instrument of his humiliation—the paper rockets flung at him by his colleagues—become the symbol not only of his fledgling company but of his ethical entrepreneurialism.

HP signs on other AYS employees for his enterprise. First is the stern but attractive receptionist Koena, who does all the work of an office manager but is told not to aspire for that kind of a position because her "talent" and "contribution" is to sit at the front of the office and look pretty. Second is the peon Chottelal Mishra, who does odd jobs and serves tea and snacks to the sales team and is therefore derogatorily called "cup-plate." Third is the technical expert Girish Reddy, who is an almost invisible presence in the office. HP signs them on as full partners, noting that the team would split the profits equally among themselves. Rocket Sales is thus composed of characters distinctly defined through their gendered, ethnic (their regional and religious backgrounds), and class status.

While the film's focus on ethics—abhorrence for cheating, bribery, and lying— alludes to the popular form that Gandhian thought has acquired in Indian public culture, the narrative of *Rocket Singh* makes clear that HP's own sense of ethics derives from his distinctly defined religious and cultural identity. As a Sikh, HP is shown to use his grandfather and the Sikh Guru Nanak as his moral compasses, guiding him through the ethically ambiguous and morally convoluted workings of AYS. The story suggests, however, that becoming an entrepreneur also frees him from being anchored to his religious identity. As he is attempting to convince a reluctant Koena to become a part of Rocket Sales, HP says that the enterprise would allow her to become an equal partner, an entrepreneur. He tells her moreover that if they didn't do this, he would always be the "joker Sardar" and she the "item girl." If Sikhs in the United States and elsewhere have been referred to in racially derogatory terms as "diaper head," then in Indian popular culture the Sikh male is at the center of jokes that pivot on his assumed stupidity. Defined through his religion, the Sikh male in Indian public culture is thus the "joker"—the man who is funny because he is stupid. The phrases "item song" and "item girl" reference the single song-and-dance routine featuring an attractive female star inserted into the narrative plot of a commercial Hindi film with the aim of attracting greater eyeballs. Koena repeatedly lets her coworkers know that she is married; she wears heavy makeup, has brown-blonde highlights in her hair, and dresses in saris that flatter her toned body. Koena may be married but she is also an attractive woman who is unabashed about her charms and her femininity, and as such she is AYS's "item girl." The narrative of *Rocket Singh* thus uses the particularities of religious, cultural, and gendered subjectivities in two divergent ways *simultaneously* to construct the subjectivity of the entrepreneur. Harpreet Singh Bedi ceases to be the "joker Sardar" when he becomes an entrepreneur, Koena is no longer an "item girl," when she becomes a partner of Rocket Sales, and Chottelal Mishra disavows the class-slur "cup-plate" when he joins the enterprise. The subjectivity of the entrepreneur is thus constituted as a universal democratic ideal, where the particular shackles of religious and gendered identities can be thrown away.

However, the entrepreneurial subjectivity as constituted in *Rocket Singh* is *simultaneously* signified by a turn to the particularities of religion and gender. What Harpreet Singh brings to Rocket Sales is ethics; these ethics are seen to be innate to him precisely because they are seen to be a derivative of his religious identity. Harpreet Singh becomes the "joker Sardar" because he was "stupid" enough to lodge a complaint of corruption against an important client, a tag he sheds when he becomes an entrepreneur. But it is precisely because he is a "joker Sardar" who believes in conducting business ethically that the entrepreneurial subjectivity that the film constructs is signified as democratic. To put it plainly, the entrepreneur is constructed as a *universal* democratic ideal by deploying the *particular* religious identity of the Sikh male and his moral code of ethics. Similarly, Koena becomes AYS's item girl because she is the attractive young female receptionist who, her boss tells her, increases their sales by a couple of percentage points simply by being there, looking pretty, and smiling at the client. Koena sheds the sexist tag when she becomes office manager and an entrepreneur, but her value to Rocket Sales derives from her position as AYS's item girl, and as such she is able to pass on clients disgruntled with AYS to Rocket Sales. Here again, the entrepreneur is constructed as a *universal* democratic ideal by deploying the *particular* gendered work of the receptionist.

The only member of Rocket Sales who is not specifically defined through a cultural identity is Nitin, the group's immediate boss at AYS. Nitin finds out that the group is running its own enterprise within the offices of AYS. When Nitin accuses the group of unethical practices and corruption and threatens to report them, he is reminded of his own many falsified receipts and documents by the man he had so often humiliated as "cup-plate." Mishra, as an entrepreneur and a partner in Rocket Sales, has been unshackled from the indignity that was his lot when he was "cup-plate" and is thus emboldened to hold Nitin by the scruff of his neck and assert that a man who did not understand ethics had no business calling another unethical. Nitin joins Rocket Sales as an equal partner instead of reporting the group. What is significant about Nitin's character to the story that the film narrates is that as an entrepreneur Nitin acquires the democratic, ethical inclusivity that he could not sustain as an employee of AYS.

Rocket Singh: Salesman of the Year links the arrival of this form of business and the entrepreneurial subjectivity to new India. The film frames the conflict at the center of the narrative—Harpreet Singh's ethics versus AYS's morally ambiguous business practices—as a battle between old and new ways of doing business. Harpreet Singh tells his boss that his ways of conducting business and running an office are a thing of the past. In fact, the writer of the film, Jaideep Sahni, mentions in an interview in the "special features" section of the film's DVD that the seed for the *Rocket Singh* story came from a conversation he had with the producer of the film about the transformation of the office and business space in India. What *Rocket Singh* does therefore is construct the entrepreneur as a mongrel subjectivity, which draws on cultural and gendered particularities and alludes to socialism's emphasis on parity and Gandhian ethics, but is always neatly linked back to the valorization of the possessive individual. Moreover, through the narrative strategies it uses to construct the entrepreneur, *Rocket Singh* constitutes a possessive investment in the subjectivity. HP finally tastes success and freedom when he takes on the persona of the entrepreneur, trading on his *own* skill and acumen (rather than that of the corporation) in the market.

If the entrepreneur of *Rocket Singh* is deeply concerned with ethical business practices, to the extent that he keeps an account of all the AYS resources he has used and pays the corporation back, the entrepreneur in the film *Guru* (Mani Ratnam, 2007) is more ethically ambiguous and is even brought before a government commission interested in investigating his creative interpretation and play with export-import regulations and bookkeeping. Yet, the story that the film *Guru* narrates goes even further than *Rocket Singh* in constructing the subjectivity of the entrepreneur as democratic and inclusive. Critics writing and commentating in various media outlets read the film as such. Rajeev Masand, in his review for CNN-IBN TV, said that "*Guru* is the story of a man who believed not only in personal growth and personal success, but in empowering the very people who contributed to his success . . . a man who understood that the growth of an enterprise, a company, a corporation must reflect not only in its owner's personal growth and success, but the growth and success of its every shareholder."[42]

One of the enduring images of this popular film adorned its posters prior to the release of the movie and draws from a key sequence in the narrative. Shot in muted, dull, gray light, in pouring rain, the image positions the entrepreneur with his back to the camera facing a mass of black umbrellas. The image links the entrepreneur, dressed in a black suit, his face unknown to us, to the mass he stands in front of but it also sets him apart. He is one of them but he is also their leader—a visual manifestation of spectacular realism. The image on the film's poster introduces its protagonist to its audience by defining him as a "villager," a "visionary," and a "winner." Gurukant Desai, the entrepreneurial character whose life story the film traces, when portrayed as a "visionary" and a "winner" is set apart from the mass of people who have bought into his promise quite literally by purchasing his corporation's shares, but as a "villager" and as a man who did not have the social, cultural, or economic capital to enter into a market dominated by those who did, he is also presented by the film's narrative as being a part of that mass. Gurukant Desai's enterprise is named "Shakti Parivar" (Shakti = strength, Parivar = family) and his shareholders are defined as members of a family. The terms *corporation*, *company*, and *enterprise* are conspicuous by their absence. As such, the audience interpellated into the subject-position of the commoner is sutured to the character of Gurukant Desai, working out its desires, aspirations, and dreams through this "visionary," this "winner." As we have been tracking in a range of different stories, in *Guru* too it is the patrilineal suture that binds the commoner with the visionary businessman. Recall that the form of this suture is identical to the one used in narratives that transformed Narendra Modi into a visionary political leader that we discussed in chapter 2. This patrilineal link that sutures the commoner to the visionary is significant therefore to the aesthetic form of spectacular realism.

Dreams or aspirations are an important motif running through the narrative of the film *Guru*. The film begins with an older Desai standing at the center of a large and empty stadium, hands on his hips, reminiscing with a smirk that he was consistently told not to dream, because dreams did not come true. The film concludes in the same location, only now the stadium is filled to capacity, the crowd roars, and fluttering banners identify this huge gathering as the shareholders's meeting for "Shakti Parivar" (the Shakti Family). A triumphant Gurukant Desai asks the gathering if they are ready to dream big, and they roar back their acquiescence; he asks them if they are ready to take on the world and become the largest corporation not just in the nation but across the globe, and again the crowd shout in affirmation. Bookended by these sequences, the narrative of the film allows the audience positioned as the commoner not only to be sutured to the protagonist, Gurukant Desai, it also enables this audience to dream *his* dream and experience catharsis through the realization of that dream. The dream acts also as a moment of pause and as a space for regrouping and rejuvenation at a time of despair and hardship within the narrative of the film. Prior to the climax, Desai is facing the biggest crisis of his life: his factories have been shuttered pending an investigation by a state-appointed commission, his shareholders (read: his family) have turned against him, and, as a last humiliation, he suffers a stroke that temporarily paralyzes half of his body. At this moment of despair and defeat within the narrative, Gurukant Desai's wife and young daughters stand strong beside him.

This is a moment of pause, a moment to rest awhile, to regroup and to dream again. The ability to dream, to aspire, the film suggests, is the opposite of defeat— it is freedom. Moreover, the ability to realize the dream and make it whole, the narrative also tells us, is the entrepreneur's unique gift.

The sequence that follows this moment places Desai in the defendant's seat at a commission hearing about the workings of his corporation. On the final day of the hearing, media and the public are invited into the room. As Desai walks unsteadily up the stairs to the hearing, a man breaks through the police cordon that is trying to keep a swelling crowd in check. The man approaches Desai and states simply, "I drive a taxi, Wadala to Churchgate [a cab route in the city of Mumbai]. I own Shakti shares. I was able to arrange my daughters' marriages with those shares.

That's all I wanted to say. I wanted to thank you. Don't be afraid. I am with you."
Guru's narrative thus suggests that the entrepreneur's unique ability to stubbornly
dream, even when he is told he has no right to do so, and to realize that dream,
despite the odds, is explicitly democratic. Moreover, the film shows us how, in
being bound to the entrepreneur and his dream, the taxi driver, the housewife,
and the commoner all make their own dream whole.

Even more importantly, perhaps, for our purposes, *Guru's* narrative using the
form of spectacular realism represents the nation, sutured in this moment to the
man of commerce (rather than to the man or woman of politics, for instance) as
being renewed, rejuvenated, and made whole—renewed through the dream of
the entrepreneur. In the climactic sequence of the film, which follows the cab
driver's encouragement of Desai, the entrepreneur speaks for the first time using
his own voice (his wife had thus far spoken on his behalf considering his weak-
ened condition following the stroke) at the hearing. Desai begins by noting the
obvious—yes, he has been accused of breaking the law—and then proceeds
to draw a deliberate juxtaposition: Forty years ago, he says, another man stood
accused of breaking a law that had been instituted by colonial masters with the
intention of maintaining slavery. When that man broke the law, he brought freedom and we now know him as "bapu" (father). The protagonist of the film *Guru*
thus juxtaposes the political mobilization against British colonialism, specifically
the civil disobedience movement inspired by M. K. Gandhi, with his own creative
manipulation of the post-independence Indian state's laws regulating capital. In
the story that the film narrates, Desai's aspiration to become a capitalist, his desire
to be the proprietor of his skills and trade these as commodities, and the realization of this dream is juxtaposed with anticolonial nationalism's aspiration for freedom. In a key moment within the monologue, Desai suggests that holding the
entrepreneur back through "license raj" and other regulations has resulted in the
nation quite literally having to stand with a begging bowl before other nations and
global institutions such as the World Bank. In other words, anticolonial nationalism's aspiration for "self-rule" is juxtaposed here with neoliberalism's possessive
individualism. As such, Desai's dream itself is defined by the narrative as a quest
for independence and as inherently democratic.

Thus, the story that the film narrates argues forcefully that capital itself is always
already democratic and concomitantly that the attempts to check its movement
are undemocratic and elitist. As more and more villagers become entrepreneurs in
new India, the story suggests, the nation itself becomes more democratic. In order
to tell this story, therefore, Gurukant Desai is narrated as a commoner, a villager
("*I am the public,*" he shouts at the commission hearing) who has kicked and broken down the doors that have kept him and others like him outside. "I would walk
around with a pail, when I was a petrol pump attendant," he says at his hearing,
"much like our state stands with a begging bowl before the World Bank so it can
build roads." "You," he says, pointing to the members of the commission hearing
the case, "want me to remain a petrol pump attendant." Just as *Rocket Singh* had

suggested that times had changed, *Guru* argues forcefully that in these "new" times, men like Gurukant Desai are not an exception but are increasingly becoming the rule. They will not remain petrol pump attendants anymore, no matter what is taken from them and which doors are slammed in their faces; they are increasingly breaking down those doors with the only instrument that they have always possessed—their courage. This courage, Gurukant Desai informs the commission, is the nation's courage, and it will not be broken. As the common person emerges triumphant as the entrepreneur, *Guru* suggests, the nation (sutured to but also embodied by this commoner) breaks through shackles imposed on it by the state and is renewed. "Why must we always be referred to as the Third World?" Desai asks at the hearing. "Why can't we hold our head high and take our rightful place at the First World table?" he demands, thus suturing the fate of the entrepreneur with that of the nation.

Guru makes distinct allusion to the life story of one of India's iconic capitalists and entrepreneurs—Dhirubhai Ambani, the man who, as the mythology goes, went from working in the petroleum industry and oil refineries in the Middle East to establishing his own cloth and petrochemical empire in India (Reliance Industries). Even as the filmmaker noted that *Guru* was not an Ambani biopic, film reviewers debated the similarities and the differences between the biography and the cinematic narrative. What is significant for our purposes here is that the film charts the story of the entrepreneur at the center of its plot using the same narrative strategies that public intellectuals like Nandan Nilekani and Gurcharan Das use to write a popular history of India's political economy. Whether *Guru* stays true to the Ambani biography or not, it makes enough allusions to it, and more importantly, its narrative weaves the same story using the form of spectacular realism about the entrepreneur in India and about the new nation that Nilekani narrates in his popular history.

What popular films like *Guru* and *Rocket Singh* do then is provide a visually and aurally aesthetic story that serves as a complement to the popular histories of India's political economy as narrated by public intellectuals like Nandan Nilekani and Gurcharan Das. They help constitute a distinctive form of hegemonic masculinity, moreover. Films from the late 1980s and 1990s, when Hindu nationalism was mobilizing its constituency to resurrect its political fortunes, narrated a form of masculinity that was defined through service to the nation and practicing a form of renunciate celibacy as hegemonic.[43] That duty-bound, aggressively patriotic form of masculinity did not disappear from public culture just as the angry young man did not. Alongside these embodiments of masculinity now arrived the businessman. In the new millennium, when neoliberalism was being constructed as an event and the nation was seen to be renewed, films helped constitute the businessman as the hegemonic male. This hegemonic businessman was not an elite, nor was he conventionally good looking, well educated, or a man of sophisticated charms and taste; rather, he belonged to the more everyday world of passing grades (even academic failure) and passable English, a man of faith and above all, a man of commerce. A film such as *Guru,* moreover, gives us an instantiation of both the commoner and his masculine ethos but also the spectacular visionary.

This businessman of post-reform India is at a distance from the angry young man of the Hindi films from the seventies and the eighties, but as a character he does not embody a disavowal or a repudiation of the angry young man. We spent some quality time with the angry young man in chapter 2 and that time has revealed to us that one of the many reasons he continues to resonate is that possessive individualism is a significant aspect of his characterization. Our businessman of new India, with his possessive investment in entrepreneurialism that is deemed apolitical, does not ostensibly need the street's extra-legal economy in the way that the angry young man did. The stories that narrate the character of the entrepreneur make this point explicitly; they suggest that in new India, the possessive individual is unshackled and the spaces of commerce have been freed too, enabling him to realize his dream of becoming an entrepreneur. Post-reform India can be represented as new precisely because hegemonic masculinity is marked by a shift from the angry young man to the businessman.

Guru and *Rocket Singh* thus valorize the shift from politics to economics that Nilekani and Das have discussed in their books by emphatically arguing that the entrepreneur is an inclusive and democratic subjectivity. Such a construction is made possible by drawing on ethnic and gendered particularities but also on class as social status more broadly *and* by defining the entrepreneur as a subjectivity that allows the melting away of difference. Moreover, films such as *Guru* and *Rocket Singh* produce a possessive investment in entrepreneurialism in an idiomatic way that is extremely affective. As such, the nation is seen to have arrived at a second potent moment in its history (the first significant moment being independence from colonial rule). In this second moment, the nation, through the commoner-turned-entrepreneur's unique ability to tap into and unleash the democratic force of capital, emerges renewed.

HINDU NATIONALISM AND THE ENTREPRENEUR

Even as the possessive individual is translated into a cosmopolitan, ethically resolute, democratic man and narrated as unshackled in new India, the Hindu nationalist story labors to suture that entrepreneur and his interests to that of the corporation. The BJP has often been referred to as the "brahmin-bania" political party because its key constituency includes communities drawn from the upper castes—the brahmins and the traditional trading and business communities, the "banias."[44] Psephological analysis of Indian general elections from 1996 to 2014 reveals that even as the BJP's dependence on upper castes for electoral gains has decreased as the party cultivates constituencies from within the Other Backward Castes and dalits, that "the affinity that many upper caste Hindu voters feel for the party has not lessened."[45] The BJP is, sometimes, critiqued in commentary circulating within the English-language press for protecting this core constituency of upper- and middle-caste business and trading communities by disallowing and/or regulating foreign direct investment in the retail sector. At the end of the year in 2018, in time for the general elections in 2019, the Modi government instituted new guidelines for foreign direct investment in the e-commerce sector, for instance, that were read as "appeasing" its core constituency.[46] Even as full foreign ownership (100 percent FDI) of online marketplaces was allowed beginning in 2016, the Modi government's guidelines two years later in its own narration aimed at "blessing" the marketplace model of e-commerce while introducing "some safe-guards" so that the same "marketplace would not act like a retailer."[47] In other words, the Modi government "blessed" the presence of mega-corporations like Amazon within the Indian market, such that Indian traders and businessmen could sell their commodities via its platform but suggested that entities like Amazon should refrain from acquiring the persona of the businessman/the retailer. Amazon and other corporations like it, such as Flipkart, fell in line. Far from being opposed to economic liberalization or even wary of it, Hindu nationalism "blesses" neoliberalism therefore and acts in concert with and for capital even as it gestures toward regulating its movement. As Hindu nationalism intersects with neoliberalism, the upper- and middle-caste trader and businessman is sutured to the mega-corporation. Or, we might say, the interests of native/local capital are narrated as aligned with global capital. This alignment must be consistently narrated to win the consent of the small trader or businessman. Indeed, this is the material instantiation of the cultural form of spectacular realism.

Key to Hindu nationalism's intersection with neoliberalism, as well as the suturing of the trader and businessman to the corporation, is its narration of the entrepreneur. In a speech at the "Youth Entrepreneurship Meet" in 2013, then–Gujarat chief minister Narendra Modi narrated a story that he hoped would be inspiring to the young people who were attending the session.[48] A man he had met several decades ago, perhaps in the late 1970s, Modi said, ran a small business in the city of Baroda or Vadodara in Gujarat. He acted as a "mediator" connecting carpenters, plumbers, cooks, and handymen with people who required this form of labor. He made his own advertising, crafting four or five banners out of large swaths of cloth, on which he wrote his address with his own hand. These banners were hung at a few different locations in the city. This entrepreneur, Modi noted, was a perfectly ordinary man of "ordinary intelligence." Modi concluded this story by noting that more recently, he had met another businessman; this second man, unlike the "ordinary entrepreneur," ran a large industrial house and talked about creating a new business venture in the capital city of Delhi. The "business model" of this new venture was identical, Modi concluded with flourish, to the one deployed by the "ordinary entrepreneur" he had met decades earlier in the city of Baroda. Using the form of spectacular realism, Modi had thus narrated the link between the ordinary possessive individual and the corporation. He had sutured the "ordinary" or common entrepreneur to the corporation and in doing so had suggested that their interests were, in fact, aligned.

In Modi's narration, the entrepreneur is an enterprising man who dares to dream, has a vision that enables him to realize that dream, recognizes the significance of possessive individualism, and does not take no for an answer. What is the "entrepreneurial quality"? Modi had asked his audience early on in his speech. As an answer to his own question, he narrated another story: In this story, which also took place several decades ago, Modi was seated in a train when a disabled boy, who could only drag himself forward, having lost the use of his legs, enters the compartment. The boy made money polishing boots and was looking for customers in the train. The man seated next to Modi asked the boy to polish his shoes. Having secured his customer, the boy took out that day's *Times of India*[49] and handed it to him. Modi tells his audience that he noticed that the boy had written a few quotable quotes and best wishes on the newspaper for his customers to read. This understanding about building a relationship with a customer and knowing "how to please him" is the entrepreneurial quality, Modi said, concluding the story. This story about a boy who could not walk and eked out a living polishing boots on trains could have been told as a tragedy. Indeed, popular cultural stories created a decade after independence or even in the 1970s used characters like the boot-polishing boy to tell the story of obstructed time and dashed hopes. In the time of Hindutva neoliberalism however, this boy is translated into an entrepreneur and features in the spectacularly real tale of renewal, aspiration, and the unshackled dream. It bears reiterating that characters like the boot-polishing boy have also featured in popular nonfiction texts by writers like Nilekani and Das and that the popular cultural story therefore reveals the processes through which Hindu nationalism intersects with neoliberalism.

Lacing his speech with various stories, drawn both from his own tenure as chief minister of the state of Gujarat and from the lives of very ordinary men in the state he had encountered over his many years as a political activist, Modi told his audience that his hope was that these stories would open their own horizons. Dreams need movement to be realized, Modi declared, because life is itself about movement and progression. "Even water, when it stops flowing, only causes disease," Modi said to great applause. He did not need to add that capital also requires constant movement, but even without that explicit allusion, the dreamscape had been aligned with capital in his narration where the possessive individual, commerce, and dreams had been linked together.

Importantly, Modi defined himself as both a commoner and an entrepreneur. Narrating a couple of other stories, Modi elaborated that even though his own work lay within the space of political and social activism, the entrepreneurial spirit underlined his work ethic. First, he noted, he conceived unconventional solutions to problems and in order to realize these solutions, he did not take no for an answer, even if it was his own administration and bureaucracy that was in the way. In other words, here the stubborn insistence on an unconventional solution articulated by the visionary is defined as entrepreneurial. In one of the stories Modi narrated to elaborate this point, he noted that to test his idea to separate the electrical "feed" to agricultural land from the household as a solution to the problem of power inadequacy in the state of Gujarat, he bypassed his own administration and entered into an agreement with a cooperative operating in a small region of the state. As we have already noted, albeit in the narrative of the film *Manthan*, the individual, indeed the visionary, is paradoxically narrated as central to the collective or the cooperative. In Modi's narration of his entrepreneurial skill, the cooperative or the collective is an instrument through which the visionary acts. The cooperative in this story is a stand-in for the people. The visionary with entrepreneurial skill along with the people, so defined, can bring change, and indeed can make electricity flow where it had not for decades—or so Modi's story goes.

In another story Modi narrated during this speech to elaborate on his entrepreneurial spirit, he brought in a familiar character—Amitabh Bachchan, superstar of the Hindi-language cinema, whom we met in his "angry young man" avatar but then also in his turn as the "brand father" of new India. In chapter 2, we also discussed the advertising campaign produced for the tourism board of the state of Gujarat that brought Bachchan and Modi together. Modi's story about Bachchan in the 2013 speech, in fact, centered on this advertising campaign. Noting that Bachchan was a "Congress man," Modi insisted to his audience that the actor's political affiliations did not lie with the BJP. He reminded his audience that Bachchan was close to the Gandhi family and had even contested an election in the 1980s on the Indian National Congress's ticket.[50] Additionally, Bachchan had no known connections or ties to the state of Gujarat. He did not live in the state nor did he work there. Modi said that since he was an entrepreneur, these details did not deter him from approaching the superstar to lend his star appeal to the state's tourism campaign. Even though Bachchan was a "Congress man," the INC did not know how to use him, Modi noted to great applause. As we already know from chapter 2, Bachchan did consent to be featured in the state's tourism campaign, showcasing its rugged landscapes, its temples, and its wildlife within a narrative that underlined Gujarati pride and fortitude. Significant to Modi's story about Bachchan and Gujarat is that he narrates the actor as a possessive individual who trades in his brand appeal, cultivated over time as a successful actor. Modi does not represent himself as a fan of Bachchan or his films, nor does he attempt to construct a connection between the actor and the state or its people (on the contrary, he insists that this connection does not exist). On the other hand, Bachchan is the brand father of new India and it is to that brand that Modi turns for the campaign. The entrepreneur, then, is also adept at recognizing and strategically deploying resources, including brands, according to the story that Modi narrates.

Dwelling on this speech that Modi made when still the chief minister of Gujarat enables us to note that the possessive individual is not inimical to Hindu nationalism. Authoritarian nationalism may paint itself in nativist colors, it may sing of the ancient, untainted past of the nation, but in its narratives it intersects with some of liberalism's key tenets. The possessive individual-as-entrepreneur enables Hindu nationalism to address its core constituency of traders and small businessmen belonging to the upper and middle castes without naming caste in an explicit manner. Additionally, Hindu nationalism, like neoliberalism, narrates the entrepreneur as a commoner, unshackled and on his way to achieve his potential in new India, and as such links his interests to those of the corporation, also deregulated and unhindered in the time of Hindutva neoliberalism.

A year into his first term as prime minister of the nation, Narendra Modi announced a new initiative called "Make in India." "I want to tell the people of the whole world: Come, make in India. Come and manufacture in India. We have skill, talent, discipline and the desire to do something," Modi declared on August 14, 2014, in his first Independence Day speech as prime minister. A month later on September 25, 2014, the Make in India initiative was formally launched. The initiative's stated goal was to make "India a global manufacturing hub by encouraging both multinational as well as domestic companies to manufacture their products within the country."[51] The goal to have the manufacturing sector contribute 25 percent of GDP was to be largely met by enabling greater foreign direct investment in twenty-five key sectors of the economy. In its narrative, the Modi government said that the state in India has always been seen as a "regulator and not as a facilitator."[52] Seeking to change this conception, the Modi government hoped that the Make in India initiative would bring about a "paradigm shift" such that the state would act as a "partner of the corporate sector" in the "economic development" of the nation.[53] Such a narrative about the state's role as well as the outlines of the policy initiative, which works to create larger openings within the economy for global capital, is in line with neoliberalism's conception of political economy, as we have been discussing through the course of the book. What I want to highlight about Make in India, in the context of the discussion of the entrepreneur, is the popular story that was attached to the initiative and the form it gave to the policy.

I have discussed the 2018 film *Sui Dhaaga: Made In India* (Needle and Thread, Sharat Katariya) earlier in the chapter to highlight its narrative's resonance with Nandan Nilekani's story about the entrepreneur and traditional caste-based occupations. We have noted that in the film, the male protagonist, Mauji, returns to his family's and community's traditional occupation of tailoring, except unlike his grandfather, he wears the tag of entrepreneur and as such is valorized and deemed unshackled. *Sui Dhaaga* was released in 2018, a year before the general elections. The complete title of the film—*Sui Dhaaga: Made in India*—combined the languages of Hindi and English, as many contemporary Hindi-language films are wont to do. More importantly, it alluded to the Modi government's Make in India initiative. The phrase "made in India" was part of the film's dialogue and was used by its protagonist Mauji at crucial moments within the film. The Make in India initiative, as we have just discussed, is about encouraging foreign direct investment; indeed, it is centrally about enabling global capital in the manufacturing sector. The film *Sui Dhaaga*, on the other hand, narrates the story of the translation of the traditional artisan into an entrepreneur. As a part of the film's marketing campaign, its production house released a video that showcased artisans from different parts of India, all working to create a logo for the film using a template provided to them by the film's marketing team. The video included the voices of the artists, and it showed their tools, instruments, and their labor and identified them only through their region and the name of their handicraft or handloom style. The video concluded with a tapestry of the work created by the different artists and their communities. The artists were given the same template to create their work, and as such, their individual pieces were of identical dimensions, type size, and style, but varied in the range of colors used, the pattern of the stitch, and the background design. This promotional video as well as the end credits of the film, which featured visuals of small business owners who work with textiles, linked the reel character Mauji to the real and material world of handicraft and handloom workers. It linked Mauji to the traditional artisan and craftsman, living in rural and small-town India. More importantly for our purposes here, the popular cultural narrative that *Sui Dhaaga* constructs for its audience affectively sutures the fictional character Mauji and the traditional craftsman to the Make in India initiative or to global capital itself via the identity category of the entrepreneur. The narrative form of spectacular realism enables and defines that suture. As such, the popular cultural story aims to suggest that the interests of the traditional artisan and the small businessman are aligned with those of global capital. Additionally, the story links or articulates locality or local particularities first to the nation and then more subtly to global capital. The diverse range of logos, which are nevertheless similar, in the promotional video allude to national integration slogans, such as "unity in diversity," that have circulated in public culture in India since the 1950s.[54] The video takes us, its audience, to the four corners of the country, audiovisually linking diverse design and craftsmanship, language, dress, and landscapes into the cartography of the nation. Stitched together, that nation is linked via the identity category entrepreneur that *Sui Dhaaga* constructs for us to global capital itself, through a subtle nod to the Make in India initiative. Hindu nationalism and neoliberalism intersect, this time through the artisan turned entrepreneur, aka the possessive individual. Through the narratives that it constructs and circulates within public culture, Hindu nationalism labors to link the commoner and his interests to the interests of capital.

THE "STRANGE CASE" OF ZAHEERA SHAIKH

What we have been tracking thus far in the chapter is the ways in which the hegemonic story in Indian public discourse narrates capital as inclusive and democratic, through the figure of the commoner. This story argues that commoners have achieved representation and become agents in new India through an unabashed desire for the accumulation of wealth, by speaking the language of consumption, and embracing possessive individualism, which necessitates an understanding of the skills an individual possesses as commodities that can then be traded in the market. In this section, I turn to the unruly narrative of a young Muslim woman, Zaheera Shaikh, in order to highlight the limits of a story that constitutes and represents the agency of a commoner through the logic of possessive individualism. In line with the discussion of dalit politician Mayawati in chapter 2, this section highlights how even as subalternity or the commoner is foundational to the constitution of the entrepreneurial subjectivity, particular embodiments of commonness also simultaneously mark the limits of that subjectivity. Indeed, the story of Zaheera Shaikh is the limit case of new India. This story marks the limits of possessive individualism espoused by both neoliberalism but also by Hindu nationalism. As we discuss this case, I want to deliberately underline my word choice, tense, and voice. I am interested here in the stories that are told *about* Zaheera Shaikh. I am therefore *not* narrating or retelling her story; I am instead re-narrating the stories that have been told about Shaikh.

Zaheera Shaikh was the star witness in the Vadodara Best Bakery Case. The case refers to a violent incident that took place on March 1, and in the early hours of March 2, 2002, when anti-Muslim programmatic violence engulfed the western Indian state of Gujarat. Fourteen people were killed when a mob set fire to the Best Bakery located in the Hanuman Tekdi neighborhood of the city of Vadodara. The carnage at Best Bakery came to exemplify both the horrific anti-Muslim violence in Gujarat in 2002 and the subsequent legal struggles to bring the perpetrators of that violence to book in legal, activist, and media discourse. In other words, the Best Bakery Case became one of a handful of symbols, a form of shorthand even, to represent the programmatic violence that engulfed Muslims and radically altered the lives of those who survived the carnage. The bakery acquired the force of symbol, in large part because a young Muslim woman named Zaheera Shaikh appeared ready to perform the labor of testifying and narrating the details of the violence and of embodying the struggle for justice against those who had inflicted that violence. The BJP and its leader Narendra Modi were in power in the state during this time. Many of those accused of the violence in the state, including in the Best Bakery case, had links to the BJP and its state machinery.[55]

Zaheera Shaikh, listed as the eighteen-year-old complainant in the "First Information Report" filed by the Vadodara police, is narrated as being a witness when her family's bakery was burned to the ground and is, moreover, believed to have seen members of her family being murdered. "Her story," as one English-language newsmagazine put it, became "the symbol of the Gujarat carnage." Shaikh used "her story" strategically, suturing herself to particular subject positions[56] at particular moments in the case: In the first trial, at the Vadodara court, she said she could not identify the accused as the perpetrators of the bakery killings. Following the acquittal of the accused by the Vadodara court, Shaikh made a statement to the media at a press conference in Mumbai organized by a group called Citizens for Justice and Peace, which included prominent writers and activists. Here, she said she had turned hostile at the Vadodara trial because of intimidation. She stated that "she had lived under a constant threat to her life" from a BJP legislator, who had even escorted her to the court and back to ensure that she gave the testimony that he desired.[57] The Supreme Court of India ordered a retrial of the case outside the state of Gujarat in response to a petition filed by the National Human Rights Commission and Shaikh's statement. In the retrial, however, Shaikh stated that her statements made in the Vadodara court were accurate—that she was unable to recognize the people accused of the Best Bakery massacre. A story published by the English-language newsmagazine *Tehelka*, known for actively pursuing exposés through covertly videotaping key players involved with particular events and issues, subsequently revealed that Shaikh was paid a sum of "Rs 18 lakhs" (approximately $40,000) by political operatives with ties to the BJP to turn hostile again at the retrial.

Why should we read the stories about Zaheera Shaikh within the context of possessive individualism and entrepreneurialism? My contention is that Shaikh's case is significant in the context of the discussion thus far precisely because it pivots on the ability to read her desire for social mobility, the aspiration for acquisition of wealth, and the alleged use of her own story as a commodity that could be traded in the market, as agency. Shaikh remained a symbol of the long struggle for justice for the victims of the violence that engulfed Gujarat in 2002 until it was alleged that she had traded her story like a commodity in the marketplace. Let us remember that the moral and ethical ambiguity defining the practices of fictional characters like Gurukant Desai in the film *Guru* were represented as subaltern maneuvering in a field of constraint, a form of benevolent reading that the story about Shaikh could not garner. Or, if you will allow me a brief detour, consider Arvind Adiga's 2008 Man Booker Prize–winning novel *The White Tiger*, which tells the story of a village tea shop waiter (the village is named Darkness by the protagonist), Balram Halwai, who kills his boss/master, robs him of a suitcase filled with cash, and becomes an entrepreneur in the tech capital of the nation, Bengaluru. The novel defines Darkness as governed by the material and cultural practices of servitude. In this world, the boss is not simply an employer, he is also the patriarch. It follows therefore that Balram Halwai did not just commit any ordinary murder, he committed patricide, in order to become an entrepreneur or, as he narrates it, "to know, just for a day, just for an hour, just for a minute, what it means not to be a servant."[58] Many critics have read *The White Tiger* as a sharp and pointed critique of the new India story. They have read it as a "story of poverty, entrepreneurialism, and postcolonial development,"[59] and as a narrative that puts the lie to the assertion and the promise that neoliberalism will "convert the destitution of the world's poorest into entrepreneurial survival and resilience."[60] *The White Tiger* argues that it isn't liberalization, neoliberalism, or global capital but the slaying of the patriarch-master that liberates the commoner, according to this reading of the novel. More importantly for our purposes here, *The White Tiger* also defines that liberated commoner as an entrepreneur. Balram Halwai talks about the "first entrepreneur" he ever knew thus: "Vijay's family were pigherds, which meant they were the lowest of the low, yet he made it up in life. Somehow he had befriended a politician. People said he had let the politician dip his beak in his backside. Whatever he had to do, he had done: he was the first entrepreneur I knew of."[61] The entrepreneur or entrepreneurialism in *The White Tiger*—the form of which is described by some critics as "unremitting realism"[62]—is similar to the entrepreneurs we have encountered in various stories we have discussed thus far. Undoubtedly, Balram Halwai is an unflinchingly darker character than some of the others we have encountered—and starkly different from *Rocket Singh's* HP— but as *The White Tiger* reminds us, "You can't expect a man in a dung heap to smell sweet."[63] What should also be of interest to us here is that the critics of the novel bore Balram Halwai's stench and read his actions, even his violence, not as nihilism, but as "enact[ing] rather than negat[ing] meaning."[64] Detour done, let us return to Zaheera Shaikh, a victim and witness of real, not fictional, violence. This young woman's trading of her story and in particular her trading of her story for wealth was not read as improvisation, *jugaad*,[65] or the semiotic violence necessary to break the bonds of servitude that shackle women like her. Instead, she was roundly condemned in the English-language news media as deserving of punishment. This is why the story about Shaikh (and not that of the fictional Balram Halwai) produces an unruly moment in our discussion of the entrepreneur.

An editorial in the *Times of India* in 2004 noted that Shaikh "should be tried and punished . . . the vigil maintained by the Supreme Court and the media as well as the change in political climate hold out hope that perpetrators of the Gujarat carnage would be brought to book . . . but unreliable witnesses like Zahira [*sic*] could derail the process of justice and healing."[66] The *Tehelka* article that had revealed that she had sold her story for money began its narrative by suggesting that Shaikh's actions raised a litany of questions: Which one of her testimonies is true? "Why is Zaheera making a mockery of one of the most important trials of the last few decades? Why did she turn hostile even though she saw her own sister Sabira and uncle Kausar Ali being killed? Is it because she wanted to move on with her life and return to Best Bakery? Or was she threatened? Or is there another reason?"[67] Having posed these questions and defined Shaikh as a perplexing figure, the magazine sets out, as it states baldly, to blow the "lid of all conjecture" through its investigation. By revealing that Shaikh was ostensibly paid a sum of money to change her testimony, the magazine vehemently states that the "brutal," "damaging" and "dismaying" truth is now out: Shaikh had claimed that she had changed her testimony and refused to identify the accused because she was threatened. "Yes, Zaheera was threatened," the magazine notes, "but she was not just threatened . . . the prime witness was also paid Rs. 18 lakh to turn hostile." In fact, *Tehelka* claimed, the money was a greater inducement than any threat of violence: "The testimony of Zaheera Sheikh [*sic*] changed *only* because Rs. 18 lakh changed hands. Zaheera retracted in the Vadodara court, not 'because she could not see what the mob was doing as she was hiding out of fear,' but because she had already counted the bucks by then."[68] Having established that money was Shaikh's primary motivation, *Tehelka*'s narrative discredits Shaikh and her agency by deeming it unethical, immoral even.

The judgment of the Special Court in Mumbai, which retried the case, sentenced nine of the accused to life imprisonment, acquitted eight, and punished Zaheera Shaikh with a year in prison for perjury. The judgment was hailed as a moment of immense significance for civil society institutions within media discourse in India. An editorial in *The Hindu* noted that "after four years of tortuous twists and turns," what was most "striking about the Best Bakery case is not the conviction of nine of the 17 accused brought to trial, but the effort that went into securing the ends of justice" and asserted that "without the active intervention of social activists, media personnel, the National Human Rights Commission and the Supreme Court, those responsible for burning to death 14 persons in a Vadodara bakery during the post-Godhra anti-Muslim pogrom in Gujarat in 2002 would have walked free from the law."[69] The eighteen-year-old Muslim woman who had filed the "First Information Report" that enabled the prosecution of the violent massacre, brought the carnage into the purview of the judiciary, and whose repeated statements to the media, nonprofit organizations, human rights groups, and activists had enabled the case to be retried after the accused had been summarily acquitted, was thus written out of the narrative. Shaikh's trading of her own story—arguably the only possession she owned that was marketable—like a commodity in the market could not be represented through the category of entrepreneurialism.

Recall the stories that we have tracked in this chapter: a differently abled boy polishing shoes on a train; a young girl selling flowers at a traffic stop; a politician bypassing his bureaucracy and using a people's co-operative to ostensibly resolve the problem of power inadequacy, and later signing a superstar to anchor a tourism campaign for his state; and the return to traditional caste-based work. All have been narrated as entrepreneurialism. The stories we have tracked through the course of this chapter would suggest a capaciousness to possessive individualism; as we have noted, the entrepreneur is narrated as a cosmopolitan, inclusive, and democratic mode of identification. The narration of the entrepreneur as unshackled enables these stories to define the nation itself as having experienced renewal. The popular histories of India's political economy authored by public intellectuals like Nandan Nilekani and Gurcharan Das have worked to construct a teleology for the entrepreneurial subjectivity, marking a movement from rejection to euphoric embrace. This teleology relies on re-signifying and representing commonness as primordial, itself on a linear trajectory towards its apogee—the cosmopolitanism of the entrepreneurial subjectivity. We have also discussed through the 1970s film *Manthan* that even when the conception of a collective in the form of a co-operative is defined and represented, it has necessitated the narration of a resolute, masculine, and moral individual. Whereas popular cinema of the new millennium—which narrates its central characters as commoners on a journey to becoming cosmopolitan entrepreneurs—can be read as disconnected from narratives like

Manthan, the centering of the morally resolute, incorruptible man in a story about the collective did not disable the narrative about the possessive individual. More importantly, as we have been tracking through this chapter and the previous one, these stories provided the narrative scaffolding for the entrepreneur. The resolute man who once worked to build a co-operative as the solution to inequity is now narrated as an embodiment of unshackled individualism and therefore freedom itself. Zaheera Shaikh's story and its inability to be narrated through hegemonic categories reveals the particularity at the heart of liberalism's possessive individualism. The possessive individual is a masculine embodiment who validates capital but also nationalist morality. The realism of Zaheera Shaikh's story could not be linked to the spectacle of capital or nation. The putative cosmopolitanism of the entrepreneur allows caste and gendered particularity to hide in plain sight. This is why Zaheera Shaikh could not be read as a possessive individual—her trading of her story as a commodity in the marketplace validated neither capital (unlike Gurukant Desai of *Guru* or even Balram Halwai of *The White Tiger*) nor the nation's renewal (unlike Mauji of *Sui Dhaaga* or the dalit entrepreneurs celebrated in the Indian and international press). Zaheera Shaikh's tragic story points to the manner in which gendered subalternity acts as the limit of the entrepreneurial subjectivity and of the possessive individual.

4 · LOVE IN NEW TIMES

There is no good love that, in speaking its name, can change the world into the referent for that name.

—Sara Ahmed

Let me tell you a story, a story about a man and a woman. They belonged to different worlds, but as a matter of chance one day they met. The man had been surprised (coerced, perhaps?) into going deep-sea diving with two of his buddies. He did not want to do it. He could not swim and was afraid, but he had to do it because he had made a pact with his friends. She was their dive instructor. He was a financial consultant, a broker, a trader, living and working in London. His well-appointed apartment was meticulously organized. Coldly logical and methodical, he had a plan for his life, and he wanted to make as much money as he could. He had lost his father young and his mother had been saddled with her husband's debt. The lesson he had learned from that early experience was that wealth and everything it entailed for those who had it was all that mattered. Consequently, he was tightly wound, closed, and insular. She was a free spirit, open to every adventure life had in store, and she believed that a man should be placed in a box only when he was dead. They were each other's foils, and they intrigued each other. She worked closely with him on the dive, gently encouraging him to overcome his fear, one breath and one step at a time. She held his hand and led him into the breathtakingly beautiful world, deep underwater. He was enchanted and moved. Something had shifted deep inside him. She continued to encourage him to absorb the wonders of each of life's moments. They fell in love. As the last challenge of their pact, the friends would run with bulls. He said if he survived, he would travel the world with her. He might lose his job; the job that he had prioritized over everything, including his most cherished relationships, the job that had given him the financial security, and indeed the social mobility, wealth, and elite status that he had desired most of his life. So what? he said, he would live, he would be alive. He survived the run. They got married. The end.

The story that I have narrated is one of the three tracks in the immensely popular 2011 Hindi film *Zindagi Na Milegi Dobara* (You Don't Live Twice, Zoya Akhtar). It is a love story in which the conflict driving the narrative is the man's emotional emptiness and incompleteness. The story links this sense of emptiness to his immersion in the new world of finance capital. Differences of class, caste, religion, or other social markers, which played a significant role in love stories made in an earlier era, are not remarked upon, and as such, they appear inconsequential to the trajectory of this love story.[1] Falling in love with a woman who cares little about money and social status saves the man from his ennui. Yet that love does not necessarily alter his relationship to capital nor does it expressly critique capital. Falling in love, recognizing love, and naming it as such, does not, as Sara Ahmed reminds us, change the world so that it becomes love's referent. Or does it?

The love story, in fact, has been read within film scholarship as the "ideal type," a uniquely suited aesthetic form for modern capitalism. As film scholar Sangita Gopal has argued: "If modern capitalism is driven by consumption (i.e. the urge to possess objects), then romantic love is the ideal type of this general desire."[2] Gopal argues that classic Hindi cinema (which for her falls within the timeline of 1947–1970) inevitably represented "desire as the reciprocal longing of two freely choosing individuals," since it is a "commercial medium subject to the laws of capital." What distinguishes the classic love story made between 1947 and 1970 from the newer iterations made post-economic liberalization is that the Hindi film industry in the decades immediately post-independence also saw itself as participating in the project of nation-building and therefore, Gopal contends, "it felt obligated to acknowledge and work with the extended family as the locus for political and cultural change." It was this "double imperative"—to represent love as desire between two autonomous individuals whom capital calls upon to identify as consumers *and* as members of a family whom kinship ties and the nation calls upon to identify with—that necessitated the "creation of a distinctive version of the couple form."[3] In other words, according to Gopal, the couple form in classic Hindi cinema "served as a mechanism that enabled the conjoining of private desires and public concerns"—"private desires" being love or romance between two individuals and "public concerns" being the imperatives of the family and the nation.

Love stories produced in the post-liberalization era work to narrate the tribulations of matrimony. Conflict is therefore located within the realm of the private. As such, or so the argument goes, the couple in the new love story, such as the one I have outlined, is formed by individuals "isolated" from the "domain of the social" but "inserted" into a "network of material objects, lifestyle attitudes, sociological trends, and financial and economic metrics," and these individuals become the idealized form of the citizen in post–economic liberalization India.[4] The argument here is that neoliberalism in India (much like neoliberalism elsewhere) demands an ideal type that centers consumption, both the actual act of consumption but also the cultivation of an attitude that desires consumption, and that new love stories narrate the couple within this mold. The love story is therefore an ineffective critique of neoliberalism, at best.

I am suggesting here that the narrative negotiations with heterosexual love are variegated and complex. For instance, the consequences of the double movement of "isolation" from the space of the social and "insertion" into the space of finance and the economy are posited as different for the male and female leads within the narratives of certain Hindi films. Films like *Love Aaj Kal* (Love Today and Yesterday/Love Nowadays, Imtiaz Ali, 2009), *Band Baaja Baaraat* (released internationally as *The Wedding Planners*) (Maneesh Sharma, 2010), and *Zindagi Milegi Na Dobara* (You Don't Live Twice, Zoya Akhtar, 2011) suggest that the post–economic liberalization male is rendered incomplete through his "insertion" into the space of finance. It is only when he learns to love—more specifically when he learns to recognize love as a sensory experience that is outside the bounds of consumerism and the vicissitudes of transactional economics—that he is rendered complete. Thus, even as neoliberalism in India is euphorically narrated as national renewal and experienced as global modernity through the form of spectacular realism, contemporary popular Hindi cinema has nevertheless in some of its recent productions ruminated and reflected on a sense of loss, a certain ennui in these new times. This kind of popular narrative constitutes femininity and the feminine ideal as the corrective for the experience of fragmentation that defines global modernity. In doing so, it continues to center masculinity as *the* gender of modernity, appropriating a particular form of femininity even as it continues to obfuscate the woman. While the cinematic love stories such as the one we began with do not decenter capital or the nation—*Zindagi Na Milegi Dobara*, in fact, can be credited with channeling the burgeoning economic might of the new Indian middle class toward global tourism and spectacular vacations that can be documented on social media—these popular cultural narratives embed a contradictory story. That other narrative impulse hints at love's radical potential to decenter the possessive individual of global modernity and at love's ability to engage deeply with difference.

In no small measure, this complex rendering of love is a consequence of the fact that Hindi cinema draws on a variety of sources and traditions when narrating love. Whereas the cinematic rendering of love in Hollywood and world cinema is crucially important to Hindi films, the repertoire of Sanskrit and Prakrit epics, lyrics, plays and stories, and the Perso-Arabic repertoire including Sufi poems, religious injunctions, poetic romances (*masnavis*), eulogies (*qasida*), lyrics (*ghazal*), and devotional bhakti poetry and philosophy are significant too.[5] Also, some love stories produced in the 1970s, particularly those that adapted regional language literature, centered the *woman's* interiority—her confusions (about an old love and the current one) and desires (for an abstract, dreamy conception of love and the "real" touch of a lover)—and some narrated the man's ineptness at wooing the woman (not necessarily his inability to recognize love). Other love stories produced in the 1970s and the 1980s narrated love using the strokes of an epic—centering conflicts on class and status, family feuds, as well as betrayals of a lover resulting in a death and an avenging rebirth.

It is imperative then to think about the ways in which the popular love story in this conjuncture is rendered by articulating together diverse allusions and conceptions—from the idea of romantic desire as consumption and the conflict between love and family (read: national) honor to love as a tale of adventure and wonder and love as transcending "social norms and restrictions and ultimately even transitory human life."[6] Also, it is necessary to think of both the continuities and discontinuities between the love stories that were produced in the four decades between the 1970s and 2015 and what these trajectories and ruptures might tell us about love in "new times."

Moreover, an analysis or discussion of love in new India must necessarily consider the Hindu Right's conceptualization of "love jihad" in addition to the form of conjugality enabled by neoliberalism. In the Hindu Right's conception of love jihad, love is conceived as the mask that hides the grotesque project of jihad. Love jihad conceives the jihadi Muslim male as strategically and cynically using love to capture and convert Hindu femininity. The phrase "love jihad" is sometimes traced back to 2007 and to the workings of the Hindu Janajagriti Samiti, an organization that is a part of the Hindu nationalist movement, in the southern Indian states of Karnataka and Kerela.[7] An argument can be made that in 2009 the division bench of the Karnataka High Court had legitimized the phrase by seeking an inquiry into the presence of a "conspiracy" that was resulting in the religious conversion of Hindu women to Islam through marriage with Muslim males. The inquiry was in response to a habeas corpus petition filed in the state's high court by the father of a Hindu woman (Silja Raj) who had eloped with a Muslim man, alleging "love jihad." The inquiry revealed that the Silja Raj had married and converted to Islam on her own volition and that there was no evidence of any "organized attempt by any group of individuals to entice girls/women belonging to Hindu or Christian religions to marry Muslim boys with the aim of converting them to Islam."[8] While empirical evidence could not be mustered, the story of love as jihad aimed at demographically depleting the numbers of Hindus while simultaneously raising the demographic might of Muslims remains in circulation, having moved in its most contemporary iteration from the southern and westerns states of Karnataka, Kerala, and Gujarat to the northern Indian states of Uttar Pradesh, Haryana, and Jharkhand.

As historian Charu Gupta reminds us, the conception of love as a strategic tool of war has a much longer trajectory. Gupta has argued that in the 1920s within the context of Hindu assertion in northern India, movements such as *shuddi* or the movement to "purify" and reclaim those who had converted from Hinduism to other religions and *sanghathan*, or the "organization in defense of Hindu interests" were launched. It is in this period that "the Hindu woman's body became a marker to sharpen communal boundaries in ways more aggressive than before." Consequently, a range of propaganda materials were circulated during this time that claimed "abductions and conversions of Hindu women by Muslim goondas, ranging from allegations of rape, abduction and elopement, to luring, conversion, love and forced marriages."[9] Working with a diverse set of resources, including "newspapers, pamphlets, meetings, handbills, posters, novels, myths, rumors and gossip, the campaign was able to operate in a public domain, and monopolize the field of everyday representation."[10] The most contemporary iteration of this discourse, which inevitably leads to programmatic violence and the displacement of Muslims,[11] uses the post-9/11 globally legible language of jihad and terrorism funded and organized by terrorist assemblages residing on foreign shores. Love in this conception is a weapon much like the car bomb, the hijacked plane, and the crude bomb in a backpack, meant to devastate the non-Muslim. Thus, while contemporary cinematic renderings narrate love and the feminine ideal as redemptive for the fragmented, adrift neoliberal male, the Hindu right's concept of "love jihad" flips the coin on love and narrates it as the danger that threatens the purity of Hindu society; the Hindu feminine body is the vulnerable breach in such a conceptualization.

How do we read these divergent narrations of love *together*? And what might such a reading reveal about the sexual and gendered ground on which neoliberalism and nationalism are formulated in India? What are the continuities and discontinuities in the love stories produced between 1970 and 2015? Why and through what ways does love trouble ethnic nationalism and neoliberalism even as it also affectively sutures them together? These are some of the motivating questions for this chapter.

As a concept, love has been read through diverse and sometimes contradictory philosophical perspectives. For instance, Elizabeth Povinelli has argued that our modern conception of love, in the shape of an event that is formed at the "intersection—and crisis—of"[12] the discourses of individual freedom and social constraint, "emerged from European Empire as a mode and maneuver of domination and exploitation."[13] As such, Povinelli stresses, the "intimate couple is a key transfer point between, on the one hand, liberal imaginaries of contractual economics, politics, and sociality and, on the other, liberal forms of power in the contemporary world."[14] This love, to follow Povinelli's argument, keeps in circulation the story that the only choice that matters and that is available to us is between individual freedom and social constraint, and moreover, that this choice is "natural, vital and irreplaceable."[15] Is the new Hindi cinematic love story that appears utterly uninterested in social constraints and foregrounds internal and internalized conflict instead a break then from the liberal imaginary? Not quite. As Povinelli reminds us, liberalism is not a "thing," but instead is a "moving target" that rolls in the ground it finds itself in, gathering and appropriating materials and taking the shape of the ground itself such that it appears "natural, vital and irreplaceable." In other words, if we are to argue that the classic Hindi cinematic love story sets in motion the couple form as the embodiment of liberal logics and aspirations (choosing between individual freedom and social constraint), then the new love story constitutes the couple as the ideal of neoliberalism. Read through this framework, the new love story twines love as spectacle to the realism of the incompleteness of the man-within-finance-capital and adjusts him to that world.

French philosopher Alain Badiou, in praise of love on the other hand, has called for its reinvention, following the poet Arthur Rimbaud. Badiou's argument is that the liberal and libertarian conceit of rendering love risk-free, much like war is sanitized and made clean, is precisely the threat that love faces. For Badiou, love is not limited to that which liberalism and neoliberalism alike have defined it as. Love must be reinvented, loosened from its suturing to liberal logics, which suggest that love must end in a contract between two freely choosing individuals. Love, Badiou argues—drawing significantly from poets and poetry more than from philosophy—is an encounter that enables you to see the world from the perspective of two rather than from the perspective of one. Love is an event, Badiou argues, but unlike Povinelli, for Badiou, this means it is "quite opaque and only finds reality in its multiple resonances within the real world."[16] In other words, love is neither identity nor the impulse to survive or thrive, and it is not communion and not an experience; instead, love is about the "paradox of an identical difference"[17] (seeing as two not one) and always about "the possibility of being present at the birth of the world."[18] "Love isn't simply about two people meeting and their inward-looking relationship: it is a construction, a life that is being made, no longer from the perspective of One but from the perspective of Two," Badiou insists.[19] For him then, love is about the construction of a world on the ground of difference, not through consumption or contract with the Other, but *with* the Other. The world that love enables, Badiou suggests, can be constructed by the event of the "I" and the "Other" coming together and constituting the Two.

In the story that this chapter narrates, we will hold the conception of love as the radical possibility of the formation of a new world that is built on the ground of difference conjointly with the conception of love as the colonial maneuver of domination and control that reified the individual and individual autonomy and the consuming couple as the ideal citizens of neoliberalism but also as the instrument of Hindu patriarchy. We will hold the narration of love as that which is outside the boundedness of global capital and the corporate boardroom together with the narration of love as a cynical mask and a tool of war. By staying with the tension, perplexity, and unease that these dissonant conceptions and narrations of love engender, rather than succumbing to the requirement to create mutually exclusive categories, the story this chapter narrates points to the instability of the conjuncture that we have been referring to as Hindutva neoliberalism. Even as love, as the tool of the hegemonic story, narrates a tale of emasculation—through either the story of the brutal masculine Other (lower-caste or Muslim male) ravaging vulnerable femininity (the upper-caste Hindu female) or the ineptness of the modern male at the art of romance—and therefore also a subsequent masculine awakening, love is also that imagining that does the politically powerful work of revealing the processes through which this hegemonic story is constituted and points to another imaginary. The love story thus reveals the persistent iterative work necessary to maintain the contours of the conjuncture and the gendered and sexed ground on which this work is carried out. The chapter will therefore follow the simple script of the heterosexual love story: it will lay out the character sketch of first the male lead, then that of the female lead, and then sing a song about their love or discuss the love song, an elemental feature of the cinematic love story. The narrative form of spectacular realism has some trouble with the cinematic love story. As we follow the script of the love story, we will also track its complex navigation with form.

THE MAN

The 1970s saw the powerful emergence of the character of the angry young man on celluloid, embodied by the actor Amitabh Bachchan. Even when he seized the wealth that would allow him to escape the street and don the well-tailored suit instead of the dockworker's uniform, neither the grit and grime of the street nor the dark and violent masculinity that he embodied when walking on it would leave him. His baritone voiced the obstructed times he lived in and the tragedy that would be his story. But the 1970s also produced another cinematic male lead. This man—whom film scholar Satish Poduval has referred to as the "affable young man" in contradistinction to the angry young man—featured in some of the love stories of the decade and was embodied by the actor (also writer and director) Amol Palekar. This young man of the 1970s—who featured in such love stories as *Rajnigandha* (The Flower, Basu Chatterjee, 1974), *Chhoti Si Baat* (A Little Matter, Basu Chatterjee, 1976), and the comedy *Golmaal* (Chaos, Hrishikesh Mukherjee, 1979)—was distinctly middle class, urban, educated, and often an employee in a corporation waiting for a promotion, affable, and endearingly inept. He embodied realism, through sociological detailing, in the manner in which we have been tracking throughout this book. Even if he was struggling to find employment, a suitable home, or a promotion at work, he belonged in this world and did not reside at its margins in the way the angry young man did. If the angry young man never smiled, *this* young man smiled all the time, and his voice—with its nasal, high-pitched twang—was the sonic instantiation of a bumbling, nonthreatening masculinity. This young man, particularly in films like *Rajnigandha* and *Chhoti Si Baat*, was unencumbered by family, and even if he was anxious about his job or whether he would secure a promotion, socioeconomic class was not a constraint on romance. Instead, either his ineptitude at expressing his ardor and at wooing the feminine Other or his involvement in a comedy of errors that needed untangling proved to be the constraint.

This young man embodied a masculinity that was deemed ill-formed and hesitant; it was feminized and therefore required tutelage, almost always from a father figure, a patriarch. The patriarch schooled him on acquiring a masculine ethos that was more aggressively articulate, was status-aware and therefore brooked no offense from those of lower status, that was intolerant toward his rivals in romance, and that took charge of the scene of romance. This was a form of masculinity that sometimes aimed to appropriate the swagger and musculature of the angry young man without a recognition of the angry young man as a political being. In several of these love stories, including *Chhoti Si Baat*, the affable young man briefly encounters Amitabh Bachchan, the actor playing himself, but in the makeup and costume of the angry young man. Often this encounter would occur on the film set or when Bachchan was ostensibly on his way to or from a film set. In some cases, the encounter between the affable young man and the angry young man occurs through a film's publicity materials, such as the poster, or in a dream. The angry young man is thus established as a spectacular cinematic persona even as the affable young man is defined as the real, and, more importantly, as the commoner or the *aam admi*. The realism of this commoner needed to intersect with the angry young man, who was transformed into a spectacle. In *Chhoti Si Baat*, the encounter between realism and the spectacle occurs at the home/school of the father figure who has consented to tutor the character played by Amol Palekar so he can correct his masculinity. The affable young man is awestruck by Amitabh Bachchan as the angry young man, and in that brief cinematic moment the narrative of the film establishes the angry young man's masculine ethos as superior. The common man can borrow and appropriate the style of the spectacularly cinematic angry young man. And because this appropriation occurs via the tutoring of the patriarch, it has the moral and social sanction that the affable young man always seeks.

Recall that we have discussed another consumption or appropriation of the angry young man when examining the concept-image of development in chapter 1. There, another cinematic middle-class character, Michael Mukherjee in the Mani Ratnam film *Yuva* (Youth), consumed the aura of the angry young man by delinking his masculinist aggression from the subaltern world of caste-based politics. In *Yuva* the angry young man embodied realism, which needed to be linked to the irrefutable and therefore spectacular moral superiority of the middle class Mukherjee in order to be legitimated. In the love stories we are discussing here, the "affable young man," a mundane and unremarkable middle-class character, is our embodiment of realism and the angry young man's unflinching and resolute masculinity is the uncontested spectacle. Both stories require the spectacle to intersect with realism and necessitate the strategic appropriation of the angry young man. To dwell on the significance of the angry young man character for these narratives, it is necessary to draw out the articulation of masculinity with modernity.

I am interested specifically in the feminist reading of modernity, which traces the *particular* processes through which the *universal* experience of modernity is constituted. Feminist analyses of modernist texts have shown how gendered symbolism has enabled the construction of quintessentially modernist tropes of (masculine) rationalization and (feminine) pleasure.[20] Some of the Hindi cinematic texts produced toward the end of the twentieth century and in the beginning of the new millennium define the normative subject of modernity as masculine, specifically a middle-class, upper-caste, and urban form of masculinity; however, as we have just discussed, this masculinity is narrated as incomplete and as a work in progress. The incompleteness of this masculinity is excavated via the love story, by positioning the masculine beside the feminine Other, and significantly, its inadequacy is also revealed by positioning this young man against the subaltern male (the angry young man).

Mediated as it has been by the experience of British colonialism, the region's encounter with modernity has involved a complex suturing of patriarchal systems (with caste and regional variations), the changes wrought on the family by colonialism,[21] the experience of travel and Western education, the institution of reform laws such as the Special Marriages Act of 1872 allowing for marriage based on individual choice, and the religious reformist movements, which in the case of Hinduism involved a " process of cultural reorientation, with a view of forming individuals who would fulfill their human (and national) potential."[22] As gender historians such as Mrinalini Sinha have shown, reform of cultural and religious practices and rituals—such as the age of sexual consent—through the machinery of the colonial state often resulted in the formation of a resistant coalition between nationalists and traditional leaders resulting in the strengthening of Hindu patriarchy. The formation of this coalition was both a reaction to and the renegotiation of the colonial binary differentiating between the "manly Englishman" and the "effeminate Bengali." Opposition to colonial social reform policies was based on the assumption that such policies were an intrusion into Indian or native domestic relations and the assertion of control over their "own" women and spaces of domesticity was the nationalist response in masculinist garb. In other words, the negotiation with modernity was enmeshed with masculinity—in its adequately manly or inadequate and feminized form.

Consider in this context the manner in which the conception of an inadequate masculinity was linked to the anticolonial nationalist movement, but more specifically to the Hindu nationalist movement in the nineteenth century. Positing a specific relationship between masculinity and the nation as well as between Vedic Hinduism and the nation, nineteenth-century Hindu reformers such as Dayanand Saraswati and Vivekananda exhorted men to "devote their body and soul to the well-being of the country." Vivekananda commanded his followers to forcefully pray to the "Mother Goddess" to take away their "weakness," their "unmanliness," and to make them "Men." The divergence here is the manner in which this conception of an inadequate masculinity and its resolution into manliness is articulated in the cinematic narrative to success in love and within the scene of heterosexual romance. As I have argued elsewhere, the nineteenth-century Hindu nationalist conception of masculinity demanded aggression and musculature but also celibacy.[23] The practice of celibacy here was defined as a form of renunciation.[24] The muscled, grim, celibate Hindu upper-caste male in the service of the nation was, in fact, a staple of nationalist cinematic narratives that represented Islam as an ideology and a threat to the nation in the 1990s, when Hindu nationalist groups were resurrecting themselves through mass mobilization campaigns.[25] In the case of the Hindi cinematic love story though, the conception of inadequate masculinity is uncoupled from the conception of renunciate celibacy, for here primacy is accorded to the scene of romance over the scene of war. The hesitant and feminized masculinity of the affable young man is thus one iteration of this protracted relationship between modernity and masculinity. Embodied by

Amol Palekar, this hesitant masculinity was endearing, even refreshingly different from the dark and brooding masculinity of the angry young man, who was nevertheless necessary for our middle-class common man to find his own sense of self. Sutured to his affability, his sense of middle-class ethics, and even his fumbling ineptitude at recognizing and overcoming the wily maneuvers of "other" men, audiences of such love stories root for his success at the scene of romance and are rewarded by the happy union of the young man with "his" woman.

The focus of love stories like *Bobby* (Raj Kapoor, 1973) or the aptly and pithily titled *Love Story* (Rajendra Kumar, 1981), which were box office mega-successes and made their protagonists overnight sensations, was not the inadequate masculinity of the modern, urban, middle-class male. Instead working with a conception of youthful masculinity that was either brash, uninhibited, and even rough (*Love Story*), or charming and wounded by parental neglect (*Bobby*), these films zoomed in on the scene of romance and the transformations it wrought in the protagonists and the worlds within which they resided. In the films that featured the affable young man, love was a matter of routine—like going to work every day, the young man would glimpse or meet his girlfriend and talk about similar matters each day—structured and organized by the time of the modern, of capital. Its fulfillment required a shift in masculine embodiment. Love was, however, cast in spectacular form in cinematic love stories such as *Bobby* and *Love Story*. Here, love was not a matter of the clock but was a profoundly revolutionary sensation that itself transformed the lovers.

In *Love Story*, where an old feud between the fathers of the protagonists is the conflict that must be resolved, love softens the arrogance and the brashness of the young man. He is transformed into a caring, sentimental, even sensitive man who struggles and fights for his love. Films like *Love Story*, *Maine Pyar Kiya* (I Loved, Sooraj Barjatya, 1989), and even *Qayamat Se Qayamat Tak* (From Doom Till Doom, Mansoor Khan, 1988) all featured male protagonists from wealthy families—sons of rich builders, businessmen or feudalists turned retailers—who take to some form of manual labor when on the run (for love) from their warring families. Love compels these young men to run away with the young women they are in love with—leaving the homes, resources, and luxuries they grew up with—and then labor with rudimentary tools at a distance from metropolitan urban landscapes. Even though the scene of work remains undefined, the cinematic narrative presents this labor-in-love as transformative.[26] If love in these stories is the spectacular sensation, then the labor-in-love performed by the man-in-love is the investment in creating a world within which that love could reside, in which that love would become the real and the mundane. In *Love Story*, abrasive youthful masculinity is ironed out by this labor-in-love into an emotional, sensitive manliness. In *Maine Pyar Kiya* and *Qayamat Se Qayamat Tak*, it gives the young man a voice and a purpose and compels him to look the patriarch in the eye and eschew that which he believes now to be wrong, unfair, or hateful. Consequently, this youthful love and its supplement the labor-in-love transforms the social world and

its relationships that had been set up by the film. In *Bobby*, the arrogant, neglect-
ful, rich father becomes a caring man and links arms with another who belongs to
a fishing community and a different faith. In *Love Story*, an old feud is forgotten
and a patriarch is reformed, and in *Maine Pyar Kiya*, the patriarch who had allowed
socioeconomic class to become a chasm reunites with his old friend. These stories
do not necessarily dismantle patriarchy, but they do challenge the patriarch. The
youthful, often immature masculinity of the male protagonist is transformed into
a forceful manliness as a consequence of this rebellion. The male protagonist does
not need to consume or appropriate a subaltern masculinity to undergo the transformation; being in love calls for that change. In fact, if the first half of this love
story is concerned with the staging of the romance and narrates love as spectacular, the second half is centrally about the conflict between a form of masculinity
that is empowered by patriarchy and wealth and a masculinity that is fueled by
labor-in-love. These narratives thus write love as transformative not just for the
lovers but their families, and specifically their patriarchs as well. Spectacular love
here transforms reality.

The antecedents of *these* love stories are rich and include the ghazal and the
masnavi (romances) drawn from the Perso-Arabic repertoire that has circulated in
the South Asian region for at least three centuries. As Francesca Orsini writes,
"Emotions distilled in a ghazal verse have long been one of the most powerful
means of sentimental education in South Asia, whether through the memorized
couplets of famous poets like Mir Taqi Mir (1722–1810) or Ghalib (1797–1869), or
the film songs of lyricists like Majrooh Sultanpuri and Sahir Ludhianvi or the
audio cassettes of Begum Akhtar, Iqbal Bano, Ghulam Ali and Jagjit Singh."[27]
Moreover, Orsini suggests that the "function of love" as seen through the universe
of the ghazal is "that of softening the heart and making it receptive to more pain,
so as ultimately to make the human heart a site for the Divine Light to be reflected
upon it and into it." The masnavi specialized in the "conflict between love and ethics or between the code of love and family honor."[28] In the stories about love that
the masnavi narrated, "The quest for self-perfection and happiness is typically
depicted as a quest for fulfilment in love and for union with the beloved."[29] Scholars have also pointed to two distinct strands within the romantic masnavi, one
that told an adventure story and a second that had a simple linear narrative about
two individuals and their emotional states. The masnavi insisted that this was a
real story by situating the characters in historically specific spaces and times and
"put forth their own doctrine of 'true love,' which disregards and transcends social
norms and restrictions and ultimately even transitory human life."[30] Cinematic
love stories like *Bobby*, *Qayamat Se Qayamat Tak*, and even *Love Story* are resonant
with this repertoire of love, as they visually and sonically narrate love as sometimes transforming the brash, arrogant man (and woman) into a caring, ethical
individual, and at other times they narrate the coming of age and maturing of masculinity through the pain and happiness of encountering love. Always, these films
posit love as greater than social hierarchies, norms, and familial restrictions. I do

not want to suggest direct correlations between these ballads and verses and the mass entertainers produced by the Hindi film industry, just as I do not want to posit a simple linkage between Vedic Hindu conceptions of masculinity and the cinematic narrative. However, it is imperative, I believe, to trace the appearance, reappearance, narration, and representation of certain themes and tropes within the love stories that circulate in the region.

The challenge to the patriarch that existed in some of the films, especially those made in the 1980s, is replaced in several classic love stories made in the 1990s, post-economic liberalization by the narration of a benevolent but conservative father figure. In films such as the popular *Dilwale Dulhaniya Le Jayenge* (The Big-hearted Will Take the Bride, or DDLJ, Aditya Chopra, 1995) or *Kabhie Khushi Kabhie Gham* (Sometimes Happiness, Sometimes Sorrow, or K3G, Karan Johar, 2001), the patriarch is an obstacle to the story of love, but when embodied by actors like Amrish Puri and Amitabh Bachchan with a commanding screen presence and a booming baritone, the father is resolute, sturdy manliness itself against which bumbling, youthful masculinity must struggle. The anger or resigned subterfuge against the patriarch that had fueled the transformation of youthful masculinity in earlier films is now replaced by earnest persuasion (DDLJ) or a sorrowful exit and a pining nostalgia (K3G). The narratives of these films are not necessarily interested in offering a challenge to the patriarch, but employ their protagonists— the ideal consuming, desiring individuals suited for a new, neoliberal India—to win the consent of these formidable fathers. The young men in love do not labor in rural or semi-urban environs with rudimentary tools; instead they are global citizens who travel unencumbered between London and the metropolitan cities of India, they conspicuously consume without compunction, and the laboring struggle that other young men in other love stories found essential to discover their own voice does not seem necessary for these young men. Even though the films conclude with the lovers united or returned to the family fold—importantly, with the consent of the father—the narrative resolutely maintains the patriarch as the centripetal force of this cinematic world. In fact, in these stories, the patriarch as much as capital and the nation, is the spectacle.

Let us read this return of the patriarch to preeminence on the cinematic screen alongside the discourse on love jihad. As mentioned, love jihad as a phrase and as a phenomenon is a creation of Hindu nationalist groups that has now been accorded a certain legitimacy by a state high court and the Supreme Court of India seeking an investigation into the phenomenon. In November 2020, the Uttar Pradesh state government passed an ordinance that placed severe bureaucratic hurdles for interfaith marriages, particularly if they involved religious conversions. This ordinance has come to be known as the "love jihad law" because it has led to the arrest of Muslim men (seen in the company of Hindu women or registering a marriage with a Hindu woman) on the charge that they were forcibly converting Hindu women. Love jihad suggests that Muslim men—backed by terrorist organizations—lure Hindu women with the promise of love, convert and marry them, and then recruit them for anti-national work. Lawsuits filed in the courts to annul the marriages between a Hindu woman and a Muslim man on the ground that the matrimony was a consequence of love jihad are always filed in the name of the Hindu woman's father, the patriarch. The demand made of the courts is that the marriage be annulled and the woman be returned to the father. In the case of a twenty-four-year-old woman, Hadiya, in the state of Kerala who had converted to Islam and then arranged a marriage for herself through a matrimonial website with a Muslim man, Shafin Jahan, the Kerala High Court noted that "though the learned senior counsel [Hadiya's lawyers] has vociferously contended that the detenue is a person who has attained majority, it is necessary to bear in mind the fact that the detenue who is a female in her twenties is at a vulnerable age . . . as per Indian tradition, the custody of an unmarried daughter is with the parents . . . we consider it the duty of this court to ensure that a person under such a vulnerable state is not exposed to further danger."[31] Having noted this, the court granted "custody" of Hadiya to her father. Not only does the Kerala High Court infantilize a twenty-four-year-old and deem her vulnerable and therefore requiring her placement in the custody of her parents, the judgment also deems her intellectually and emotionally incompetent at worst, immature at best, on the evidence that she failed her first-year exams in her undergraduate program in homeopathic medicine, that she had subsequently failed to enroll in and complete the final-year residency that would have completed her requirements for the degree, and had instead chosen to convert to Islam—and that while she claimed an interest in Islam, she had only completed a two-month-long course on the religion. The Kerala High Court judgment on the Hadiya case is significant in the context of the love story for two reasons: first, the High Court insisted that the marriage between Hadiya and Shafin Jahan was fraudulent because there was *no* evidence of love; the couple had met through a matrimonial website, and in the court's opinion the marriage appeared to have been arranged by a third party— with whom Hadiya was living—and not by the parents of the couple. Moreover, the court noted that Shafin Jahan was a political activist and therefore the marriage was a sham, a maneuver to remove Hadiya from the purview of the parens patriae (the court acting as the "father of the nation") and the patriarch (her father). As such, the court suggested that it knew what love *looked* like—the young woman and man meet, spend time together, and decide to get married despite parental opposition—and since Hadiya and Shafin did not follow this cinematic script of love, the court could not read it through the frame of a "love marriage." The marriage was therefore arranged and because this arrangement did not involve the participation of the woman's Hindu family, in the court's eye it was fraudulent.

Second, the court, in exercising its power of parens patriae, deemed it necessary to treat a healthy, competent, educated twenty-four-year-old woman as its ward. Here, Hadiya did not become the court's ward because she lived in an abusive, violent, or inhumane environment but because she had acted out of the bounds of daughterly practice demanded of an unmarried daughter in what the court called a middle-class Hindu home. In other words, because she had converted to Islam, had not completed the requirements for her degree, and then arranged a marriage for herself with a Muslim male, she required the persistent and unrelenting gaze of the patriarch and the court acting as parens patriae. At various instances in this tragic case, the court dictated where Hadiya should live, what she should do (complete the requirements for her degree and secure employment as a homeopathic doctor), who could visit her, and even whether she could carry a cell phone. Pointing to Hadiya's temerity in not keeping the court informed about her marital plans and arranging the wedding without its (or her father's) consent, the court deemed it a sham and annulled it. What was most significant about the way in which the Kerala High Court bench of Surendra Mohan and Abraham Mathew *saw* not-love and love and exercised its jurisdiction of parens patriae in this judgment passed in 2017 (in a case that had seen several turns and diktats from the court over the year and a half prior), was the embodiment of patriarchal power. Both in its cinematic iteration in the love stories made posteconomic liberalization and in the legal arguments made in cases involving "love jihad," it is this sociocultural and legal preeminence of patriarchal power that is revealed as foundational to Hindutva neoliberalism in India.

Finally, I want to turn to yet another iteration of love and the love story on the Hindi cinematic screen to highlight a narrative about love and masculinity that links global capital and neoliberal "new times" with the embodiment of an anguished and incomplete masculinity. These films draw heavily from the Perso-Arabic repertoire of love discussed earlier and therefore narrate love as transformative. In fact, love here is narrated as requisite for the completion and fulfillment of the self. These films zoom in on the two individuals; families, when present, are given short shrift and remain insignificant to the plot of the love story and the patriarch is often absent.

Love Aaj Kal (Love Yesterday and Today/Love Nowadays, Imtiaz Ali, 2009), an instantiation of this kind of love story, suggests that a debilitating loss has accompanied the coming of new times in India. The film marks this loss as the transnational Indian male's inability to first comprehend and then to express feelings, specifically the feeling of love. The film follows the tortured routes of the male protagonist—a mobile, young Indian male at home in London, San Francisco, and Delhi—who must first understand and then find an expression of his love. The film suggests that the cosmopolitan, modern, and new subjectivities of "new times" that have emerged from what is seen in the film as a completed and successful tussle against older social hierarchies such as caste, class, and religion have a harder time comprehending feelings. Moreover, the film ironically suggests that this incomprehension may be a consequence of the absence in new times of the very identity struggles that made it possible for the protagonist to be a cosmopolitan, secular, modern youth. In other words, *Love Aaj Kal* suggests that in the India of new times, youth are *not* constrained by social hierarchies in the same way their counterparts in old times were. In the conflict between social constraint and individual freedom that Povinelli talks about, freedom and the individual have been declared victors. This is precisely what is new and today (*aaj*), *Love Aaj Kal* suggests. However, *Love Aaj Kal* also argues, quite emphatically, that the globally modern, unmoored individual of these new times is lost, incapable of recognizing and comprehending love. This individual, the film argues, is, in fact, unfree. A song sequence—titled *Mein Kya Hoon* (Who and what am I?)—encapsulates some of the film's key narrative arguments. The song sets up a dissonance. While the lyrics and the melody signify dizzying masculinist exhilaration of living in new times— there is an emphasis on possession and possessing, of desire and desiring and of conquest—the visuals, while initially in sync with these sonic signifiers, quickly reveal the absolute unraveling of the self-possessed young man. The visuals suggest that the mundane routine of calendrical time created by global capital, coupled with the isolation (in the midst of a crowd) it engenders, leave the man anguished, bereft, utterly despondent, and adrift.

> The horizon of my dream now kisses my feet
> Earlier I was behind/Earlier I followed, now the world follows me.
>
> How do I tell you what and who I am,
> I am the one who gets/possesses that which I desire
> I am the one who keeps promises made to myself alone
> I am the one who gets/possesses that which I desire....[32]

This song appears toward the midpoint of the narrative and serves to define the climactic conflict of the story. By this point in the cinematic narrative, Jai, the male protagonist of *Love Aaj Kal*, can be seen as an embodiment of new India. He is at home in the world, moving effortlessly between London, San Francisco, and Delhi; he is self-assured, confident, and materially successful, and he has conquered the world in the way that he believed he had to. In its lyrics, the song makes allusions to the India Poised commercial discussed in detail in chapter 2. It emphasizes the globally modern new Indian male's ability to possess his dreams of material success. This man of new times does not follow—as the India Poised commercial had predicted—but leads the world, and perhaps most importantly, unlike the denizen of old India who is in the thrall of time, this man of new India has time itself in his grasp. Much like the narrative figure of the entrepreneur discussed in chapter 3, whose newly minted subjectivity was defined through the narrative strategy of dreams and dreaming, in the lyrics of this song the ability to dream and possess that desire is what defines Jai's success. And yet, as the visuals inform us, this confident composure unravels into a crisis and Jai plunges into a deep and anguished depression. The film's argument suggests that this is a consequence of an incompleteness that plagues his masculinity (that trope again). Here though, the incompleteness is not a consequence of his middle-class unmanliness, but rather it is the result of his inability to know or understand love and romance. It is only when he begins to comprehend love through the feminine ideal that his masculinity can overcome the crisis that had plagued it. Love, here, is transcendent and spectacular—beyond the limits of social hierarchies, yes, but also outside the bounds of capital. Moreover, these filmic narratives suggest that the feminine ideal—who is complete in her femininity in the way that man is not in his masculinity, and who is self-assured, confident, and also at home in the world—must teach the successful but crisis-ridden male the lesson of love and true happiness.

The story of the male lead within the love story is thus varied but reveals the significance of the story of masculinity itself for this conjuncture. The man-in-love works to reinforce the salience of Hindu patriarchy and capital, but when love (rather than nation or capital) is narrated as the spectacle then the man-in-love through his labor-in-love also presents a certain challenge to that patriarchy. The man-in-love in his unremarkable, middle-class avatar in the 1970s narrates a crisis in masculinity that is resolved through the appropriation of subaltern masculinities. We return to that crisis in masculinity in the new millennium but this time, the love story narrates disaffection and a sense of incompletion in new times.

THE WOMAN

The narration and representation of femininity, and in particular the feminine figure in love, is also crucial to the formation of the conjuncture. Specifically, this figure is significant to the narration of modernity. The decade of the 1970s is often defined by film scholars as constituting a rupture in the cinematic rendering of sexuality, sex, and gender because the female lead in several Hindi films made in this decade embodied a cosmopolitan, desiring, consuming femininity that was at odds with the heroine-vamp (virgin-whore) dichotomy set up by cinematic narratives in previous decades. Popular actress, model, and beauty queen Zeenat Aman's filmography is often used as evidence for this argument. Ajay Gehlawat notes that even as Aman was "touted as heralding the 70s look of Westernized, 'liberated' young woman in Hindi film," she was also one of the first female leads to "show that good girls could be unashamedly sexual while fulfilling all the requirements to ultimately become wife to the hero."[33] In other words, this female body—as the actress Zeenat Aman came to inhabit it—could function to titillate the audience *and* could give voice, texture, and a visual to desires, dreams, and hopes (that were sometimes contradictory) that were narrated as definitive of the modern female lead. While conceptions of modernity have defined it as a time, an identity, and a process that either liberates or represses women, film scholars have questioned such a narrative that sets up a neat binary and trace the processes through which the figure of the vamp in Hindi cinema is subsumed by the "consuming and desiring female subject" to draw out a more complicated picture, both of femininity and the modern.[34]

Even as the decade of the 1970s is identified within this scholarship as a significant historical moment for the emergence of the kind of feminine modern epito-
mized by women like Zeenat Aman, the Modern Girl Around the World Research
Group marks the turbulent period between World War I and II as a crucial temporal node for the examination of the conjunctions between modernity, gender, and
the expressions of sexuality.[35] Using the "modern girl" as a heuristic device, the
Research Group traced her emergence in different regions around the world during this time. This is a period marked, as they argue, by "two contradictory forces:
increasing global economic interdependence and ascendance of forms of political
nationalism that often challenged such interdependence."[36] The modern girl of
the interwar years dressed in provocative fashions, consumed specific commodities, was explicitly erotic, and pursued romantic love. Hegemonic nationalisms
therefore consistently policed and aimed to control the modern girl, who was a
historical agent as well as an image. Priti Ramamurthy, writing about the starlets
or *sitaras* of the silent movies and early talkies in India in the 1920s and 1930s,[37]
reveals that while these modern girls in early cinema engaged with global modernity through "multi-directional citational" practices that involved bodily and fashion
aesthetics, were cosmopolitan, and expressly enjoyed the pleasures of heterosexual romance, they also performed and embodied an aesthetic hybridity that was
encoded as a "global *and* Indian modern."[38] The modern girl's radical play with
convention and tradition was managed within the films through the violent death
of her character, and within historiography this feminine engagement with modernity was "eclipsed," Ramamurthy notes, by an "all-consuming nationalism" that
has always obscured "alternative and more complex stories about gender, nationalism, and modernity."[39] In other words, the modern girl disappeared from both
the films that were made in the first decade after independence from British colonialism *and* from film history.

Echoes of the modern girl remain however, and she is narrated at crucial temporal nodes. In fact, I read the woman-in-love in the cinematic 1970s as an iteration of the modern girl, signifying yet another entanglement between modernity,
the gendered body, sexuality, and the nation. In the film *Roti, Kapda aur Makan*
(Food, Clothing and Shelter/Bread, Cloth and a House, Manoj Kumar, 1974), a
middle-class woman played by Zeenat Aman dreams of a car (which would enable
her to quit the tribulations of traveling in a bus), a mansion, closets filled with
clothes, fine jewelry, and the ability to travel the world in an airplane. Her boyfriend, the male lead (named Bharat, which is also the moniker of the Indian
nation in Hindi), also a middle-class man with a coveted engineering degree, is
the route through which she hopes to realize her dream. Right after she articulates
this desire for wealth, consumption, and global travel that can only be achieved
if her boyfriend and the male lead of the film secures employment (he has been
trying in vain for four years), Aman invites him to dance with her in the rain.
When he reluctantly refuses, noting that he has an interview in thirty minutes, she
dances alone and sings about the incommensurability of sensuous youth, love, and

romance with the mundane and drab routines of seeking employment. In this sequence in particular and in the film's narrative more generally, it is Aman's character Sheetal who provides the audience with an instantiation of the national modern that could be linked to the global modern. She spectacularly intertwines an uninhibited exhibition of sexual desire with the desire for conspicuous consumption. More importantly, she has the ability to *articulate* or express this intertwining. As such, Sheetal is a modern girl, but even more importantly for our purposes, she is also an early embodiment of the new India that advertising, brand campaigns, films, and commentary spoke more explicitly about in the first decade of the new millennium. Through her performance, Aman linked present time (the turbulence of the 1970s) with the past (early entanglements with modernity in the interwar years) and the future (the tryst with neoliberalism at the turn of the new millennium). The newness of new India was narrated as articulate desire (both sexual and fiscal) and ambition in the new millennium. This articulate desire was linked to narratives of global modernity. Thus, even as the male lead in this film, made in the mid-seventies, narrated the present time of the narrative as obstructed where food, clothing, and shelter were scarcities for even the educated middle classes, it was through femininity and the female body that desire, both for an uninhibited exhibition of sexuality and conspicuous consumption, was conveyed. In the film, Sheetal's strategic maneuvers to realize her desires are deemed immoral and therefore illegitimate: Sheetal gets engaged to a wealthy businessman at the time when her boyfriend finds it nearly impossible to secure employment befitting his skills and educational qualifications. Bharat compromises his ideals for the sake of wealth too, but within the moral universe of the film, his compromise—because it is forced and in the interest of his family and friends—does not taint him as it does Sheetal. Her decision to leave Bharat is defined as desire for her own material comfort and is thus deemed as compromised. She attains redemption when she sacrifices herself for the larger cause of national good. The film scripts an obstructed present and points the finger at the greed of the community of big and small tradesmen who control the market and therefore the trade of food, clothing, and land. This greed, the film suggests, spectacularly pits this community against both the state and the common man and woman. In fact, the wantonness of this greed is represented through the violence of rape, within the film. The grocer, the tailor, and the landlord rape a poor woman (Tulsi) who lives alone with an aged and disabled father in a sequence that is central to the moral and political arc of the film. In the world established by the film, therefore, Sheetal's ethical compromise motivated by the desire for her own material success necessitates both repudiation and punishment.

The characters embodied by Zeenat Aman are discussed as complicating the binary distinctions between the vamp and the legitimate female lead and instituting a mode of cinematic femininity that both titillates (like the vamp) and is expressive about her own perspective. While this is evident, it is imperative to also recognize the ways in which Sheetal as the woman-in-love is mobilized to embody a form of femininity that is timely and therefore an instantiation of the real. Unlike Bharat, Sheetal's love interest and the male lead in the film's narrative, whose travails and tragedies fill the frame and are spectacularized, Sheetal participates *in* the world within which she is located. Bharat feels the inequities of the time as a form of oppression that is attempting to emasculate him—he cannot pay for the education of his younger male siblings, and he cannot get his sister married or pay for his ailing father's healthcare. He cannot provide for his girlfriend's dreams and aspirations. His is a spectacular battle with the conditions that threaten both his masculinity and his morality. As a set of images and sonic signs, his struggle is a spectacular one because even as it references the obstructions and inequities of the 1970s, it also signifies a timelessness (i.e., a struggle untethered to the timeliness of materiality or the historicity of the social formation). Sheetal, though, is of her time, and she understands that modernity *here* in the time of the narrative takes the form of conspicuous consumption and the self-assured articulation of desire. Modernity beckons her. She hears that call in all its clarity, responds to it, and attempts to suture herself to the identifications that will make the modern possible for her. Being a woman-in-love is also a sign of the modern. The social formation within which Sheetal resides puts these signs of modernity into conflict—Sheetal is in love with Bharat but being a woman-in-love will not bring her material comforts and wealth. In this moment, she deliberately chooses to accept the proposal of marriage extended to her by a wealthy businessman, who is also her employer. This man is both moral and wealthy, and most importantly, *he* is in love with her. Her decision puts her in conflict with her own love and her family but it also works to signify and identify her as a modern woman. In another moment, when the articulation of loyalty both to love and the nation (when both romantic love and the nation are embodied by the same man) becomes paramount, Sheetal responds to this call too, and sacrifices her life.

Linked to commodity capitalism, Sheetal was akin to the "modern girl" of the interwar years. Her femininity serves to mark the emergence of a modernity linked to consumption, commodity capitalism, globalization, and the articulation of erotic desire. She is the female lead (and not the vamp) and therefore the sensorium of the film enables and encourages the audience's identification with her desiring body. Ultimately, however, hegemonic nationalism aims to control this femininity and her body is sacrificed for the nation. Love becomes the instrument through which hegemonic nationalism disciplines this modern girl. It is for love that Sheetal sacrifices herself. Her identification as woman-in-love represses her identification with consumerism and the commodity. Sheetal as "modern girl," is also akin to the angry young man, such that even as an identification with his angry, brooding, violent, vigilante masculinity is encouraged by the film's narrative, it is sacrificed in service of hegemonic nationalism. The decade of the 1970s thus gives us two cinematic embodiments—one spectacularly masculine in the form of the vigilante, and the other sensuously real in the form of the modern, desiring woman—that become central to public discourse in the new millennium.

In films made in the first decade of the new millennium, such as *Love Aaj Kal* (Love Today and Yesterday/Love Nowadays, Imtiaz Ali, 2009), *Band Baaja Baaraat* (released internationally as *The Wedding Planners*, Maneesh Sharma, 2010), and *Zindagi Milegi Na Dobara* (You Don't Live Twice, Zoya Akhtar, 2011), the "modern girl" returns in yet another iteration. She is modern because her professional ambitions are linked to the desires associated with the globally hegemonic project of neoliberalism. As such, she is an entrepreneur, as Shruti is in *Band Baaja Baarat*. Or she is at home in the world, a global traveler familiar and comfortable in different parts of the world, like Meera in *Love Aaj Kal* or Laila in *Zindagi Milegi Na Dobara*. Unlike Sheetal though, Shruti, Meera, and Laila are the moral centers of the cinematic universe within which they reside. These films constitute femininity and the feminine ideal as the corrective for the experience of fragmentation that defines neoliberalism. The feminine ideal here is unmoored from the nation and tradition. She is not a mother or a goddess. She is, in fact, the modern girl in the guise of Shruti, the entrepreneur who sets up an event-planning business; Laila, a diver and scuba instructor who travels the world; and Meera, an art historian who works to restore heritage structures. All of them are also women-in-love.

Through these women-in-love who are also "modern girls," these popular cinematic narratives *hint* at love's radical potential to decenter the possessive individualism of neoliberalism as well as its ability to engage deeply with difference. Even as femininity is rendered already complete and at home in the globalized world, these texts suggest that an appropriation of the feminine through the mediation and the experience of love is necessary for the masculine subject to be complete himself. In doing so, the films continue to center masculinity as the gender of neoliberalism. As is central to the narrative form of spectacular realism, here too the feminine (this time the feminine ideal) functions as the ground on which hegemonic masculinity constitutes itself. The narration of the crisis of masculinity and its resolution lies at the core of the story. As such, these popular love stories ultimately constitute love as a somewhat painful but ultimately fizzy affect.

Filmmakers such as Zoya Akhtar and Imtiaz Ali have been lauded for the representations of their female characters; the women in *Zindagi* and *Love Aaj Kal* are certainly pivotal in a way that they have not been in some other examples of Hindi cinema. However, these female characters appear entirely too neat, too complete. While the transformed worlds within which they live, work, and love produce a crisis for the men around them, these women—the moral centers of the stories—are not affected in the same way. The industries spawned by the neoliberal political economy have engendered new opportunities *and* a new unease for the working woman in India. News reports of the working conditions of call center workers, rape in urban areas, sexual harassment, and wage inequities narrate both the newness of the opportunities and the anxiety that the working woman in India experiences. And yet Laila of *Zindagi* and Meera of *Love Aaj Kal* seem at a distance from such realities. The feminine modern, as it is embodied by these women, is also not uneasy or torn by her own desires and aspirations as Sheetal from *Roti, Kapda aur Makaan* was. Through her costuming, her makeup, her body stylization, and her dialogue she signifies the time of the modern and as such she is a character constituted by historical time. But as the feminine ideal, as the muse, she is timeless, set outside of history. And hence, the idealization of the feminine ironically serves to make invisible the historical woman.

What is significant here, though, is the ways in which these cinematic narratives extricate their male leads from what has been represented as the soul-crushing grip of global capital and its routines, via this feminine ideal and the experience of love. Arjun, one of the male leads in *Zindagi Na Milegi Dobara*, is so embedded within global finance capital that he is either an automaton or a caricature of an erstwhile human being. This was the world that he had aspired to and longed for since he was a child being raised by a single mother, and for much of the film it is the routines of the financial markets that provide him with his own sense of a self. This sense starts to unravel when he meets Laila and falls in love with her. By the end of the film, this experience of love and intimacy with the feminine ideal enables Arjun to simply walk away from the world of global capital that he had yearned to be a part of most of his life.

The long discursive line that connects Sheetal from *Roti, Kapda aur Makaan* with Laila, Meera, and Shruti had to pass through characters like Simran from *Dilwale Dulhania Le Jayenge* (The Big-Hearted Will Take Away the Bride, or DDLJ, Aditya Chopra, 1995). DDLJ is regarded as an iconic love story, a cinematic milestone, and one of the best-loved of the set of films made in the 1990s that focused on the diaspora and catered to it. In fact, the love story between Raj and Simran is the narrative node through which Babuji—Simran's father and a Punjabi immigrant living in London—wrestles with questions of home, nation, modernity, and tradition. The film begins with him, a tall, brown-skinned Punjabi man in London's Trafalgar Square musing about the rootlessness of the immigrant who leaves home in search of opportunity in alien lands and pines for the sensory and affective experience of the homeland. The film concludes with him at a train station in a small town in Punjab, in northern India, where he had compelled his wife and daughters to come so his older daughter could enter into an arranged marriage and reproduce the traditional values that he felt untethered from in London. At that train station, though, he lets his daughter go so she could "live *her* life" with the man she had fallen in love with—a second-generation *desi* like herself who lived in London. Here, the struggle between tradition and modernity and anxieties about the vulnerability of the patriarchal family and the boundaries of the nation in the context of globalization and global travel are mapped onto Simran's femininity. As both Purnima Mankekar and Rupal Oza have argued about this period within Indian public discourse, "the concern with the vulnerability of open borders was mapped onto the subjectivity" of what Oza has termed the "new liberal Indian woman." In other words, in the decade of the 1990s in particular, the anxiety about globalization was displaced onto women's bodies and representational politics. As Oza has argued, "since women's subjectivity has historically been framed as vulnerable, pure and a repository of culture, it is primarily toward women that this concern was directed as opposed to men whose encounter with the 'West' is not framed in terms of purity."[40]

While Simran as a character differs from the women we have discussed thus far, her femininity nevertheless also functions as the ground on which a crisis of masculinity is played out. As the woman-in-love, she comes to embody the threat to the patriarchal familial unit that an engagement with modernity may bring, and as a woman in love with a man residing outside the nation's boundaries, she also embodies a threat to sovereignty. DDLJ works to resolve this crisis by underlining the power of the patriarch. Simran only runs and joins the man she loves when her father gives her his consent. Love here is the threat and the woman-in-love is its embodiment. In DDLJ, the woman-in-love is not eliminated or vanquished as she is in other popular films made during this time,[41] but is managed so that Hindu patriarchy through its ostensible consent for love remains all-powerful.

A word here about the cinematic rendering of Muslim women in love in the 1990s, which was the precise moment of both the neoliberal turn and the rise of Hindu nationalism: The representation of Muslim femininity, and particularly the Muslim woman-in-love, works as a complement to Hindu masculine patriotism in popular cinematic stories to manage the anxieties produced by Islam deemed as ideology and the presence of ostensibly violent Muslim masculinity.[42] While her subjectivity as a Muslim constitutes her as the Other within such stories, the Muslim woman's femininity works to manage the threat of otherness. As such, she is rendered as the desirable, consumable Other. The private space of the Muslim household is represented as being unequivocally oppressive for the Muslim female, who bears her oppression with a silent and dignified forbearance. Even as the cinematic Muslim woman makes otherness consumable largely through a display of silent intensity, these stories spectacularize the nation and narrate it as facing trouble from an ideological Islam.

Significantly, the Hindu woman is rendered in the garb of the Muslim woman within stories that narrate the conception of love jihad. Hadiya, discussed earlier as the subject of one of the most (in)famous cases where the conception of love jihad was sought to be upheld, was incessantly referred to as a gullible, naive child who needed protection from her Hindu patriarch and patriarchal institutions. The gullibility of the woman-in-love is the vulnerable breach into the community (read: Hindu nation), and the erotic consumption of the feminine, in this case Hindu femininity, is the act of war within such stories. Since femininity is assumed to be the breach, Muslim femininity (particularly the Muslim woman-in-love) is also rendered as consumable or, as in the writing of Hindutva ideologues like V. D. Savarkar, an exhortation is made to "pay the Muslim fair sex in the same coin" through "conversion even with force" and then "absorption."[43] Love jihad is thus a Hindu nationalist concept that relies on the assumption that femininity is vulnerable and gullible and can be worked upon through the instrument of love to breach the purity of the nation in an act of war. The most explicit account of this war strategy emerges in Hindu nationalist texts in fact, and the foundational assumptions of this strategy that link masculinity, femininity, and the heteronormative couple to the ideal of the nation and are audiovisually rendered by some popular cinematic narratives.

But, love as an emotion and an experience associated with the normatively male and female cinematic body during this period also had the ability to point to a space and time that was utopic, in the sense that this space and time was outside the bounds of global capital, colonialism, caste and social hierarchies, and patriarchy. As such, the love story had the potential to capture its audience's imagination. Precisely for this reason, cinematic, heteronormative love was also a narrative mode through which to tell the story about benevolent patriarchy, the Hindu nation, hegemonic masculinity, and, perhaps most importantly, to tell the story about adjusting to the oppression of both patriarchy and global capital. Here, the stories follow the form of spectacular realism, spectacularizing the nation, the patriarch, and/or capital with the realism of the couple-in-love sutured to the spectacle. In other words, love is the narrative and affective node where both the material struggle to redefine the world in terms that are outside the bounds of violent hierarchies *and* the maneuvers necessary to reproduce the world in ways that do not disrupt normativity can be observed. Love is therefore that which is outside global capital, the corporate boardroom, and patriarchy *and* a cynical mask and a tool of war.

THE LOVE SONG

Of all the diverse forms of popular media artifacts made during the conjuncture that begins in the 1970s and reaches its most coherent form after the first decade of the new millennium, the circulating film song, specifically the love song in Hindi cinema, is particularly enabled in constituting love as an affect and an experience that inaugurates a radically new world. According to the love song, space and time in this new world constituted by love do not follow the diktats of global capital or Hindu patriarchy. Here, a lifetime is lived in a few moments of calendrical time;[44] here, walls tumble and a path is opened;[45] here, open vistas and panoramic landscapes can signify the intimate space of an embrace;[46] and here, the lover is recognized both as the "other" (not-I), the stranger, the foreigner who is alien to the world of the "I" (*begaana, anjaana*) and as an intimate fellow traveler (*humsafar*).[47] In the spatiotemporal world of the Hindi cinematic love song, the spectacular world of the dream melds with the waking (real) world.[48] The melodic structure of the love song combines the incessant ticking of clock-time with the slow, lilting, and repeating beat of its internal rhythm.[49] As an audiovisual, it combines the sonic tensions of a crescendo with the visually sensual pleasures of lovers walking together in a field of tulips.[50] The cinematic love song conjugates the modern with the folk, the time and space of the dream with the spatiotemporality of the material world, hope with fatalism, and ecstasy with tragedy in its poetry, its rhyme and meter, and its sliding, melodic notes. It focuses on the couple in love, and visually this often means the couple are filmed alone amid majestic landscapes, fields, and sometimes even cityscapes emptied of the jostling crowds. More than representing a conception of individualism that is then linked with freedom, the purpose of the love song's deep interest in the intimate couple is to dwell on the moment when one becomes two. The love song insists that *in* this moment when the other/not-I walks *with* the I, lies a world and a lifetime. The love song is clear that love is both spectacular and real; here realism is not used cynically to prop up the spectacle. Instead a melding of the spectacle with realism is suggested, which makes the world anew.

Many popular cinematic love songs circulate long after the film itself has receded from public memory. Some love songs attain a kind of popularity that the film within which they reside never manages. Music and song has been intertwined with Hindi cinema since the advent of the talkie in the 1930s. As historians of both film and popular music have pointed out, the integral presence of song in cinema is a legacy of the influence that Marathi and Parsi urban theater as well as folk forms like *nautanki* and *jatra* had on early cinema in India. These performative forms all mixed dialogue with song and dance. Though the film song derives from traditional and folk forms, it is also defined as a modern form. The film song, through its association with cinema and its deep ties to "the technologies of recording and reproduction," comes to be positioned as the "modern antithesis to the so-called traditions of Indian music, both folk and classical."[51] In this context, film scholar Samhita Sunya, tracing the genealogy (between 1934 and the early 2000s) of the phrase *prem nagar* (or city of love) in film songs shows that while prem nagar is a "literary trope derived from folk songs and poetry attributed to ascetic and mystic *sant* (saint-singer) poets, namely, Kabir (15th century) and Bulleh Shah (18th century),"[52] in the incorporation of the trope within the film song, it became "reconfigured as an epithet for the romantic pleasure spaces of motion pictures and the milieu of urban life in which cinema was embedded."[53] In other words, city of love, through its travels within the audiovisual trajectories of the film song, came to be associated with urbanity, modernity, and cinephilia. Since the 1930s, film music has dominated the market for music itself.[54] Film scholars have argued that the "open-ended poetics" of the film song, its "repeatability," and its "infinite catchiness" enable the "collective participation of audiences."[55] This participation is enabled by the heterogeneous form of the film song, with lyrics penned by poets and writers, a composition assembled by artists, sung by popular vocalists, and rendered on screen with the aid of choreographers, costume designers, production designers, cinematographers, and popular actors who lip-sync and are often also dancers.

The political economy of the music industry in India has seen many shifts and changes since the 1890s when the phonograph became merchandise in the commercial and industrial cities of Bombay and Calcutta, a couple of which are worth mentioning here since these events are significant to the prevalence and presence of film music within public discourse. In the 1980s, Gulshan Kumar, then a small cassette manufacturer, exploited loopholes in the Indian Copyright Act of 1957 as well as licensing and taxation regulations and began recording and selling "version recordings." These were popular, iconic film songs sung by lesser-known artists. Moreover, these version recordings were cheaply marketed at "every possible retail outlet," including stalls that sold chewing tobacco and tea and neighborhood grocery stores. The cassette and the cassette player were new technologies for the music industry in the 1980s and were cheaper to access than the record and the record player. Favorite film music, including old classics, could therefore be owned, played, and replayed in the home without the former dependence on radio's playlists. Secondly, in the late 1980s and the early 1990s, music companies began financing films by paying an advance on the film's music. The producers of the film used this advance as working capital and the music company owned the rights to the music even before the film was made and the music produced. The music of the film was then heavily marketed in its own right by the music company when it was produced. One of the biggest successes of this new arrangement for the company that bought the music rights (Gramco) at the time was the music of the love story *Maine Pyar Kiya* (I Fell in Love, Sooraj Barjatya, 1989).[56] These practices point to the manner in which the film song is simultaneously twined with the film and is separate from it. The love song in cinema conjugates poetry and melody with the moving image. It circulates through the cassette, the CD, and as digital notes creating an affective sonic and melodic world around itself, and in linking back to the film of which it is a part, it also intermixes the visual with melodic poetry.

As a consequence of these characteristics, the film song is particularly enabled to narrate love in ways that are different from the story about love that the film within which it is located tells. The film *Gharonda* (Dwelling, Bhimsain Khurana, 1977), for instance, tells a cynical story about love. Here, love is more concerned with the pragmatic and immediate project of home ownership in an urban metropolis where land is at a premium. The couple at the center of the film's narrative are in love and work toward buying a home, but when they are cheated of not only that dream but their savings as well, they plan a scheme wherein the woman would marry an older, ailing, wealthy man. They would await this man's death and then live the life they had planned together, complete with wealth and a home. Love here is simply a step toward attaining the trappings of urban modernity and middle-classness. The film's narrative instrumentalizes the love story to focus on the struggles around housing, the land mafia, and the con games that defined the housing market in an urban metropolis like Bombay in 1970s. In the song "Mujhe Pyar Tumse Nahin Hai" ("I am not in love with you")[57] from the film, however, love is defined as that relationship that has the ability to constitute a space that is both a part of the material, historical world but also incongruent with it. Love, in other words, is poetic world-making. While playfully claiming certainty about *not* being in love, the feminine voice in this song sings about the warmth and joy of her companion's presence, so much so that his absence casts shadows of sadness on her heart. She sings about the dreams—some large and towering like the sky-scrapers around them, others timid and small—that have enveloped her now that she is with him and she sings about constantly moving between warm, bright light and cool, shadowy darkness. The melody of the song also consistently shifts between a playful, teasing refrain where the lyrics cheerfully claim a position of not being in love, to a deeper, wistful, even melancholic note in the stanzas where the poetry reflects on the affective spaces that companionship with the young man has made her dwell in. The visuals that accompany this song, which provides the sonic and melodic backdrop for a slice-of-life glimpse into the world of this couple, consistently signify two-ness. The camera zooms out from close shots of a pair of bicycles or two pairs of sandals and a woman's bag to capture the couple walking together on the beach. The camera also pans from shots of the cityscape—streaming lines of cars and lights on busy city streets, tall skyscrapers and their tiny windows—to the intimate space that the couple has created for themselves through their love and companionship. The interactions between the couple cap-tured by the ostensibly unobtrusive camera are playful, joyful, and familiar. The conjunction of the poetry, the melody, and the moving image create a world for the couple. While this world exists within the reality of the narrative world of the film as well as within the reality of the material world, the song contends, it is not coterminous with it—precisely because, the song suggests, this world of love has been brought into being by the couple themselves. Moreover, the song suggests that the presence of this world is evidence of love. For the audience, this world is aspirational; it is joyous, hopeful, fragile, and companionate. It is both spectacular and real, material.

Similarly, in the song, "Tujhe Dekha..."[58] ("When I saw you...") from the film *Dilwale Dulhaniya Le Jayenge* (The Big-Hearted Will Take the Bride Away, Aditya Chopra, 1995), the man- and woman-in-love sing about looking into each other's eyes and being overwhelmed by the realization that love was madness. This ecstatic madness had a spatiotemporal quality to it: "Where do I go from *here, now*? In your arms, will I breathe my last," they sing, standing alone in a field bursting with yellow flowers. The intimate embrace of the lover is the space of love—in *this* space (*yahaan*), the man- and woman-in-love state they will remain until they die, and the present-time (*ab*) of that embrace is love's temporality. The spatiality of love in the cinematic love song also enfolds exquisite landscapes and dreamscapes unfettered by the materiality of distance and borders. Love's tempo-rality is similarly not bound by the diktats of clock-time. The present-time of love is full, such that a moment is a lifetime, and time moves seamlessly between the calendrical past, the future, and the timescapes of the dream. Love, acknowledged and recognized as such by the lovers, composes future-time and alters the past. The visuals of the song not only take the couple into a dreamscape where they walk alone through magical landscapes but also takes them (and the audience) back to scenes of their past, which now stand altered by love. Thus, while the couple had argued or stood distantly apart in those scenes in the past (the narrative/ cinematic past), they now playfully engage with each other as lovers in precisely those same scenes now replayed in the song. Simran, now a woman-in-love, appears in a red wedding dress in one of these scenes from the past. The recognition of love via the lyrics and melodic refrain of the song visually remakes the couple's scenes together in the narrative past as iconic of their love story. Here again, in a film that uses love to reinforce the moral might of Hindu patriarchy and define global capital and globalization as integral to the project of Hindu nationalism itself, the love song carves out a world that is unbounded by Hindutva neoliberalism.

Let us dwell on this idea for a bit, for it can be argued, as it has been, that the Hindi cinematic song, particularly from the 1990s on, is constitutive of neoliberalism and globalization, through the exotic foreign locations it traverses, the celebration of fashion and the runway, and the melding of the world of fantasy with the material world.[59] While this is an entirely accurate analysis, certain cinematic *love* songs exceed this remit. Consider the song "Dekha Ek Khwab To Yeh Silsile Hue"[60] (A Dream I Dreamt Started This Series of Events) from the film *Silsila* (A Series of Events, Yash Chopra, 1981). The song and the film arguably inaugurate the Hindi cinematic aesthetic that combines exquisite, aspirational foreign locations with glamourous female actors. The film tells the story of desire and transgressions to the moral code of Hindu patriarchy only to ultimately reaffirm the Hindu family. This formula is much like the one we encountered in *Deewar*, that quintessential angry young man film we discussed in chapter 2, where the audiences are sutured to the vigilante *and* the vigilante is killed, so the nation (the mother) and the state (the police) are reaffirmed as the moral centers of the narrative. It is not a coincidence therefore that the director of both films is Yash Chopra, the actor is Amitabh Bachchan, and the lyricist is Javed Akhtar (one-half of the duo Salim-Javed who scripted the angry young man films). Salim-Javed had split as a writing duo and Akhtar reinvented himself as a lyricist; *Silsila* was an important project in carving out this trajectory. *Silsila* was also a break from the working-class, lumpen-vigilante characters that had established Bachchan as a superstar in the 1970s. While Yash Chopra had worked on small-budget films when he worked for his brother's B. R. Chopra Films, his own independent productions were richer, lusher stories featuring romances between upper-class, upper-caste characters. "Dekha Ek Khwab . . ." in *Silsila* was shot in tulip fields in the Netherlands, for instance. The visual, affective, cultural memory of those tulip fields signifying romance is as integral a part of public discourse as the angry young man character representing the anger of an obstructed present. The melodic and lyrical structure of the song follows the convention for Hindi film songs. It begins with a prose couplet that is voiced by the famous Bachchan baritone, which resonantly notes, "that beyond suspicion and doubt and closer to the boundaries of certainty, the heart had acquired the illusion that they [an "other," *unko*, a gender-neutral pronoun] loved me."[61] This understanding of being reciprocally loved by the one who he (the masculine I) loves becomes the preface for the love song.

The song itself is composed of a *mukhada*—a short couplet that defines the central thought of the song—that repeats after every *antara*, a longer, distinct verse that elaborates on the concept introduced (and repeated) by the mukhada.[62] "Dekha Ek Khwab . . ." is a duet, sung and enacted by a masculine voice and a feminine one. There are, in essence, two mukhadas: the first and definitive one from which the song derives its title, voiced by the masculine voice, and the second in dialogue with it, voiced by the feminine. In the mukhada, whereas the man sings about how a dream (about love) had produced a series of events, such that a field of flowers bloomed for as far as the eye could see, the woman lyrically composes a complaint against his eye, for even flowers between lovers constitutes distance. It is these dual thoughts, entirely in dialogue with each other, that are central to the experience of this love song.

Visually, the camera-eye follows the complaint voiced by the woman in the song, in the sense that it continuously pans over the landscape of mountains, trees, and fields of tulips to find the couple; once it does, the camera-eye zooms into the world that is created by their embrace and intimacy. Lyrically and visually, the song suggests that the realization and acknowledgement of love opens magnificent vistas (the tulip fields in the Netherlands make this chain of signification overt and literal) but also that the most significant aspect of love is the couple at the center of this landscape. In other words, the song suggests that of all the exquisite worlds that love composes, the one formed by the embrace of the lovers is most magnificent. Moreover, in the context of this song, it is the feminine voice that defines love for its audience in this manner.

The movement of the camera-eye in the song is dizzying and frantic, continuously panning left or right or downward as it searches for the couple; it is only after it zooms in on the couple, walking together, embracing or sitting together, that it steadies itself. The melody that accompanies these dizzying visuals is, on the other hand, lilting in some of its repeated rhythms and sparkling in other parts, calling forth the sonic memories of rippling, refreshing, flowing waters. The audiovisual experience created by "Dekha Ek Khwab . . ." thus combines the dynamic movement of the melodic notes and the camera-eye with sensuous spaces, both the bountiful fields of tulips captured by the camera and the intimate space of the embrace as seen through the camera and felt through the poetry. As such, this love song creates a spatiotemporal world. This lush world is certainly concerned with what film scholar Anustup Basu, writing about Hindi cinema post–economic liberalization (and in the specific context of another Yash Chopra film, *Darr* [Fear]), has called a collection of "male desires for money, goods, women and power which are presently retailed but yet to be named or given community recognition."[63] The world created by the love song with its exotic foreign locales, a glamorous woman, and wealth, is an intimation of the "irresistible" world neoliberalism promises.

However, the love song exceeds this ideological remit. It ultimately insists that the spatiotemporality that is most significant is that which is constituted by the intimate embrace of two-ness; the "I" and its "other" in love.

"Naino Mein Sapna" (In My Eyes, I Have a Dream) from the film *Himmatwala* (A Brave Man, K. Raghavendra Rao, 1983) is different from the songs we have discussed thus far.[64] It is a kitschy set piece in which the male and female leads perform an elaborately choreographed dance sequence, complete with extras, on a beach kitted out with painted pots, large cutouts, and feathers. *Himmatwala* is a remake of a Telugu-language film and is credited with both transforming its female lead, Sridevi, then an extremely popular star in cinema made in the south, into a national superstar, and with being one of many southern film remakes made during the 1980s that set the Hindi film industry "back."[65] *Himmatwala*, like some other remakes, was hugely popular and a commercial success. However, as Tejaswini Ganti points out, such films were often derided in later decades by members of the Hindi film industry itself, including filmmakers and actors, for being too kitschy and for catering to the audience's baser instincts. This derision served to distinguish these filmmakers and actors as more "modern" and "professional" and as such did what Ganti calls "boundary-work" constituting "processes of gentrification and rationalization" as an integral aspect of Hindi film production culture.[66] All of this is to say that the performative quality, the production values, and the sensory experience of "Naino Mein Sapna" is at a variance from both "Tujhe Dekha To" and "Dekha Ek Khwab" and yet that difference is often overstated. As a love song, "Naino Mein Sapna" stays on a single location, and it does not focus on exotic landscapes or vistas; it is, in fact, utterly uninterested in creating a spatial juxtaposition to the expression and experience of love. What it does instead, much like many other love songs of this variety, is constitute a spectacle that is focused on the dancing body, in particular the feminine dancing body (although the male lead dances with the female lead throughout, *she* and her body are most significant). The song itself is visualized as a spectacle: the kitschy set decorations are reminiscent of Hindu religious festivals and rituals that are staged publicly. In these public festivals, a stage is set up in a neighborhood and decorated, an idol of the relevant god placed at the center, music (mostly film music) is played via a public-address system, and at certain key moments dance is integrated into the spectacle as well. As a staged spectacle, these public festivals have an audience that queues up both for *darsan* as well as to engage with the entertainment. A song like "Naino Mein Sapna" is specifically staged for the scopophilic pleasure of its audience. Unlike the songs featuring vamps from films made in the 1960s and the 1970s, these performances are not located in a nightclub, onstage with an audience or a bar; here the diegetic spectator who stands between the performers and the "real" audience of the film sitting in the cinema hall is completely missing. The male and female leads dance ostensibly for themselves but really, the audience knows, they dance for us. Here, the acknowledgement or recognition of love, or the fantasy about it, triggers the spectacle of the dancing body. Songs like "Naino

Mein Sapna" often begin after a look is exchanged between the male and female leads or when they embrace for the first time or a piece of dialogue acknowledging their love is voiced for the first time. The film cuts to the song and returns to the main narrative after its conclusion. The song itself acts as a bracket within the narrative—it emphasizes certain conceptions and presents them in a distinct audio-visual form, and as such the song (particularly the love song) creates a distinctive spatiotemporality within the time-space continuum of the cinematic narrative. This distinctive and joyous spatiotemporality that has been engendered by love is here signified through the choreographed, costumed, dancing body. While the sensual pleasure of beautiful landscapes is conjoined with the glamorous bodies of the man and woman-in-love in songs like "Dekha Ek Khwab" to signify the new worlds that love reveals, here the sensuality of the dancing body does that work of signification. Most importantly, the audience of the film and this love song are enjoined to this chain of signification.

By directly gazing into the camera and then walking toward it as the camera itself zooms past them, the couple at the core of the song "Tum Ho . . ." (You Are . . .) from the film *Rockstar* (Imtiaz Ali, 2011) invite the film's audience into the world that is engendered by love, *their* love.[67] This is a radically disruptive moment in which the screen that separates the dramatic world of the film from the audience that watches and listens to it is broken. "Tum Ho" has been described by its director Imtiaz Ali as the "epilogue" or the "end glossary" of the film. In a narrative that tells the tragic love story of a musician, "Tum Ho" is the only love song. This is the only song that the musician, Janardhan/Jordan, a boy belonging to one of the agrarian castes and who lives in a lower-middle-class neighborhood in the city of Delhi, sings for his love Heer, a Kashmiri brahmin girl from an elite Delhi-based family (in every way, Janardhan/Jordan's "other.").

Through the tear in the screen, the audience is invited into a world that until that moment belonged only to the lovers—this is a world, Heer proclaims, that is without rules and limits, that is not structured by a society or policed by the apparatus of the law and ideology; it is a world that exists here (*yahaan*) in the now (*abhi*) and is forever (*hamesha*). The visuals that compose the world the audience enters are uncanny. They are familiar and strange—familiar because the visuals that make up the song are drawn from events, scenes, and sequences that the film's audience has just finished viewing, and strange because even though the audience has been to these spaces and has witnessed these events through the film's narrative, the *particular* visuals that make the song had been cut and concealed from that viewing. The tear in the screen thus invites the audience into a world that is constituted by the couple and their love—they walk alone surrounded by magnificent mountains amid an open field, they embrace in a claustrophobic apartment against a wall, they run toward each other on a bridge in Prague, they gently interlace their fingers. This is a world constituted by their loving intimacy and as such has been deemed taboo; so taboo, in fact, that Heer refers to it early in the narrative as "playing in filth" (*gandh machana*) and compels her partner to take her to "filthy" places, such as the red-light district, a cinema hall playing pornographic films, a strip club, and a seedy bar, literally translating the offensive or taboo-like quality of their relationship into a journey through distasteful spaces. *Rockstar* charts the processes through which this love, which is deemed "filthy," infects the male and female characters at the center of the film. Because this love across caste and class lines is deemed distasteful and impossible by the societal hierarchies that structure the lives of the characters, this love is repressed for most of the narrative. It is not acknowledged completely, left only partially recognized, and concealed even by the characters themselves. This repressed love, in turn, infects them. In other words, because their love can only be described as profane (gandh machana) within the political economy in which the characters reside and must therefore be repressed, it in turn profanes their bodies. The love song, "Tum Ho," is the visual-sonic space that is outside or unbounded by a political economy founded on caste and class, and it is therefore in *this* space that Heer and Jordan's love can return. "Tum Ho" is uncanny but in a manner that reverses the term's logic within the paradigm of Freudian psychoanalysis. According to Freud, when the familiar (homely) returns as strange (unhomely), it produces fear and is deemed monstrous. Rooted in a political economic context, *Rockstar* suggests that the repression of love, so that the familiar structure of societal hierarchies is reproduced, is what is strange, fearful, and monstrous. The return of that which had been repressed and concealed—love as radical two-ness—in the space of the song is joyous. This space is created by loving and poetic world-making and it is precisely for this reason that the audience is invited into it through that disruptive tear in the screen.

The five love songs I have briefly discussed here are diverse and feature in very different films made between the 1970s and 2014. This is therefore not an exhaustive listing but does point to the significant ways in which the cinematic love song creates a spatiotemporality through the intersection of visual and sonic notes that is distinct from Hindu patriarchy and neoliberalism. Even when the films within which these love songs reside produce and reproduce Hindutva neoliberalism, the song itself acts as a bracketed space—linked to but also separate from that filmic story. The love song's spectacular realism diverges from the narratives of which it is a part. It melds the realism of the couple-in-love with the spectacle of love and in doing so transforms their reality. The love song, even more so than some of the love stories within which it resides, tells an unruly story.

LOVE, LOVE JIHAD

Nagraj Manjule, a filmmaker whose Marathi-language 2016 film *Sairat* (Unfettered) was an unflinching critique of caste narrated through the love story between a lower-caste boy from a fishing community and an upper-caste girl from a family of politically connected landlords, had caustically noted in an interview that:

We Indians are so twisted that we oppose lovers in real life but love to watch them on screen. It is a sign of split personality. The same people who will stone lovers on the street will whistle and dance when they see lovers on screen. There is a strange duplicity to this.[68]

Manjule's comment about the Indian public's "strange duplicity" brings us back to the question that I began this chapter with: How do we read these divergent narrations of love *together*? How do we read the radical world-making that the love song—hummed and sung by millions—speaks about in conjunction with the narratives about love being subservient to Hindu patriarchy and the nation? As I write this concluding section of the chapter and contemplate my own questions in juxtaposition with Manjule's important and insistent critique, I am struck by the uncanny: News reports in the Indian media today (July 2018) reveal that a Muslim man was assaulted outside a court in the northern city of Ghaziabad when he and his partner, a Hindu Rajput woman, were speaking to a lawyer to ascertain details regarding the process to register their marriage through the Special Marriages Act. While family and personal law in India are separate and governed by the customs and scriptures of major religions, the Special Marriages Act passed by the Indian parliament in 1954 enables Indian citizens to marry and register their marriages legally, irrespective of the religious identities of the individuals involved. The mob that assaulted the Muslim man in Ghaziabad alleged love jihad.

In 2017, in another northern Indian city (Jaipur) a "spiritual fair" was organized by the Hindu Spirituality and Service Foundation, a group associated with the Hindu nationalist movement. The "spiritual fair" was designed to "propagate Hindu culture" and to this end educate Hindu students, particularly young Hindu girls, about love jihad. A booklet that was distributed at one of the stalls and later removed (in fact, it was denied that the booklet was ever distributed) following criticism attempted to outline the process of love jihad—the Muslim man, this booklet alleged, would ingratiate himself to both the Hindu woman and her family by running errands, speaking to the parents of the young woman as if they were his own family, and gaining their trust by suggesting that he was, in fact, a Hindu.[69] He might wear certain markers on his body, such as a red thread around his wrist, which would falsely attest to his Hinduness. Gaining entry and trust, the man would regularly speak to the young woman in private, suggest that he was in love, and propose marriage. If the woman's parents objected, the woman, now completely in his thrall, would stubbornly elope. She would be converted to Islam and the Muslim man would gain kudos from his community for having "served his religion." Love jihad would be complete. Hindi film actors Saif Ali Khan and Aamir Khan, both of whom are Muslim men married to Hindu women, are cited as examples of men who use love as an instrument of jihad. Muslim women—classmates, hostel-mates, workers at beauty salons, and so on—are defined as allies of Muslim men, who will befriend Hindu women and introduce them to their co-religious men, thus aiding the process of love jihad.

The booklet propagates religious homogeneity and patriarchy. Hindu fathers are advised to instruct their daughters about the virtues and morals of Hinduism; relatedly, they are advised to consistently define Muslim men as bearded terrorists, traitors, supporters of Pakistan, untrustworthy, wastrels, opportunists, men who consume women as offerings, and lumpen elements. It suggests that daughters be raised to study and then marry within the community and advises fathers to use every tool in the tool kit, including surveilling their daughters, befriending them, and resorting to extreme emotional blackmail (pretending to attempt suicide through an overdose of sleeping pills) to ensure that their wards do not fall victim to love jihad. This story is entirely closed to the experience of love; it reads love cynically and can only narrate it as a weapon of war. It is this sociopolitical cultural context that compels an artist like Manjule to state that while love is popular on screen, on the street lovers are viciously opposed.

In his film *Sairat*, Manjule depicts both the radical possibilities of love as well as the unrelenting violence with which it is ruthlessly murdered. In the film, the new world opened up by love, constituted by and forged through living with caste and class difference, is fundamentally marked by struggle. In other words, the film evocatively narrates that living with difference (without subsuming, appropriating, or repressing it) necessitates struggle. It is love that enables the protagonists of this film to fashion themselves and their world through this struggle, which often incapacitates them. The intensity and brutality of living both with difference and poverty, for a moment, even drives the young man to suicide. It is the radical affect of love that enables the couple to continue to strive and build a world that they could inhabit as a twosome. That world, motivated by love and forged through struggle, is violently sundered in the conclusion of the film, when the couple are murdered for breaching caste and patriarchal codes.

The stories that we have discussed here have, without exception, been about heterosexual love. Dominant religious and cultural discourse as well as Freudian psychoanalysis will have us believe that heterosexuality is love as difference while homosexuality is conflated with sameness (same sex desire, love etc.). There is a danger here then of reiterating and underlining this conception. This is a tension and a danger that I want to confront, rather than elide or obfuscate. Scholars like Sara Ahmed, Judith Butler, and Michael Warner have worked and reworked the ground prepared by Freudian psychoanalysis to show us the ways in which the conflation of homosexuality with sameness constitutes 1) heterosexuality as the norm, and 2) transforms sameness into perversion and pathology. Most significantly, Ahmed in particular has also shown us that the narrative of heterosexuality conceals its own investment in sameness by foregrounding difference. She has argued that heterosexuality for the male, here following but also critiquing Freud, is the desire to *have* the loved "object," which in turn is a means of "self-exaltation" or narcissism because "what one 'has' elevates what one 'is.'"[70] In other words, Ahmed argues that despite the conflation of heterosexuality with difference, it has more to do with sameness, self-love, and likeness than we might imagine. Moreover,

Ahmed contends that the "lover and the object approximate an ideal, an approxi-
mation which binds them together." That ideal involves the "creation or making of
likeness."[71] Heterosexuality might be a relationship between different genders but
it can also be a bond that is founded on what the "two have *in common*." And following the normative conflation of hetero-sex with reproduction, *that* which the
heterosexual couple have in common is desired to be reproduced. As Ahmed
notes, "Good reproduction is premised around a fantasy of 'making likeness.'"[72] In
short, love masquerades as being about difference but conceals the fantasy and
desire for sameness.

The love story that works in the service of the nation, of a homogenous community, and of patriarchy, as well as the liberal ideal of multiculturism, is using the
positive valence that is associated with the emotion of love in order to constitute
sameness. Both Hindu nationalism and neoliberalism are invested in constituting sameness, the former by brutally and violently repressing difference while
simultaneously cultivating a love for sameness (the Hindu nation) and the latter
by incorporating and appropriating difference while ensuring that that difference
does not radically alter its social, cultural, and economic hierarchies. The heterosexual love stories that constituted the "affable young man" and the "modern girl"
as well as the stories that used love in the service of Hindu patriarchy and the
nation that we have discussed have concealed the desire for the production of
sameness by speaking about difference. While some of these love stories used the
affect of love to reiterate the preeminence of the nation and the patriarch, others
(the so-called new love stories) used love to center capital and liberalism. *This* is
the hegemonic function of the heterosexual love story.

However, there is a conception of love that draws on long poetic and prose
traditions in South Asia and also reworks them—in some of the cinematic love
stories we have discussed but especially in the love song—that, I contend, defines
the emotion as poetic world-making. The world that *this* conception of love creates does not repress or appropriate difference. Difference, in fact, is constitutive
of this world. At a remove from Freudian psychoanalysis, the difference that this
conception of love speaks about is not defined by and limited to hetero-sex. Nor is
this love a metaphysical conception, even though it often draws on metaphysical
poetry to narrate itself. No, this love is this-worldly, rooted in a political-economy
that often violently forbids its presence and imagines another world, which it
hopes and desires to create. This world that *this* love desires to create cannot be
about self-making and sameness because *this* love would not exist in the absence
of difference.

In the film *Sairat*, the young male protagonist in love (Prashant or Parshya) has
two close friends, one a differently abled lower-caste youth (Pradeep/Langdya/
Balya) and the other a Muslim (Salim or Sallya). When they realize that their
friend is in love with the upper-caste landlord's daughter, Pradeep in particular
encourages and supports Parshya in honing and defining his conception of love.
While Salim is correctly wary of the consequences of this love for his friend in the

beginning, he too actively supports first his friend and then the couple-in-love. Risking their own lives and those of their families, Pradeep and Salim run away from their village and home with the couple. "They (Parshya and Archi) are doing what they are doing because they are in love, why are you doing this [running away and risking your lives]? For friendship?" Salim and Pradeep are asked by another character with some derision at a crucial moment in the film. Even when Parshya tells them that they should return home to their families, Salim and Pradeep continue to stand with the couple and even land in jail. I think that Pradeep and Salim's support and encouragement of not only their friend but the couple-in-love should be read as an investment in love's radical potential for poetic world-making. A world that would enable Parshya and Archi to live together is a world that has to have been reconstituted with a radically different political-economic structure and sociality. In such a world, a poor Muslim young man like Salim and a differently abled lower-caste man like Pradeep might also have the possibility to live without being the targets of violence, systemic discrimination, and derision. This conception of love, rooted as it is in difference and invested in world-making, is a threat; it is therefore either defanged by celebrating it on screen, appropriating it so the adjustment to patriarchy and capital is made easier, or by labeling it jihad and violently repressing it.

CONCLUSION

The 2015 Hindi film *Tamasha* (Spectacle, Imtiaz Ali) is about stories, the storyteller, and storytelling. It is also a film about love. The film is about spectacles—both the staging of spectacles as well as the experience of becoming one. It also dwells on the conception of realism. It narrates the painful struggle of its male protagonist, Ved, who believes he is suspended between the heart and the world (*"dil aur duniya ke beech"*). I will use *Tamasha* as a narrative node and think with (as well as against) its grain to conclude the range of discussions that have made up this book. *Tamasha*'s Ved experiences the heart and the world as the poles of a binary. The film's dialogue and song lyrics make allusions to various types of binaries: "yours and mine" (*tera mera*), "feminine and masculine" (*zanana mardana*), "bipolar," "heart and the world" (*dil aur duniya*). Often, these allusions are made playfully or in jest, in song, but the narrative also insists that living with and within binaries threatens to unravel our protagonist. Binaries are a mechanism of power, *Tamasha* suggests. From Ved's point of view, the world (*duniya*) is the dominant story, it dominates and controls him: It is the story told by the patriarch and every institution he encounters including the school, the university, and the corporation. Because this controlling story defines and gives meaning to the world, this story is understood as realism—the actual, the factual, the sociologically real (*dar asl*). Ved therefore also believes that if he lives his part within the narrative webs of the dominant story—running to the beat of the clock, the calendar, the heteronormative family, and the corporation—he will be legible. He will, in fact, be perceived as real, a common man, *the* common man, only if he resides within the narrative framework of the dominant story. And therefore, he insists that this is who he *really* is. He is Ved.

No, says the woman who loves him. You are someone *else*. Ved is a character you are playing. The real Ved, she tells him, resides in the tale that the heart spins. In saying so, she echoes back to him his own suspicions. Our protagonist has known this but he has always believed and has been led to believe that the story of the heart must be hidden from the world, it must be repressed. In other words, his real self is and must remain shackled. In the way that I have summarized it thus far, the form of *Tamasha* could be an echo of several stories we have encountered through the course of this book. Our protagonist is shackled; he has been weighed down by regulations and his true self remains repressed. In order to discover that true self (is that the unshackled entrepreneur?), he must find the narrative within which this self can find voice. In the framework of the stories we tracked in the chapter that focused on development as a concept-image, Ved could be described as stuck in obstructed time, spinning his wheels but going nowhere. As the common man, he is awaiting the freedom that unshackling will bring, enabling him to take the iconic journey that will suture him to the spectacular visionary and the spectacle of success, as the stories that helped us decipher iconicity suggested. Or, the stories featured in the chapter on the entrepreneur would argue, the unshackling that our protagonist awaits will enable him to realize his heart's desire and he will emerge as the possessive individual. Or as some of the love stories featured in the previous chapter would have it, Ved would acknowledge and recognize love and allow the ideal femininity of his lover to help him adjust and adapt better to the world. In each of these sets of stories that we have encountered, Hindutva neoliberalism is narrated as the political-economic intersection that will unshackle and free the common man. To put it differently, Hindutva neoliberalism is the narrative that would finally enable Ved (named, after all, in honor of the Hindu scriptures known collectively as the Vedas) to free his repressed but true self. This is true, these stories insist, because both neoliberalism and Hindu nationalism are foundationally about the common man. *Tamasha*, however, does something different.

Despite the polysemy of *Tamasha*'s text, it labors to make an argument that is at a distance, if not at odds, with the stories that have given shape and form to Hindutva neoliberalism. Even though the film uses a form that appears familiar, Ved does not find his happily-ever-after in Hindutva neoliberalism. Where does he find it, then? Central to *Tamasha*'s argument is its conception of realism and the spectacle. Through the course of this book, we have been tracking the form of spectacular realism, which performs the discursive labor of suturing the commoner (the *aam aadmi*) to the spectacle of capital and authoritarian nationalism. That discursive labor aims to win consent for Hindutva neoliberalism. *Tamasha* inverts the discursive logic of spectacular realism as a form. The film suggests that it is capital and patriarchy that translate and transform our protagonist into the commoner, as such that *commoner* is a falsehood, the opposite of realism. Our protagonist is powerfully acted upon to play the character of the commoner. Enacting that character is a traumatic experience, a trauma that is staged and experienced every single day. In order to unshackle himself from the trauma of living a lie, our protagonist must find realism.

This brings us to the binary of heart-world (*dil-duniya*) that *Tamasha*'s plot sets up for its protagonist. To unshackle himself from the lie that the world has enforced upon him, he must turn to the heart. Or to find his happily-ever-after, he must find the heart. But, what is the heart? What does it want? If Ved is caught between the heart and the world, and if the world (*duniya*) is the dominant story, the story of capital, then the heart (*dil*) appears to be the symbol for the story that does *not* labor to reproduce capital.[1] Thus, the dil-duniya binary would suggest that where duniya or the dominant story is the history mapped out by capital, dil, the story that the heart spins, is that which interrupts duniya and creates an unease in our protagonist. In duniya, our protagonist is a commoner in groveling service of capital and patriarchy; he mouths the jargon of the corporation and is asked to be an individual even as he is simultaneously told to be a cog in the wheel. In the world, he must be his father's son and capital's knave, displaying his unique selling point (USP) at all times. As such, Ved-in-the-world labors to reproduce the very structures and institutions that alienate him from himself. But, like Ved, we must circle back to the question that continues to elude a response: What exactly is the heart? Is it a mirage, as Ved suggests at one point in the narrative, that appears restorative like water but is actually parched like sand? Is it the lover standing, beckoning from a distance? Does the heart's story reside in "unselfconscious collective practices"?[2] Is the heart a space outside the bounds of capital and patriarchy? Does it always already exist? Does it require discovery?

Having set up the dil-duniya binary, *Tamasha* does a curious thing. It aims to sidestep and bracket the bipolarity of binaries. *Tamasha* suggests that the self that is not alienated from itself, the real self, does not simply exist as the polar opposite of the dominant story. It must be crafted through careful storytelling. It must be constituted through a journey of deliberately asked questions (*safarnama, sawaalon ka*). There is nothing "unselfconscious" about the heart. This journey of question and answer, call and response that our protagonist must undertake in order to construct the story of the heart also reveals to him that the world is, in fact, a hegemonic story. It is not an immovable reality, but a powerfully constructed imperative. It must consistently work to win consent. If duniya is a story that becomes hegemonic because it is told, retold, and circulated in myriad different ways, then dil is a story too. Moreover, it is a story that reveals the world's mythologies and must also therefore be narrated, re-narrated, and circulated. In order to draft this story, our protagonist must give up on the certainties (including the certainties of binaries) promised by capital and patriarchy. Along the way, he meets people who do not conform to binaries—a rickshaw driver who is a singer, a wise hijra who begs at the traffic light—who act as uncanny intuitions and confirmations of the impossibility of binaries. Ved must surrender to the spectacular joys and sorrows of love. He must also allow himself to become a spectacle (*tamasha*). The spectacle, *Tamasha* suggests, helps unravel the tangled web of the hegemonic story, and that deconstruction, in turn, can lead to the constitution of a self that is not alienated from itself (realism). In the narrative logic of the film, realism requires the spectacular. In the hegemonic story of Hindutva neoliberalism that we have been tracking, capital and authoritarian nationalism are constituted as spectacular and the commoner (the *aam aadmi*) is constituted as realism; that which is spectacular is then cynically sutured to that which is real, so that consent can be won for Hindutva neoliberalism. In the narrative logic of these stories, the spectacular requires realism.

As we have been tracing through the course of this manuscript, popular stories from film, advertising, journalism, and commentary provide the paradigmatic structure through which the political-economic formation of Hindutva neoliberalism narrates itself. Spectacular realism emerges as an aesthetic form of Hindutva neoliberalism through the patterning of a diverse range of stories. In the hegemonic form of spectacular realism, authority and authoritarianism often enact the spectacle and a patrilineal relationship sutures realism to the spectacle. In the film *Tamasha*, popular stories are crucial to our protagonist. He has listened to stories and popular myths through his childhood. He used to, in fact, seek out a storyteller so he could hear these stories drawn from literature and mythology from all over the world in all their various iterations. Listening to those stories makes our protagonist a storyteller too; he is attuned to the many stories swirling around him, he hears the patterns and the intersections among those stories, and he is a listener first, narrator second. He can play with storylines, merging, blending, and mixing plotlines that the world categorizes as disparate and incommensurable. Because he is playful, is enabled to be playful in the story of the heart, there are no limits (*teri na hadeh*). He can move like the sky, like thought itself (*aasmaan hai, khayal hai*). Here, he does not have to struggle to find his USP and market himself convincingly; he *is* without precedent, without parallel (*bemisaal*), just like everyone else. In the heart's story, moreover, he is never alone or lonely. It is only because he listens that he can narrate and only because he is called, can he respond. Here, he lives within a collective, quite specifically a theater group, which includes the rickshaw driver-singer, even his lover sometimes, among many others. He is not a lone writer or a lonely photographer consuming the world through his lens. He crafts his stories within the experience of collectivity afforded by theater—a form, some have argued, that is different from every other popular cultural form because it is not constituted by the processes of mechanical reproduction.[3] What he creates with his theater group is a tamasha, a theatrical spectacle. That tamasha crafts and tells the story of the heart by narrating the hegemonic story of the world. In doing so, it links the heart with the world, the intimate with the public, the particularly local with the globally universal.[4] The spectacle of love and the staging of spectacles allows our protagonist to eschew the bipolarity of heart and world (*dil aur duniya*). The popular story, but especially the play with both the form and content of the popular story, is crucial to the protagonist's understanding of the world as a hegemonic story and to the crafting of his own.

The unruly stories that we have examined in each of our chapters, including the debate about the concept of equity in development, dalit politician Mayawati's genealogical construction of iconicity, Zaheera Shaikh's trading of her tragic story like a commodity, and the love song that conceives of love as creating new worlds, are narratives that reveal the crafting of the hegemonic story. In other words, these unruly stories make the familiar hegemonic story strange. They are unruly because they appear to fit into the weave of the hegemonic narrative, but in order to truly accommodate these stories the hegemonic narrative would need to be disrupted.

As such they reveal the form or weave of the hegemonic story. These unruly stories are not the polar opposites of the hegemonic story and do not a constitute a binary with the story that comes to define the conjuncture. Therefore, relief from or resistance to the hegemonic story for those seeking it cannot be simply found within these unruly stories. Popular cultural stories are often read as serving one of two possible functions—an ideological or a resistant function (*dil aur duniya*, heart and world). My aim throughout the book has been to trouble this binary. I have attempted to reveal how the popular cultural story provides the form, the shape, and the template through which neoliberalism and authoritarian nationalism define themselves, as well as to reveal the trouble stories sometimes create for hegemonic formations. As such, I have argued for a critical-reading practice without guarantees.

I began the book by asking how our contemporary time has come to be defined by ostensibly contradictory sets of political projects—authoritarian nationalism, which emphasizes nativism, and neoliberalism, which champions the deregulation of markets, trade, and borders and fosters globalization. Through a focus on the popular story, we have tracked the intersection of neoliberalism with Hindu nationalism in India as an aesthetic form, namely spectacular realism. Both neoliberalism and Hindu nationalism use, appropriate, and formulate similar discursive strategies in order to narrate themselves as political-economic projects that center the commoner. The focus on narratives or stories reveals that authoritarian nationalism and neoliberalism are not incommensurate projects. These political projects have, in fact, labored to strengthen each other. The spectacular failures of the projects—the global financial crisis of 2008 for neoliberalism, for instance, and the deep political-economic crises including agrarian distress and unemployment in the first term of the Modi government—did not lead to the collapse of either project. The intertwining of Hindu nationalism with neoliberalism was only strengthened. In the specific context of India, we have also tracked the significant ways in which the popular discourse of pre-liberalization India set the stage for the narrative maneuvers of both liberalization and Hindu nationalism. Even though Hindutva neoliberalism often narrates itself as an event and therefore as a radical break from the past, its continuities with that past are as crucial as its disjunctures.

ACKNOWLEDGMENTS

The story that these acknowledgments weave is about relationships: relationships with people, institutions, cities, and towns, and with textual, visual, and sonic signs without which this book was impossible. The story is also about the journeys that these relationships enabled me to take without a thought about destinations. My relationship with my doctoral dissertation committee at the University of Washington in Seattle allowed me to meander along intellectual trajectories that kindled my curiosity and move between disciplinary spaces as if that were normative. Thanks to Ralina Joseph, Priti Ramamurthy, Chandan Reddy, Crispin Thurlow, and Gerry Baldasty for their mentorship, friendship, and warm embrace. They made the academy home. I could not have conjured up a better doctoral adviser than Ralina. Her belief in me sustained me in ways I cannot count. Reading Black Cultural Studies and Women of Color Feminisms with Ralina enabled me to carve out a space in Media Studies. Priti and Gowri are my family in Seattle. Writing a paper with Priti and Amy Bhatt for a special issue of *Signs* was crucial to the journey of this book.

Seattle has become my home city in the United States—those overcast skies, that misty rain, that filtered golden light, the evergreen trees, the cherry blossoms on the quad at UW, the Seattle Metro, watching Hindi films on the screen, Starbucks, Elliott Bay Book Company, the Ave. Those spaces were brought alive by the companionship of Jameel Ahmad, Jennifer Dubrow, Kristin Gustafson and Jean Miller and their daughter Davis, Keith Snodgrass, Tapoja Chaudhuri, Amy Bhatt, Phelps Feeley, Mark Hungerford, Monique Lacoste, Kate Bell, Leah Werbel, and Tabitha Hart. Manoucheka Celeste's insight, brilliance, and energy changed everything. The Women of Color Collective that she helped create alongside Sara Diaz, Martha Gonzalez, Noralis Rodrigues, and Monica De La Torre, at UW, sustained me and conceptualized an unparalleled space for camaraderie and interdisciplinary conversations that none of us have quite found since. The Marx and Madeira group (Amy, Kevin, Aamir, Juned, Sahar, and Sandra) made so many evenings lively and memorable. Memories of *addas* with my *sahelis* Sahar Romani and Sandra Gresl always bring joy. My thanks also to Amanda Swarr, Lynn Thomas, Vince Rafael, Phil Howard, and Matt Sparke for being such wonderful teachers and interlocutors. The Simpson Center for the Humanities at UW was a dynamic intellectual space and I was lucky to have been a part of the Society of Scholars at a crucial stage in the dissertation writing process. The South Asia Center was yet another wonderfully interdisciplinary space at UW that helped me hone the questions I was asking and understand their stakes, thanks to Sareeta Amrute, Christian Novetzke, Sudhir Mahadevan, Sunila Kale, Anand Yang, Sonaal Khullar, Cabeiri Robinson, and Keith Snodgrass. A teaching fellowship in the

Interdisciplinary Arts and Sciences program at UW, Bothell taught me how inter-disciplinarity could productively work in the academy, I will always be grateful to Bruce Burgett and Ron Krabill and especially my students in BIS 413: Nations and Nationalisms for that experience.

Before Seattle though, it was the chilly climes and warm hospitality of Minne-apolis and the University of Minnesota that introduced me to the academy in the United States. Linda Jean Kenix, Hazel Dicken-Garcia, Brian Southwell, and Ajay Skaria first helped me understand how to read critically and write analytically. Hazel reacquainted me with Stuart Hall and introduced me to the joys of archival research and textual analysis. I used to dream so many times of flying out to Min-neapolis to meet you, Hazel. In my dream, I always had my book in hand. I lin-gered and you left too soon, but what you taught me is, I hope, resonant in what is productive in these pages.

The postdoctoral year at Yale University was rejuvenating and all about sump-tuous meals, kettles of tea, the heartiest of laughs, and the joys of community. K. Sivaramakrishnan and Inderpal Grewal afforded me that opportunity. Durba Mitra, Aniket Aga, Chitrangada Choudhury, Arupjyoti Saikia, Tariq Thachil, Piyali Bhattacharya, and Sahana Ghosh made even the hallowed, ivy-covered environs of Yale feel like home. My dearest friends, my pals for life—Rochisha Narayan, Rene Saran, Kasturi Gupta, and Sumati Sundaram—because of you Taft Apart-ments in New Haven will always hold a special place in my heart. Rochi, I cannot wait for my autographed copy of your book!

At Virginia Tech, where I first began to outline the shape and scope of this book, in my colleagues I had the most wonderful interlocutors. I cannot thank Emily Satterwhite and Nicole Zhang enough for being such warm colleagues and friends. Peter Schmitthenner, Brian Britt, Rachel Scott, Elizabeth Malbon, Betty Fine, Francois Debrix, Matt Gabriel, Petra Rivera Rideau, and Ben Sax were gen-erous colleagues. I workshopped a very nascent draft of what would become chap-ter 4 of the book at VT and I was lucky to have a mentoring grant that allowed me to bring Arvind Rajagopal to campus there. I learned so much—including about Appalachian Studies and post-secularism—from the work my colleagues were doing at VT and so many of our conversations shaped my own thinking.

I grew up in bustling, jostling Mumbai, in a suburb called Santacruz. I live and work now in a forest in a town in California called Santa Cruz! I am surrounded by wildlife—deer, raccoons, coyotes, snakes, owls, banana slugs, birds of all nature, sea lions, and even mountain lions. The distance between Santacruz, Mumbai, and Santa Cruz, California, could not be greater and yet, on some days in the summer, the way the sun's light hits the ocean's water and sparkles or the burbling crash of a wave on the rocks reminds me of that warmer, saltier sea—the Arabian—and its beaches from my childhood. I think I have put down some roots in Santa Cruz, California! Feminist Studies at UCSC welcomed me; it has been a joy to teach in the department. And for that, I have Bettina Aptheker, Anjali Arondekar, Neda Atanasoski, Karen Barad, Gina Dent, Nick Mitchell, Felicity Schaeffer, and Marcia

Ochoa to thank. Neel Ahuja and Gina Athena Ulysse joined the department after I did and have been supportive senior colleagues. Colleagues across other departments at UCSC, including Gail Hershatter, Lisa Rofel, Vanita Seth, Herman Gray, Debbie Gould, David Anthony, Chris Connery, Shelley Stamp, Ben Leeds Carson, Tanya Merchant, Dard Neuman, Carla Freccero, Lisbeth Haas, Bali Sahota, Veronica Tonay, Mayanthi Fernando, Megan Moodie, Nidhi Mahajan, and Muriam Halle Davis have helped make UCSC home. The Cultural Studies colloquium, where I had the opportunity to present a draft version of chapter 1, remains a uniquely dynamic intellectual space. The revisions for the manuscript were completed while I was part of a Writing Circle for junior faculty of color. Thanks to Sylvanna Falcon, Chris Benner, Jody Greene, and Sikina Jinnah for all their work in getting us together. Thanks to Kel Weinhold! And thanks to my mates, Nidhi, Yasmeen, Savannah, Kat, Justin, Anjuli, and Roberto! Thanks also to my students from whom I always learn so much—Yizhou Guo, Halima Kazem, Radhika Prasad, Yoel van de Sande, Rosa Lee Petterson, Jasmine Simone, and Deanna Duffy.

The Center for Education and Documentation in Mumbai was a treasure trove and became an important archive for this project. The knowledgeable staff of CED are a tremendous resource for any researcher interested in public discourse in India! Thanks also to Aswin Punathambekar, Radhika Gajjala, Radhika Parameswaran, Purnima Mankekar, Arvind Rajagopal, Amanda Weidman, and Usha Iyer for their support over the years. Nicole Solano at Rutgers University Press is a warm, supportive, and enthusiastic editor. Thanks to my anonymous reviewers for an insightful engagement with the manuscript. Your comments and critiques were incredibly productive for me as I revised the book. In the able hands of my production editor, Kristen Bettcher, copy editor, Brett Keener, and indexer, Alex Trotter, the manuscript that had lived in my computer for some years was transformed into a book, whose pages can be turned. A very early version of chapter 3 appeared in the journal *Communication, Culture & Critique* and the feedback from the anonymous reviewers then was productive.

My other teachers, Jeroo Mulla, P. Sainath, Smriti Koppikar, Anupamaa Joshi, and George Jose, thank you! In so many ways, the journey that led to this book began with you. It also began with my SCM comrades, Natasha Hemrajani, Nishantni Josson, Lara Bhalla, Georgina Maddox, Smitha Deans, Saritha Thomas, Meera Jacob, Preetiarti Parija, Sohoni Bhattacharya, and Tinaaz Nooshian. Haaris Shaikh and Deepa Kadam are not just warm friends, they are comrades who helped me source materials for the book. To my oldest and bestest friends, Amol Shah, Revati Venkatesh, and their beautiful daughter Sana, and Darakhshan Khan, Davide Motta, and their sweet daughter Soraiya: your friendship has sustained me. Darakhshan, we have traveled together, my friend, and look how far we have come! Here's to all the many miles that lie ahead!

My parents, Mohan and Gayatri, had me when they were in their early twenties. We have grown together and they have supported me in all the ways they could, even when the paths I took terrified them. My grandmothers, Sarojini and

Kalyani, were and are my inspiration and my grandfathers, P.B.K. and Mohan Rao, were some of my favorite storytellers. My brother, Anand, is my friend. Thank you, Babs, for your unstinting support, your wit and humor. It has been an absolute joy to witness you grow into the man you have become. Keep singing your song and we'll always have pizza and Maggi! To the other elders—Moinuddin and Khairunissa—and siblings—Shaziya, Aatif, and Moiz—in my life, thank you for your welcoming embrace. Your love, encouragement, and support, your strength, courage, and good humor even in the face of life's vagaries inspire me. Naila and Aasiya are sisters forever. Rida, Yaseen, Haaris, and Farhan, you have brought so much love and joy into our lives. Dadi Abba, I miss you; I especially miss your mirthful laugh. Bade amma, your fortitude and hospitality I can never forget. Rizwan, my Bombay-brother, our time together was short but it was so full; time cannot be accounted for by the clock and the calendar alone.

Juned Shaikh is my partner, my friend, and my comrade. I love our story, Juned. It is the best! It has romance, a touch of drama, lots of laughs, songs—even some dancing—a few exotic locales, and a sprinkling of magic. Its form feels familiar but not derivative. Without our story, without you, this book, this version of myself, this world that we now inhabit would have remained the whisper of a dream. Sahar, you are our joy. You entered our story and transformed it, you added color, glitter, and rainbows. This book is dedicated to you, Sahar, and to your baba, Juned.

NOTES

INTRODUCTION

Barack Obama, text of the presidential address to the joint session of the Indian parliament, http://www.deccanherald.com/content/111081/text-president-barack-obamas-address.html.

I have translated the Urdu verse penned and recited by Gulzar into English.

1. Walter Benjamin, "The Work of Art in the Age of Mechanical Reproduction" in *Illuminations* (New York: Schocken Books, 1968), 217–251.

2. Ideologues of Hindu nationalism, such as V. D. Savarkar, have drawn inspiration and political frameworks specifically from Nazism.

3. Caroline Levine argues, for instance, that "literary forms and social formations are equally real in their capacity to organize materials, and equally unreal in being artificial, contingent constraints." Caroline Levine, *Forms: Whole, Rhythm, Hierarchy, Network* (Princeton, NJ: Princeton University Press, 2015), 14.

4. W. J. T. Mitchell conceives of "pictures" in this form as "worldmaking rather than world mirroring." See W. J. T. Mitchell, *What Do Pictures Want? The Lives and Loves of Images* (Chicago: University of Chicago Press, 2005), xv.

5. See Shankar Gopalakrishnan, *Neoliberalism and Hindutva: Fascism, Free Markets and the Restructuring of Indian Capitalism* (Delhi: Aakar Books, 2009) for an argument against such a conceptualization from the perspective of the Indian Left.

6. Alys Weinbaum et al. note that a heuristic device "cannot be taken as given a priori; rather, it emerges in and through the research process and possesses a future orientation." Alys Weinbaum, Lynn Thomas, Priti Ramamurthy, Uta Poiger, Madeleine Yue Dong, and Tani Barlow (The Modern Girl Research Group), eds., *The Modern Girl Around the World: Consumption, Modernity, and Globalization* (Durham, NC: Duke University Press, 2008), 2.

7. See, for instance, the work of David Harvey on neoliberalism.

8. See, for instance, Purnima Mankekar, *Screening Culture, Viewing Politics: An Ethnography of Television, Womanhood, and Nation in Postcolonial India* (Durham, NC: Duke University Press, 1999); Rupal Oza, *The Making of Neoliberal India: Nationalism, Gender, and the Paradoxes of Globalization* (New York: Routledge, 2006); and Shanti Kumar, *Gandhi Meets Primetime: Globalization and Nationalism in Indian Television* (Urbana: University of Illinois Press, 2006).

9. Clare Hemmings, *Why Stories Matter: The Political Grammar of Feminist Theory* (Durham, NC: Duke University Press, 2011).

10. Robert J. C. Young, *Colonial Desire: Hybridity in Theory, Culture and Race* (London, New York: Routledge, 1995).

11. See Peter Holley, "KKK's Official Newspaper Supports Donald Trump for President," *Washington Post*, November 2, 2016, https://www.washingtonpost.com/news/post-politics/wp/2016/11/01/the-kkks-official-newspaper-has-endorsed-donald-trump-for-president. Holley discusses white nationalist support for Trump, the Trump campaign's disavowal of the *Crusade*'s (the Klan's newspaper) statement of support, as well as Trump's more ambiguous response to former KKK grand wizard David Duke's support of his candidacy and the eviction of people of color from campaign rallies.

12. See the *Atlantic*'s discussion of Donald Trump's October 2016 speech on lobbying and ethics reform where he used the phrase "drain the swamp": https://www.theatlantic.com/politics/archive/2016/10/donald-trumps-plan-to-drain-the-swamp/504569/.

13. See, for instance, Pippa Norris, "It's Not Just Trump. Authoritarian Populism is Rising Across the West. Here's Why," *Washington Post*, March 11, 2016, https://www.washingtonpost .com/news/monkey-cage/wp/2016/03/11/its-not-just-trump-authoritarian-populism-is -rising-across-the-west-heres-why/?utm_term=.d3d7a47ce9b7.

14. See, for instance, Pippa Norris, *Cultural Backlash: Trump, Brexit and Authoritarian Populism* (Cambridge: Cambridge University Press, 2019).

15. Stuart Hall, "The Great Moving Right Show," *Marxism Today*, January 14–20, 1979.

16. For an excellent summation of Stuart Hall's conceptualization of authoritarian populism and Nicos Poulantazas's theorization of authoritarian statism, see Ian Bruff, "The Rise of Authoritarian Neoliberalism," *Rethinking Marxism: A Journal of Economics, Culture & Society* 26, no. 1 (2014): 113–129.

17. See Hall, "The Great Moving Right Show"; Stuart Hall, "Authoritarian Populism: A Reply to Jessop et al," *New Left Review* 1, no. 151 (May–June 1985): 115–24; Stuart Hall, *Hard Road to Renewal: Thatcherism and the Crisis of the Left* (London: Verso, 1988); and S. Hall, C. Critcher, T. Jefferson, J. Clarke, and B. Roberts, *Policing the Crisis: Mugging, the State and Law and Order* (London: Macmillan, 1978).

18. See Ernesto Laclau, *On Populist Reason* (London: Verso, 2005), 105. Defining both Mao Tse-Tung's "Long March" and the political mobilizations of the followers of Brazilian politician Adhemar de Barros (who espoused clientalism as a form of politics—votes in exchange for political favors—in the 1950s as populism), Ernesto Laclau directly defines populism as the "presence of an anti-institutional dimension," "a certain challenge to political normalization, to 'business as usual,'" and an "appeal to the underdog" (122, 123).

19. Laclau, 105.

20. Ranabir Samaddar, "Fifty years ago: How pro-poor politics became an integral part of Indian democracy," *Scroll.in*, February 26, 2021. https://scroll.in/article/985058/fifty-years-ago -how-pro-poor-politics-became-an-integral-part-of-indian-democracy.

21. Samaddar, "Fifty years ago."

22. Samaddar, "Fifty years ago."

23. Samaddar, "Fifty years ago."

24. David Harvey, *A Brief History of Neoliberalism* (Oxford: Oxford University Press, 2005).

25. Alfred Saad-Filho and Deborah Johnston, "Introduction," in *Neoliberalism: A Critical Reader*, ed. Alfred Saad-Filho and Deborah Johnston (London: Pluto Press, 2005), 1–6.

26. Saad-Filho and Johnston.

27. David Harvey, *A Brief History of Neoliberalism* (Oxford: Oxford University Press, 2005).

28. Harvey, 2.

29. Aihwa Ong, *Neoliberalism as Exception: Mutations in Citizenship and Sovereignty* (Durham, NC: Duke University Press, 2006), 3.

30. Ong, 3.

31. Ong, 4.

32. Antonio Gramsci in Hall, "The Great Moving Right Show."

33. Nancy Fraser, *The Old is Dying and the New Cannot Be Born* (London: Verso, 2019), 11.

34. See Ruth Wilson Gilmore, *Golden Gulag: Prisons, Surplus, Crisis, and Opposition in Global-izing California* (Berkeley: University of California Press, 2007).

35. Chandan Reddy, *Freedom with Violence: Race, Sexuality and the US State* (Durham, NC: Duke University Press, 2011), 20.

36. Cedric Robinson, *Black Marxism: The Making of the Black Radical Tradition* (London: Zed Press, 1983; Chapel Hill: University of North Carolina Press, 2000). Also see Robin D. G. Kelley, "What did Cedric Robinson Mean by Racial Capitalism?" *Boston Review: A Political and Liter-ary Forum*, January 12, 2017, http://bostonreview.net/race/robin-d-g-kelley-what-did-cedric -robinson-mean-racial-capitalism.

37. See Juned Shaikh, *Outcast Bombay: City Making and the Politics of the Poor* (Seattle: University of Washington Press, 2021), 5.

38. Shaikh, 5.

39. The recent case brought against Cisco Systems Inc. by the California Department of Fair Employment and Housing for caste discrimination distinctly reveals that global capital (and new technology corporations) is not outside the "old" bounds and binds of caste. In this case, it has been alleged that Cisco discriminated against an Indian American employee and allowed him to be harassed by two managers because he was a dalit. See Anahita Mukherji, "California's Legal Ground in Battling Caste Discrimination Takes Center Stage in Historic Cisco Case," *The Wire*, March 10, 2021, https://thewire.in/caste/cisco-case-caste-discrimination-silicon-valley-ambedkar-organisations.

40. Shankar Gopalakrishnan, *Neoliberalism and Hindutva: Fascism, Free Markets and the Restructuring of Indian Capitalism* (Delhi: Aakar Books, 2009), 44–45.

41. David Ludden, "Ayodhya: A Window on the World," in *Contesting the Nation: Religion, Community, and the Politics of Democracy in India*, ed. David Ludden (Philadelphia: University of Pennsylvania Press, 1996), 4.

42. Tapan Basu, Pradip Datta, Sumit Sarkar, Tanika Sarkar, and Sambuddha Sen, *Khaki Shorts and Saffron Flags* (New Delhi: Orient Longman, 1993), 1.

43. Achin Vanaik, *The Furies of Indian Communalism: Religion, Modernity and Secularization* (London, New York: Verso, 1997), 39–40.

44. Ludden, "Ayodhya," 5.

45. Thomas Blom Hansen, *The Saffron Wave: Democracy and Hindu Nationalism in Modern India* (New Delhi: Oxford University Press, 1999), 4.

46. Hansen, 4.

47. Arvind Rajagopal, "Advertising, Politics and the Sentimental Education of the Indian Consumer," *Visual Anthropology Review* 14, no. 2 (Fall–Winter 1998): 14–31. Rajagopal argues that the BJP—more expertly than the Indian National Congress—fashioned a political rhetoric drawing from Hindu symbolism and ritual as a mass mobilization tool; Indian advertising, which until the 1980s only focused on the urban elite, did the same when economic liberalization necessitated larger markets and sets of consumers.

48. Manisha Basu, *The Rhetoric of Hindu India: Language and Urban Nationalism* (Cambridge: Cambridge University Press, 2016), 25.

49. Basu, 15–16.

50. It must be noted that other terms have been used to describe our present conjuncture. Nancy Fraser, for instance, uses the term "hyperreactionary neoliberalism." See Nancy Fraser, *The Old is Dying and the New Cannot Be Born* (London: Verso, 2019).

51. Using concepts such as "the shock doctrine," "disaster capitalism," and "corporatist," Naomi Klein has famously argued that natural disasters and economic and political crises become the spatiotemporal node within which deregulation is enacted to "liberate corporations." Catastrophic events, Klein has argued, thus come to be defined as "exciting market opportunities." The spectacular failure of neoliberalism can be conceptualized as one such catastrophic event, which paradoxically became an opportunity for its greater salience. See *The Shock Doctrine: The Rise of Disaster Capitalism* (New York: Picador, 2007), 18, 6.

52. Ian Bruff, "The Rise of Authoritarian Neoliberalism," *Rethinking Marxism: A Journal of Economics, Culture & Society* 26, no. 1 (2014): 113–129. From a different vantage point, Naomi Klein has argued that the economic doctrines named as neoliberalism in fact require authoritarianism for their complete implementation. See Klein, *Shock Doctrine*.

53. See Martin Saar, William Callison, and Anne Gräfe, "Spinoza and the Political Imaginary," *Qui Parle: Critical Humanities and Social Sciences* 23, no. 2 (2015): 115–133. The authors argue that many seventeenth-century writers thought about the "imaginary and image-mediated

nature of political relationships," Spinoza being the most thorough and systematic of these writers.

54. Oza, *The Making of Neoliberal India*, 15. See Shankar Acharya and Rakesh Mohan, eds., *India's Economy: Performance and Challenges: Essays in Honor of Montek Singh Ahluwalia*, (Delhi: Oxford University Press, 2010); and I. A. Ahluwalia and I.M.D. Little, eds., *India's Economic Reforms and Development: Essays for Manmohan Singh* (Delhi: Oxford University Press, 1998).

55. A group of industrialists, including Rahul Bajaj, Hari Shankar Singhania, Keshub Mahindra, S. K. Birla, Ashok Jain, and L. M. Thapar submitted a memorandum to finance minister Manmohan Singh expressing concern about foreign direct investment in Indian markets and import duty cuts in 1993. This group has come to be known as the Bombay Club. See footnote 64 in Jairam Ramesh, *To the Brink and Back: India's 1991 Story* (Delhi: Rupa Publications, 2015), 103.

56. Bhabhatosh Dutta, Hanumantha Rao et al., "Devaluation and IMF Loan: Leading Economists' Alternative View," originally published in *Mainstream*, July 13, 1991, republished as Annexure 6 in Jairam Ramesh, *To the Brink and Back: India's 1991 Story* (New Delhi: Rupa Publications, 2015).

57. Ramesh, *To the Brink and Back*, 93.

58. Pheng Cheah, *Spectral Nationality: Passages of Freedom from Kant to Postcolonial Literatures of Liberation* (New York: Columbia University Press, 2003), 7.

59. Ajay Gudavarthy, "Brahmanism, Liberalism and the Postcolonial Theory," *Economic and Political Weekly* 51, no. 24 (June 11, 2016): 15–17.

60. Gudavarthy, 17.

61. Shefali Chandra, *The Sexual Life of English: Languages of Caste and Desire in Colonial India* (Durham, NC: Duke University Press, 2012), 16.

62. See, for instance, Nandan Nilekani, *Imagining India: Ideas for the New Century* (New York: Penguin Press, 2008); and Gurcharan Das, *India Unbound: The Social and Economic Revolution from Independence to the Global Information Age* (New York: Anchor Books, 2000, 2002).

63. Montek Singh Ahluwalia, "The 1991 Reforms," *Economic and Political Weekly* 51, no. 29 (July 2016).

64. Oza, *The Making of Neoliberal India*, 11.

65. Nivedita Menon and Aditya Nigam, *Power and Contestation: India Since 1989* (Hyderabad: Orient Longman, 2008), 4–5.

66. Lisa Lowe and David Lloyd, "Introduction," in *The Politics of Culture in the Shadow of Capital*, ed. Lisa Lowe and David Lloyd (Durham, NC: Duke University Press, 1997), 1.

67. Franco Moretti, *Modern Epic: The World System from Goethe to Garcia Marquez* (London: Verso, 1996), 6.

68. Lauren Berlant, *The Queen of America Goes to Washington City: Essays on Sex and Citizenship* (Durham, NC: Duke University Press, 1997), 12.

69. Sarah Banet-Weiser, *Authentic: The Politics of Ambivalence in a Brand Culture* (New York: New York University Press, 2012), 3.

70. Banet-Weiser, 4.

71. See William Mazzarella, *Shovelling Smoke: Advertising and Globalization in Contemporary India* (Durham, NC: Duke University Press, 2003) for a detailed discussion of this term. Also see Arvind Rajagopal, "The Commodity Image in the (Post) Colony," *Tasveer Ghar: A Digital Archive of South Asian Popular Visual Culture*, http://www.tasveergharindia.net/cmsdesk/essay/100/index.html, for a different emphasis on the term. Rajagopal in particular has argued, following the work of Wolfgang Haug, that use value is translated into exchange value through the mediation of the image. However, in the relationship that is thus formed between the commodity and the image, neither does the commodity remain a purely economic entity nor does the image function as only aesthetic.

72. John Fiske, *Understanding Popular Culture* (New York: Routledge, 1989, 1990, 2011).

73. Bishnupriya Ghosh, *Global Icons: Apertures to the Popular* (Durham, NC: Duke University Press, 2011).

74. See Pheng Cheah, *Spectral Nationality: Passages of Freedom from Kant to Postcolonial Literatures of Liberation* (New York: Columbia University Press, 2003).

75. Seyla Benhabib, *The Claims of Culture: Equality and Diversity in the Global Era* (Princeton, NJ: Princeton University Press, 2002), 6.

76. Benhabib, 15.

77. See Raymond Williams, who had argued that "realist art or literature is seen as simply one convention among others, a set of formal representations, in a formal medium to which we have become accustomed. The object is not really lifelike but by convention and repetition has been made to appear so." Raymond Williams, *Keywords: A Vocabulary of Culture and Society* (New York: Oxford University Press, 1976, 1983), 185.

78. Issues such as the capture of essential commodities to create monopolies within the market, the entanglement of political power with capital, land grabbing, and violence between religious and caste communities may have historical specificity but Mogambo as the fountainhead and embodiment of evil is a spectacular supervillain.

79. See M. Madhava Prasad, *Ideology of the Hindi Film: A Historical Construction* (Delhi: Oxford University Press, 2000). Prasad has noted that mainstream Indian cinema has struggled with the advance definition of it as "not-yet cinema" because realism has circulated as an imperative for film as a mode of representation (2). Indian cinema did not necessarily submit to the realist imperative. This is why it was deemed "not yet." And yet, the dominance of the realist imperative "proved to be indispensable . . . as the site that enables discourse *about* Indian cinema, providing the tools for critical intervention, determining at an unconscious level, the reading practices we bring to bear on Indian film texts, as well as serving as an ideal for film-making to aspire to" (5). Film criticism in India chided filmmakers for not working within the realist imperative and filmmakers aspired to make realist cinema. It is within this discursive and social climate that the enumeration of sociological characteristics and the embodiment of simple commonness in *Mr. India* can be read as realism even in a film that will not be classified within the realist category.

80. George Steiner, "George Lukacs—A Preface" in George Lukacs, *Realism in Our Time: Literature and the Class Struggle*, trans. John Mander and Necke Mander (New York: Harper and Row, 1962), 13.

81. In film scholar Priya Jaikumar's evocative terms, the promise of classical realism is "to disturb the bounds of ideology, to humanize, and to bring the audience into astonishing proximities with the world and its social relations." Priya Jaikumar, *Cinema at the End of Empire: A Politics of Transition in Britain and India* (Durham, NC: Duke University Press, 2006), 109.

82. Jaikumar, 109.

83. Lukacs, in fact, accused the realism of modernist writers such as James Joyce of precisely this mode of storytelling, and as such regarded this literature as "modernist anti-realism." The consequence of this type of modernist literature was, Lukacs argued, to render and conceive the human being as ahistorical.

84. See M. Madhava Prasad for an iteration of this aspect of realism and melodrama in the context of film theory and Indian cinema.

85. L. K. Advani, *My Country, My Land* (New Delhi: Rupa and Co., 2008), 373.

86. Advani, 355.

87. Advani, 376.

88. Advani, 376.

89. Advani, 377.

90. Fredric Jameson, *The Political Unconscious: Narrative as a Socially Symbolic Act* (Ithaca, NY: Cornell University Press, 1981), 79.

1. THE DEVELOPMENT STORY

1. Marc Edelman and Angelique Haugerud, "Introduction: The Anthropology of Development and Globalization" in *The Anthropology of Development and Globalization: From Classical Political Economy to Contemporary Neoliberalism* (Malden: Blackwell Publishing, 2005), 1–74, 2.

2. Edelman and Haugerud.

3. James Ferguson, "Decomposing Modernity: History and Hierarchy after Development," in *Postcolonial Studies and Beyond*, ed. Ania Loomba et al. (Durham, NC: Duke University Press, 2005), 169 (166–181). The idea of the Great Chain of Being can be traced back to ancient Greece and remained powerful up to the eighteenth century, as evident in European philosophy.

4. See the introductory chapter of David Scott, *Omens of Adversity: Tragedy, Time, Memory, Justice* (Durham, NC: Duke University Press, 2014).

5. Scott, 5, 6.

6. See Arturo Escobar, *Encountering Development: The Making and Unmaking of the Third World* (Princeton, NJ: Princeton University Press, 1995).

7. In mathematics education, concept-image references the mental images and cognitive structures built over time that are associated with a mathematical concept. David Tall and Shlomo Vinner give the example of subtraction, which is first encountered as a "process involving whole, positive numbers." In this case, subtraction may get associated with reduction, which could pose problems when negative numbers are subtracted and there is, in fact, an increase. As a concept-image therefore, subtraction can be understood not just as a mathematical process but also as a set of mental images and cognitive structures that come to bear on that process. David Tall and Shlomo Vinner, "Concept Image and Concept Definition in Mathematics with Particular Reference to Limits and Continuity," *Educational Studies in Mathematics* 12, no. 2 (1981): 151–169.

8. See Srirupa Roy, *Beyond Belief: India and the Politics of Postcolonial Nationalism* (Durham, NC: Duke University Press, 2007).

9. See Subrata Ghoshroy, "Taking Stock: The US-India Nuclear Deal 10 Years Later," *thebulletin.org*, February 16, 2016, https://thebulletin.org/2016/02/taking-stock-the-us-india-nuclear-deal-10-years-later.

10. Statement on the Indo-U.S. Bilateral Nuclear Cooperation Agreement, signed on August 7, 2007, by Prakash Karat (Communist Party of India (Marxist)), A. B. Bardhan (Communist Party of India), G. Devarajan (All India Forward Bloc), and Abani Roy (Revolutionary Socialist Party) and published in *Left Stand on the Nuclear Deal: Notes Exchanged in the UPA-Left Committee on India-U.S. Civil Nuclear Cooperation* (New Delhi: Progressive Printers, 2008).

11. Barack Obama, text of the presidential address to the joint session of the Indian parliament, http://www.deccanherald.com/content/111081/text-president-barack-obamas-address.html.

12. See Amit Maitra, "It's True, India has Emerged," *Economic Times*, November 11, 2010, http://economictimes.indiatimes.com/opinion/guest-writer/its-true-india-has-emerged/articleshow/6904295.cms?curpg=1.

13. Benedict Anderson, *Imagined Communities* (London: Verso, 2006 edition), 187.

14. Anderson, 187.

15. Jawaharlal Nehru, Speech On the Granting of Indian Independence, August 14, 1947. Modern History Sourcebook, http://www.fordham.edu/halsall/mod/1947nehru1.html.

16. Manmohan Singh, Address at the Indira Gandhi Conference—"India: The Next Decade," New Delhi, November 19, 2004, *Prime Minister Manmohan Singh: Selected Speeches*, Volume I: May 2004 to May 2005 (Publications Division: Ministry of Information and Broadcasting, Government of India).

17. India Poised campaign, English-language version featuring Amitabh Bachchan.

18. India Poised campaign, Hindustani-language version featuring Gulzar.

19. See, for example, Gurcharan Das, *India Unbound: The Social and Economic Revolution from Independence to the Global Information Age* (New York: Anchor Books, 2002).

20. See Wendy Brown, *In the Ruins of Neoliberalism: The Rise of Antidemocratic Politics in the West* (New York: Columbia University Press, 2019).

21. Swaminathan Ankelasari Aiyar, "West's Discovery of India," *Times of India*, June 25, 2006.

22. Bennett Coleman & Co. is the flagship company of the Times Group.

23. Vanita Kohli-Khandekar, *The Indian Media Business*, 2nd ed. (New Delhi: Response Books, 2006), 35.

24. Kohli-Khandekar, 34.

25. Kohli-Khandekar, 34.

26. Kohli-Khandekar, 34.

27. Kohli-Khandekar, 34.

28. Arvind Rajagopal, "Introduction," in *The Indian Public Sphere: Readings in Media History*, ed. Arvind Rajagopal (New Delhi: Oxford University Press, 2009), 1–30.

29. Rajagopal, 4. See also Shanti Kumar, *Gandhi Meets Primetime: Globalization and Nationalism in Indian Television* (Urbana: University of Illinois Press, 2006) for a detailed discussion on the changes in the television industry or "electronic capitalism."

30. From a personal interview with Shankar Raghuraman, head of the Times Insight Group, Delhi, 2009.

31. Sagarika Ghose, "2 ½ Years, 8 Per Cent of What?" Bloody Mary, *Hindustan Times*, November 24, 2006.

32. Ghose.

33. See Kennith Rosario, "Parmanu Review: Billowing Plume of Jingoistic Smoke," *Hindu*, May 25, 2018, https://www.thehindu.com/entertainment/movies/parmanu-review-billowing-plume-of-jingoistic-smoke/article23992975.ece.

34. I have translated the Urdu verse penned and recited by Gulzar into English.

35. Sucheta Dalal, "Great Rip-off in the Name of Development," Cheques and Balances, *Indian Express*, April 10, 2006.

36. Laksmisree Banerjee, "Merit will craft the future," *Hindustan Times*, July 13, 2007.

37. Pradipta Chaudhury, "Don't Put in a Caste," *Times of India*, June 26, 2007.

38. Editorial, "Beyond Quotas," *Times of India*, October 24, 2007.

39. Kirit Parekh, "A Fair System," *Times of India*, February 10, 2007. Emphasis mine.

40. Barkha Dutt, "An Inconvenient Truth," *Hindustan Times*, March 3, 2007.

41. John Gledhill, "Neoliberalism," in *A Companion to the Anthropology of Politics*, ed. David Nugent and Joan Vincent (Malden, MA: Blackwell Publishing 2004), 340.

42. I would suggest here that in the Indian case, neoliberal audit culture draws from and is legitimated by the Indian state's modernization drive in the first couple of decades after independence, which stressed the importance of a "scientific temper" and instituted engineering as the most significant profession for social mobility.

43. Wendy Brown, *In the Ruins of Neoliberalism: The Rise of Antidemocratic Politics in the West* (New York: Columbia University Press, 2019), 42.

44. Arjun Appadurai has argued that the uncertainty about the "Other," including the characteristics of the Other and the incompleteness of the homogenous pure national community are perceived as even greater threats to the nation in the time of globalization. In Appadurai's argument, violence becomes the pursuit of certainty and completeness. I am using the conception of uncertainty and certainty differently here but am also noting that certitude—irrefutability—is necessary for both neoliberalism and authoritative nationalism in India. See Arjun Appadurai, *Fear of Small Numbers: An Essay on the Geography of Anger* (Durham, NC: Duke University Press, 2006).

45. See Madhavi Murty, "Representing Hindutva: Nation, Religion, and Masculinity in Indian Popular Cinema from 1990s to the Present," *Popular Communication* 7, no. 4 (Fall 2009) for a discussion of the constitution of a hegemonic masculinity that valorizes the Hindu male over the Muslim male in the time of Hindu nationalism.

46. See Leela Fernandes, *India's New Middle Class: Democratic Politics in an Era of Economic Reform* (Minneapolis: University of Minnesota Press, 2006).

47. Nandini Chandra, "Young Protest: The Idea of Merit in Commercial Hindi Cinema," *Comparative Studies of South Asia, Africa and the Middle East* 30, no. 1 (2010), 119–132 (122). Chandra, 121.

48. Partha Chatterjee has, influentially, drawn a distinction between civil and political society, arguing that whereas civil society "will appear as the closed association of modern elite groups, sequestered from the wider popular life of the communities, walled up within enclaves of civic freedom and rational law," political society is the realm of the subaltern classes. This political society is seen as a set of mediating institutions and practices between the state and subaltern groups; such a society is composed of "population groups" rather than "citizens." See Partha Chatterjee, *Politics of the Governed: Reflections on Popular Politics in Most of the World* (New York: Columbia University Press, 2004), 4.

49. Thomas Blom Hansen notes in his book *The Saffron Wave* that with the decline of the Indian National Congress in the 1970s, smaller regional political parties began to gain clout. The 1980s saw a further decline of the Indian National Congress—the dominant political party until this time—and concomitant strengthening of regional parties. Hansen states that the Indian middle classes felt increasingly threatened by what they saw as the rise of unworthy, plebian political leaders and began to grow skeptical about the viability of democracy and were inclined towards more authoritative forms of governance. He states that the growth and political success of Hindu nationalism must be understood in the context of the "larger disjuncture between democratic mobilization and democratic governance." See Thomas Blom Hansen, *The Saffron Wave: Democracy and Hindu Nationalism in Modern India* (New Delhi: Oxford University Press, 1999), 17.

50. See Sara Spary, "Bill and Melinda Gates Foundation Under Fire Over Award to Indian PM Modi," CNN, https://www.cnn.com/2019/09/12/asia/bill-melinda-gates-modi-intl-scli/index.html.

51. Rebecca Klenck, "Difficult Work: Becoming Developed," in *Regional Modernities: The Cultural Politics of Development in India*, ed. K. Sivaramakrishnan and Arun Agarwal (Stanford, CA: Stanford University Press, 2003), 102.

52. Nandan Nilekani, *Imagining India: Ideas for the New Century* (New York: Penguin Press, 2008), 169.

53. Nilekani, 169. Emphasis mine.

54. Nilekani, 165.

55. Nilekani, 165.

56. "Modi Wins as Gujarat Gets Tata's Nano Plant," *Business Week*, October 8, 2008, http://www.businessweek.com/globalbiz/content/oct2008/gb2008108_390634.htm.

57. Ratan Tata interview on the TV news channel *Times Now*, October 2008, accessed February 21, 2011, http://www.youtube.com/watch?v=oKjkDynHNps&feature=related.

58. "Narendra Modi Becomes India Inc. Poster Boy," *Economic Times*, January 15, 2009, http://economictimes.indiatimes.com/articleshow/3983994.cms.

59. Harit Mehta, "Moditva to Modi-nomics," *Times of India*, January 23, 2009.

60. This interview is part of a ten-page spread that the magazine devoted to Gujarat, which it described as being "in a state of success," and reads very much like a press release. *Business India*, January 25, 2009, 68–84.

61. "The Entire Gujarat is a Golden Corridor," interview with Narendra Modi by Daksesh Parikh and Nachiketa Desai, *Business India*, January 25, 2009.

62. "The Entire Gujarat." Emphasis mine.

63. Praful Bidwai, "The Road to Gujarat," *Frontline*, November 7, 2008, 110–112.

64. Bidwai.

65. Nandini Oza, "In Full Steam: Modi Rocks With His Development Drive," *The Week*, January 11, 2009, 20–22.

66. Oza.

67. Rajdeep Sardesai, "The New Advani?" Beyond the Byte, *Hindustan Times*, December 26, 2007.

68. Sardesai.

69. Ashis Nandy, "Power Defangs [Politics has blunted the edge of his ideology, making him less dangerous]," *Outlook*, December 24, 2007, 50–52.

70. Ronojoy Sen, "From Chaiwala to Chowkidar: Modi's Election Campaigns Online and Offline," *Economic and Political Weekly* 54, no. 51 (December 28, 2019), https://www.epw.in/node/155797/pdf.

71. World Bank, "An Overview," *Equity and Development: World Development Report 2006* (Washington, DC: World Bank), 1.

72. World Bank.

73. Emma Mawdsley and Jonathan Rigg, "A Survey of the World Development Reports 1: Discursive Strategies," *Progress in Development Studies* 2, no. 2 (2002), 93–111.

74. Mawdsley and Rigg.

75. World Bank, "An Overview," 1.

76. World Bank, "An Overview," 2. Emphasis mine.

77. Panagariya teaches at Columbia University where he is the Jagdish Bhagwati Professor of Indian Political Economy, International and Public Affairs and Economics and is the author of *India: The Emerging Giant*, a book much like Nilekani's *Reimagining India*, that discusses economic reforms, poverty, and government. Panagariya writes a monthly column for the *Economic Times*.

78. Arvind Panagariya, "World Bank's Discovery of Equity," *Economic Times*, October 19, 2005.

79. Panagariya.

80. Francisco Ferreira and Michael Walton, "Why Growth Requires Greater Equity" in *Economic Times*, December 23, 2005.

81. Ferreira and Walton. Emphasis mine.

82. Ferreira and Walton.

2. ICONICITY

1. W. J. T. Mitchell, *Iconology: Image, Text, Ideology* (Chicago: University of Chicago Press, 1986), 9.

2. See Christopher Pinney, *Photos of the Gods: The Printed Image and Political Struggle in India* (Chicago: University of Chicago Press, 2004).

3. See Pinney in particular, but also Sumati Ramaswamy, *The Goddess and the Nation: Mapping Mother India* (Durham, NC: Duke University Press, 2010); Kajri Jain, *The Gods in the Bazaar: Economies of Indian Calendar Art* (Durham, NC: Duke University Press, 2007); and Diane Eck, *Darsan: Seeing the Divine Image in India* (New York: Columbia University Press, 1998).

4. Eck, *Darsan*, 3.

5. This argument for distinction is made even when canonical Western philosophy is used within these texts to explicate such practices as darsan, as is the case of Christopher Pinney's use of Merleu-Ponty's conception of "double sensation" (touch and being touched) to draw the meaning of darsan and corpothetics.

6. Pinney, *Photos of the Gods*, 193.

7. Ramaswamy, *The Goddess and the Nation*, 35.

8. Bishnupriya Ghosh, *Global Icons: Apertures to the Popular* (Durham, NC: Duke University Press, 2011), 5.

9. Ghosh, 6.

10. Michael Warner argues that the bourgeois public sphere requires a "self-abstraction." It necessitates that you participate not as a particular body, but as the abstract, universal anybody; this is both the radically utopic potential of the bourgeois public sphere and its profound impossibility (for, as we know, the universal anybody in liberal, bourgeois Europe and North America was always the very particular body of the white male with property). In Warner's argument, the iconic public figure is a response to this "immanent contradiction in the bourgeois public sphere." The public figure as icon satisfies the desire of the citizen and thus maintains the equilibrium of the conjuncture and simultaneously gives form to that indeterminate but invariably and inevitably called-upon category, the people. See Michael Warner, *Publics and Counterpublics* (New York: Zone Books, 2002).

11. One could argue also, following W. J. T. Mitchell's rigorous analysis of the "rhetoric of the image," that idolatory and the reverence accorded to the icon as a magical technology was and is as central to Western modes of apprehending the visual as it has been for the colonial Other. As Mitchell shows us, the emphasis for continental philosophy's musings about the image and the icon has been an iconoclastic claim for a more scientific (and therefore less magical) eye and modes of representation in conjunction with the reification of text over image. See W. J. T. Mitchell, *Iconology: Image, Text, Ideology* (Chicago: University of Chiacgo Press, 1986).

12. Here I am specifically thinking of the films featuring the superstar of Hindi language cinema Amitabh Bachchan, who as we shall read in some detail in this chapter became iconic as the "angry young man." The angry young man was both a commoner but also larger-than-life or mythic.

13. Tejaswini Ganti, writing in the context of Hindi cinema, has termed this move a process of gentrification. See Tejaswini Ganti, *Producing Bollywood: Inside the Contemporary Hindi Film Industry* (Durham, NC: Duke University Press, 2012).

14. Arvind Rajagopal, *Politics After Television: Hindu Nationalism and the Reshaping of the Public in India* (Cambridge: Cambridge University Press, 2001).

15. Satish Poduval, "The Affable Young Man: Civility, Desire and the Making of a Middle-class Cinema in the 1970s," in *The 1970s and its Legacies in India's Cinemas*, ed. Priya Joshi and Rajinder Dudrah (New York: Routledge, 2014). Poduval describes the "affable young man" as the counterpoint to the "angry young man." While the affable young man was a product of middle-class cinema and helped center it as such, the angry young man belonged to the world of the masala social. Poduval states that "middle-class cinema sought to promote the self-identification between its characters and audiences, installing a verisimilitude based on individuated desire and action, and avoiding what it regarded as the un-real phantasms that burdened the masala social. These films and the affable young man suggested that the 'key site of power and economic mobility is located not in organized political action or social mobilization but in the bourgeoisie's discreet charm—that is, in its civility'" (44).

16. The blockbuster films of filmmaker Rohit Shetty would be an example here. While speaking about the success of his 2013 *Chennai Express*, Shetty stated in a press interview, "The so-called intellectuals don't like my films. They are a minority but I am happy about the way aam junta [ordinary people/the masses] has reacted to my film." See Fahim Ruhani, "I have proved it seven times, the reviews of my films don't matter: Rohit Shetty," *India Today*, September 3, 2013, http:// indiatoday.intoday.in/story/rohit-shetty-interview-chennai-express/1/305322.html.

17. In an interview with media and film studies scholar Tejaswini Ganti, filmmaker Aditya Chopra notes that, "Here, the common man—his ultimate dream is an escapism, is to watch films. He goes for three hours; he sees a world which he probably will never get, or he'll see

women whom he'll never meet, or he'll see stuff where he's never going to go to, and for him that's it. That's his ultimate, because you're dealing with a country of have-nots." Tejaswini Ganti, *Producing Bollywood: Inside the Contemporary Hindi Film Industry* (Durham, NC: Duke University Press, 2012), 296.

18. The critically acclaimed films of filmmaker Anurag Kashyap would be an example here.

19. This representation finds resonance in other mass-media texts as well—Gurcharan Das's discussion of subaltern entrepreneurs, for instance.

20. Gurcharan Das, *India Unbound: The Social and Economic Revolution from Independence to the Global Information Age* (New York: Anchor Books, 2000, 2002), 346.

21. Das, 346.

22. Formerly known as "untouchables." The term *dalit* quite literally means "broken down" and has been adopted as a name by dalit groups to reference their historic oppression.

23. Das, 347.

24. Das, 347.

25. See a summary and timeline for Infosys's troubles: https://economictimes.indiatimes .com/magazines/panache/employee-morale-hurt-reputation-at-stake-timeline-of-how-infosys -handled-whistleblower-complaints/articleshow/71749785.cms. See a summary of Ranbaxy's troubles here: https://economictimes.indiatimes.com/industry/healthcare/biotech/pharma ceuticals/ranbaxy-to-ruins-how-the-singh-brothers-turned-from-business-whizkids-to-fraud -accused/articleshow/67176061.cms.

26. "Big B Prepares to Unveil TOI's India Poised Campaign," *Times of India*, January 1, 2007.

27. Rachel Dwyer, *Yash Chopra* (London: British Film Institute, 2002), 72.

28. See Dwyer, 73.

29. Dwyer, *Yash Chopra*, 74.

30. Priya Joshi and Rajinder Dudrah, "Introduction," in *The 1970s and its Legacies in India's Cinemas* (London: Routledge, 2014), 1, 2.

31. Joshi and Dudrah, 74–75.

32. Joshi and Dudrah, 75.

33. Priya Joshi, "Cinema as Family Romance," in *The 1970s and its Legacies in India's Cinemas*, ed. Priya Joshi and Rajinder Dudrah (London: Routledge, 2014), 8–22.

34. Vinay Lal, *Deewar: The Footpath, the City and the Angry Young Man* (New Delhi: Harper-Collins, 2012), 63.

35. See http://www.businesstoday.in/magazine/cover-story/goodbye-abcl,-hello-ab-corp /story/5201.html.

36. See http://www.rediff.com/news/1996/2011vir2.htm.

37. Inderpal Grewal, *Transnational America: Feminisms, Diasporas, Neoliberalisms* (Durham, NC: Duke University Press, 2005), 87.

38. http://indiatoday.intoday.in/story/after-dream-venture-abcl-go-bankrupt-amitabh -bachchan-faces-legal-battle-with-creditors/1/253830.html.

39. http://www.realbollywood.com/news/2006/10/bachchan-is-the-king-of-endorsements .html.

40. Jaideep Bose, "A Passage from India" *Times of India*, January 1, 2007.

41. Bose.

42. "Big B Gives Baritone to Big Idea," *Times of India*, January 2007.

43. "Big B Gives Baritone to Big Idea."

44. See Asghar Ali Engineer, "Communal Riots in 2002: A Survey," in *Economic and Political Weekly* 38, no. 4, (January 2003): 280–282, for a brief summary and analysis of the violence.

45. In an election campaign speech several months after the Gujarat pogrom, Modi referenced reports about Hindu terror and addressed Pervez Musharraf, then president of Pakistan, as a stand-in for the Muslim Other, saying that Hindus could never be terrorists, but if the "miyah's"

actions lead the Hindu on that path, then Musharraf should "open his ears" and listen, for if Hindu terror were to be born then Pakistan would be wiped off the world map. Modi's turn of phrase that captures the open and aggressive threat would have been all too familiar for audiences of Hindi cinema.

46. See https://time.com/collection-post/3823155/narendra-modi-2015-time-100/.

47. Yogendra Yadav, "The Patterns and Lessons," *Frontline*, January 3, 2003.

48. Editorial, *Frontline*, January 3, 2003.

49. Mushirul Hassan, "Engulfed by the Tidal Wave," *Indian Express*, December 25, 2002.

50. Editorial, *Frontline*, January 3, 2003.

51. Harsh V. Pant, "Lethal Weapon: Gujarati *gaurav*, Parivar prejudice," *Indian Express*, December 27, 2002.

52. Darshan Desai, "Slog-over Batsman," *Outlook*, December 23, 2002.

53. Referring to the then president of Pakistan, Pervez Musharraf, as "miyah Musharraf" was deliberate. It reduced the head of the state of Pakistan to his religious identity—a Muslim, a "miyah"—and as such categorized all Muslims through their religious identification.

54. Sujan Dutta, "Media and the Message," *Telegraph*, December 22, 2002.

55. Dutta, "Media and the Message."

56. The normative citizen within this discourse is specifically gendered male.

57. V. D. Savarkar, "Presidential Address at the 19th Session of the Akhil Bharatiya Hindu Mahasabha," in *Hindu Rashtra Darshan* (A Collection of the Presidential Speeches delivered from the Hindu Mahasabha Platform) (Bombay: V. V. Bambardekar, India Printing Works, 1949), 27, 28.

58. Parul Dave Mukherji, "Popular Festivals, Populist Visual Culture and Modi Masks," in *Democratic Culture: Historical and Philosophical Essays*, ed. Akeel Bilgrami (London: Routledge, 2011), 205, 206.

59. Prahlad Kakkar narrated the history of the campaign to me during an interview in August 2015.

60. "Narendra Modi Becomes India Inc. Poster Boy," *Economic Times*, January 15, 2009, http://economictimes.indiatimes.com/articleshow/3983994.cms.

61. Rajdeep Sardesai, *2014: The Election that Changed India* (New Delhi: Penguin Books, India, 2015), xvii.

62. Benedict Anderson, *Imagined Communities* (London: Verso, 2006 edition), 54.

63. In a set of speeches given in April 1965, ideologue and leader of the RSS (and later the Jana Sangh) Deendayal Upadhyay argued for the supremacy of a national culture ("*Bhartiyata*," sometimes referred to in this argument as *chiti* or the soul of an individual and the nation), which is articulated with *Dharma* or the "laws of life" in all matters of governance, including economic policy.

64. See http://www.dicci.org/about.php.

65. V. D. Savarkar, *Six Glorious Epochs of Indian History* (Mumbai: Savarkar Sadan, 1971), 156.

66. Savarkar, 158.

67. Savarkar, 158.

68. Venkitesh Ramakrishnan, "Dalit Power," *Frontline*, June 1, 2007.

69. Gurcharan Das, "A Sobering Lesson," *Times of India*, June 3, 2007. https://timesofindia.indiatimes.com/gurcharan-das/men-ideas/a-sobering-lesson/articleshow/2094804.cms.

70. Within mainstream press coverage this alliance was seen as an opposition to the OBC (Other Backward Castes, or the middle castes) bloc that is consistently marked as powerful within such stories.

71. Barkha Dutt, "Art of reinvention," Third Eye, *Hindustan Times*, May 12, 2007.

72. Dutt, "Art of Reinvention."

73. Rajdeep Sardesai, "Lady in Waiting," Beyond the Byte, *Hindustan Times*, April 27, 2007.

74. Sardesai, "Lady in Waiting." Emphasis mine.

75. Badri Narayan, *Women Heroes and Dalit Assertion in North India: Culture, Identity and Politics* (New Delhi: Sage Publications, 2006), 31.

76. Sardesai, "Lady in Waiting."

77. Sagarika Ghose, "Look Back in Hatred," Bloody Mary, *Hindustan Times*, April 8, 2008.

78. Ghose, "Look Back in Hatred." Emphasis mine.

79. Subhash Mishra, "Dalit Icons, Indian Idols," *India Today*, October 22, 2007.

80. Mishra, "Dalit Icons, Indian Idols."

81. Mishra, "Dalit Icons, Indian Idols."

82. Mishra, "Dalit Icons, Indian Idols."

83. Subhash Mishra, "Poor Little Rich Girl," *India Today*, July 9, 2007.

84. Sardesai, "Lady in Waiting."

85. Sagarika Ghose, "Uttar Pradesh Pvt Ltd," Bloody Mary, *Hindustan Times*, May 11, 2007.

86. Sardesai, "Lady in Waiting."

87. See Gayatri Spivak, *Critique of Postcolonial Reason: Toward a History of the Vanishing Present* (Cambridge, MA: Harvard University Press, 1999) for a rumination on the (im)possibility of the native informant.

88. Michael Warner, "The Mass Public and the Mass Subject," in *Habermas and the Public Sphere*, ed. Craig Calhoun (Cambridge, MA: MIT Press, 1992), 395.

89. Warner, 384.

90. Michael Warner, *Publics and Counterpublics* (New York: Zone Books, 2002).

91. Scholars and critics have discussed dalit writing—in the form of fiction, poetry, social and political commentary, or autobiography—as collectively constituting a public that eschews the narrative that caste belongs to a dead past and that works out an analysis of the ways in which caste functions in and structures the everyday. See Sarah Beth, "Hindi Dalit Autobiography: An Exploration of Identity," *Modern Asian Studies* 41, no. 3 (May 2007): 545–574; and K. Satyanarayana and Susie Tharu, eds., *The Exercise of Freedom: An Introduction to Dalit Writing* (New Delhi: Navayana, 2013). Mayawati's *Safarnama* is a part of this body of work in its critique of caste but also distinct from it in its narration of Mayawati as the descendent of those political activists who first constituted the dalit public.

92. This became particularly evident to me when I visited monuments and parks built in the Mughal era, such as the Humayun's Tomb in Delhi. Much like the Mughal monuments in Delhi and its surrounding areas, the *Prerana Sthal* commands a respectful gaze, in part through its sheer size.

93. Kajri Jain has discussed the "big statue genre" as an assemblage that "brings together a postcolonial socioeconomic formation, a type of object/body/image; a political system; a dominant political ideology; a building material; relations to land; and a mode of transport tied to systems of manufacturing and infrastructure and, at another scale, to natural resources and geopolitics" (12). She discusses big statues as indexing emergence, "which refers both to the (re) appearance of the monumental statue form in time and to the literal coming out of religious icons from temples into public space" (5). See Kajri Jain, *Gods in the Time of Democracy* (Durham, NC: Duke University Press, 2021). My argument is that the BSP's statues are distinct from statues constructed by Hindutva neoliberalism because they are an investment in constructing a genealogy for the Bahujan samaj in public in ways that retool the narrative form of spectacular realism.

94. See, for instance, Saidiya Hartman, *Lose Your Mother: A Journey Along the Atlantic Slave Route* (New York: Farrar, Straus and Giroux, 2007).

95. See Badri Narayan, *Women Heroes and Dalit Assertion in North India: Culture, Identity and Politics* (New Delhi: Sage Publications, 2006) for an elaboration of this argument.

96. See https://www.bbc.com/news/world-asia-india-48389130.

97. See https://economictimes.indiatimes.com/news/elections/lok-sabha/india/stable-govern ment-to-boost-economic-growth-foreign-fund-flow-india-inc/articleshow/69459604.cms.

98. https://economictimes.indiatimes.com/news/elections/lok-sabha/india/stable-govern ment-to-boost-economic-growth-foreign-fund-flow-india-inc/articleshow/69459604.cms.

3. THE ENTREPRENEUR

Nandan Nilekani, *Imagining India: Ideas for a New Century* (New Delhi: Penguin Books, 2008), 61–62.

1. The entrepreneur, as we shall see, is gendered male within these narratives. Masculinity— freed and unshackled—is at the core of the identity category, even when the female and femi- ninity is sometimes appropriated to signify renewal.

2. Manmohan Singh, Address at the Indira Gandhi Conference—"India: The Next Decade," New Delhi, November 19, 2004, *Prime Minister Manmohan Singh: Selected Speeches*, Volume I: May 2004 to May 2005 (Publications Division: Ministry of Information and Broadcasting, Government of India).

3. See Manmohan Singh's extensive interview to PBS a decade after the institution of eco- nomic reforms in India in 2001: http://www.pbs.org/wgbh/commandingheights/shared/mini textlo/int_manmohansingh.html.

4. See Lydia Polgreen, "Scaling Caste Walls With Capitalism's Ladder in India," *New York Times*, December 21, 2011, http://www.nytimes.com/2011/12/22/world/asia/indias-boom-creates -openings-for-untouchables.html?pagewanted=all.

5. See the introduction in Nandini Gooptu, *Enterprise Culture in Neoliberal India: Studies in Youth, Class, Work and Media* (New York: Routledge, 2013).

6. See the special report on the "entrepreneurial society" in *Economist*, 2009, accessed March 21, 2012, http://www.economist.com/node/13216087.

7. William Deresiewicz, "Generation Sell," *New York Times*, November 12, 2011, https://www .nytimes.com/2011/11/13/opinion/sunday/the-entrepreneurial-generation.html.

8. Deresiewicz, "Generation Sell."

9. Wendy Brown, *In the Ruins of Neoliberalism: The Rise of Antidemocratic Politics in the West* (New York: Columbia University Press, 2019), 38–39.

10. Brown, 37.

11. Political theorists and theorists of neoliberalism, for instance, will suggest that the late twentieth century is significant to the rise of the entrepreneur.

12. C. B. Macpherson, *The Political Theory of Possessive Individualism, Hobbes to Locke* (New York: Oxford University Press, 1962), 3.

13. Macpherson, 3.

14. Macpherson, 263, 264.

15. Harish Damodaran, *India's New Capitalists: Caste, Business and Industry in a Modern Nation* (New York: Palgrave Macmillan, 2008), 2.

16. Damodaran, 2.

17. Damodaran, 2.

18. Pankaj Mishra, "Donald Trump is Going to India to Find Himself," *New York Times*, Febru- ary 21, 2020, https://www.nytimes.com/2020/02/21/opinion/trump-india.html.

19. Nilekani, *Imagining India*, 63.

20. "What Makes Shyam Special . . . ," *The Hindu*, January 17, 2003, https://www.thehindu.com /todays-paper/tp-features/tp-fridayreview/what-makes-shyam-special/article28572365.ece.

21. Madhavi Murty, "Representing Hindutva: Nation, Religion, and Masculinity in Indian Popular Cinema from 1990s to the Present," *Popular Communication* 7, no. 4 (Fall 2009).

22. Nandan Nilekani, foreword to *India's New Capitalists: Caste, Business, and Industry in a Modern Nation,* by Harish Damodaran (New Delhi: Permanent Black, 2008), ix, x.

23. As discussed in the introductory chapter, historians of urban spaces, labor, and caste such as Juned Shaikh have made an argument about caste hiding in plain sight in the context of the built environment of the city as well as in language.

24. Pheng Cheah, *Inhuman Conditions: On Cosmopolitanism and Human Rights* (Cambridge, MA: Harvard University Press, 2006), 18. Cheah questions the prematurity of an argument that claims the demise of the nation in the emergent face of cosmopolitanism, and aims to show that despite the claims of "newness" of such arguments, that these accounts rely on rather old humanist notions of reason and imagination having the cognitive powers to overcome "contingent, finite limitations."

25. George Lipsitz, "The Possessive Investment in Whiteness: Racialized Social Democracy and the 'White' Problem in American Studies," *American Quarterly* 47, no. 3 (Sept. 1995): 369–387, 371.

26. Lipsitz, 370.

27. Nilekani, *Imagining India,* 61–62.

28. See a report on the Indian publishing industry in http://www.telegraphindia.com/1090726 /jsp/graphiti/story_11281512.jsp. As I observed during my fieldwork in India, pirated copies of *Imagining India,* priced at a few dollars apiece, were being sold at almost every traffic light and marketplace in the bustling cities of Mumbai, Pune, and Delhi; the unofficial sales figures of *Imagining India* will therefore be significantly higher than the official statistics.

29. Nilekani, *Imagining India,* 82.

30. Make in India official website, http://www.makeinindia.com/about.

31. Gurcharan Das, *India Unbound: The Social and Economic Revolution from Independence to the Global Information Age* (New York: Anchor Books, 2000, 2002).

32. Das, 245.

33. Das, 228.

34. See, for instance, Shilpa Phadke, Sameera Khan, and Shilpa Ranade, *Why Loiter? Women and Risk on Mumbai Streets* (Mumbai: Penguin India, 2011).

35. Phadke, Khan, and Ranade, 231.

36. Phadke, Khan, and Ranade, 235.

37. Nilekani, *Imagining India,* 78.

38. Nilekani, 82.

39. Nilekani, 78.

40. Achin Vanaik, "The Puzzle of India's Growth Rate," *Telegraph,* June 22, 2006.

41. Raja Sen, "Plain and Simple," review of *Rocket Singh: Salesman of the Year,* rediff.com, December 11, 2007, http://movies.rediff.com/report/2009/dec/11/review-rocket-singh-salesman-of-the -year.htm.

42. Rajeev Masand, "Masand's Verdict: Guru," review of *Guru,* CNN-IBN, April 18, 2011, http://ibnlive.in.com/news/masands-verdict-thumbs-up-for-guru/31056-8.html.

43. Madhavi Murty, "Representing Hindutva: Nation, Religion, and Masculinity in Indian Popular Cinema from 1990s to the Present," *Popular Communication* 7, no. 4 (Fall 2009).

44. See Rukmini S., "The BJP's Electoral Arithmetic" in *The BJP in Power: Indian Democracy and Religious Nationalism,* ed. Milan Vaishnav (Washington D.C.: Carnegie Endowment for International Peace, 2019), 37–50, https://carnegieendowment.org/files/BJP_In_Power_final.pdf.

45. Rukmini S., 39.

46. Varsha Bansal and Gireesh Chandra Prasad, "What New Guidelines Mean for the E-commerce Ecosystem," *livemint.com,* December 31, 2018, https://www.livemint.com/Companies/5to8JnDk EBZw9mXU1Pwd3I/What-new-FDI-guidelines-mean-for-the-ecommerce-ecosystem.html.

47. Asit Ranjan Mishra and Mihir Dalal, "Govt. defines e-commerce marketplace rules, allows 100% FDI," *livemint.com*, March 30, 2016, https://www.livemint.com/Politics/hglep85yZO QzChj6KRrrCK/Govt-allows-100-FDI-in-ecommerce-marketplace-model.html.

48. The speech is available on Narendra Modi's YouTube channel: https://www.youtube.com /watch?v=fWuVLkmRBJ8. Modi made the speech in Hindi, with a sprinkling of English. The speech uses the English word *entrepreneur*. The translation of the speech into English is mine. Narendra Modi's website includes a summary as well as a complete translation of the speech into English: https://www.narendramodi.in/we-are-a-youthful-nation-our-dreams-must-be-on-that -scale-we-must-fill-the-vacuum-that-exists-in-the-world-cm-at-young-entrepreneurs-meet-5026.

49. The English-language newspaper *Times of India* is linked to an English-speaking middle-class, upper-caste readership in India.

50. Bachchan had, in fact, contested an election in 1984 from the northern Indian city of Allahabad. He won with an overwhelming majority but resigned his seat three years later.

51. https://www.makeinindia.com/article/-/v/make-in-india-reason-vision-for-the-initiative.

52. https://www.makeinindia.com/article/-/v/make-in-india-reason-vision-for-the-initiative.

53. https://www.makeinindia.com/article/-/v/make-in-india-reason-vision-for-the-initiative.

54. See Srirupa Roy, *Beyond Belief: India and the Politics of Postcolonial Nationalism* (Durham, NC: Duke University Press, 2007).

55. One example here is the violence in Naroda Patiya. The Sessions Court found a number of the accused, some of them with known connections to the BJP, guilty of the violence. Some of these convictions were later overturned by the Gujarat High Court. The Sessions Court judgment can be read here: https://cjp.org.in/wp-content/uploads/2018/05/Naroda-Patiya-Trial -Court-Judgement.pdf. This *India Today* article reports on the acquittal by the Gujarat High Court of Maya Kodnani, a key accused in the Naroda Patiya case and the former Minister of State for Women and Child Development in the state government: https://www.indiatoday.in /india/story/naroda-patiya-massacre-how-maya-kodnani-s-fortune-changed-over-2-verdicts -in-16-years-1216416-2018-04-20.

56. Stuart Hall has argued that "an effective suturing of the subject to a subject-position requires, not only that the subject is 'hailed', but that the subject invests in the position"; in other words, he theorizes identities/subjectivities as "sutures" and "suturing" as an articulation. See Stuart Hall, "Introduction: Who Needs 'Identity'?" in *Questions of Cultural Identity*, ed. Stuart Hall and Paul Du Gay (London: Sage Publications: 1996), 6.

57. Uday Mahurkar with Sumit Mitra, "I Wanted Justice," *India Today*, July 21, 2003, 27–36.

58. Aravind Adiga, *The White Tiger* (New York: Free Press, 2008), 276.

59. Ananya Roy, "Afterword: Entrepreneurs of Millennial Capitalism," in the Book Review Symposium section for *Poverty Capital: Microfinance and the Making of Development* (London: Routledge, 2010), *Antipode: A Radical Journal of Geography* 44, no. 2 (March 2012): 545–553.

60. A. Roy, 545–553.

61. Aravind Adiga, *The White Tiger* (New York: Free Press, 2008), 26.

62. Stuart Jeffries, "Roars of Anger," *The Guardian*, October 15, 2008, https://www.theguardian .com/books/2008/oct/16/booker-prize.

63. Adiga, 28.

64. A. Roy, 547.

65. See Stephen Young, Satendra Kumar, and Craig Jeffrey, "Beyond Improvisation? The Rise and Rise of Youth Entrepreneurs in India," *Transactions of the Institute of British Geographers* 42, no. 1 (March 2017): 98–109, for one elaboration of *jugaad* and improvisation in the context of entrepreneurship.

66. Editorial, "Trust on Trial: Try Zahira Shaikh for Perjury," *Times of India*, November 5, 2004, http://articles.timesofindia.indiatimes.com/2004-11-05/edit-page/27145399_1_zahira-sheikh -retrial-apex-court. Accessed March 22, 2011.

67. Ashish Khetan, "The Buying of Zaheera Shaikh," *Tehelka*, accessed March 21, 2011, http://www.tehelka.com/story_main10.asp?filename=ts010105The_Buying.asp.
68. Khetan. Emphasis mine.
69. Editorial, "A Torturous Quest for Justice," *Hindu*, February 27, 2006, http://hindu.com/2006/02/27/stories/2006022701841000.htm.

4. LOVE IN NEW TIMES

Sara Ahmed, *The Cultural Politics of Emotion* (New York: Routledge, 2004), 141.

1. A number of prominent filmmakers and film commentators have recently argued that the classic Indian film love story, which featured a heteronormative couple and a central conflict around socioeconomic class, caste, and/or religion against which love triumphed or was violently extinguished, had been deemed irrelevant or had undergone a transformation in new times. Anthropologist and film scholar Tejaswini Ganti, for instance, notes that new love stories feature protagonists from the same socioeconomic class—the wealthy, global elite—and the "source of dramatic tension and narrative conflict is internalized and centers on the conflict between individual desire and duty to one's family." New love stories, particularly those made in the new millennium, this argument continues, are entirely and deliberately focused on the individual, unmoored from family, community, and even nation. See Tejaswini Ganti, *Bollywood: A Guide Book to Popular Hindi Cinema* (New York: Routledge, 2004), 40.
2. Sangita Gopal, *Conjugations: Marriage and Form in New Bollywood Cinema* (Chicago: University of Chicago Press, 2011), 17.
3. Gopal, 17.
4. Gopal, 17.
5. For a detailed reading of these repertoires, see Francesca Orsini, ed., *Love in South Asia* (Cambridge: Cambridge University Press, 2006).
6. Orsini, 22.
7. See Ajoy Ashirwad Mahaprashasta, "Sensational Grist," *Frontline*, November 29, 2013, http://www.frontline.in/cover-story/sensational-grist/article5338432.ece#test.
8. See Lalmani Verma and Johnson T. A., "Who Loves Love Jihad," *Indian Express*, September 7, 2014, http://indianexpress.com/article/india/india-others/who-loves-love-jihad/.
9. Charu Gupta, "Hindu Women, Muslim Men: Love Jihad and Conversions," *Economic and Political Weekly* 44, no. 51 (December 19, 2009): 13–15.
10. Gupta, "Hindu Women, Muslim Men."
11. The chronology of events includes the rapid transmission of a story of abduction, marriage, and conversion of a Hindu woman by a Muslim male, followed by targeted violence against Muslims in the community and the filing of a police complaint against the Muslim male and his family, often leading to the forcible removal of the woman from her marital home and "return" to her natal home. This was true in the 1920s as well as in the new millennium.
12. Elizabeth Povinelli, *An Empire of Love: Toward a Theory of Intimacy, Genealogy, and Carnality* (Durham, NC: Duke University Press, 2006), 4.
13. Povinelli, 17.
14. Povinelli, 17.
15. Povinelli, 9.
16. Alain Badiou, *In Praise of Love* (Paris: Flammarion SA, 2009), 28.
17. Badiou, 29.
18. Badiou, 30.
19. Badiou, 33.

20. Discussing the "gender of modernity," Rita Felski says that even as our sense of the past is shaped by the "explanatory logic of the narrative," the stories that we create "reveal the inescapable power of gender symbolism," and that nowhere is this "saturation of cultural texts with metaphors of masculinity and femininity more obvious than in the case of the modern." Rita Felski, *The Gender of Modernity* (Boston: Harvard University Press, 1995), 1. Also see Arif Dirlik, *Global Modernity: Modernity in the Age of Global Capitalism* (Boulder, CO, and London: Paradigm, 2007) for an argument about the proliferation of modernities in the time of globalization. This last argument is at a variance from our discussion here.

21. As Orsini and others show, the colonial bureaucracy sent young, educated men to live apart from the extended family with or without their wives.

22. Orsini, *Love in South Asia*, 31.

23. Madhavi Murty, "Representing Hindutva: Nation, Religion and Masculinity in Indian Popular Cinema, 1990 to 2003," *Popular Communication* 7 (2009): 267–281.

24. See Caroline Osella, Fillipo Osella, and Radhika Chopra, "Introduction: Towards a more nuanced approach to masculinity, towards a richer understanding of South Asian men," in *South Asian Masculinities*, ed. Radhika Chopra, Caroline Osella, and Fillipo Osella (New Delhi: Kali for Women, 2004), 1–25.

25. Murty, "Representing Hindutva."

26. These young men chop a lot of wood but it is unclear whether they work for a timber mill, a factory, a trucking business, or something else.

27. Francesca Orsini, "Introduction," in *Love in South Asia*, ed. Francesca Orsini (Cambridge: Cambridge University Press, 2006), 18.

28. Orsini, "Introduction," 20.

29. Orsini, 20.

30. Orsini, 21, 22.

31. From Kavita Krishnan's commentary on thewire.in: https://thewire.in/169356/love-jihad-nia-probe-kerala-court/.

32. Song lyrics in Urdu-Hindi by Irshad Kamil, translated into English by the author.

33. Ajay Gehlawat, "The Construction of 1970s Femininity, or Why Zeenat Aman Sings the Same Song Twice," in *The 1970s and its Legacies in India's Cinemas*, ed. Priya Joshi and Rajinder Dudrah (London: Routledge, 2014), 50.

34. Ranjani Mazumdar, *Bombay Cinema: An Archive of the City* (Minneapolis: University of Minnesota Press, 2007), 108.

35. Indeed, the figure of the "new woman" of the nineteenth century negotiating nationalist imperatives around tradition as well as modernity is an even older iteration. See Partha Chatterjee, *Nation and Its Fragments: Colonial and Postcolonial Histories* (Princeton, NJ: Princeton University Press, 1993).

36. Alys Weinbaum, Lynn Thomas, Priti Ramamurthy, Uta Poiger, Madeleine Yue Dong, and Tani Barlow, eds., *The Modern Girl Around the World: Consumption, Modernity, and Globalization* (Durham, NC: Duke University Press, 2008), 16.

37. Priti Ramamurthy, "All-Consuming Nationalism: The Indian Modern Girl in the 1920s and 1930s," in *The Modern Girl Around the World: Consumption, Modernity, and Globalization*, ed. Alys Weinbaum, Lynn Thomas, Priti Ramamurthy, Uta Poiger, Madeleine Yue Dong, and Tani Barlow (Durham, NC: Duke University Press, 2008), 153.

38. Ramamurthy, "All-Consuming Nationalism," 157, 158. Emphasis mine.

39. Ramamurthy, 151.

40. Rupal Oza, *The Making of Neoliberal India: Nationalism, Gender, and the Paradoxes of Globalization* (New York: Routledge, 2006), 23.

41. Sanjay Leela Bhansali's *Hum Dil De Chuke Sanam* is an example here.

42. Here, I am especially thinking of two films made by Mani Ratnam in the 1990s that received critical and popular acclaim: *Roja* (1992) and *Bombay* (1995). In *Roja*, it is the Kashmiri militant, Liaqat's sister, who has a silent but significant presence in the film. Even as the protagonist Rishi sings of yearning and his lost love (his wife, Roja), the brief encounters he has with Liaqat's sister sans dialogue/conversation or any physical contact are nevertheless intense and charged with sexual tension. In these encounters, Liaqat's sister embodies an "otherness" that is exotic, desirable, and, as a consequence of her mute intensity, completely consumable. In *Bombay*, the female protagonist, the woman-in-love Shaila Bano, exudes a silent intensity throughout the film. The man-in-love, Shekhar, deliberately and vocally battles his father's prejudiced conservatism, and as a journalist he questions the rhetoric of politicians raising tensions and the inactivity of the police. In the final scenes of the film, as a parent, he makes an impassioned plea for peace and the end of violence. Shaila, on the other hand, quietly emotes. The audience watches her toiling in her parents' home, dancing at a wedding, negotiating her father's anger with trepidation, secretly running away from her home and village, and then nervously managing her way through a new city and a new home. While not completely mute like Liaqat's sister in *Roja*, Shaila's character in *Bombay* is similarly not a threatening presence in the narrative and is the enabler of the Hindu male patriot who puts nation above all else. See also Tejaswini Niranjana, "Integrating Whose Nation? Tourists and Terrorists in 'Roja,'" *Economic and Political Weekly* 29, no. 3 (January 15, 1994): 79–82; and K. Chadda and A. P. Kavoori, "Exoticized, Marginalized, Demonized. The Muslim 'Other' in Indian Cinema," in *Global Bollywood*, ed. A. Punathambekar and A. P. Kavoori (New York: New York University Press, 2008). For the socioeconomic consequences of this form of minoritization for Indian Muslims, see Rajinder Sachar et al., "Social, Economic and Educational Status of the Muslim Community in India," report prepared by the Government of India (2006), 13, http://minorityaffairs.gov.in/reports/sachar-committee-report.

43. V. D. Savarkar, *Six Glorious Epochs of Indian History* (Bombay: Savarkar Sadan, 1971), 180.

44. Consider the line "Do pal ke jeevan se ek umar churani hai" (we [in love] have to steal a lifetime from a life that lasts a couple of moments) in the song "Ek Pyar Ka Naghma Hai" (A Song About Love) in the film *Shor* (Noise, Manoj Kumar, 1972).

45. Consider the line "pyaar ne jahan pe rakha hai choomke kadam ek baar, vahin se khoola hai koi rasta, vahin se giri hai dewaar" (where love has placed us with a kiss, there has a wall crumbled and a path opened up) in the song "Ae Mere Humsafar" (My Companion) in the film *Qayamat Se Qayamat Tak* (From Doom Until Doom, Mansoor Khan, 1988).

46. Consider the song "Tujhe dekha to . . ." (When I saw you . . .) from the film *Dilwale Dulhaniya Le Jayenge* (The Big-Hearted Will Take Away the Bride, Aditya Chopra, 1995).

47. Consider the line "Akela tha magar ban gayi voh humsafar, voh mere saath ho gayi" (I was alone, but she [a beautiful stranger] became my companion, she walked with me) from the song "Ek Ajnabee Haseena" (A Beautiful Stranger) from the film *Ajnabee* (Stranger, Shakti Samanta, 1974).

48. Consider the songs "Dekha Ek Khwab" (When I saw a dream) and "Ye Kahaan Aa Gaye Hum" (Where have we come) in the film *Silsila* (A Sequence of Events, Yash Chopra, 1981).

49. Here again, consider the song "Ae Mere Humsafar" (My Companion) in the film *Qayamat Se Qayamat Tak* (From Doom Until Doom, Mansoor Khan, 1988).

50. Here again, consider the song "Ye Kahaan Aa Gaye Hum" (Where have we come) in the film *Silsila* (A Sequence of Events, Yash Chopra, 1981).

51. Samhita Sunya, "Moving Toward *Prem Nagar*: An Intimate Genealogy of the 'City of Love' and the Lyrical Worlds of Hindustani Film Songs," *positions* 25 (2017): 1.

52. Sunya, 1.

53. Sunya, 1.

54. Vanita Kohli-Khandekar, *The Indian Media Business*, 3rd ed. (Thousand Oaks, CA: Sage Publications, 2010), 180.

55. Kohli-Khandekar, 180.

56. See Kohli-Khandekar for a fuller history and elaboration of these practices.

57. Lyrics by Naqsh Lyallpuri, music by Jaidev, performed by the popular singer Runa Laila.

58. Lyrics by Anand Bakshi, music by Jatin-Lalit.

59. See, for instance, Ranjani Mazumdar's work in *Bombay Cinema*.

60. Lyrics by Javed Akhtar, music by the renowned duo of classical musicians Shiv-Hari (Shiva Kumar Sharma and Hariprasad Chaurasia). The singers are Kishore Kumar and Lata Mangeshkar. The song features the actors Amitabh Bachchan and Rekha.

61. Translation from the original Urdu is mine.

62. See Ravi Vijaykar, "The Role of a Song in a Hindi Film," *The South Asianist* 2, no. 3: 48–73, http://www.southasianist.ed.ac.uk/article/view/167/992.

63. Anustup Basu, *Bollywood in the Age of New Media: The Geo-Televisual Aesthetic* (Edinburgh: Edinburgh University Press, 2010), 15.

64. Lyrics by Indeevar, music by Bappi Lahri, performed by Kishore Kumar and Lata Mangeshkar.

65. See Tejaswini Ganti, *Producing Bollywood: Inside the Contemporary Hindi Film Industry* (Durham, NC: Duke University Press, 2012).

66. Ganti, *Producing Bollywood*.

67. Lyrics by Irshad Kamil, music by A. R. Rahman, performed by Mohit Chauhan (male version).

68. Shilpa Jamkhandikar, "Q&A: 'Sairat' director Nagraj Manjule on the duplicity of Indians on love," Reuters, https://www.reuters.com/article/sairat-nagraj-manjule/qa-sairat-director -nagraj-manjule-on-the-duplicity-of-indians-on-love-idUSKBN1HX18U.

69. Various Indian news sites reported this story. The *Republic World* photographed and published long extracts of this booklet, which was subsequently withdrawn. See https://www .republicworld.com/india-news/city-news/kareena-kapoor-is-a-victim-of-love-jihad-says -fringe-groups-magazine.

70. Ahmed, *The Cultural Politics of Emotion*, 128.

71. Ahmed, 128. Emphasis mine.

72. Ahmed, 128.

CONCLUSION

1. Such a reading of *Tamasha* is reminiscent of historian Dipesh Chakrabarty's argument following a close reading of Marx's critique of capital. Thanks to Juned Shaikh for reminding me of this resonance. Coining the concepts of "History 1" and "History 2," Chakrabarty had contended that Marx had distinguished between two kinds of histories, one "posited by capital" (History 1) and the second (History 2) that does not "belong to capital's 'life process.'" In other words, if History 1 is the kind of history that writes the teleological story of capital, thereby enabling its reproduction, History 2 is that story that does not comply. Moreover, in this argument, History 2s are "not pasts separate from capital; they inhere in capital and yet interrupt and punctuate the run of capital's own logic," and History 1 must therefore always work to "subjugate or destroy the multiple possibilities that belong to History 2." Dipesh Chakrabarty, *Provincializing Europe: Postcolonial Thought and Historical Difference* (Princeton, NJ: Princeton University Press, 2000), 64, 65, 66.

2. Chakrabarty, 66.

3. Aparna Dharwadker, *Theatres of Independence: Drama, Theory, and Urban Performance in India Since 1947* (Iowa City: University of Iowa Press, 2004).

4. This is, in fact, in the best traditions of the melodrama, as we have discussed through Ravi Vasudevan's work in the previous chapter.

BIBLIOGRAPHY

Acharya, Shankar, and Rakesh Mohan, eds. *India's Economy: Performance and Challenges: Essays in Honor of Montek Singh Ahluwalia*. Delhi: Oxford University Press, 2010.

Adiga, Aravind. *The White Tiger*. New York: Free Press, 2008.

Advani, L. K. *My Country, My Land*. New Delhi: Rupa and Co., 2008.

Ahluwalia, I. A., and I.M.D. Little. *India's Economic Reforms and Development: Essays for Manmohan Singh*. Delhi: Oxford University Press, 1998.

Ahluwalia, Montek Singh. "The 1991 Reforms." *Economic and Political Weekly* 51, no. 29 (July 2016).

Ahmed, Sara. *The Cultural Politics of Emotion*. New York: Routledge, 2004.

Aiyar, Swaminathan Ankelasari. "West's Discovery of India." *Times of India* (Mumbai), June 25, 2006.

Anderson, Benedict. *Imagined Communities*. London: Verso, 2006.

Badiou, Alain. *In Praise of Love*. Paris: Flammarion SA, 2009.

Banerjee, Laksmisree. "Merit will craft the future." *Hindustan Times* (New Delhi), July 13, 2007.

Banet-Weiser, Sarah. *Authentic: The Politics of Ambivalence in a Brand Culture*. New York: New York University Press, 2012.

Bansal, Varsha, and Gireesh Chandra Prasad. "What New Guidelines Mean for the E-commerce Ecosystem." *livemint.com*, December 31, 2018. https://www.livemint.com/Companies/5to8Jn DkEBZw9mXU1Pwd3I/What-new-FDI-guidelines-mean-for-the-ecommerce-ecosystem .html.

Basu, Anustup. *Bollywood in the Age of New Media: The Geo-Televisual Aesthetic*. Edinburgh: Edinburgh University Press, 2010.

Basu, Manisha. *The Rhetoric of Hindu India: Language and Urban Nationalism*. Cambridge: Cambridge University Press, 2016.

Basu, Tapan, Pradip Datta, Sumit Sarkar, Tanika Sarkar, and Sambuddha Sen. *Khaki Shorts and Saffron Flags*. New Delhi: Orient Longman, 1993.

BBC News. "Indian Election 2019: Narendra Modi thanks voters for 'historic mandate.'" May 23, 2019. https://www.bbc.com/news/world-asia-india-48389130.

Benhabib, Seyla. *The Claims of Culture: Equality and Diversity in the Global Era*. (Princeton, NJ: Princeton University Press, 2002.

Benjamin, Walter. "The Work of Art in the Age of Mechanical Reproduction," in *Illuminations*, 217–251. New York: Schocken Books, 1968.

Berlant, Lauren. *The Queen of America Goes to Washington City: Essays on Sex and Citizenship*. Durham, NC: Duke University Press, 1997.

Bidwai, Praful. "The Road to Gujarat," *Frontline*, November 7, 2008, 110–112.

Bose, Jaideep. "A Passage from India," *The Times of India*, January 1, 2007, 2.

Brown, Wendy. *In the Ruins of Neoliberalism: The Rise of Antidemocratic Politics in the West*. New York: Columbia University Press, 2019.

Bruff, Ian. "The Rise of Authoritarian Neoliberalism." *Rethinking Marxism: A Journal of Economics, Culture & Society* 26, no. 1 (2014): 113–129.

Business India. "In a State of Success." January 25, 2009, 69.

Business Week. "Modi Wins as Gujarat Gets Tata's Nano Plant." October 8, 2008.

Chadda, K., and A. P. Kavoori. "Exoticized, Marginalized, Demonized. The Muslim 'Other' in Indian Cinema." In A. Punathambekar and A. P. Kavoori, eds., *Global Bollywood* (New York: New York University Press, 2008).

Chakrabarty, Dipesh. *Provincializing Europe: Postcolonial Thought and Historical Difference.* Princeton, NJ: Princeton University Press, 2000.

Chandra, Nandini. "Young Protest: The Idea of Merit in Commercial Hindi Cinema." *Comparative Studies of South Asia, Africa and the Middle East* 30, no. 1 (2010): 119–132.

Chandra, Shefali. *The Sexual Life of English: Languages of Caste and Desire in Colonial India.* Durham, NC: Duke University Press, 2012.

Chatterjee, Partha. *Politics of the Governed: Reflections on Popular Politics in Most of the World.* New York: Columbia University Press, 2004.

Chaudhury, Pradipta. "Don't Put in a Caste." *Times of India* (Mumbai), June 26, 2007.

Cheah, Pheng. *Inhuman Conditions: On Cosmopolitanism and Human Rights.* Cambridge, MA: Harvard University Press, 2006.

Cheah, Pheng. *Spectral Nationality: Passages of Freedom from Kant to Postcolonial Literatures of Liberation.* New York: Columbia University Press, 2003.

Chen, Kuan Hsing. *Asia as Method: Toward Deimperialization.* Durham, NC: Duke University Press, 2010.

Dalal, Sucheta. "Great Rip-off in the Name of Development." Cheques and Balances, *Indian Express,* April 10, 2006.

Damodaran, Harish. *India's New Capitalists: Caste, Business and Industry in a Modern Nation.* New York: Palgrave Macmillan, 2008.

Das, Gurcharan. *India Unbound: The Social and Economic Revolution from Independence to the Global Information Age.* New York: Anchor Books, 2000, 2002.

Das, Gurcharan. "A Sobering Lesson." Men and Ideas, *The Times of India* (Mumbai), June 3, 2007.

Deresiewicz, William. "Generation Sell," *New York Times,* November 12, 2011. https://www .nytimes.com/2011/11/13/opinion/sunday/the-entrepreneurial-generation.html.

Desai, Darshan. "Slog-over Batsman." *Outlook,* December 23, 2002, 40.

Dharwadker, Aparna. *Theatres of Independence: Drama, Theory, and Urban Performance in India Since 1947.* Iowa City: University of Iowa Press, 2004.

Dirlik, Arif. *Global Modernity: Modernity in the Age of Global Capitalism.* Boulder, CO, and London: Paradigm Publishers, 2007.

Dutt, Barkha. "Art of Reinvention." Third Eye, *Hindustan Times,* May 12, 2007.

Dutt, Barkha. "An Inconvenient Truth." *Hindustan Times,* March 3, 2007.

Dutta, Bhabhatosh, and Rao Hanumantha et al. "Devaluation and IMF Loan: Leading Economists' Alternative View." Originally published in *Mainstream,* July 13, 1991; republished as Annexure 6 in Jairam Ramesh, *To the Brink and Back: India's 1991 Story* (New Delhi: Rupa Publications, 2015).

Dutta, Sujan. "Media and the Message," *Telegraph,* December 22, 2002.

Dwyer, Rachel. *Yash Chopra.* London: British Film Institute, 2002.

Eck, Diane. *Darsan: Seeing the Divine Image in India.* New York: Columbia University Press, 1998.

Economic Times. "India Inc says time for transformation as Modi looks set for second term." May 23, 2019. https://economictimes.indiatimes.com/news/elections/lok-sabha/india/stable -government-to-boost-economic-growth-foreign-fund-flow-india-inc/articleshow/69459 604.cms.

Economic Times. "Narendra Modi Becomes India Inc. Poster Boy." January 15, 2009.

Economist. "The Entrepreneurial Society." March 14, 2009. http://www.economist.com/node /13216087.

Edelman, Marc, and Angelique Haugerud. "Introduction: The Anthropology of Development and Globalization," in *The Anthropology of Development and Globalization: From Classical Political Economy to Contemporary Neoliberalism* (Malden, MA: Blackwell Publishing, 2005).

Engineer, Asghar Ali. "Communal Riots in 2002: A Survey." *Economic and Political Weekly* 38 no. 4 (January 2003): 280–282.

Escobar, Arturo. *Encountering Development: The Making and Unmaking of the Third World.* Princeton, NJ: Princeton University Press, 1995.

Felski, Rita. *The Gender of Modernity.* Boston: Harvard University Press, 1995.

Ferguson, James. "Decomposing Modernity: History and Hierarchy after Development." In *Postcolonial Studies and Beyond,* edited by Ania Loomba et al., 166–181. Durham, NC: Duke University Press, 2005.

Fernandes, Leela. *India's New Middle Class: Democratic Politics in an Era of Economic Reform.* Minneapolis: University of Minnesota Press, 2006.

Ferreira, Francisco, and Michael Walton. "Why Growth Requires Greater Equity." *Economic Times,* December 23, 2005.

Fiske, John. *Understanding Popular Culture.* New York: Routledge, 1989, 1990, 2011.

Fraser, Nancy. *The Old is Dying and the New Cannot Be Born.* London: Verso, 2019.

Freeman, Elizabeth. *Time Binds: Queer Temporalities, Queer Histories.* Durham, NC: Duke University Press, 2010.

Frontline. Editorial, January 3, 2003, 9.

Ganti, Tejaswini. *Producing Bollywood: Inside the Contemporary Hindi Film Industry.* Durham, NC: Duke University Press, 2012.

Gehlawat, Ajay. "The Construction of 1970s Femininity, or Why Zeenat Aman Sings the Same Song Twice." In *The 1970s and its Legacies in India's Cinemas,* edited by Priya Joshi and Rajinder Dudrah. London: Routledge, 2014.

Ghose, Sagarika. "Look Back in Hatred." Bloody Mary, *Hindustan Times,* April 8, 2008.

Ghose, Sagarika. "2 ½ Years, 8 Per Cent of What?" Bloody Mary, *Hindustan Times,* November 24, 2006.

Ghose, Sagarika. "Uttar Pradesh Pvt Ltd." Bloody Mary, *Hindustan Times,* May 11, 2007.

Ghosh, Bishnupriya. *Global Icons: Apertures to the Popular.* Durham, NC: Duke University Press, 2011.

Gilmore, Ruth Wilson. *Golden Gulag: Prisons, Surplus, Crisis, and Opposition in Globalizing California.* Berkeley: University of California Press, 2007.

Gledhill, John. "Neoliberalism." In *A Companion to the Anthropology of Politics,* edited by David Nugent and Joan Vincent. Malden, MA: Blackwell Publishing, 2004.

Gooptu, Nandini. "Introduction." In *Enterprise Culture in Neoliberal India: Studies in Youth, Class, Work and Media,* edited by Nandini Gooptu. New York: Routledge, 2013.

Gopal, Sangita. *Conjugations: Marriage and Form in New Bollywood Cinema.* Chicago: University of Chicago Press, 2011.

Gopalakrishnan, Shankar. *Neoliberalism and Hindutva: Fascism, Free Markets and the Restructuring of Indian Capitalism.* Delhi: Aakar Books, 2009.

Grewal, Inderpal. *Transnational America: Feminisms, Diasporas, Neoliberalisms.* Durham, NC: Duke University, Press, 2005.

Gudavarthy, Ajay. "Brahmanism, Liberalism and the Postcolonial Theory," *Economic and Political Weekly* 51, no. 24 (June 11, 2016).

Gupta, Charu. "Hindu Women, Muslim Men: Love Jihad and Conversions." *Economic and Political Weekly* 44, no. 51 (December 19, 2009): 13–15.

Hall, Stuart. "The Great Moving Right Show." *Marxism Today,* January 14–20, 1979.

Hall, Stuart. *Hard Road to Renewal: Thatcherism and the Crisis of the Left.* London: Verso, 1988.

Hall, Stuart. "Introduction: Who Needs 'Identity'?" In *Questions of Cultural Identity,* edited by Stuart Hall and Paul du Gau. London: Sage Publications, 1996.

Hall, Stuart, C. Critcher, T. Jefferson, J. Clarke, and B. Roberts. *Policing the Crisis: Mugging, the State and Law and Order.* London: Macmillan, 1978.

Hansen, Thomas Blom. *The Saffron Wave: Democracy and Hindu Nationalism in Modern India.* New Delhi: Oxford University Press, 1999.

Hartman, Saidiya. *Lose Your Mother: A Journey Along the Atlantic Slave Route.* New York: Farrar, Straus and Giroux, 2007.

Harvey, David. *A Brief History of Neoliberalism.* Oxford: Oxford University Press, 2005.

Hassan, Mushirul. "Engulfed by the Tidal Wave." *The Indian Express,* December 25, 2002.

Hemmings, Clare. *Why Stories Matter: The Political Grammar of Feminist Theory.* Durham, NC: Duke University Press, 2011.

Hindu. "A Torturous Quest for Justice." Editorial, February 27, 2006.

Hindu. "What Makes Shyam Special..." Friday Review, January 17, 2003. https://www.thehindu.com/todays-paper/tp-features/tp-fridayreview/what-makes-shyam-special/article28572365.ece.

Holley, Peter. "KKK's Official Newspaper Supports Donald Trump for President." *Washington Post,* November 2, 2016. https://www.washingtonpost.com/news/post-politics/wp/2016/11/01/the-kkks-official-newspaper-has-endorsed-donald-trump-for-president.

Jaikumar, Priya. *Cinema at the End of Empire: A Politics of Transition in Britain and India.* Durham, NC: Duke University Press, 2006.

Jain, Kajri. *Gods in the Bazaar: The Economies of Indian Calendar Art.* Durham, NC: Duke University Press, 2007.

Jain, Kajri. *Gods in the Time of Democracy.* Durham, NC: Duke University Press, 2021.

Jameson, Fredric. *The Political Unconscious: Narrative as a Socially Symbolic Act.* Ithaca, NY: Cornell University Press, 1981.

Jeffries, Stuart. "Roars of Anger." *The Guardian,* October 15, 2008.

Karat, Prakash, A. B. Bardhan, G. Devarajan, and Abani Roy. "Statement on the Indo-U.S. Bilateral Nuclear Cooperation Agreement." *Left Stand on the Nuclear Deal: Notes Exchanged in the UPA-Left Committee on India-U.S. Civil Nuclear Cooperation.* New Delhi: Progressive Printers, 2008.

Kelley, Robin D. G. "What Did Cedric Robinson Mean by Racial Capitalism?" *Boston Review: A Political and Literary Forum,* January 12, 2017. http://bostonreview.net/race/robin-d-g-kelley-what-did-cedric-robinson-mean-racial-capitalism.

Khetan, Ashish. "The Buying of Zaheera Shaikh." *Tehelka.*

Khindaria, Brij. "Beware the backlash of the poor." *Business India,* April 23, 2006.

Klenck, Rebecca. "Difficult Work: Becoming Developed." In *Regional Modernities: The Cultural Politics of Development in India,* edited by K. Sivaramakrishnan and Arun Agarwal. Stanford, CA: Stanford University Press, 2003.

Kohli-Khandekar, Vanita. *The Indian Media Business.* 2nd ed. New Delhi: Response Books, 2006.

Kumar, Shanti. *Gandhi Meets Primetime: Globalization and Nationalism in Indian Television.* Urbana: University of Illinois Press, 2006.

Laclau, Ernesto. *On Populist Reason.* London: Verso, 2005.

Lal, Vinay. *Deewar: The Footpath, the City and the Angry Young Man.* New Delhi: HarperCollins Publishers, 2012.

Levine, Caroline. *Forms: Whole, Rhythm, Hierarchy, Network.* Princeton, NJ: Princeton University Press, 2015.

Lipsitz, George. "The Possessive Investment in Whiteness: Racialized Social Democracy and the 'White' Problem in American Studies." *American Quarterly* 47, no. 3 (September 1995): 369–387.

Lowe, Lisa, and David Lloyd. "Introduction." In *The Politics of Culture in the Shadow of Capital,* edited by Lisa Lowe and David Lloyd. Durham, NC: Duke University Press, 1997.

Ludden, David. "Ayodhya: A Window on the World." In *Contesting the Nation: Religion, Community, and the Politics of Democracy in India,* edited by David Ludden. Philadelphia: University of Pennsylvania Press, 1996.

Lukacs, George. *Realism in Our Time: Literature and the Class Struggle.* Translated by John Mander and Necke Mander. New York: Harper and Row, 1962.

Macpherson, C. B. *The Political Theory of Possessive Individualism, Hobbes to Locke.* New York: Oxford University Press, 1962.

Mahaprashasta, Ajoy Ashirwad. "Sensational Grist." *Frontline,* November 29, 2013. http://www.frontline.in/cover-story/sensational-grist/article5338432.ece#test.

Mahurkar, Uday, with Sumit Mitra. "I Wanted Justice." *India Today,* July 21, 2003, 27–36.

Maitra, Amit. "It's True, India has Emerged." *Economic Times,* November 11, 2010. http://econo mictimes.indiatimes.com/opinion/guest-writer/its-true-india-has-emerged/articleshow /6904295.cms?curpg=1.

Mankekar, Purnima. *Screening Culture, Viewing Politics: An Ethnography of Television, Womanhood, and Nation in Postcolonial India.* Durham, NC: Duke University Press, 1999.

Masand, Rajeev. "Masand's Verdict: Guru," review of *Guru,* CNN-IBN, April 18, 2011. http://ibnlive.in.com/news/masands-verdict-thumbs-up-for-guru/31056-8.html.

Mawdsley, Emma, and Jonathan Rigg. "A Survey of the World Development Reports 1: Discursive Strategies." *Progress in Development Studies* 2, no. 2 (2002): 93–111.

Mazumdar, Ranjani. *Bombay Cinema: An Archive of the City.* Minneapolis: University of Minnesota Press, 2007.

Mazzarella, William. *Shovelling Smoke: Advertising and Globalization in Contemporary India.* Durham, NC: Duke University Press, 2003.

Mehta, Harit. "Moditva to Modi-nomics." *Times of India,* January 23, 2009.

Menon, Nivedita. *Recovering Subversion: Feminist Politics Beyond the Law.* Urbana: University of Illinois Press, 2004.

Menon, Nivedita, and Aditya Nigam. *Power and Contestation: India Since 1989.* Hyderabad: Orient Longman, 2008.

Mishra, Asit Ranjan, and Mihir Dalal. "Govt. defines e-commerce marketplace rules, allows 100% FDI." *livemint.com,* March 30, 2016. https://www.livemint.com/Politics/hglep85y ZOQzChj6KRrrCK/Govt-allows-100-FDI-in-ecommerce-marketplace-model.html.

Mishra, Pankaj. "Donald Trump is Going to India to Find Himself." *New York Times,* February 21, 2020. https://www.nytimes.com/2020/02/21/opinion/trump-india.html.

Mishra, Subhash. "Dalit Icons, Indian Idols." *India Today,* October 22, 2007.

Mishra, Subhash. "Poor Little Rich Girl," *India Today,* July 9, 2007.

Mitchell, W.J.T. *Iconology: Image, Text, Ideology.* Chicago: University of Chicago Press, 1986.

Mitchell, W.J.T. *What Do Pictures Want? The Lives and Loves of Images.* Chicago: University of Chicago Press, 2005.

Moretti, Franco. *Modern Epic: The World System from Goethe to Garcia Marquez.* London: Verso, 1996.

Mukherji, Parul Dave. "Popular Festivals, Populist Visual Culture and Modi Masks." In *Democratic Culture: Historical and Philosophical Essays,* edited by Akeel Bilgrami. London: Routledge, 2011.

Murty, Madhavi. "Representing Hindutva: Nation, Religion, and Masculinity in Indian Popular Cinema from 1990s to the Present." *Popular Communication* 7, no. 4 (Fall 2009).

Nandy, Ashis. *The Intimate Enemy: Loss and Recovery of Self Under Colonialism.* 2nd ed. New Delhi: Oxford University Press, 2009.

Nandy, Ashis. "Power Defangs [Politics has blunted the edge of his ideology, making him less dangerous]." *Outlook,* December 24, 2007, 50–52.

Narayan, Badri. *Women Heroes and Dalit Assertion in North India: Culture, Identity and Politics.* New Delhi: Sage Publications, 2006.

Nehru, Jawaharlal. "Speech on the Granting of Indian Independence" (August 14, 1947). In *Internet Modern History Sourcebook,* edited by Paul Halsall. New York: Fordham University, 1998. http://www.fordham.edu/halsall/mod/1947nehru1.html.

Nilekani, Nandan. Foreword to *India's New Capitalists: Caste, Business, and Industry in a Modern Nation* by Harish Damodaran. New Delhi: Permanent Black, 2008.

Nilekani, Nandan. *Imagining India: Ideas for the New Century.* New York: Penguin Press, 2008.

Niranjana, Tejaswini. "Integrating Whose Nation? Tourists and Terrorists in 'Roja.'" *Economic and Political Weekly* 29, no. 3 (January 15, 1994), 79–82.

Norris, Pippa. *Cultural Backlash: Trump, Brexit and Authoritarian Populism.* Cambridge: Cambridge University Press, 2019.

Norris, Pippa. "It's Not Just Trump. Authoritarian Populism is Rising Across the West. Here's Why." *Washington Post,* March 11, 2016. https://www.washingtonpost.com/news/monkey-cage/wp/2016/03/11/its-not-just-trump-authoritarian-populism-is-rising-across-the-west-heres-why/?utm_term=.d3d7a47ce9b7.

Obama, Barack. "Text of the Presidential address to the joint session of the Indian parliament." White House, November 8, 2010. https://obamawhitehouse.archives.gov/the-press-office/2010/11/08/remarks-president-joint-session-indian-parliament-new-delhi-india.

Ong, Aihwa. *Neoliberalism as Exception: Mutations in Citizenship and Sovereignty.* Durham, NC: Duke University Press, 2006.

Orsini, Francesca, ed. *Love in South Asia.* Cambridge: Cambridge University Press, 2006.

Osella, Caroline, Fillipo Osella, and Radhika Chopra. "Introduction: Towards a More Nuanced Approach to Masculinity, Towards a Richer Understanding of South Asian Men." In *South Asian Masculinities,* edited by Radhika Chopra, Caroline Osella, and Fillipo Osella. New Delhi: Kali for Women, 2004.

Oza, Nandini. "In Full Steam: Modi Rocks With His Development Drive." *The Week,* January 11, 2009, 20–22.

Oza, Rupal. *The Making of Neoliberal India: Nationalism, Gender, and the Paradoxes of Globalization.* New York: Routledge, 2006.

Panagariya, Arvind. "World Bank's Discovery of Equity." *Economic Times,* October 19, 2005.

Pant, Harsh V. "Lethal Weapon: Gujarati *gaurav,* Parivar prejudice." *Indian Express,* December 27, 2002.

Parekh, Kirit. "A Fair System." *Times of India,* February 10, 2007.

Parikh, Daksesh, and Nachiketa Desai. "The Entire Gujarat is a Golden Corridor: Interview with Narendra Modi." *Business India,* January 25, 2009.

Phadke, Shilpa, Sameera Khan, and Shilpa Ranade. *Why Loiter? Women and Risk on Mumbai Streets.* Mumbai: Penguin India, 2011.

Pinney, Christopher. *Photos of the Gods: The Printed Image and Political Struggle in India.* Chicago: University of Chicago Press, 2004.

Poduval, Satish. "The Affable Young Man: Civility, Desire and the Making of a Middle-class Cinema in the 1970s." In *The 1970s and its Legacies in India's Cinemas,* edited by Priya Joshi and Rajinder Dudrah. New York: Routledge, 2014.

Polgreen, Lydia. "Scaling Caste Walls With Capitalism's Ladder in India." *New York Times,* December 21, 2011. http://www.nytimes.com/2011/12/22/world/asia/indias-boom-creates-openings-for-untouchables.html?pagewanted=all.

Povinelli, Elizabeth. *An Empire of Love: Toward a Theory of Intimacy, Genealogy, and Carnality.* Durham, NC: Duke University Press, 2006.

Prasad, M. Madhava. *Ideology of the Hindi Film: A Historical Construction.* Delhi: Oxford University Press, 2000.

Rajagopal, Arvind. "Advertising, Politics and the Sentimental Education of the Indian Consumer." *Visual Anthropology Review* 14, no. 2 (Fall–Winter 1998): 14–31.

Rajagopal, Arvind. "The Commodity Image in the (Post) Colony. *Tasveer Ghar: A Digital Archive of South Asian Popular Visual Culture.* http://www.tasveergharindia.net/cmsdesk/essay/100/index.html.

Rajagopal, Arvind. "Introduction." In *The Indian Public Sphere: Readings in Media History*, edited by Arvind Rajagopal, 1–30. New Delhi: Oxford University Press, 2009.

Rajagopal, Arvind. *Politics After Television: Hindu Nationalism and the Reshaping of the Public in India* (Cambridge: Cambridge University Press, 2001).

Ramakrishnan, Venkitesh. "Dalit Power." *Frontline*, June 1, 2007.

Ramamurthy, Priti. "All-Consuming Nationalism: The Indian Modern Girl in the 1920s and 1930s." In *The Modern Girl Around the World: Consumption, Modernity, and Globalization*, edited by Alys Weinbaum, Lynn Thomas, Priti Ramamurthy, Uta Poiger, Madeleine Yue Dong, and Tani Barlow. Durham, NC: Duke University Press, 2008.

Ramaswamy, Sumati. *The Goddess and the Nation: Mapping Mother India*. Durham, NC: Duke University Press, 2010.

Ramesh, Jairam. *To the Brink and Back: India's 1991 Story*. Delhi: Rupa Publications, 2015.

Rangarajan, Mahesh. "Polity in Transition: India after the 2004 Elections." *Economic and Political Weekly*, August 6, 2005, 3598–3605.

Reddy, Chandan. *Freedom with Violence: Race, Sexuality and the US State*. Durham, NC: Duke University Press, 2011.

Robinson, Cedric. *Black Marxism: The Making of the Black Radical Tradition*. Chapel Hill: University of North Carolina Press, 2000. First published 1983 by Zed Press (London).

Rosario, Kennith. "Parmanu Review: Billowing Plume of Jingoistic Smoke." *The Hindu*, May 25, 2018. https://www.thehindu.com/entertainment/movies/parmanu-review-billowing-plume -of-jingoistic-smoke/article23992975.ece.

Roy, Ananya. "Afterword: Entrepreneurs of Millennial Capitalism." *Antipode: A Radical Journal of Geography* 44, no. 2 (March 2012): 545–553.

Roy, Srirupa. *Beyond Belief: India and the Politics of Postcolonial Nationalism*. Durham, NC: Duke University Press, 2007.

Ruhani, Fahim. "I have proved it seven times, the reviews of my films don't matter: Rohit Shetty." *India Today*, September 3, 2013. http://indiatoday.intoday.in/story/rohit-shetty -interview-chennai-express/1/305322.html.

S., Rukmini. "The BJP's Electoral Arithmetic." In *The BJP in Power: Indian Democracy and Religious Nationalism*, edited by Milan Vaishnav, 37–50. Washington D.C.: Carnegie Endowment for International Peace, 2019. https://carnegieendowment.org/files/BJP_In_Power_final.pdf.

Saad-Filho, Alfred, and Deborah Johnston. "Introduction." In *Neoliberalism: A Critical Reader*, edited by Alfred Saad-Filho and Deborah Johnston. London: Pluto Press, 2005.

Saar, Martin, William Callison, and Anne Gräfe. "Spinoza and the Political Imaginary." *Qui Parle: Critical Humanities and Social Sciences* 23, no. 2 (2015): 115–133.

Samaddar, Ranabir. "Fifty years ago: How pro-poor politics became an integral part of Indian democracy." *Scroll.in*, February 26, 2021. https://scroll.in/article/985058/fifty-years-ago-how -pro-poor-politics-became-an-integral-part-of-indian-democracy.

Sardesai, Rajdeep. "Lady in Waiting," Beyond the Byte, *Hindustan Times*, April 27, 2007.

Sardesai, Rajdeep. "The New Advani?" Beyond the Byte, *The Hindustan Times*, December 26, 2007.

Sardesai, Rajdeep. *2014: The Election that Changed India* (New Delhi: Penguin Books, India, 2015).

Savarkar, V. D. "Presidential Address at the 19th Session of the Akhil Bharatiya Hindu Mahasabha." *Hindu Rashtra Darshan* (A Collection of the Presidential Speeches delivered from the Hindu Mahasabha Platform), (Bombay: V. V. Bambardekar, India Printing Works, 1949).

Savarkar, V. D. *Six Glorious Epochs of Indian History*. (Mumbai: Savarkar Sadan, 1971).

Scott, David. *Omens of Adversity: Tragedy, Time, Memory, Justice*. (Durham, NC: Duke University Press, 2014).

Sen, Raja. "Plain and Simple." Review of *Rocket Singh: Salesman of the Year*, rediff.com, December 11, 2007. http://movies.rediff.com/report/2009/dec/11/review-rocket-singh-salesman -of-the-year.htm.

Sen, Ronojoy. "From Chaiwala to Chowkidar: Modi's Election Campaigns Online and Offline." *Economic and Political Weekly* 54, no. 51 (December 28, 2019).

Singh, Manmohan. "India: The Next Decade" (New Delhi, Nov 19, 2004). In *Prime Minister Manmohan Singh: Selected Speeches*, Volume I: May 2004 to May 2005 (Publications Division: Ministry of Information and Broadcasting, Govt. of India).

Shaikh, Juned. *Outcaste Bombay: The Urban Habitations of Caste and Class, 1896–1984* (Seattle: University of Washington Press, 2021).

Spary, Sara. "Bill and Melinda Gates Foundation Under Fire Over Award to Indian PM Modi," *CNN*, September 12, 2019. https://www.cnn.com/2019/09/12/asia/bill-melinda-gates-modi -intl-scli/index.html.

Spivak, Gayatri. *A Critique of Postcolonial Reason: Toward a History of the Vanishing Present* (Cambridge, MA: Harvard University Press, 1999).

Steiner, George. "George Lukacs—A Preface." In *Realism in Our Time: Literature and the Class Struggle*, by George Lukacs, translated by John Mander and Necke Mander. New York: Harper and Row, 1962.

Sunya, Samhita. "Moving Toward *Prem Nagar*: An Intimate Genealogy of the 'City of Love' and the Lyrical Worlds of Hindustani Film Songs." *positions* 25, no. 1 (2017).

Tata, Ratan. Interview on the TV news channel Times Now, October 2008. http://www .youtube.com/watch?v=oKjkDynHNps&feature=related.

Times of India. "Big B Gives Baritone to Big Idea." Times City, January 2007, 4.

Times of India. "Big B Prepares to Unveil TOI's India Poised Campaign." January 1, 2007, 3.

Times of India. "Beyond Quotas." Editorial, October 24, 2007.

Times of India. "Trust on Trial: Try Zahira Shaikh for Perjury." Editorial, November 5, 2004. http://articles.timesofindia.indiatimes.com/2004-11-05/edit-page/27145399_1_zahira -sheikh-retrial-apex-court.

Vanaik, Achin. *The Furies of Indian Communalism: Religion, Modernity and Secularization*. London, New York: Verso, 1997.

Vanaik, Achin. "The Puzzle of India's Growth Rate." *Telegraph*, June 22, 2006.

Vasudevan, Ravi. *The Melodramatic Imagination*. New Delhi: Permanent Black, 2010.

Verma, Lalmani, and T. A. Johnson. "Who Loves Love Jihad." *Indian Express*, September 7, 2014. http://indianexpress.com/article/india/india-others/who-loves-love-jihad/.

Vijaykar, Ravi. "The Role of a Song in a Hindi Film." *The South Asianist* 2, no. 3: 48–73. http:// www.southasianist.ed.ac.uk/article/view/167/992.

Warner, Michael. "The Mass Public and the Mass Subject." In *Habermas and the Public Sphere*, edited by Craig Calhoun. Cambridge, MA: MIT Press, 1992.

Warner, Michael. *Publics and Counterpublics*. New York: Zone Books, 2002.

Weinbaum, Alys, Lynn Thomas, Priti Ramamurthy, Uta Poiger, Madeleine Yue Dong, and Tani Barlow (The Modern Girl Research Group), eds. *The Modern Girl Around the World: Consumption, Modernity, and Globalization*. Durham, NC: Duke University Press, 2008.

Williams, Raymond. *Keywords: A Vocabulary of Culture and Society*. New York: Oxford University Press, 1976, 1983.

World Bank. *Equity and Development: World Development Report 2006*.

Yadav, Yogendra. "The Patterns and Lessons." *Frontline*, January 3, 2003, 10–12.

Young, Robert J. C. *Colonial Desire: Hybridity in Theory, Culture and Race*. London, New York: Routledge, 1995.

Young, Stephen, Satendra Kumar, and Craig Jeffrey. "Beyond Improvisation? The Rise and Rise of Youth Entrepreneurs in India." In *Transactions of the Institute of British Geographers*, 42, no. 1 (March 2017), 98–109.

INDEX

"Achche Din Aane Wale Hain" [Better Days Are Coming] (song), 63
Achche Din series (BJP commercials), 62–63, 92
Adiga, Arvind, 142
Advani, L. K., 25–26
advertising, 3, 12, 18, 184, 193n47; Hindu symbolism and, 73, 74; obstructed time and, 39; public persona constituted via, 79
aesthetics, 2, 71, 72, 73, 162
affable young man, in Hindi cinema, 74, 152–55, 179, 200n15
affirmative action policies, 6, 32, 44, 49; Hindu nationalist opposition to, 5, 42; Mandal Commission Report and, 18; protests against, 48
Agarwal, Anil, 108
agency, 60, 104, 125; of the commoner, 60, 75, 140, 141; consumerism and, 125; dalit, 100, 104; masculinized, 47; subaltern, 120, 125
agrarian rebellion, 8–9
Ahluwalia, Montek Singh, 16, 17, 109
Ahmed, Sara, 146, 147, 178, 179
Ajnabee [Stranger] (film, dir. Shakti Samanta, 1974), 209n47
Akhtar, Begum, 156
Akhtar, Farhan, 52
Akhtar, Javed, 40, 80, 172, 210n60
Akhtar, Zoya, 146, 165
Ali, Ghulam, 156
Ali, Imtiaz, 31, 159, 165, 175
Ali, Shaad, 43, 75
All India Backward and Minority Communities Employee Federation (BAMCEF), 106
All India Institute of Medical Sciences (AIIMS), 48
Aman, Zeenat, 161, 162, 163
Amar Akbar Anthony (film, dir. Manmohan Desai, 1977), 112
Ambani, Anil, 60, 94
Ambani, Dhirubhai, 126, 127, 134
Ambedkar, B. R., 104, 105, 106
Amin, Shimit, 119
Amitabh Bachchan Corporation Ltd. (ABCL), 83–84
Anderson, Benedict, 37, 95

angry young man, in Hindi films, 14, 29, 40, 172; Bachchan in role of, 79, 80–81, 83, 85, 138, 152; businessman of post-reform India and, 134, 135; emergence of, 152; as iconic figure, 73; possessive individualism and, 112; upward mobility as concern of, 53
anthropology, 19
Appadurai, Arjun, 197n44
artisans, 139–40
Aurangzeb (Mughal emperor), 25
authenticity, 7, 13; class versus caste as indicator of deprivation, 49; of the commoner, 3, 28; realism and, 73, 77; story defined through, 21
authoritarian nationalism, 9, 11, 51, 182; development and, 29, 57; intersecting narratives with liberalism, 138; intersection with neoliberalism, 2; nativism and, 3, 185
Avantibai, 100
Ayodhya, city of: as birthplace of Ram, 26; in Hindu nationalist discourse, 25; mosque destruction in (1992), 17, 25, 89–90
Azad, Chandrashekhar, 55

Babur (Mughal emperor), 25
Bachchan, Abhishek, 53, 76
Bachchan, Amitabh, 29, 40, 78, 172–73, 200n12, 210n60; ABCL corporation of, 83–84; as angry young man, 79, 80–81, 83, 85, 138, 152; as brand father of neoliberal India, 29, 78, 79, 83–87, 138; bridge as symbol of iconicity of, 85–86, 87, 91; in *Deewar*, 76, 81; as electoral candidate, 138, 206n50; Gujarat tourism advertising campaign and, 87; as iconic figure, 71; Modi's story about, 138; television industry and, 84, 85; as voice of India Poised campaign, 84–87
Badiou, Alain, 150–51
bahujan samaj (marginalized majority), 99–100, 104, 106–8, 203n93
Band Baaja Baaraat [*The Wedding Planners*] (film, dir. Maneesh Sharma, 2010), 165
Banerjee, Mamata, 100–101
Banet-Weiser, Sarah, 19
Bangalore, city of, 83
Bangladesh War (1971), 36, 80

sign systems, 2, 5, 15

Sikhs, 55, 129, 130

Silsila [A Sequence of Events] (film, dir. Yash Chopra, 1981), 172–73, 209n48, 209n50

Singh, Arjun, 49

Singh, Bhagat, 55

Singh, Jagjit, 156

Singh, Manmohan, 14, 35, 126; alienated from the common man (*aam aadmi*), 59; economic liberalization and, 83, 88, 109; on "epochal" reforms, 38

Singh, Pravinder, 77

Singh, Shree Narayan, 57

Sinha, Mrinalini, 154

slavery, 51

social, the: narrated through realism, 48, 51; realism and, 77; sharp delineation from the economic, 44; spectacular realism and, 58; structured by axes of difference, 42

socialism, 111, 112, 128

social media, 64

Somnath, city of, 25

South Africa, 67

South Asia, 10, 72

Soviet Union: collapse of, 34, 35, 46; relationship with India, 35

Special Marriages Act (British India, 1872), 154

Special Marriages Act (1954), 177

spectacular realism, 2, 18, 21–28, 54–55, 96, 108, 183; as aesthetic form of Hindutva neoliberalism, 184; cinematic love song and, 169, 176; commoner's Modi mask and, 92; craftsman linked to global capital, 140; gender and, 165; in *Guru*, 131, 133; in Hindi films, 112; iconicity and, 29, 71; love stories and, 168; narration of movement and, 80, 85; neoliberal development policy and, 67; ordinary men transformed into heroes, 127; resolution of obstruction and, 64; rural–urban divide and, 59

Spivak, Gayatri, 48

state, the, 10, 20, 61, 82; British colonial state, 55, 58; caste-based affirmative action and, 51; complicity in anti-Muslim violence, 90; iconicity and, 72; industrialization strategy and, 17; modernization drive and, 197n42; nation and, 34; policy makers as embodiment of, 15; populism and, 7; as "supreme principle," 11

Stone, Oliver, 128

stories, 18, 28, 75, 181; as archive, 3, 21; consciousness and, 20; culture and, 18–21; development,

1; of development, 36; as epiphenomena, 2, 3; hegemonic, 101, 140, 151, 183, 184–85, 185; as heuristic device, 3, 21, 191n6; narration of political-economic formations through, 2; national "emergence," 1; worldmaking function of, 2, 191n4. *See also* narratives

subalternity, 77, 78, 108, 117; angry young man and, 82, 85; gendered, 145; possessive individualism and, 30, 120

subalterns/subaltern classes, 60, 72; cinematic representations of masculinity and, 53–54; cosmopolitanism and, 123; demands for equity, 48; development and, 55; feminized, 114; linked with middle class, 55; possessive individualism and, 126; transformed into commoners, 77

subjectivity: entrepreneurial, 110, 117, 118–28, 130–35, 141, 144; gendered, 99, 100, 102

Sufi poems, 148

Sui Dhaaga: Made in India [Needle and Thread] (film, dir. Sharat Katariya, 2018), 119, 125–26, 139–40, 145

Sultanpuri, Majrooh, 156

Sunya, Samhita, 169

surplus value, 24

Swades [Homeland] (film, dir. Ashutosh Gowariker, 2004), 64–66, 70, 114–15, 125

symbolic overloads, 19

Tall, David, 196n7

Tamasha [Spectacle] (film, dir. Imtiaz Ali, 2015), 31, 181–83, 210n1

Tata, Ratan, 60

Tata Motors, 60

Tehelka (English-language newsmagazine), 142, 143–44

television, 80, 84

Tendulkar, Sachin, 92, 93

terrorism, 89, 150

Thatcherism, 7, 11

Times of India, The (newspaper), 44, 45, 50, 79, 205n55; India Poised campaign and, 85, 86; upper-caste readership of, 137, 206n49; on Zaheera Shaikh, 126

time/temporalities, 70, 86; cinematic love song and, 168, 171; as destiny, 2; feminized, 47; global capital and, 160; messianic, 4, 66; "newness" and, 18; story about coming of new time, 33; suturing of multiple temporalities, 4, 109; as teleological progress, 33. *See also* new times; obstructed present

ABOUT THE AUTHOR

MADHAVI MURTY is an assistant professor in the feminist studies department at the University of California, Santa Cruz.